SCYTHIAN ELEMENTS
IN
EARLY INDIAN ART

SCYTHIAN ELEMENTS IN EARLY INDIAN ART

Swati Ray

2009
Kaveri Books
New Delhi - 110 002

First Published in 2009
ISBN-13 : 978-81-7479-102-3

Kaveri Books
4697/5-21 A, Ansari Road
New Delhi - 110 002 (India)
Tel.: 011-2328 8140, 2324 5799
E-mail: kaveribooks@vsnl.com

Laser Typesetting by
Aarati Computers, Delhi - 110 009.

Printed at
Salarsar Imaging Systems, Delhi-110 035.

PRINTED IN INDIA

PREFACE

I have tried to bring back the Saka/Scythian art motifs to life as integral part of the ancient art of the subcontinent and attempted representing art forms without bias. It is impossible for one to know the final truth and other views and methodological obsessions persist. My debt to scholars, art historians and archaeologists will be apparent to every reader.

Diacritical markings have been used to a minimum. I have assumed that modern names of towns and cities in Central Asia and the Indian subcontinent are in sufficiently current usage and do not, therefore, require any diacritical definition. The diacritical marking - Saka/Śaka has been used only in the Indian context.

I am grateful to my teachers, colleagues and students. I specially thank Prof. Yaroslav Vasilkov of the Institute of Oriental Studies, St. Petersburg, Prof. Guriev, and Prof. J.D. Kimball of the Centre for Eurasian Studies for Nomads, Berkeley, U.S.A. I am equally beholden to Dr. Arundhuti Banerji and Dr. Rupendra Kumar Chattopadhyay. I am also grateful to Dr. Purabi Ray, Surja Sankar Ray and Riddhi Sankar Ray.

I wish to thank my family for their active cooperation especially my brother Dr. Kshounish Sankar Ray, my sister-in-law Dr. Sucharita Ray and my mother Dr. Jayasree Ray. A special thanks to my great nieces Rajasee Ray and Sreemoyee

Ray for helping me to understand the nomadic way of life. I am also grateful to Sh. Rakesh Goel of Kaveri Books, New Delhi for its publication. I wish to dedicate this study to my great-great grandfather, Parbati Sankar Roy Choudhury, honoured with the Kaiser-i-Hind in 1912, my grandfather Keshab Sankar Ray and my father, late Kanak Sankar Ray.

— Swati Ray

Contents

List of Plates

Plate 35: Gold torque with terminals in the form of recumbent lions from Kul-Oba. Fourth century B.C.

Plate 36: Gold torque decorated with ring-shaped bands, with sculptured scenes of a lion tearing Karagodeuashkh barrow. Late fourth century B.C.

Plate 37: Gold torque with sculptured figures of lions at both ends from Chertomlyk barrow. Last quarter of the fourth century B.C.

Plate 38: Gold torque with two groups of sculptured lions and terminals in the form of foreparts of deer from Tolstaya Mogila barrow. Fourth century B.C.

Plate 39: Gold torque decorated with sculptured figures of lions and applied jagged ornament from Chertomlyk barrow.Last quarter of the fourth century B.C.

Plate 40: Gold and bronze (with traces of enamel) bracelets having bronze plaits covered by gold leaves and decorated with sculptured figures of lionesses at the ends from Bolshaya Bliznitsa. Fourth century B.C.

Plate 41: Gold, bronze and enamel twisted bracelet (bronze base covered with gold leaf) with terminals in the form of sculptured half-length figures of sphinxes from Kul-Oba barrow. Fourth century B.C.

Plate 42: Gold spiral-shaped link bracelets each with relief figures of hippocampi at the ends from Karagodeuashkh barrow. Late fourth century B.C.

Plate 43: Gold comb with battle scene from Solokha barrow. Fifth century B.C.

Plate 44: Gold plaque depicting a bird of prey from Litoy barrow. Late seventh or early sixth century B.C.

Plate 45: Gold sewn-on plaque from a vestment with a brotherhood ritual of two facing Scythians drinking from the same rhyton, from Solokha barrow. First half of the fourth century B.C.

Plate 46: Gold plaque with a brotherhood ritual scene in high relief showing two Scythians drinking from the same rhyton from Kul-Oba barrow. Fourth century B.C.

Plate 47: Gold plaque from a vestment depicting a winged goddess with branched off scrolls instead of legs and with palmettes from Bolshaya Bliznitsa. Fourth century B.C.

Plate 48: Gold plaque from a vestment depicting a dancing woman wearing a short tunic and holding a calathus from Bolshaya Bliznitsa. Fourth century B.C.

1 INTRODUCTION

More than 2000 years ago, the presence of the Śakas ruled in early India. India, unless otherwise indicated, denotes the Indian subcontinent comprising the territories of India, Pakistan and Bangladesh. The Śakas had some political dominations in North-West India from circa first century B.C. and, along with the Parthians, they were continually in power in parts of North-Western India, Gujarat, parts of central India and upper western Deccan till the latter part of the second century A.D. The territories of the Śaka-Kshatrapas in the western Deccan were eventually incorporated into the mighty Gupta Empire by Chandragupta II (A.D. 376 to A.D. 414) at the end of the fourth century A.D.

It is well-known that the Śakas were a part of the Scythians. The term *Scythian* is generally employed to denote numerous groups of nomadic tribes from the borders of China to the Carpathians. Also, the Scythians constituted a subdivision within the larger group of Scytho-Siberian early nomads inhabiting the Eurasian steppes and forest steppe-zones during the first millennium B.C. This broad cultural grouping is identified with the early Eurasian Iron Age and is believed to have emerged from the Bronze Age cultures that dominated Siberia, Kazakhstan and adjoining steppes of Central Asia, Western China and the Southern Russian steppes with its adjoining regions, in the late second and early first millennium B.C. This broad Scythian cultural group included the Śakas in the eastern section. In the eastern section, the Śaka/Scythians ruled over portions of the Indo-Iranian borderlands including the area of modern Afghanistan and the north-western part of the Indian subcontinent. The regions which were incorporated into Afghanistan in the late pre-Christian and early Christian centuries were Bactria, Paropanisadai, Arachosia, Gedrosia and Drangiana. Bactria[1] (in Northern Afghanistan) was bounded on the north and also on the east by Sogdiana (situated in Uzbekistan), on the west by Margiana (part of modern Turkmenistan), and on the south or south-west by a part of Aria (modern Herat region in Afghanistan). Below it was Drangiana[2] (or Śakastāna, modern Seistan). According to Ptolemy, *India Intra Gangem*[3] (Indian subcontinent minus the area to the north and north-east of the Ganges) lay on the east of Paropanisadai[4] (modern Kabul-Begram region to the south-east of the Hindu Kush was within its limit), Arachosia[5] (south-eastern Afghanistan around Ghazni and Kandahar) and Gedrosia[6] (in a part of Baluchistan). The territory of Afghanistan outside the Hindu Kush was generally called Ariana.

The historiography devoted to the Scythians and their art is vast. The "animal style" was the chief characteristic of the art of the Scythians, Scytho-Siberians, Śaka and other Eurasian nomads. Throughout the twentieth century, this "animal style" has been studied in specialist and general works like *The Scythians and Greeks* by E.H. Minns, *Scythian Art* by G. Borovka, *Iranians and Greeks in South Russia* by M. I. Rostovtsev, *The Splendour of Scythian Art* by M. I. Artamonov and others. Minns' book is invaluable for the study of Black Sea antiquities of the Scythians. Texts representing museum exhibitions or publications of major burials (as for example, L. K. Galanina's work on Kurdzhipskiy Kurgan, 1980 etc.) are mostly in Russian or Ukrainian, and they contain the soul and body of Scythology. Veronique Schiltz in *Les Scythes et les Nomades des Steppes* speaks of the Scythian animal style as a precise lexicon of forms and she identifies individual elements of the Scythian art language, which has made its syntax possible. On the other hand, Russian archaeologists have worked extensively on Śaka burials, in the territories of the Commonwealth of Independent States.

Indologists have studied extensively Śaka/Parthian assemblages/artifacts in various forms such as numismatics, art and other archaeological evidences. The increasing number of the known Indo-Parthian and Scytho-Parthian coins were taken into account for discussing the history of the Indo-Scythians. In this connection, special reference may be made to A. Cunningham's *Coins of Alexander's Successors in the East*, originally published in a few numbers of the *Numismatic Chronicle* from 1868-1873, and subsequently published in a book form in London in 1884 with a reprint from Delhi in 1970.

An account of the Śakas with cogent arguments was published by B. N. Puri in his chapter 'The Śakas and Indo-Parthians' in Volume II of the *History of Civilizations of Central Asia*, New Delhi, 1999. It is, however, to be noted that almost all the writings on Scythian art deal with its forms in the western section and parts of the eastern section. Archaeological reports from India and Pakistan and elsewhere also contain materials for writing an art history of the Śaka/Scythians in India and its borderlands. Indeed a more comprehensive study in this respect seems to be a crying need to understand the impact of the artistic activities related to the Scythian elements in the Indian subcontinent.

The Scythian/Śaka power in the annals of the ancient Orient is at least apparent from the numerous widely known sources (both literary and archaeological) alluding to them.

The archaeological discoveries, which initiated from the latter half of the eighteenth century, continue unabated till now. The archaeological discoveries till 2007 as found from the reports of the Academics of Sciences of different territories belonging to the Commonwealth of Independent States (former Soviet Central Asian republics) have added new dimensions to the relevant study. The archaeological reports of India and Pakistan have also added new dimensions. John Marshall's *Taxila* and V. Sarianidi's *Bactrian Gold* have provided exhaustive information. The Asian connections of the Scythian culture, which were formerly not easily traceable, are now studied with fresh perspectives as revealed by new archaeological data. Certain methodologies have been used by archaeologists, especially, in relating archaeological evidence with ethnological probabilities. It is often found that the conflicts raised by archaeological data are persistently ignored *vis-a-vis* the data obtained from literary sources. There has also been a tendency for continued reconsideration of unprovenanced materials, for strengthening hypotheses. There is also the problem of translating the archaeological terminology into a language customary in the historical social life. But one thing is certain. The archaeologists are unanimous on the fact that the steppe desert zones of Central Asia, Sinkiang, Mongolia and South-Western Siberia are to be grouped together as one on the basis of vegetation and topography.[7] It is important to state that much of the North-

Western Himalayas are also considered to belong to the steppes of Central Asia.[8] Another common yardstick of the archaeologists (and also used here) is the theory of the homogenization of the steppes. The entire steppes shared an economy based on stock dependency, having a measured mobility and portability of goods. According to David Christian, the diagnostic features[9] of Scythic culture are as follows:

1. Adoption of iron metallurgy;
2. The use of the akinakes, a short sword, of specific design and systematic development;
3. The customary conservative use of certain artistic motifs;
4. The pastoral nomadic life and a patriarchal, little-centralized social organization;
5. Use of improved compound bows;
6. Use of bronze cauldrons;
7. The appearance of complex horse harnesses; and
8. Deer stones on most burial sites.

Coins and inscriptions (Persian and Indian) have also provided significant data, regarding the Śaka/Scythian way of life. Literary sources like Greek and Roman texts, Chinese literary accounts, Middle Iranian accounts and Sanskrit literary works have provided information about the Śaka/Scythians besides the political development of South Asia in relation to Central Asia.

The Greek and Roman texts include Agatharchides' *Peri Tes Erythras Thalasses*, Ammianus Marcellinus' *Res Gestae*, Arrian's *Anabaseos Alexandrou*, Diodorus's *Bibliothekes Historikes*, Herodotus's *Historiae*, Isidore of Charax's *Stathmoi Parthikoi*, Orosius' *Historiarum Adversum Paganos Libri VII*, Pliny's *Naturalis Historiae*, Ptolemy's *Geographike Huphegesis*, Strabo's *Geographikon*, and *Periplous Tes Erythras Thalasses* or *Periplus Maris Erythraei* of anonymous authorship. Many Scythians like Toxaris settled in Greece. He went to Athens to practise medicine but the tales of his native Scythia as recorded by Lucian[10] gives us valuable information about Scythia. Herodotus's work is a major source and indeed much of Book IV, and scattered sections of Books I and III of his *Historiae* are devoted to the Scythians and to related nomadic groups. However, it is not sufficient to continue to insist on the model offered by Herodotus as an understanding of the art of the Śaka/Scythians is often highly complicated by the historical perspectives of the literary sources. Archaeology provides a safer terrain.

Chinese literary sources include Fan Yeh's *Hou Han-shu*, Pan Ko's *Ch'ien Han-shu* and Ssu-ma Ch'ien's *Shih-chi*. It is probable that the Chinese had a restricted idea of the western regions of the present Indian borderlands (which included Shen-tu, probably the lower Indus valley, Ferghana and Bactria).[11]

Middle Iranian literary accounts of Al-Tabari and Ibn-Khurdādbeh are useful for corroborations. Sanskrit and Prakrit sources include *Kālakāchārya- kathānaka*, and Patañjali's *Mahābhāsya*. It must be accepted that literary sources carry both their inherent problems and prospects.

In the history of art, the Scythian art, the Scytho-Siberian art and the Śaka/ Scythian art occupy a special place. These broad elements not only added several interesting facets but also a general evolution of their own. Such is the fame of Scythian Art that its influence can be seen in Pan-Asian and Pan-European art as well.

Although the excavated barrows of the Śakas-Scythians-Siberians and the extant remains from there are quite extensive, archaeology will probably never be able to provide, like the proverbial tip of the iceberg, more than a hint of the wonder that was nomadic art or animal art.

Scythian and Scytho-Siberian-Śaka antiquities have been obtained from many sites. The basic nature of the antiquities (in spite of the plurality of sites) remained the same. This was due to tribal movements and the gradual process of acculturation in a diverse population matrix. Primarily it was the pre-historic exchange system, which was responsible for the spread of cultural materials before the arrival of controlling authorities. Scholars like Colin Renfrew have strengthened our understanding of the prehistoric exchange system with special reference to the Anatolian context.

The problem of how culture was conceived and its survival strategy can be solved by understanding the tradition of a given particular culture. In India, the beginning of Śaka-Sātavāhana, Śaka-Kshatrapa and Śaka-Kushāṇa culture is a dichotomy. The survival of Śaka cultural antiquity in different geographical zones exhibit the power structure of that particular geographical zone during a particular period. The contemporary Kushāṇa or Sātavāhana empire mattered especially in the nature of royal patronage and enroute the socio-cultural-economic base.

Throughout the twentieth century, a series of imposing researches attracted the attention of the world. However, as with so many contested issues in academe, we have reached an impasse of sorts. In spite of such researches at our disposal, some aspects of the Śaka art of the Indian subcontinent and its borderlands are not properly documented. It needs to be stressed since it holds a key position in understanding Indian art, its composite culture and reconstructing its history and also its crosscurrents with the art of the neighbouring countries. In spite of so many years of excavations, archaeologists, historians, and art historians still face a major task in exposing the Saka (Śaka) art forms in the Indian subcontinent *vis-a-vis* a broader context in the macro level, i.e. Indian art, along with Oriental art and their extensions.

In addition to the art objects themselves, the epigraphic evidences are of basic importance. With the help of the latter, some speculations have been cleared and corroborations made on information based on literary sources, both indigenous and foreign. Often, in the methodology of this study, it becomes imperative that the chronological attribution of some artifacts has to be based entirely on their stylistic elements. We have tried to take due notice of the decorative details (the individual or set of motifs) which were usually drawn from a common repertoire of the period and definitely have been current in a much wider geographical area or zone. Hence it has been necessary to undertake occasional visual explorations of other art centres pertinent to this study, so as to have a better understanding of the Śaka/Scythian elements in early Indian art. After all, no art can possibly develop in total isolation, and Śaka/Scythian art was no exception to this general rule.

References

1. *Geog. Cla. Pt.*, p. 142.
2. *Ibid.*, p. 147.
3. *Ibid.*
4. *Agr. So. Imp. Par. Hist.*, p.2.
5. *Geog. Cla. Pt.*, p. 147.
6. *Ibid.*, p. 148.
7. Kwang-Chih Chang, *The Archaeology of Ancient China*, New Haven and London, 3rd ed., 1977, p. 205.
8. George B. Schaller, *Mountain Monarchs, Wild Sheep and Goats of the Himalaya*, London 1977, p. 11.
9. *Hist. Rus. Cen. Asi. Mon.*, Vol. I, p. 127.
10. *Gol. De. Eur.*, p. 58.
11. Haraprasad Ray, *Trade and Trade Routes between India and China*, Calcutta 2003, p. 27.

2 Scythia and Śaka: Territories and Connotations

The geographical connotations of Scythia and the Saka/Śaka territories, as revealed from archaeological and literary sources are coucial in ascertaining the mechanism involved in the migration of art forms. Archaeologists have often taken the help of theorizations regarding the theory of nomadism in studying the nomadic cultures of different regions (widely spaced and belonging to different time spans). Primarily, nomadisation occurs in response to environmental inability and political insecurity (both are interrelated) in an unstable subsistence strategy based on pastoral economy. According to some social anthropologists and historians, nomadism occurs as a result of the specialization and integration of pastoralism and cultivation and this was solely possible with the growth of complex urban societies.[1] On the other hand scholars[2] have pushed the search for nomadic origins to the neolithic[3] phase. A thorough study of the objects of Scythian culture found from Ukraine (North Black Sea region), North Caucasus and Siberia shows that they were closely related in style and form. These objects date from the sixth century B.C. onwards. At the same time they are again similar to the artifacts from Siberia and Altai dated in the ninth century B.C. onwards.

It was firstly Herodotus (fifth century B.C.) who devoted a large part of his *Historiae* to a description of the lands of the Scythians and to their traditions, and from him we come to know that the land of the Scythians was confined to the flat lands north of the Black Sea, the Thracian coastlands and adjoining Asia Minor. Speaking of Asia Minor, it may be mentioned that the nomadic presence in West Asia was also noted in Assyrian chronicles. As early as the seventh century B.C. the nomads were known in Assyrian sources as the Sakas, Ashguzāi. Assyrians labelled them as Ashguzāi, Asguzāi, or Ishkuzāi (=Scuthai). Scythians are first mentioned by the Assyrians in 676-652 B.C., in a fragmentary series of questions made by the Assyrian king Esarhaddon to the oracle of the god Shamash.[4] The Scythians appeared near the north-eastern frontiers of Assyria during this time and, because of their war-like mobility and fighting skills, they justifiably dominated the political scenario and held important positions in the military hierarchy of the near East. The Scythians in all probability settled in the northern Caucasus region after leaving Assyria. Northern Caucasus was near Assyria. It is noteworthy that the famous early kurgans of Kelermes and Ulski (dated in the mid-seventh century B.C.) were situated in northern Caucasus. The Scythian presence in the north Black Sea region is also well reflected in stone inscriptions, coins, and in the writings of many observers following Herodotus. Many Greek writers referred to all the nomads of Eurasia, including those of Central Asia, as Scythians. Although the Scythians were not the only non-Greeks in this large region, it came to be known as Scythia.

However, the name Scythia was probably also extended to some eastern areas including Kazakhstan, Uzbekistan, Turkmenistan, Kyrgyzstan and Tajikistan, i.e., a major portion of Central Asia. By Central Asia we mean the present territories of Afghanistan, North-Eastern Iran, Pakistan, Northern India, Western China, Mongolia and the former Soviet Central Asian Republics. It is significant that much of the North-Western Himalayas belong to the steppes of Central Asia. Archaeologists have grouped together the steppe-desert zones of Central Asia, Sinkiang, Mongolia and South-Western Siberia as one, on the basis of vegetation and topography. The Śaka territory needs some mention here. The Persians designated all the nomadic tribes of the Eurasian steppes, including the Scythians, as the Śakas. We already know that the Achaemenid empire had established the Syr Darya as its northern frontier against the nomadic Śakas. It might be mentioned here that Central Asia during the first half of the first millennium B.C. had experienced the changes that followed the introduction of iron. The process of learning to produce iron was facilitated by the previous experience of working in bronze. The predecessors of the Scythians (the inhabitants of Arzhan in the eighth century and the people of the Tagar culture) had developed a sophisticated bronze metallurgy. The scholarly world believes that the early Scythian archaeology indicates that this mastery was inherited by the Scythians along with the common object typology and iconography. Herein the new technology of iron was assimilated slowly and the obvious advantages of the new metal were not immediately recognized (as revealed by archaeology). The protagonists of the Indo-European theory feel that the lands of the Avesta most probably correspond to the ethno-geological connotations of its name — the Aryan territory. Its socio-cultural character includes the entire Aral and Syr Darya belt, stretching from Chorasmia (the Chorasmians are incidentally mentioned by Herodotus and Hecataeus of Miletus) to Ferghana in the east. Between the seventh and fifth centuries B.C., Chorasmia and Ferghana witnessed rapid urbanization and at the height of its power under Darius I, the Achaemenid empire included Chorasmia, the *Śakā Tigraxaudā*, Sogdians and the 'Śakas who are beyond Sogdiana'. The first three are recorded in the list of countries subordinate to the next Persian king, Xerxes (486/465 B.C.), in the inscriptions and reliefs at Persepolis, Susa and Naqsh-i-Rustam. As a result, a significant proportion of the sedentary zone of northern Central Asia was included in the Achaemenid empire at the height of its prosperity. Only Ferghana lay beyond its borders as mentioned earlier. Chorasmia with Sogdiana and others made up the sixteenth satrapy, while the satrapy of the Śakas paid two hundred and fifty silver talents to the Persians. Thus they played a considerable role in the economy and politics of the Achaemenid empire. Sources record the Śaka presence in Nippur and other Babylonian cities. A Śaka detachment fought in Darius's army at the Battle of Marathon (490 B.C.) and in other engagements. Incidentally, terracotta figurines of Śaka warriors in pointed caps and long narrow trousers have been found in excavations at various places in the Achaemenid empire, ranging from Egypt to Central Asia.[5] By the second half of the fourth century B.C., the Śakas had become independent in the valleys of oases of northern Central Asia, as revealed by stable strata details. A Śaka community arose between the lower Amu Darya and the Syr Darya and in the hill country of the upper Syr Darya. Valuable evidence for its anthropological and ethnic characters come from the Bisutun, Persepolis and the Naksh-i-Rustam reliefs. To judge from these, the Central Asian peoples and tribes were virtually indistinguishable in clothing, head-gear and armaments. Their dress was much the same, consisting of short tunics, a broad belt and narrow trousers, only the *Śakā Tigraxaudā* were set apart by their sharp-pointed caps.

We come back to Herodotus. According to him, the Sakai (i.e. the Śakas) were in truth the Amurgioi Skutha (i.e. the Amyrgian Scythians).[6] Strabo indicates that the Sakai and several other peoples were known by the general name Skuthai (i.e. the Scythians).[7] Arrian refers to the Sakai (i.e. the Śakas), "a Skuthon" (i.e. Scythian people) "of the Skuthai" (i.e. the Scythians) "who inhabit Asia".[8] Ptolemy describes not only Skuthia (i.e. Scythia) "within the Imaos"[9] and "beyond the Imaos"[10] but also speaks of the "Land of the Sakai" (i.e. the Śakas).[11] It appears that to these classical authors the Śakas were Scythians, but not all Scythians were Śakas. The Sakai or the Sakas of the classical sources have been universally identified with the people called by the name Saka (also spelt Śaka) in Indian sources. It is apparent, therefore, that the Scythians were not wholly identical with the Śakas of Indian sources. It should, however, be noted here that there was a tendency in different quarters from an early period to identify the Scythians with the Sakas (Śakas). Herodotus observed that the Persians used to call all Skuthai (or Scythians) by the name Saka.[12] Pliny stated that to some tribes of the Scythae (i.e. the Scythians) "the Persians have given the general name of the Sacae" (=Sakas), "from the tribe nearest to them".[13]

This probably explains why the Scythians began to be known as Sakas (=Śakas). Originally and fundamentally the names Saka or Saca (Śaka) and Skutha or Scytha did not have one and the same connotation. The question of the distribution of the Śaka tribes is extremely complex. Literary evidence presents the most varied and contradictory points of view. The location of the different tribes is mainly determined from the extant archaeological data. The archaeological data are mainly complemented by the Nakshi-i-Rustam inscription of Darius I (522-480 B.C.) which lists the following three Śaka tribal confederations: a) The *śakā Haumavargā*, in Ferghana, where we have seen that the Sakas had begun to change over to a settled form of life; b) The *śakā Tigrakhaudā*, in the region beyond the Syr Darya and in Semirechye; and c) The *śakā tayaiy paradraya*, or European Sakas (Scythians).[14] In his list of Darius' satrapies, Herodotus also mentions the Caspians and the Sacae as belonging to the fifteenth province. As suggested by Oswald Szemerenyi, the Greek term Skythai is the earlier Iranian Skuta i.e. an archer.[15]

The Scythians were culturally related to the Sauromatians in the Volgo-Ural region. Herodotus incidentally writes of the Sauromatians as pastoral nomads living on the steppes to the east of the Scythians. Excavations (concluded in 1990) in the Volgo-Ural region have revealed the marvellous finds from the twenty-five barrows at Filippovka. These finds have been dated by K.F. Smirnov to the late fifth and early fourth century B.C. According to Herodotus, the Sauromatians arose from the union of Scythians and Amazons. The Scythians are often related with the Sarmatians who probably arose from a union of nomadic invaders from the east and Sauromatians.[16] The Scythians were also related to the Massagetae in the region east of the Caspian Sea.

Herodotus[17] describes the Pontic Scythian tribes partly as sedentary agriculturalists but he says[18] that the Massagetae of Central Asia "sow no grain but live by keeping herds and fishing; they also drink milk". Excavations at Chirik-Rabat, a site associated with the Massagetae on the north-west of the Kyzyl Kum desert, showed that in their economy the ancient traditions of fishing were combined with farming and semi-nomadic pastoralism.[19] A whole range of Scythian-type cultures have been associated with the Śaka sites in Central Asia on the Syr Darya, in the Pamirs, and in Semirechye (east of Lake Balkash). The Pazyryk culture in the Altai, the Tagar culture in Southern Siberia and the stock-breeding cultures of Mongolia constituted the Scytho-Siberian tradition, the main predecessor of the Śaka/Scythian art forms. Thus the geographical area of southern Siberia and adjoining lands constitute possible extensions during the time of the early Śakas.

The classical sources knew about the conquest of the Graeco-Bactrian kingdom by nomadic tribes around 130 B.C. These nomadic tribes were referred to as peoples who came from beyond the Jaxartes (now the Syr Darya).

Strabo mentions four tribes: the Asioi, the Pasianoi, the Tokharoi and the Sakarauloi.[20] Pompeius Trogus notes briefly that the Asiani, kings of the Tochari laid waste the Sacaraucae.[21] The Śakas were driven out from the Greco-Bactrian kingdom by the Yýeh-chih (as mentioned in *Shih-chi* of Szu-ma Ch'ien, the *Han-shu*, the *Hou Han-shu* and the *Pei-shih*). Thereafter the Śakas established a series of kingdoms in eastern Iran and north-western India as known from archaeological data, Graeco-Roman literary works and occasional references in Sanskrit texts. In the first century A.D. along with the Parthians or Pahlavas they ruled a territory stretching from the Seistan to the north-western India.

It is interesting to note that Herodotus's references to the Scythians and modern archaeological finds suggest trade in gold from Siberia and silk from China through the routes in Central Asia. When the Greeks began to rule in Bactria it was already a potential trading zone.[22] It was at the meeting point of various trade routes which were important in long distance trade in which India was also a participant. Among the suggested sources of the supply of gold to Bactria, ancient Scythia (which included parts of the southern section of the former U.S.S.R.) may be included. Along with ancient Scythia, the Ural and Altai regions may also be included.[23] On the other hand the Chinese treatises of the first century B.C. and early centuries of the Christian era refer to China's communications with the Western countries. From the report of Chang Ch'ien as quoted in the *Shih-Chi*[24] (completed in c. 100 B.C.), it appears that it was possible to travel from the mainland of China (Eastern China) to the area on the Kuei river (Oxus) through a route passing over the northern section of the Taklamakan desert in Sin-Kiang.[25] It appears from certain Greek texts of the fourth and third centuries B.C. (as quoted in later writings) that a route from West Asia passed through Aria (the area of Herat in north-western Afghanistan including Kandahar) to Hortospanum (Kabul). From there it passed through Peucolatis (Charsada in the Peshawar District), Taxila (near Rawalpindi), and finally reached Palibothra.[26] Bactra (Balkh), the capital of Bactria (to the north-west of the Hindu Kush and south of the Oxus) must have been connected with Aria (Herat area) and Margiana (Merv area in Turkmenistan) on the west, Sogdiana (to the north of the Oxus) on the north, and Kubhā (Kabul), Kapiśā (Begram) and Lampaka (Lamghan) in the south-west and then beyond the Hindu Kush. This West Asian route was probably referred to as Krpty (Kārāpath?) in two edicts[27] of Asoka (c.272-236 B.C.). The *Stathmoi Parthikoi*[28] of about the end of the first century B.C. suggests the continuation of the use of the route from Aria and through Zarangiana (Seistan) to Arachosia (Kandahar region). Eratosthenes (c. 275-194 B.C.) also mentions the Royal Road.[29]

In Central Asia the Śakas still ruled in pockets. Like the Scythians, the Sakas/ Śakas also had different ethnic groups. Between the third and the eighth centuries of the Christian era, one of the oldest local ethnic groups in Chach, Ilak (eastern bank of Syr Darya) and Ferghana consisted of Śaka tribes from beyond the Syr Darya.[30] They probably spoke Iranian (Saka dialect) as recorded in medieval Arabic and Persian literature and corroborated by numismatic sources. Saka documents dating from the seventh to the tenth century A.D. have been found in Khotan and Tumshuq, both oases around the Tarim Basin.[31] Oases around the Tarim Basin include Kashgar, Yarkand, Karghalik, Khotan, Kerya, Niya, Aksu and Kucha. These documents, written in Brāhmi script, represent several dialects. It is interesting to note that at an early date, people known to the Chinese as the Sai (derived from archaic Chinese 'sak') sought a home in the west and south of the Tarim. Patient studies of the geographic, literary and epigraphic evidence have identified the Sai with the Sakā known to the Achaemenid Persians, Greek geographers and historians, and with the Śakas in Indian texts. The Śakas must have come to Khotan long before the second century B.C. According to the *Han-shu*, the Sai tribes split and formed several states. The people of Tashkurgan in the Pamirs may perhaps been a branch of the Śakas since they could have spoken a language close to the Khotanese. Excavations have revealed Śaka cemeteries in this region. As late as the eleventh century the people of the Kashgar area spoke a dialect that can be classified as the Śaka language.[32]

Thus, the coordinates of space and time which define Scythian/Saka history boast of an amazing ancestory. How ever, there is enough evidence to encourage further investigations and to point to archaeology (as there is paucity of written sources) as the principal medium enquiry.

References

1. A.M. Khazanov, *Nomads and the Outside World,* Cambridge, 1984, p.209.
2. A.S. Gilbert, 'On the origins of specialized nomadic pastoralism in Western Iran', *World Archaeology*, Vol.15, pp.105-119.
3. Roger Cribb, *Nomads in Archaeology,* Cambridge, 1993, p.10.
4. *Gol. De. Eur.*, p.42.
5. Our information regarding the political history is partially based on the Volume. *Hist. Civ. Cen. As.*, Vol.II, p.45.
6. *Hist.*, VII. 64.
7. *Geographikon*, VI. 8, 2.
8. Anabaseos Alexandrou, III. 8, 3. ; cf. also Historarium Alexandri Magni Macedonis, VII. 8 and VIII. 4.
9. *Geog. Hup.*, VI. 12, 1f.
10. *Ibid.*, VI. 15, 1f.
11. *Ibid.*, V. 13, 1f.
12. *Hist.*, VII. 64.
13. *Nat. Hist.*, VI. 19, 50.
14. *Hist. Civ. Cen. As.*, Vol. II, p.44.
15. *Gol.De.Eur.*, p.19.
16. *Ibid.*, p.3.
17. *Hist.*, IV. 17-18.
18. *Ibid.*, I. 216.
19. *Hist. Civ. Cen. As.*, p.30.
20. *Geographikon*, XI. 8, 2.

21. *Prologus XLI* of the *Historiae Philippicae.*
22. F. Holt, *Alexander the Great and Bactria: The Formation of a Greek Frontier in Central Asia,* Leiden, 1988, p.32.
23. G. Adhya, *Early Indian Economics*, Bombay, 1966, p.180.
24. *H.H.S.,* Ssu-pupei-yao edition, Ch. 118.
25. *Shih-chi,* Ssu-pupei-yao edition, Ch 123; cf. also B.Watson, *Records of the Grand Historian of China,* Vol.II, New York, 1961, pp.266f.
26. *Nat. Hist.*, VI. 21, 61-64.
27. B.N. Mukherjee, *Studies in the Aramaic Edicts of Asoka*, Calcutta, 1984, pp.12, 14, 16.
28. *Stat.Par.*,1.
29. *Geographikon*, XV. 1,77; cf. also *Indike*, III. 1-5.
30. *Hist. Civ. Cen. As.*, Vol. III, p.279.
31. *Ibid.*, p.283.
32. H. W. Bailey, *The Culture of the Śakas in Ancient Iranian Khotan*, New York,1982, p.56.

3 THE ŚAKAS AND THE ŚAKA-PAHLAVAS IN THE INDIAN SUBCONTINENT

It appears that the Scythians invaded India from at least three directions. Since all Śakas were Scythians but not all Scythians were Śakas, and since some sources indicate that the Scythians in the east were called Śakas, as the literary and epigraphic texts of ancient India and Iran often mention, the Scythians in Indian territories will also be referred as Śaka/Scythians. The three major directions from which the Śaka/Scythians invaded India were, in the first place, from the former Sai country (to be placed in the modern Ili basin) through Hsien-tu to Chi-pin or Kashmir. Secondly, there was a Scythian migration across the Hindu Kush into the north-western borderlands of the Indian subcontinent. Thirdly, they came from Seistan via Arachosia and the Brahui mountains into the lower Indus country.[1]

As a result of tribal movements, as well as due to the aggression of neighbours, the Scythians who were originally Central Asian nomadic tribes, formed a number of ethnic groups. They appear to have founded various settlements in different regions even in very ancient times. In the early records of the Achaemenid dynasty of Persia, reference is made to no less than three settlements of the Śakas who were subjects of the Achaemenids. These were the *Śakā Tigrakhaudā* (Śakas with pointed helmets), *Śakā Haumavargā* and *Śakā tayaiy paradraya* (Śakas beyond the sea).

The Śakas with pointed helmets are probably also referred to in the Achaemenian records. They lived beyond Suguda or Sogdiana (modern Bukhāra region). According to Herodotus, they were the neighbours of the Bactrians[2]. They are supposed to have lived in the plains of the Jaxartes or Syr Darya. The *Śakā Haumavargā* have been identified by scholars including D.C.Sircar with the Scythian settlers of Drangiana in the Helmund valley which was known later as Śakastān (modern Seistan). The Śakas of the land beyond the sea are usually believed to have been those who lived in the Russian steppes to the north of the Black Sea.[3]

As mentioned above[4], the first major direction from which the Śaka/Scythians invaded India was from the north, from the former Sai country.The *Ch'ien Han-shu* (ch. 96B) states that the territiory of the Wu-sun (in the lli basin and including the area on the lake Issyk-kul) was originally the country of Sai (Sakas).When the Great Yueh-chih went to the west and defeated and drove away the Sai wang (Śaka king), the latter went southwards and crossed Hsûan-Tu and the great Yýeh-chih occupied their country. This happened during the reign of the Hsiung- nu ruler Mao-dun (171-158 B.C.). This migration probably took place between 174 and 160 or 158 B.C.[5] The *Ch'ien Han-Shu* (ch. 96A) further records that the Sai king went southwards and became ruler of Chipin[6] and indicates that the Śakas following their leader migrated through the area of Su-le (Kashgarh). It appears that a section of the Śakas migrated southwards from the Lake Issyk-kul and through Kashgarh and the Pamirs entered Chipin the name of which can be phonetically related to that of Kaśmira, included a part of the north-western section of the Indian subcontinent (incorporating the Kashmir valley). Thus, the earliest Saka (Śaka) invasion of India, which came from the north, resulted in the establishment of a Saka (Śaka) kingdom in the extreme north-west (including Swat and Darel and also the Gilgit and Chilas areas) by c. 158 B.C. At that time (100 B.C. - A.D. 50) the Indo-Greeks were a major power in that part of the subcontinent. This inference is supported by Patañjali, who, in about the first half of the second century B.C. indicated in his *Mahābhāsya* (II, 4, 10), that the Śakas lived outside Āryāvarta situated to the south of the Himavat or the Himalayan region.

Secondly, they came from the north-west. The Yýeh-chih occupation of the Śaka territory on the Lake Issyk-Kul might have also compelled a section of the Śakas to move westwards from the Lake issyk-Kul region in the direction of the Jaxartes river or Syr Darya and beyond (as indicated by the *Prologus* XLI of the *Historiae Philippicae* of Trogus, which refers to the Scythian invasions of Bactria (or the

Bactrians and Sogdiana between the Jaxartes and Oxus).[7] The Greeks ruled over these territories or at least Bactria.

The Bactrian Greeks of the post-Alexandrian period were a significant power. The Seleucid house of the Alexandrian legacy ended sometime between c. 246 and 237 B.C. when Diodotus, a Greek satrap of Bactria, revolted and became independent of the Seleucid empire.[8] About a hundred years later, the Śaka-Scythians gave the final blow to the Greeks. He was succeeded by his son Diodotus II who was defeated by Euthydemus. Euthydemus probably had established his authority over Sogdiana (between the Oxus and the Jaxartes river). One of his coin-types showing a bust and seated Heracles is known to have been imitated by the Tokharian nomads in the territory of Sogdiana.[9]

Chang Ch'ien saw the Yueh-chih in occupation of Ta-hsia or roughly, eastern Bactria, in c. 130/129 B.C. By or before this year, the Greek rule must have ended in Bactria.[10] According to Strabo,[11] Bactriana was taken away from the Greeks by the Scythian nomads like the Asioi, Pasianoi, Tokharoi and the Sakarauloi, who had originally come "from the country on the other side of the Jaxartes river that adjoins that of the Sakai and the Sogdianoi and was occupied by the Sakai". Thus, it appears, that the Śakas had occupied a part of Transoxiana before conquering Bactria. Bactria, at that time was a centre of Greek culture. Thus the nomads came in direct contact with the Greek culture and naturally the latter influenced these tribes. Round about this time (130-125 B.C.) the Imperial Parthians began to take some interest in the Indus region. Attempts of such an expansion of power were in the logic of their struggle against their enemies, the Greeks, who were contemporary masters of the territory in question. Mithradates I conquered at least a part of Arachosia from the Greeks.[12] From the same power he perhaps captured an area on the lower Indus, perhaps including Patalene. From Bactria the Sakas migrated across the Hindu Kush into the north-western borderlands of the Indian subcontinent.[13]

From the west, the Śaka migration involved the Arsacid emperor, Mithridates II (c.123-88/87 B.C.), who according to Justin,[14] scored success against the Scythians and added many new provinces to the Parthian empire. He could have subdued the Scythian (Saka) nomads in western Bactria. A section of them could have ultimately settled in about Drangiana or Śakastāna of *Stathmoi Parthikoi* towards the end of the first century B.C. The Parthian philhellenism had an impact over another group of Śakas who lived in Śakastāna or Seistan owing allegiance to the Arsacids. In course of its description of an itinerary of a caravan trail, the *Stathmoi Parthikoi*[15] states that in the city of Sigal in Śakastāna, a part of the Parthian empire "is the royal residence of the Sakai" (i.e. the Śakas). This certainly means the existence of a Śaka feudatory state in Śakastāna or the Seistan region in or about the last quarter of the 1st century B.C. In Seistan, the Scythians (including the Śakas) and the Parthians mingled with each other forming a composite people whom we may call the Scytho-Parthians. Thus the Śakas of Śakastāna was within the limits of the Parthian empire and were likely to develop a close relationship with the Pahlavas or Parthians who were the ruling groups in India hailing from that direction in the first century B.C. as well as first century A.D. Hence, they may be called Śaka-Pahlava or Scytho-Parthians. The activities of the different groups of Śakas and Śaka-Pahlavas in the subcontinent can be enumerated on the basis of numismatic, epigraphic and literary sources. The names of the Śaka-Pahlava and Scytho-Parthian rulers are furnished mainly by their coins, several varieties of which can be attributed to different areas on the basis of their types and major findspots. Such attributions help us in determining the limits of the domains of different rulers. There was an increase of alloy in the metallic currency of North-Western India during the period between c.50 B.C. and A.D. 50. This has been attributed to the absence of a strong monarch or political authority in a commercially important zone like North-Western India. This factor probably tempted private moneyers to mint coins.[16] In the Scytho-Parthian period, the tendency to replace good money by sub-standard coinage became so popular and powerful that an important ruler like Azes II could not check it. However, in the Kushāna period, coinage got reformed.

Against the above noted background of the advent of the Śakas in India and its borderlands, the activities of different groups of Śakas and Śaka-Pahlavas in the subcontinent can be studied.

The earliest Śaka kingdom was established by c. 158 B.C. in a region of the extreme north-western section of the Indian subcontinent, which included Darel and Swat on the Indus and also Gilgit and the Chilas area. The area was then known as a part of Chi-pin. It is not certain whether the Kashmir valley was a part of the Śaka kingdom. We also do not know the name of the earliest Śaka king in India. However, there is an indication that the Śaka power spread southwards via the Hazara region. A Kharoshti inscription on a rock near Shahdaur in the Hazara country refers to a king called Damijada (or Namijada) as a Śaka. Obviously the king had the Hazara area under his sway.[17] Regarding the extension of Śaka inroads into India, it may be noted that they must have been aware of the existing trade routes penetrating the Indian subcontinent. For example, the Audambaras and the Indo-Greeks had busy trade relations based on favourable commercial routes joining Kashmir with the Gangetic valley.[18]

The extension of the Śaka rule to the Shah Dheri (ancient Taxila) area is suggested by an inscription found in that locality. It records a pious act at or near Takhaúilā by Patika, the son of Liaka Kusuluka, a scion of the Kshaharātam (family) and the *Kshatrapa* of Chukhsa,[19] in the year 78 and during the reign of the Great King, the Great Moga. The name indicates Scythian affiliation.

It appears that the territory of Chukhsa or the Sind Sagar Doab between the Indus and Jhelum (including Taxila or Shah Dheri near Rawalpindi) was ruled by a governor named Moga in the year 78. The year can be attributed to the so-called old Śaka Era of 170 B.C. Thus, by c.92 B.C. Moga, probably of a group of Śakas, occupied a part of the Punjab (now in Pakistan). Moga has been universally identified with Moa and Maues of legends on several varieties of coins.[20] Maues probably conquered Gandhāra to the west of the Indus from the Indo-Greek ruler, Artemidorus. From the group of Maues, if not from the Greeks themselves, the hegemony over Arachosia passed to the Imperial Parthians. With the end of the hegemony of the group of Maues towards the close of the first quarter of the first century B.C. ended the first phase of the Śaka or Śaka-Pahlava rule in India. In Sind Sagar Doab and Gandhāra, the Indo-Greek rule was re-established. The Indo-Greeks to the east of the Jhelum, which had not been disturbed by Maues, continued to rule in that zone.

In about the second quarter of the first century B.C. Arachosia passed into the hands of another group of rulers.[21] Their coins have been discovered mainly within the limits of its territory. On the basis of the inscriptions on the coins of the group of rulers concerned, they can be divided into several classes. The first class bears the names of Vonones and Spalahora. The second class bears the names of Vonones and Spalagadama. The third class of coins mentions the name of Spalyris and Spalagadama. The fourth class of silver coins refers to Spalirises and Spalirisa. The fifth group of copper coins mentions Spalirises and Spalirisa.[22] Thus Indo-Parthian coins show the rule of Parthian or Scytho-Parthians like Vonones and Spalirises in Arachosia (Kandahar area in South-east Afghanistan).Together with the above classes of coins we should consider another group of coins[23] bearing the name of Azes on the obverse and on the reverse Azilises. Another group has these names in the reverse order. These groups of coins ultimately prove the existence of Azes I, Azilises and Azes II. Azes I, who probably began to rule in c. 58 B.C. hailed from

Arachosia. He conquered Gandhāra[24] and the Sind Sagar Doab including Taxila.[25] Azilises, his co-ruler and successor, controlled an area to the west of the Indus. On the east, he probably extended his rule up to Mathurā.

The coins of the Scytho-Parthian ruler Vonones and his associates carry the device of Herakles on the reverse of their coins (naked, beardless Herakles with a lion skin over his left raised club in the half raised left hand and right hand crowning his head with a wreath). These coins are found mainly in the regions of Kandahar, Ghazni (both included in ancient Arachosia).[26] Hence the Vonones type may be referred to that territory. Some coins of Vonones are found in Seistan, Kabul, Taxila and different places of the Punjab area of Pakistan. Thus, the provenances of coins locate the kingdom of the group concerned only in Arachosia and its vicinity. This inference is corroborated by the fact that not a single coin of Spalirises, who is to be associated with the Vonones group, has been discovered at Taxila. Only three coins of Spalirises and two of Spaliris, another member of that group, were found at Begram . The number is too small to indicate the rule of the Vonones group in the Begram area. One Azes was associated with Spalirises,[27] but his direct relation with Vonones is not known and this Azes may not be taken as one of Vonones' associates.

The names of the rulers of the group of Vonones as found in Indo-Parthian coins betray Scythic as well as Parthian affiliations. Therefore, it should have its origin in the Śaka-Pahlava or Scytho-Parthian area of Śakastanā. Spalrises served as an associate of Vonones before becoming the sole ruler of Arachosia. Later he had to accept Azes I as his co-ruler. The coins of Azes I struck independently with the devices (seated Herakles, etc.) used earlier by the group of Vonones in Arachosia can be attributed to that region. There are clear numismatic evidences that Azes I extended his authority to the north-western section of the Indian subcontinent. The "City goddess of Pushkalavati : bull" type coins[28] of Azes I indicate his presence in the area of Pushkalavati (Charsada in the Peshawar district). Azes I had for sometime a co-ruler in Azilises. On the basis of the coins it appears that Azilises extended the Scytho-Parthian power to Mathurā. Azilises was succeeded by Azes II. No coin-type of Azes II can be found at Arachosia. On the other hand, the *Stathmoi-Parthikoi* of Isidore of Charax, compiled on the basis of the information collected up to c. first B.C., includes Śakastāna and Arachosia within the Parthian empire. The *Stathmoi Parthikoi* of Isidore of Charax (in the closing decades of the first century B.C.) states that "beyond (Zarangiana) is Sakastana of the Skythian (or

Scythian) Sakai (or Sacae), which is also Paraitakene, 63 schoeni. There are the cities of Banda, Min, Palacenti and Segal; in that place is the royal residence of the Sakai (or Sacae).... As far as this place, the land is under the rule of the Parthians."[29]

Thus from the testimony of Isidore, we come to know that by the last quarter of the 1st century B.C. Śakastāna or Seistan and Arachosia including the Kandahar area were within the Parthian empire.[30] This inference is in a way supported by a section of chapter 96A of the *Ch'ien Han-shu*.[31] So Arachosia was lost by the group of Azes I either towards the close of the reign of Azilises or rather in the beginning of the rule of Azes II. There is no indication of the reign of Azes II in the Mathurā area. The Mathurā region was under the *Mahākshtrapa* Rajula (Rājuvula).[32] Sodāsa succeeded him. Since Sodāsa, the son of Rājuvula was a *Mahākshatrapa* in the year 72 (A.D. 13-14), as indicated by the Āmohini votive tablet inscription, Rājuvula might have conquered the territory of the Strato family either in the last quarter of the first century B.C. or in the first decade of the first century A.D. It appears that in the first quarter of the first century A.D. the satraps of Mathurā ruled without acknowledging the supremacy of the Azes group. Ultimately, the Śaka/Pahlava satrapal dynasty of Mathurā seems to have been overthrown by Kanishka.

Finally, the Śaka migration from the west was effected by the Gondophares group. The Takht-i-Bahi inscription[33] found near Mardan (Peshawar district) and the evidence from numismatic data suggest that the group of Gondophares more or less captured the kingdom of the Azes group. The group of Gondophares might well have come to the north-west in the wake of the Parthian invasion. Its presence in Arachosia and Śakastāna, the two regions of the Parthian empire, are attested to by numismatic evidences. On some copper coins of Gondophares, we find the name of one Orthagnes.[34] It appears that Orthagnes commenced his rule in Seistan swearing allegiance to the imperial Parthian throne sometime before the rule of Gondophares, the first year of which corresponds to A.D. 20/21. The coins of Gondophares, based typologically on the issues of Orthagnes in Sakastana and Arachosia, allude to his rule in these areas. Gondophares also ruled over the lower Indus country.[35] His family probably extended its authority up to the Mathurā area.[36]

Syrastrene or Saurashtra is mentioned by Ptolemy as a province of Indo-Scythia and is described as the region about the mouths of the Indus and the Gulf of Kanthi or Gulf of Kutch.[37] In the second or the third quarter of the 2nd century A.D.,

Ptolemy enumerated Patalene, Syrastrene, and Aberia or Sabeiria as the provinces of Indo-Scythia.[38] As a tract is not likely to be called after a people until some time after their first settlement in it, Ptolemy's evidence should indicate that the Scythian colonization of these provinces probably started long before the date of his *Geographike Huphegesis* i.e. the second or third quarter of the second century A.D. Thus the advent of the Śakas in the territory concerned might have taken place even before the dawn of the Christian Era.[39] There is no evidence of a Śaka migration to the lower Indus area in the period of the Achaemenids of Persia. So the Arsacid dynasty or the Imperial Parthians of the East, which ruled from c. 250 B.C. to c. A.D. 227 or A.D. 228/29, after ousting the Greek successors of the Achaemenids and Alexander, witnessed the first Śaka activities in the lower Indus country. Ptolemy's provinces of Indo-Scythia coincides with two of the three territories indicated in the Jaina *Kālakāchārya-kathānaka* which were colonized by the Sagas[40] or Śakas by the first century B.C. before the latter settled in Saurashtra. Also the *Periplous Tes Erythras Thalasses* (or the *Periplus Maris Erythraei*), a text probably of the first century A.D. locates Scythia in the lower Indus area.[41]

Thus, the testimonies of the *Kālakāchāraya-kathānaka* and *Geographike Huphegesis* not only indicate the presence of a Śaka colony on the lower Indus including Patalene probably under the rule of the Imperial Parthians but also the activities of the Śakas or Scythians in Saurashtra.

That Parthian rule continued in the Sindhu valley as late as the eighth decade of the first century A.D. is evidenced by the *Periplus* which says, "Before it (Barbaricum on the principal mouth of the Sindhu) there lies a small island and inland behind it is the metropolis of Scythia, Min-Nagara; it is subject to Parthian princes who are constantly driving each other out."[42]

The Scythian satrapal dynasty of Mathura seems to have been overthrown by Kanishka. The Kushānas did not totally uproot the numerous Śaka principalities under subordinate chiefs. In the Rajasthan area, several tribal states appear to have submitted to the Śaka-Scythians. During the early part of the first century B.C., the Mālavas had settled in the Ajmer-Mewar region while the Indo-Greek kingdoms of the Punjab were well on the way of decline. They were gradually displaced by the Sakas and Pahlavas who were in turn overthrown, at least in north-western and northern India, by the Kushānas in the second half of the first century A.D. The kingdom of the Śaka-Kshatrapas of western India continued to exist along with the rule of the imperial Kushāṇas. While the Śakas and Kushāṇas dominated portions of northern and western India, the Satavahanas of central Deccan enjoyed imperial status in the South. In western Uttar Pradesh and the adjoining region of Punjab, the Śakas dominated till the time of the early kings of the Gupta dynasty. The Śakas under Chashana and Rudradāman ruled over parts of western Maharashtra. The continuation of Śaka rule over Rajasthan (till the end of the first quarter of the third century A.D.) is indicated by the discovery of the coins of the successors of Rudradāman I from this region. Their successors were finally defeated by Chandragupta II and the Śaka dominions were annexed to the Gupta empire.

References

1. *Agr. So. Imp. Par. Hist.*, p. 205.
2. According to Arrian, a chief named Mauaces or Mavaces (i.e. Maues) who led the Sacians (Śakas), a Scythian tribe dwelling in Asia not far from Bactria and Sogdiana, was an ally of Darius III.
3. *The Age of Imperial Unity*, edited by R.C. Majumdar, Bombay, 1970, p.120.
4. See p.29, above.
5. B. Watson, *Records of the Grand Historian of China*, New York, 1961, Vol. II, pp.173-175.
6. *C.H.S.*, ch. 96A, p.10; ch. 96B, p.76.
7. P. Trogus, *Prologus XLI, Historiae Philippicae* (quoted in Justin's *Epitome*).
8. *Ibid.*, XLI. 4.
9. B.N. Mukherjee, *The Kushāṇa Genealogy*, Calcutta, 1967, p.25.
10. *Epitome*, XLII. I.
11. *Geographikon*, XI. 8, 2.
12. *His. Ad. Pag.*, V. 3, 16-17.
13. A.D.H. Bivar, 'Maues at Taxila', *JCA*. 7, pp.5-15.
14. *Epitome*, XLII. 2.
15. *The Parthian Stations by Isidore of Charax*, edited by W.H. Schoff, Philadelphia,1 9 1 4 , p.17.
16. B.N. Mukherjee, 'The Usefulness of Modern Economic Theories for The Study of Economic History of Ancient India-An Illustration', *J.A.S.*, Vol. X, No. 1, 1967, p.15.
17. *The Parthian Stations by Isidore of Charax*, edited by W.H.Schoff, Philadelphia, 1914, p. 207.
18. Osmund Bopearachchi, Wilfried Pieper, 'Ancient Indian Coins', *Indicopleustoi: Archaeologies of the Indian Ocean*, II, Turnhout, 1998, p.47.
19. *Cor.Ins.Ind.*, Vol. II, Pt.I, pp. 23f.
20. *C.H.I.*, Vol. I, p.570.
21. *C.C.G.S.K.*, pp., 98-100.
22. *Pun.Mus.Cat.*, Vol. I, p.143 and Pl. XIV, No. 397.

23. *Cat..Co.Ind.Mus.*, Vol.I, pp. 43f.
24. *Jour.Num.Soc.Ind.*, 1955, Vol. XVII, pt. II, pp. 5-8.
25. *Taxila*, Vol. II, p. 781; cf. also *P.M.C.*, Vol. I, p. 130.
26. *Num.Chr.*, 1890, pp. 106-107 and 109; cf. also *C.I.I.*, Vol. II, pt. I, p. XL.
27. *Num.Chr.*, 1890, pp.107 and 139.
28. *C.C.G.S.K.*, Pl. XXIX, No. 15; cf. also *Pun.Mus.Cat.*, Vol. I, Pl. XII, No. 308.
29. *Stat.Par.*, Sec. 19.
30. *Loc.cit.*
31. *C.H.S.*, ch. 96A; cf. also *J.A.I.*, 1881, Vol. X, p.23.
32. *Ep. Ind.*, Vol. II, p.199.
33. *Cor.Ins.Ind.*, Vol.II, pt. I, p.62.
34. *Pun.Mus.Cat.*, Vol. I, pp.155-156.
35. *Ibid.*, p.156.
36. J. Allan, *A Catalogue of the Indian Coins in the British Museum, Catalogue of the Coins of Ancient India*, p. CXV.
37. *Geog. Hup.*, VII. I, pp.55-61.
38. *Loc. cit.*
39. E. H. Bunbury, *A History of Ancient Geography* [2nd edition], Vol. II, p.548.
40. N. Brown, *The Story of Kālaka*, Washington, 1933, p.40.
41. *Periplus*, Section 38, translated by W. H. Schoff, New York, 1912.
42. *Ibid.*, Section 38.

4 THE SAGA OF THE SCYTHIAN-ŚAKA ART

The Scythians were an integral part of a broad cultural group that dominated the Eurasian Steppe zone between the eighth and fifth centuries B.C. They are often taken as a component of the Scytho-Siberian groups. This group included the semi-nomadic peoples, whose habitat extended from the borders of Greece and Persia to the borders of China (Zhou dynasty). The entire region was known as Scythia, although the Scythians were not the only non-Greeks in this region. The Scythians were the westernmost of these peoples, inhabiting the Crimea, the steppe and forest steppe to the north of the Black Sea, and the Kuban river basin. Herodotus in his *Historiae* has given a vivid description of the lands of the Scythians and their traditions. Their presence was also attested in stone inscriptions and coins of various dynasties and in the writings of many classical authors after Herodotus.

The western section of Scythian art includes different groups like the Kuban, Taman, Crimean, Don, Kiev and the bordering Ural group, the latter being the marking point for the eastern section of the Śaka/Scythian art. The region forming the western section included the Pontic steppes and European Russia, i.e. from the Ukraine to the River Volga. Scythian artifacts found from kurgans, east of Volga onwards till the frontiers of China and southwards till India have been coined as the eastern section of Scythian art or Saka/Scythian or Saka-Pahlava/Scythian art.

A. WESTERN SECTION

Early Scythian art objects are found from burials from the west of the Caspian Sea, often, west of the Caucasus Mountains till the borders of Eastern Europe, from the north of the Black Sea region in the south and eastwards till the borders of West Asia, in the north, till Western Siberia, and in the north-east till the land of the Sarmatians in South Siberia. What archaeologists find is hardly ever representative of the total materials and artifacts used in the past. The Scythians had no grand funerary structures temples over the burials of their dead.

The early stage of the Scythians saw the nomadic steppe origins which continued in the middle phase (beginning of the transition) and then the later Scythic phase saw the cultural transition from nomadic steppe origins to a partially settled way of life. All these three stages are well reflected in the materials from the burials or Kurgans. The Scythian antifacts may be broadly classified into four major types: 1. Utility objects, 2) Horse trappings, 3) Ornaments and 4) Weapons. These antifacts reveal that the Scythian culture was same how sandwiched between Central Asian, South Siberein, West Asian, Greek and other influences. The age covered by these objects is spread over centuries.

One is fascinated by the almost heraldic use of gold in Scythian art. They almost overshadow the bronze and silver antifacts. The early Scythian buoials reveal horse trappings of finely carved bone, indicative of an ancient carving tradition applied on wood or other parts of dead animals. The horse trappings of finely carved bone include eye-bars (Plate 1) for linking bridle reins in the shape of rams and ram-birds' heads as found from Kelermes.[1] They can be dated in the late seventh or early sixth centuries B.C. In this early Scythian or archaic period, the animal style seemed to be a natural blend of the unique Scythian artistic tradition and certain borrowed forms, mostly of ancient Oriental origin. Two imaginary creatures, specific to the Scythians, were predominant in their art, especially from the early period- 1) a flying ram with the beak of a bird of prey, and 2) the griffin or a winged lion, generally with an eagle's head. Another quiver ornament common to the early Scythian period included a curled-up beast of prey usually made of bone (Plate 2).[2] The style of the curled-up beast was rudimentary compared to later manifestations.

The introduction of the Bronze Age brought about great changes to the mountain peoples. In Asia, bronze, having spread into the basin of the Indus and into Iran, gave rise to the Tazabagyab culture south of Lake Aral (eighteenth to tenth century

B.C.). In Kazakhstan, it was bronze that united the pastoral tribes of the area under the Andronovo Culture (eighteenth to thirteenth century B.C.). Still, further east on Lake Baikal, the Glazkovo Culture (seventeenth to twelfth century B.C.) transmitted the secret of bronze metallurgy to China during the same period.[3] In ten centuries, the ancient Near Eastern bronze conquered the Eurasian economy. An equal passage of time was necessary for the aesthetic formulas of this bronze art to recross the continent in the opposite direction. The process was favoured by the persistence of the old Iranian-Anatolian formulas subsequently modified by the Karasuk culture near Minusinsk (tenth to seventh century B.C.) and by the Scythians (eighth to third century B.C.), in forming the basis for the subsequent nomadic art.

Advancement in the creation of useful objects does not necessarily mean an accompaniment of artistic development. Moreover, it can be definitely established that given art forms do not always determine the creation of analogous forms (in similar, parallel and different artistic environments) as exemplified by the bronzes of Scythia and Luristan and other assemblages of the earlier period.

Before classifying the Scythian objects it is important to note the organization of nomadic material culture in relation to their surviving strategy over a long period of time and space. Cribb refers to the three key dimensions in the context of conceiving nomadic material. Premierly, the extent to which the cultural assemblage is found on the site, i.e. (i) fixtures, (ii) portables. Secondly, material culture ranges from durables on the one hand to perishables on the other. A third dimension is about the value of the concerned items measured according to their economic need (i.e. valuables as opposed to expendables).[4] Considering the above factors, the Scythian nomadic material culture holds a significant place for a long period of time. The Scythian repertory made skillful use of bone, wood, wool, leather, precious metals, stones, etc. The Scythian nomads had developed an independent reflection of their encompassing world and religious ideas. Gold casting, hammering and stamping the gold foil or plate were widespread and gold was used to decorate bone artifacts and wooden objects. Their distinctive 'animal style' art is of a kind which is widespread in Central Asia as far east as Kazakhstan and Siberia. Excavations at Arzhan in Tuva, Mayemir kurgan in Altay Republic, and the Golden Barrow at Chiliktin in East Kazakhstan revealed that the early nomads were well acquainted with the technology of gold work. By the fifth and fourth century B.C. the Scythian nomads roamed over the vast, almost crescent-shaped steppe, which stretches from the confines of China to the banks of the Danube. The Scythians were highly mobile horse soldiers war parties and breeders of cattle and horses. In the north eastern section many of these peoples often displayed a tendency preserved by time, to migrate to the west or south-west of their starting point. The other side was perhaps inaccessible due to geographical barriers. Inner Asia provided long distance communication, or overland movement, in as much as no region on earth as it is landlocked by the absence of feasible maritime alternatives. The major movements of peoples, cultural innovations and goods have been through Inner Asian land routes far removed from the Pacific, Arctic and the Indian Oceans. It might be noted, however, that parts of the early Silk Road traffic was channeled through Indian Ocean ports. The use of the Black Sea and Caspian Sea routes were confined to margins of Inner Asia. The lists of tribes or peoples inhabiting the northern and north-eastern shores of the Black Sea during the Scythian period is long and complex and made all the more so by the fact that literary references are not always supported by archaeology.

On the basis of archaeological excavations, it is deduced that the Scythians settled around the northern shores of the Black Sea, and later spread to the neighbouring regions and beyond. It is difficult to trace the place of origin of the Scythians. As the controversy continues, it is to be noted that nomads before the Scythian age roamed over vast areas of the steppe from a still earlier period, and those nomads who had settled around the northern shores of the Black Sea were termed Scythians by Herodotus. Later archaeological discoveries have linked many nomadic tribes with the Scythians. Even the identity of archeological finds have been frequently disputed, by some scholars. Recent excavations at Tli-Bagrat in the Koban have revealed numerous bronze artifacts classified as follows:

a) Pre-Koban artifacts — end of 3000 B.C. till middle of 2000 B.C.;

b) Ancient Koban artifacts—1400 B.C. to 1300 B.C.;

c) Classical Koban bronzes — 1200 B.C. to 1000 B.C.;

d) Artifacts of transition period from Bronze to Iron Age — 9th century B.C.;

e) Artifacts of a period of wide Iron Age or Koban-Scythian 8th century B.C. to 6th century B.C.

The Koban findings have sometimes been labelled as Scythian.

An interesting bronze object from Tli-Bagrat dated in the ninth century B.C. is perhaps a symbol of eternal motion. It has three animal-headed curving projections, bent in clockwise direction with a hole in the centre (similar to the driving wheel of a car).[5] There is also an animal and bird plaque, showing a definite organization of space as in later Scythian work such as the bronze bridle plaques in Seven Brothers dated in the mid-fifth century B.C. Also found in Tli-Bagrat is a fragment of a saddle decoration having animal designs and circular geometrical patterns. The fragment also shows a design of men on horsebacks and significantly all men are headless, which reminds one of the Scythian custom of cutting off the enemies' heads.

Leaving behind Koban, Scythian zoomorphic ornamentation as found from sites in the region of the middle Don river has often been interpreted as Sauromatian art but a careful analysis shows that there was a marked influence of Scytho-Siberian traditions of Central Asia and South Siberia.

The art of the steppes reflected a tenacity by which non-Scythian elements (Persian, Greek, and Hellenistic elements) were absoated by Scythian traditions of ornamentation and object typology. The efficient reception and reworking is amazing to the viewers. The Scythian patrons and craftsmen sought out and made use of the styles, motifs and even techniques of their neighbours. This determined adoption and adaptation are evident in the imported objects found in such abundance within the grave furnishings of both the eastern and western sections of Scythian art and in the burials of both commoners and the aristocrats. Scythian and Hellenic mythology shared many images amongst themselves, and in early Scythian art one could understand the West Asian and Greek elements alongside elements belonging to a steppe nomadic tradition.

Scythian art can be classified under three phases, i.e. the early Scythian phase, middle and late Scythian phase. The orientation and relationship between the groups are difficult to comprehend, that is, it is difficult to give importance to any particular group or to assign the beginning of Scythian art to any group. Different types of artifacts like objects of utility, ornaments, trappings and weapons belong to different periods of Scythian art. According to the sites excavated (in the western section proper), the concentration of kurgans has been found to be on the Dneiper, Don, Kuban, Taman and Crimean groups, and they are all to be seen as a whole in the evolution of Scythian art. The earliest major burials include those of Kelermes, Litoy and Kostromskaya. The artifacts found at Kelermes reflect Near Eastern style and attests to the presence of the Scythians in the region north of the Caucasus prior to the decline of Nineveh and Urartu.

The major types of Scythian artifacts will now be discussed to trace the evolution of the Scythian art style.

1. OBJECTS OF UTILITY

Mirrors constitute an integral part of Scythian objects of utility. A knob-handled mirror from the Tagar burials indicates that by the early Iron Age, mirror was a significant part of the early nomadic burial ritual. A knob-handled mirror from the Mayemir steppe is ornamented with the raised line representations of five deer and a goat around the central knob.[6] Kelermes 2 has yielded a bronze mirror with a coiled feline on the loop handle. The predecessors of this coiled feline has been excavated from Arzhan, Mayemir and Chiliktin all signifying the purest Siberian style. The Kelermes mirror is similar to two bronze mirrors from Smela.[7] From Kelermes 4, a rounded mirror made of silver covered with electrum plate having a central knob or loop has been found. It exhibits Ionian and West Asian motifs and styles.[8] The back of the mirror has eight wedge-shaped sections depicting a number of individual and grouped images, like the Mistress of Animals holding two panther-like felines, two lions confronting each other over a back-turned ibex, two seated sphinxes facing each other, winged griffin, a dog-like creature with a bear and an eagle-like bird over the bear's back. The latter is similar to the Litoy bird plaques. In the last wedge before the Mistress of Animals, a lion savages the body of a bull over the body of a standing boar (Plate 3).[9] The mirror is a useful indication of the manner in which native Scythian and non-native traditions were beginning to be merged. Another mirror of the early Scythian period was found at Annovka on the left bank of the Ingulets River in the Ukranian Steppe and it was dated in the late sixth century B.C. It is of bronze,[10] and the handle is in the form of a female caryatid and this is similar to a bronze mirror handle in the form of a goddess with dogs and lions on her shoulders from Kherson[11] . Seven Brothers barrow, (mid fifth century B.C.) yielded a mirror handle in the form of a youth caryatid with rams on his shoulders. The technique is reminiscent of the Greek style. Also of the early Scythian period is the mirror found at the necropolis of Olbia (sixth century B.C.). It is of bronze, with a handle having a ram head and attached to the disk by a recumbent stag.[12]

Cauldrons are found in Scythian kurgans from the seventh century B.C. onwards. Herodotus wrote about the well-known Scythian bronze or copper cauldrons. A cauldron with a caprid handle has been found from Kelermes (late seventh or early sixth century B.C.).It is made of cast bronze and is decorated by a raised zig-zag band below the lip. A similar cauldron was found from Kelermes having a rhomboid pattern in raised bands.[13] In Raskopana Mogila, of the Dnepropetrovsk Region in the Ukrainian Steppe (early fourth century B.C.), a cauldron of cast bronze with semi-spherical handles and applied bucrania, circles and palmettes has been found. It has a narrower mouth than the Kelermes type. A cast bronze cauldron with six squared caprids on the rim and a relief lozenge-shaped pattern was found at Chertomlyk on the right bank of River Dniepr (fourth century B.C.). The Chertomlyk cauldron also bears comparison with a cauldron from the earlier burial of Solokha. The Solokha cauldron has a well-proportioned body with a simple and broad pattern of raised lines depicting zig-zags, and the rim is marked by six semi-spherical loops with protuberances.

Another important utility object is the rhyton. Kelermes has yielded a silver rhyton with engraved images of griffins; large birds, fronds, palmettes and lotus-petal border. It belongs to the late seventh or early sixth century B.C. Seven Brothers barrow has yielded three rhytons belonging to the fifth century B.C. One of them is a silver rhyton with ridged horn terminating in the protome of a winged goat. The other two are gold rhytons, one with beaded ornamental bands terminating in a ram head and the other terminates in the protome of a dog. The lower portion of the third rhyton has an engraved lozenge pattern topped by a feather pattern.[14] The use of gold overlays was an early Scythian tradition. Also belonging to the middle Scythian period was a horn rhyton having an encircling of gilded silver found at Elizavetovsk 9 (fifth or fourth century B.C.). The metal overlay is ornamented with the repeated pattern of an eagle-griffin tearing at a fish or dolphin. Another gold overlay for a rhyton, with a band of deer heads, two bands of modified twisted-rope pattern, and a lion-head tip was found at Velikaya Znamyanka (mid-fifth century B.C.). The latter is ornamented with a modified twisted-rope pattern, depicting archaic carving techniques.[15]

Poletops are also distinctive object types of the Scythian material culture. Poletops probably signified a magico-religious purpose. Kelermes yielded a pair of bronze poletops having horse heads (Plate 4).[16] The horses have large protruding eyes, nostrils and mouths indicated by raised bands and partitioned heart-shaped motifs depicting upright ears. A similar style may be gauged from several psalia zoomorphic images in the early Scythian period and also in the horse-headed bone psalia from the Urartian site of Norshun-Tepe.[17] Two bronze poletops in the shape of large bird-heads with hanging bells was found from Ullsky 2, Kuban group (sixth century B.C.). Both these poletops are fashioned in great beak-heads forms with superimposed smaller beak-heads along the sides of the birds' ceres. Both the beak-heads and backturned caprids are common motifs in early Scythian art. Along the projecting fold of the cere smaller birds' heads have been represented by parallel lines in relief (Plate 5).[18] On the more elaborately decorated specimen the scroll of the beak has also been adorned with such parallel lines in relief. In the middle of this figure yet another birds' head has been depicted, facing the opposite way. Below it, the figure of a wild goat in the already familiar attitude (of the Scythian deer) with head turned back and legs tucked up, has been moulded in relief. These two poletops are among the finest achievements of Scythian art especially in the ornamented treatment of organic bodily forms. A pole top terminating in a griffin head with an openwork body made of bronze (Plate 6) was found from Kelermes.[19] The body takes the form of a bulbous openwork over a squared socket. A poletop terminating in a stag on a spherical bottle (Plate 7) has been found from Makhoshevsky barrow (Kuban, late seventh century B.C.). The strangely positioned standing stag having long ears, a sensitive mouth and rounded cell eyes can be seen in archaic Scythian conventions and in the stylization of deer images of the Altai region. This poletop is also made of bronze.[20] An interesting poletop surmounted by a bull head over a bell-shaped rattle has been found from Ulsky 2 (sixth century B.C.). A thick twisted rope separates the bull head from the rattle.

Scythian barrows have yielded many wooden vessels. These vessels were specially ornamented by a variety of gold plaques. Gold plaques for a wooden-bowl in the form of beak-heads and recumbent deer have been found from Ak-Mechet, Crimea from early fifth century B.C. The plaques are filled with images of recumbent deer with raised antlered heads, but, in its surface treatment there are still remnants of the earlier traditions of bone or wood carving. The alert vitality of the deer on the Ak-Mechet plaques attests to a characteristic feature of Scythian art, i.e. the ability to capture the essence and dynamics of a living creature. This vitality lost its vigour during the middle period of Scythian art and there were changes from the archaic style. The vessels with their basic wooden material had almost lost all their wooden portions. The wooden versions were ornamented with gold overlays, which were raised and secured to the wooden bowls by means of small gold nails. The gold plates would be used to cover the wing handles with which many of the vessels were provided and to ornament sections of the body. The tradition of ornamenting wooden bowls with gold plated works, most probably with repoussê and chasing techniques, seems to have been common among the Scythians of the seventh to fifth centuries B.C. and to have lasted even into the fourth century B.C.

Other than wooden vessels, metal ones have also been found. A vessel with scenes of Scythian youths fighting lions and mythic beasts have been found from Solokha (early fourth century B.C.). It is made of silver gilt and the handles are ornamented by two attached rams' heads with large horns. Separating the rams' heads is a small tri-lobed palmette. The ornamental decoration is gilded and the base line is identified by a gilded twisted-rope pattern (a common feature in Scythian art). Below that, the bowl is covered with a raised lotus pattern. A vessel with images of Scythian men (Plate 8) was found at Gaymanova Mogila, north of Melitopol of the Ukrainian Steppe (fourth century B.C.). It has a notable frieze in high relief, depicting Scythian warriors and in it Blavatskiy had seen only scenes from everyday life.[21] Two of the Scythian men on the Gaymanova silver vessel wear thick, twisted torques visible on one side of their heavy beards, without indicating their terminals. The sides of this bowl-shaped vessel are filled with scenes of six Scythian males whose images along with all the applied ornaments are gilded. A raised lotus—petal pattern, separated from the larger representations by a narrow band of lotus petals, covers the base of the vessel. The relief treatment of the ram's heads on the handles is occasionally high.[22] Gaymanova Mogila served as the burial vault for Scythian royalty and the funeral objects discovered in it correspond in many details to the customs associated with the burial of Scythain kings as described by Herodotus (even the bowl with images of Scythian men corresponds to the Scythian legend narrated by Herodotus). The images at Gaymanova Mogila have been interpreted by Rayevskiy[23] to have belonged to the myths of Scythian origin.

A spherical gold or electrum vessel without handles, having representations of Scythian males was found at Kul Oba (Plate 9). It is divided vertically into three sections and could have been a Scythian ritual vessel (the shape is similar to that of Indian ritual vessels, made of copper) having scenes of Scythian mythology and with ornaments in the lower part. Separating the lower part of the vessel from the figural frieze is a wide pattern of twisted rope. The figures represented on the upper section of the vessel body are rendered in a relatively high repoussê technique. These well-spaced images are all Scythian males, presented with their weapons: bows, arrows, goryti, spears and shields, and the entire composition show the armed men in quiet interchange; therefore, the warlike accoutrements are but daily accessories of Scythian life. On one side of the vessel, two figures seated on hummocks or rocks are engaged in conversation (Plate 12) holding their spears. In another section (Plate 10), one hooded Scythian helps a companion bandage his left leg. In the next section (Plate 11) one man seems to be prying into the other's mouth in an assisting gesture. The rendition of their clothing i.e. the soft boots, pants and belted jacket are stylistically similar in all the sections. The gold spaces separating the individuals and groups add to the overall sense of compactness and there is a feeling of monumentality born in that restricted space. These scenes may illustrate a legend recorded by Herodotus, which relate how the three sons of Heracles (apparently identical to the first Scythian king, Targitaus) decided the question of succession by stringing his bow[24].

A spherical vessel with representations of Scythian males found at Chastyye Mogily 3, near Veronezh, upper Don basin, fourth century B.C. is another masterpiece of the western section. It is made of silver gilt.[25] Like the vessel from Kul Oba, this vessel (Plates 13,14 and 15) is divided into three main sections. The lower section has a pattern of expanding lotus petals. Separating the main figural section from both the base and the throat are two friezes of engraved double-edged lotus petals. Stylistically, this vessel is less refined than that from Kul Oba. The subject matter of this vessel is similar to that of Kul Oba and Gaymanova Mogila and perhaps the origin lies in a common source, perhaps a myth or legend or epic. There are six male figures grouped in three paired scenes, and one of the figures reappears in all. He is an elderly Scythian with long hair and a beard.[26] The men wear long kaftans, with triangular gussets, trimmed with fur and embroidered on the shoulders and chest with fantastic designs. These ornamentations perhaps suggest that they were Scythian leaders of the highest rank. There is the typical combination of the Scythian appearance—men wearing gorytus, quiver and bow cases. All the figures are gilded and distinct in style and only the faces and hands are silver.

The amphora is a typical utility vessel of the late Scythian phase i.e. fourth century B.C. onwards. There is only one significant vessel of this group, and that being the great amphora from Chertomlyk, on the right bank of the river Dniepr. All other amphorae found in burials are plain ceramic vessels. The amphora (Plate 16) is dated in the late fourth century B.C. It has floral ornaments, a frieze of men and horses and griffins savaging stags. It is made of silver gilt and its height is 70 cm. It has faucets in the form of sculptured heads of lions (two) and of a hippocampus (one)[27] . Regarding the frieze in the Chertomlyk vase, all the figurines of men and horses were moulded separately and only arranged in a composition when they were soldered to the vessel. It is one of the best-known utility objects from the Scythian world having lion head pour-spouts. The body of the amphora is divided into three principal sections and is covered with a broad tendril motif in gilded repoussê. The tendrils bear stylized flowers and palmettes and the vines are graced by a variety of birds. Below the neck of the vessel is a frieze of separately cast figures of Scythian males and horses and the available space above the frieze is filled with images of griffins savaging stags. These beautifully modelled and gilded heads are similar to the Kul Oba torque terminal.[28] The raised images of griffins have similar counterparts on the Tolstaya Mogila pectoral. The images of griffin and deer, the large tendril design and birds were done by repoussê.

Regarding the Scythian utility objects, one may continue that in the Kul Oba cup series, and in the Chertomlyk amphora, there are images of Scythian males represented alone or in groups of two or more, and that these images appear only in the late fifth or early fourth century B.C. These male images appear to be ordinary mortals, and it is not clear whether they represent deities or semi-divine figures.

Phials are also an important utility object of the late Scythian period. Phials are saucer shaped vessels. Gold and silver phiale were recorded in the inventories of the Parthenon beginning in the late fifth century B.C.[29] A gold phial with three bands of lions attacking horses and deer was found at Solokha (Dniepr group—fourth century B.C.).[30] The underside of the phial is divided into three registers containing interwoven images of lions and lionesses attacking horses and deer. The animals were executed in repoussê technique. Around the upper edge of the outer register of animals is an ivy leaf tendril. Another gold phial with Gorgon-Medusa masks, snakes, feline heads, fish, porpoises and dolphins was found at Kul Oba, Kirch Peninsula, fourth century B.C.[31]

2. ORNAMENTS

Besides utility objects, the ornaments found in Scythian burials form an important section of the Scythian art. Like the utility objects, the ornaments could also be classified under the early, middle and late Scythian periods. Within the context of West Asian traditions, the Scythians' interest in earrings and pendants as forms of personal adornments was hardly unusual. Earrings were a highly elaborate form of female adornment in Egypt and the Near East. Such objects were generally absent from early Scythian burials. The earliest earring types appearing in Scythian burials were boat-shaped or circular in form. This form elaborated and combined with the disc-pendant, resulting in elaborate earrings and temple pendants (worn hanging from a diadem or crown, over the wearer's temples). From fifth to third centuries B.C., there are a number of usual Greek earring forms, such as the splayed spiral with granulated terminals and earrings with posts ornamented with disks or rosettes from which dangle miniature figures such as Erotes, Nikai, or dancing figures, as at Juz Oba, Bolshaya Bliznitsa and Artjukov's barrow.[32] Most of the earrings reflect an elaborate use of filigree, granulations and enamel. Their techniques continued to be followed at Tillya-Tepe, a site in Afghanisthan and belonging to the first century A.D. The other earrings found in Scythian burials mostly belong to the later period i.e. 4th century onwards. The earrings of the middle Scythian period include the boat-shaped earrings with rosette-ornamented terminals as found from Volkovtsy 4 on the left bank of the Dniepr river, and they belong to the fifth century B.C. They are made of gold with granulation work. The boat-shaped earrings (Plates 17 and 18) have filigree ornaments and triangles of granulated surfaces and rosette terminals.[33] Each earring is ornamented with a border of braid pattern. These, boat-shaped and ornamented with granulation, are associated with Ziwiyeh and Karmir Blur finds. As in the utility objects, so also in the ornaments, the Scythian sensibility is revealed much by the pleasingly smooth surfaces of the boat elements, contrasted with the piled granulation. Boat-shaped earrings with perched and hanging birds were found at Novoseltsy 4 (Dniepr group, fourth century B.C.). They were made of gold with granulation techniques as in the earlier periods.[34] They were actually crescent-shaped earrings (Plates 19 and 20) decorated with granulated triangles and sculptured figurines of water birds at the ends and suspended on chains. The differences from the earlier ones are marked, with water birds sitting on each of the terminals. At Dort Oba 2, Crimea, fourth century B.C., was found a boat-shaped earring with griffin-headed terminals and ornamented with a traditional braid pattern and triangular masses of granulation. This is quite similar to the boat-shaped earring with griffin head from Nymphaeum dated in the fifth century B.C.[35]

Pectorals constituted an important part of the ornament assemblage in Scythian burials. The pre-existence of the pectoral tradition has been attested to by the gold pectoral from Ziwiyeh.[36] With goats, fantastic animals, and winged genii on both sides of a stylized Tree of Life, the pectoral reflects the grand legacy of the Near Eastern representational tradition. The crouching felines found at both ends of the pectoral was essentially due to a prevailing style of the proto-Scythian tradition, or at least to a Central Asian nomadic tradition. Significantly, Urartu has yielded a number of silver and bronze pectorals.

At Kelermes 3 dated in the seventh or early sixth century B.C. there has been found a diadem, with a griffin-headed protome, pendants and rosettes. It is made of gold with filigree and enamel.[37] The gold diadem has flowers attached to it and there is a centrally located griffin protome. The filigree work on the diadem is heightened by the pendants hanging from loops in the lower part of the band. The Kelermes griffin diadem is similar to the diadems from ancient Egypt, dating to the Hyksos period and to the New Kingdom.[38] A gold diadem of aptik form (Plate 21) with stamped band and pendants in the form of three-lobed blades or pods, was found from Three Brothers 1 (latter half of the fourth century B.C.).[39] This diadem takes the form of an aptik characterized by a low curved band that encircled the head. The band ornamentations include egg-and-dart motifs, alternating upright palmettes and acanthus motifs and feline motifs. The Scythian universal use of geometrical patterns like rows of punched dots can also be seen. The hanging and dangling elements are also present. In ornamental motifs and in the combination of band, worked by stamps or a die, and hanging elements, this headdress is a typical Scythian diadem. Remains of a gold ritual headdress with tendril and acanthus patterned band, hanging buds and dancing maenads were found at Deyev, fourth century B.C.[40] The bands have been embossed or stamped with a tendril motif having acanthus heads and flowers. From Bolshaya Bliznitsa, fourth century B.C., was found a gold crown in the form of a low calathus decorated with scenes of griffins battling Amazons.[41] The crown (Plates 22, 23 and 24) is entirely covered with pieces of worked gold sheets with separately attached figures. The upper portion of the crown shows an egg-and-dart ornament while the lower border is filled with a motif of rosettes within squared meanders. Human figures on the crown are executed in high relief. They wore close fitting pants ornamented with a lozenge pattern or with small floral motifs. From Karagodeuashkh (late fourth century B.C.), was found a gold plaque for a lost cone-shaped headdress.[42] This triangular plaque (Plate 25) was evidently used to ornament a tall cone-shaped headdress and was cut from a larger piece of gold. In the upper section of the plaque appears the frontal figure of a woman in a chiton and in the middle there is another frontally standing woman with two horses on either side. The two sections are separated by an egg-and-dart pattern. In the lowest section of the plaque appears a centrally placed and frontally seated female. She wears a long gown and a tall conical headdress. There are standing males in Scythian clothings .An openwork cone-shaped gold headdress (Plate 26) decorated with volutes and floral designs (fourth century B.C.) was found from Ak-Burun barrow, Crimea.[43] It has an unusual form.

The Kul Oba (fourth century B.C.) pendants with relief Athena heads, dangling chains, rosettes, and amphora shaped elements are made of gold with filigree, granulation and enamel.[44] One of the temple pendant (Plate 27) has a disk with a relief head of Athena in a helmet. The amphora-shaped elements are picked out with granulation. "The style is perfectly Greek, but as nothing exactly like them has been found elsewhere we should probably regard them as a local peculiarity, possibly even made by Greeks for barbarian customers."[45] A pendant (Plate 28) with a relief image of a woman riding a hippocampus, dangling chains, rosettes, and amphora shaped elements has been found from Bolshaya Bliznitsa.[46] At Karagodeuashkh, Kuban, fourth century B.C. was found a pendant or earring in the form of a disk with hanging inverted pyramids.[47] This motif will again be encountered at Tillya-Tepe. It is of gold with filigree and granulations. The disk is ornamented with filigree tendrils and bordered by circles of filigree work.

A beautiful example of later Scythian art is a pectoral[48] with four twisted ropes, having three representational friezes, and lion-headed terminals. It was found from Tolstaya Mogila (fourth century B.C.), and is made of gold with filigree and enamel. This pectoral (Plates 29, 30 and31) terminating with lions' heads and decorated with scenes of Scythian life in the upper frieze, fighting animals in the lower frieze and floral ornament in the middle is considered a masterpiece. The pectoral impresses one by the massive use of gold and the technicalities associated with its working. Most of the flowers were made from gold sheet including the figures of animals, men and birds. Another pectoral, impressive in its features was found at Bolshaya Bliznitsa, Taman Peninsula, fourth century B.C. It is of gold with enamel. The pectoral has a frieze of animals and floral elements, two twisted ropes and lion head terminals.[49] It is a crescent-shaped pectoral (Plate 32) with fifteen, sculptured figurines of animals (goats, rams, dogs and hares) and filigree flowers, petals between two twisted plaits and clasps in the form of relief heads of lions. Solokha revealed a twisted-rope torque[50] with lion head terminals, datable to the early fourth century B.C. It is of gold with filigree work and enamel and similar to the single torque terminal from Kul Oba. At Kul Oba was found a twisted rope torque with terminals in the form of Scythian riders, datable to the fourth century B.C. It is of gold with enamel and filigree.[51] The torque(Plate 33) is made of twisted gold wire with ornamentations of palmettes, lotus flowers and egg-and-dart ornaments inlaid with coloured enamels. The terminals are in the form of half-length facing horsemen—two bearded Scythian riders. The collars behind the riders combine a number of elements, which are found elsewhere and frequently on the Scythian goldwork of the fourth century B.C. like braided wires, lotus-petal friezes, and S-shaped spirals having granules of gold. A torque with smooth ropes having lion-head terminals was found at Talayev barrow, Crimea (fourth century B.C.).[52] This torque (Plate 34) is based on a solid gold rope having braided patterns, ornamentation with long S-shapes of wire and scrolled centres marked with granules. The same technicalities are apparent from the artifacts found from Central Asian burials, like the Issyk Kurgan and other Siberian burials.[53] At Kul Oba a gold smooth rope torque,[54] with terminals in the form of recumbent lions (Plate 35), reveals realistic treatment. The form is that of a single band with predatory felines at the ends and it is reminiscent of the torque traditions from the Altay and Pazyryk culture. It is similar to the Karagodeuashkh spiralled torque (Plate 36).[55] A spiralled smooth rope torque (Plate 37) terminating in recumbent lions, and made of gold was found from Chertomlyk.[56] According to Kubarev, the torque is reminiscent of those with carved panther terminals from the Altay region, such as those from Kurgan 12, Ulandryk I.[57] A spiralled, gold, smooth-rope torque (Plate 38) terminating in deer and approached by felines, was found at Tolstaya Mogila (fourth century B.C.).[58] The torque has two groups of sculptured lions whose musculature is being treated. The motif of several panthers approaching a deer recalls the treatment of the same theme on a carved wooden diadem from Ulandryk, in the Altay.[59] Another spiralled smooth-rope torque (Plate 39) with felines was found at Chertomlyk. It was made of gold and had applied jagged ornamentations,[60] As in the case of the torque from Tolstaya Mogila, the terminals are edged by a triple line and an added frieze of triangular designs. Sculptured figures of six panther-like felines, extremely smooth, recall carved wooden precedents from Altay burials of the Pazyryk culture. They are also reminiscent of the manner in which the Śakas would border their bronze altars with rows of felines. In many cases, however, these felines would be winged as found from a square altar with winged felines from Semirechiye and a round altar with long-legged standing felines from East Kazakhstan.[61]

From Bolshaya Bliznitsa was found a pair of bracelets (Plate 40) with doubled twisted ropes and rampant lion-terminals. It is of gold plate over bronze, with filigree and enamel[62] beneath the animals' legs. From Kul Oba was found a gold-over-bronze bracelet with twisted rope (Plate 41) terminating in the half-bodies of sphinxes.[63] On this bracelet, the bronze interior is visible through a number of breaks in the gold. The same technique is still in use in the fabrication of Indian jewelleries. From Karagodeuashkh, Kuban, fourth century B.C., was found a gold, two-spiralled and flattened bracelet (Plate 42) terminating in hippocampi.[64] The gold bands are thin and appear to have been cut and hammered into their ridged shape. Hippocampi appear frequently in late Scythian art, as on the scabbard from Kul Oba and the confronting hippocampi on a gold openwork plaque from Alexandropol.[65]

From Solokha, early fourth century, the famous gold comb (Plate 43) crested with recumbent lions, fighting figures and horses, has been found.[66] The men, lions and horses were all cast separately and then soldered together. The squared teeth were also separately cast. It is a small but monumental comb. The comb derives its style from the wooden or bone comb types of Scythian and Scytho-Siberian tradition. The crests of simpler Scythian combs may have been covered with gold, as the early comb with a crest in the form of stylized bird heads, from the Khanenko Collection, and the remains of gold covered combs found from Mastyugino and Chastyye Mogily.[67] The squared teeth of the comb are like the formation of a colonnade (in a micro form).

Clothing plaques were a major sub-group of ornaments as innumerable Scythian burials have revealed thousands of gold plaques intended to be sewn to clothing. The actual ornamentation of clothing with plaques is well attested to by representations on Scythian objects— primarily, rosettes, stars, rings, disks, stepped ornaments, squares, floral elements, and animal motifs. The Scythians must have derived their tradition of gold clothing plaques from the Assyrians and Achaemenids, but the fact remains that this decorative tradition was widespread within the nomadic world of the Eurasian steppe, and there are indications that it may have gone back to a period preceding significant contact between the nomadic and Achaemenid worlds. The intact burial at Issyk and other Śaka burials establish the existence of a tradition at least as early as the fifth century B.C., of using gold plaques to so ornament a garment as to acquire the appearance of gold cloth. Evidences are also found at Tillya-Tepe. Plaques representing spread-winged birds (late seventh—early sixth century B.C.) were found from Litoy (Plate 44).[68] Seven Brothers 2 (mid-fifth century B.C.) yielded plaques showing representations of recumbent ibexes, crouching sphinxes, back-turned roosters, Silenus heads, ram's and bull's heads, owls, flying boars with palmette bodies, Janus head with a helmeted warrior on one side and a lion's face on the other, youth kneeling and rampant lions. Solokha has yielded the important plaque (Plate 45) showing two Scythians kneeling and drinking from a rhyton within a squared frame (fourth century B.C.).[69] Kul Oba plaques have representations of two Scythians drinking from a single rhyton (Plate 46),[70] two Scythians standing back to back with drawn bows, and various animal motifs. Bolshaya Bliznitsa (fourth century B.C.) plaques (Plates 47 and 48) show various forms.[71] There are plaques in the shape of dancing women in long robes and nude youths, plaques in the shape of women on animals (Plate 49), similar to several images from the Tillya-Tepe burials,[72] a robed woman on a panther and others.

3. WEAPONS

From Kelermes 4, Kuban, late seventh or early sixth century B.C., was found a gold overlay[73] for gorytus (Plate 50). It is ornamented with the images of recumbent deer and crouching felines. It is in the form of a gold sheet and it would have been attached by nails along the edges, as is indicated by the small holes. The images on the Kelermes overlay (Plates 51 and 52) are indicative of the early Scythian skill at monumentcraft. Their antlers and bodies reveal the techniques of wood or bone carving, and the crouched feline images are similar to those found from Ziwiyeh.[74] In the late period of Scythian art, from Chertomlyk (late fourth century B.C.) was found a gorytus cover[75] with scenes from Greek mythology. Its replication in almost identical goryti covers from Melitopol, Five Brothers, suggests the existence of workshops. The combinations of ornamental bands, reveal a standardized vocabulary of motifs, common to both the eastern and western sections of Saka/Scythian art. The remains of a gorytus cover with scenes of a battle were found from Karagodeuashkh (late fourth century B.C.).[76] It is made of silver-gilt, and has borders of conventionalized lotus buds, stylized lotus petal pattern, and triple twisted rope pattern. The figural style is similar to that of the Chertomlyk gorytus. A scabbard casing, with a procession of fantastic animals on the shaft, winged genii on the top, and recumbent deer on the hanging plates,[77] was found at Kelermes 1, Kuban, late seventh or early sixth century B.C. A similar gold type was found at Litoy kurgan of the same date. The fantastic animals and the presence of winged genii on the gold scabbard casings suggest a general Near Eastern iconographic tradition. In representations of warriors in regalia, the sword in the Śaka/Scythian repertoire hangs on the right front of the man's belt. This can be clearly seen on the carved images of the Śakas and Persians on the Persepolis Apadana.[78] An axe overlay (Plates 53 and 54) with stacked images of fantastic animals, goats, boar and deer was found at Kelermes 1.[79] It used gold over an iron core. Earlier the bronze alternative was encountered. The beasts appear to be variations on the theme of the recumbent animal. A scabbard casing (Plates 55 and 56) for an iron sword, with raised images of felines and caprids was found at Shumeiko (late sixth or early fifth century B.C.).[80] It was made of gold with surface granulation. The lower section of the sheath is of plain gold, ornamented at its upper edge by three tiers of triangulated masses of granulation. Another gold scabbard casing (Plate 57) with lions savaging humans and deer heads was found at Solokha (early fourth century B.C.).[81] A beak-head in the shoulder of the feline is suggestive of the Scythian tradition (from early sixth to fifth century B.C.). From Tolstaya Mogila (fourth century B.C.), a scabbard casing (Plates 58, 59, 60 and 61) with scenes of lions and griffins savaging deer and horses, was found.[82] Images here are treated with greater realism with respect to the musculature, texture and a more massive treatment.

The Scythians ornamented not only their clothing but also their weapons and horses with plaques of bronze, gold and silver. The most famous plaques, associated with weaponry, are those attached to shields. They include the large gold panther plaque (Plate 62) from Kelermes,[83] the deer plaques from Kostromskaya (Plate 63),[84] and Kul Oba (Plate 64).[85] A bronze bridle cheek piece (Plate 65) from Elizavetinskaia[86] depicts the stylized head of a stag amidst the openwork of the plaque-like cheek piece. The head is almost lost among the enormous antlers which form an intricate, seemingly pure ornamental composition. Perhaps more than any other material from Scythian burials, the ornamental plaques from horse harnesses seem to reflect the changes from the native archaic tradition, which gradually transformed into new nomadic traditions in the fifth century. It will now be seen how these nomadic traits would be encountered and absorbed at various Saka/Scythian sites with the accompanying changes in the eastern section.

B. EASTERN SECTION

In the eastern section, as mentioned above, the name Scythia or Śaka/Scythia was extended to the areas east of the Caspian Sea, including Siberia, Mongolia and the western borders of China. It also included Kazakhstan, Uzbekistan, Turkmenistan, Kyrgyzstan, Tajikistan, Afghanisthan, Pakistan and India.

Before entering the eastern section proper one comes to Filippovka, a nomadic cemetery in the foothills of the Ural Mountains, at the eastern edge of the western section of the Scythian art. The reason for including the Filippovka burial in the eastern section is that most of the objects found here have stylistic affinity with the objects found from the tombs of the Altai region, Siberia and Western China.[87] Spectacular gold and silver objects dating from the fifth to the fourth century B.C. were excavated between 1986 and 1990 from the burial mound at Filippovka, which lies on the open steppe in the southern Ural Mountains region, sixty miles west of Orenburg. These finds constitute a brilliant new chapter in the history of the art of the nomads. Among the precious works of art from the funerary deposits are also gold and silver vessels of foreign manufacture resembling in both form and style works from the Achaemenid Iran. Other gold and bronze plaques exhibit similarities with the art of both ancient Bactria and modern Kazakhstan. The presence of the Scythians is evident in the horse trappings and the great cast-bronze cauldrons found in the central tomb chamber at kurgan I in Filippovka. The subjects commonly represented on the Filippovka finds are similar to those in the animal repertoire of contemporary Scythian art. The stylistic affinity of the Filippovka deer, lie to the east, in Bashadar, Tuekta and Pazyryk. The overall ornamentation on bodies of animals was also common on the eastern steppes not only in wood carving but also in gold work found from the Issyk kurgan.[88] Filippovka was ideally located so that it could master both east—west travel along the steppes and the north-south routes, control the Uralic and Altaic gold mines from Central Asia to the borderiands of the Achaemenid empire.[89] Various gold attachments for wooden vessels have been found. In pit 2 of kurgan 1, four different types of hammered gold plaques in the so-called animal style were found. Hammering the metal over a wooden form produced them. Weapons include a sword inlaid with gold (Plate 66),[90] a dagger like the typical akinakes (Plate 67),[91] and a whetstone (Plate 68).[92] The horse trappings include a gold buckle (Plate 69)[93] and gold bridle decorations in the form of griffins or griffins' heads (Plates 70,71 and 72).[94] Two bronze roundels depicting a combat between two camels (Plate 73)[95] were perhaps ornaments for horse trappings. There are only few garment plaques and jewellery.

Scholars love to attribute the materials of the Altai group of nomads to the Scythians. The great connecting factor was the animal motifs common to the products of the western section. The present day Altay Republic was home to the early nomads of the Pazyryk culture. To the north, in the Minusinsk basin lived the people of the Tagar culture. Bronze stags cast in relief and hammered were common in the Tagar repertoire. (Plate-197) Present day Tuva was the centre of the Aldi-Bal' and Saglin cultures, while northern and central Mongolia are identified with the so-called Chandman culture. The early nomadic tribes of Mongolia lived in khýrees, or circles (an idea of steppe nomad tribes from 800 B.C.) in the centre of which the elder's hooded cart (gerlug) was surrounded by an encampment of gers or tents. The later Khāns adopted this but instead of the gerlug, they built a palace (butchord) and monastic compound in the centre and surrounded the whole camp with a fortified wall or fence.

Noin Ula in Mongolia is an important Scytho-Siberian centre. Over 200 kurgans dated in the third to first century B.C. contained precious objects like golden pendants, silver plaques, table like structures[96] with animal motifs, bronze artifacts, pottery, textiles and utensils. Bronze objects include plaques, belt-buckles, horse trappings, bronze cauldrons and bronze candleholders. A significant felt rug decorated with chain-stitch designs showing typical steppe motifs like the elk and griffin locked in combat has been found in Noin Ula.[97] The presence of lacquered cups, silk and other objects reveals links with China during the Han period. (206 B.C. — 220 A.D.). The effect of Scythian art is especially marked in the Hunan art of the Chu age. It largely contained animal motifs like stylized tigers, horned lions and other beasts, which had been depicted in the western section like eagle-headed griffins. Under the Hans, the influence of Siberian art of the Scythian type became for a time so forceful that some of the oriental bronze plaques scarcely differed in arrangement and form from the nomadic works, whilst the Chinese dragon became twisted into an altogether Scythian posture, its head turned in one direction and its body in another. At much the same time the Chinese metal-workers began to stylize the tails and extremities of many of their beasts in accordance with the characteristic convention of the Altaian and Scythain art. The pole and furniture finials, which had flourished in early Scytho-Siberian art appeared in China. Forty graves excavated at Xiangbaobao[98] in the grasslands near River Tashkurgan have yielded bronze bridle pieces and gold plaques executed in the Scytho-Siberian style. This locality borders the Śaka territory of the Tarim basin in the west. Interestingly, the territory of Khotan had, like the rest of the Tarim Basin, been under Chinese supremacy both under the Han and Tang dynasties. Intaglios from Yotkan reveal careful delineations of a warrior of the Indo-Scythic type.[99] In the Lou-Lan graves at Lop

Nor the deceased wear a peaked brown felt hat[100] much similar to the Śaka type. At Alagou (Turfan county) bone ornaments are carved with the heads of animals in a style reminiscent of the Scythian art.[101]

We have seen the stag motif very much used in the Scythian art. In Siberia, the so-called stag figures (surely of elk, as confirmed by the heavy drooping muzzle) are very common. The peculiarities of the elk, like the heavy muzzle, broad palm antlers, and exaggerated long limbs, have all influenced the Scythian art. The ceres and the hooked beak are characteristic marks of birds of prey and at the same time typical features of Scytho-Siberian stylization. Their territory was merged into the steppe belt and land of forest and tundra, mostly inhabited by Finno-Ugrian tribes. The Scythian connection with Asia Minor is clearly reflected in the so-called Ziwiyeh treasure from the Saqqez tomb in Iranian Kurdistan (seventh century B.C.), which contains outstanding artifacts in which images characteristic of both ancient Near Eastern and Scythian art are combined. The golden objects in the Scythian style found at Ziwiyeh are similar to the finds from the Scythian burial mounds, such as the sword with a gold covered hilt and the scabbard in the Elizavetgrad kurgan, Ukraine, and the gold-handled sword and axe (Plate 53) from the Kelermes kurgan in the Kuban region.[102] As seen, all these objects combine Scythian motifs (reclining deer) with ancient Eastern imagery (the holy tree with its attendant divinities and fantastic animals) and it is probably correct to consider that they are imitations of Urartian artifacts, modified by the addition of elements in purely Scythian style. Art historians have tried to relate the birth of the Scythian art to the period of Scythian campaigns in Asia Minor, but on the other hand, we find examples of the pre-Scythian and Scythian art discovered in Siberia, which predate those from Ziwiyeh (i.e. seventh century B.C.) and are also decorated in the animal style.

It is to be noted that throughout Eastern Europe extending to Inner Asia, there existed a nomadic animal art, practised by the vast hordes of tribes, mingling to form a whole nomadic system. The term "Scythian" is now applied to a large number of ethnically unrelated tribes characterized by a strong Iranian influence in their personal and place names. Its application is frequently limited to the tribes inhabiting the coastal flatlands of the Black Sea region as seen in the western section. But archeologists have shown that the early Scythian monuments of this region are related to ancient steppe culture, which belongs to the middle of the second millennium B.C. The term Scythian denotes a vast mass of tribes sharing the same economic and cultural existence and spread over a much wider area. From the sixth to the third century B.C., the steppe lands between the Don, the Volga and the Urals were the home of a culture similar to that of the Black Sea Scythians. The bearers of this culture, whom the Greeks called Sarmatians, were in turn linked with the tribes of Eastern Kazakhstan, whose own culture is brilliantly represented by a series of gold plaques depicting reclining deer found in the sixth century Chiliktinsky kurgan. Beyond the steppes of Kazakhstan, these tribes stretched to High Altai, whose frozen burial mounds perfectly preserved objects in wood, bone, felt and metal and in which the Chinese, Iranian and Scythian influences are clearly apparent. That the nomads manufactured carpets and rugs in antiquity is well illustrated by the world's oldest carpets and felt objects found in Altaian Scythian barrows. They were made of sheep's wool, goat hair and camel hair. Pile weaving traditions still continue in Kirghyzia and in Kazakhstan, and felt carpets executed in the mosaic technique are of great artistic worth.[103] Imagery at Altai had much to contribute to the Scytho-Siberian-Śaka art. Four carved figures of walking tigers cover the length of a sarcophagus lid (Plate 74) [104] found from Altai dated in the sixth century B.C. Beneath the legs of the predators are depictions of hoofed animals: three rams, two boars, and two elk. The proportions are not to scale; the tigers are much larger than the other animals and dominate the composition. The tiger's fur is indicated by flame patterns, and the bodies of the hoofed animals are suggested by spiraliform designs. This stylistic approach is characteristic of the early Altai art of the sixth century B.C. and illustrates the high level of the artisans wood carving.

In a recent discovery of a 2700 years old tomb of a noble couple in Tuva, there is a marked evidence of the Scythian's reverence for their mounts. Some 5,700 pieces of gold artifacts were found, which prompted the Russian archaeologist Chugunov to comment-"Tuva has always been an archaeological white spot. Now it has a colour; gold."[105] In the western section, plenty of gold has been found in the Scythian tombs in the Ukraine, but those pieces were produced in later centuries, either by or under the influence of the Greeks. These new pieces[106] predate the other and display a unique Scythian style, indicating that the Scythians were skilled gold-smiths even before they encountered the Greeks. Included in the cache from Tuva were two magnificent neck pieces, a buckle from an arrow quiver, a headpiece ornament and foil fish used to decorate a horse's bridle. There is abundant evidence that the nomads had the preference for gold objects in both the western and eastern section. Bits and pieces of gold and turquoise were recovered from Arzhan, in

Tuva. In the republic of Tuva the number of barrow burials far exceeds that of all other groups in the eastern section. A burial complex of the Scythian time was found near Mount Kazylgan, and S. I. Vainstein, the archaeologist, suggested the name of the Kazylgan culture for the Scythian-type culture of Tuva.[107] Other Scythian sites include the area on the river Ij in Todzhin region, as well as the burial complexes of Ozen-Ala-Belig and Kokaael. The Kazylgan culture spans from the seventh to the third centuries B.C. From the seventh to the sixth centuries B.C. the earliest Scythian-type burials are found. L. R. Kyzlasov invented another name for the Scythian culture of Tuva: the Ujuk culture,[108] in the Ujuk valley dated in the seventh to the third centuries B.C. Different ethnic groups had inhabited Tuva in the Scythian period. Typical Scythian bronze bridle-bits with cheek-pieces, a saddle-girth buckle and strap distributors were found from a hoard in the mound of Aldy-Bel', a barrow at the burial site of Ortaa-Khem in Central Tuva.[109] The goods from the grave include the so-called "Scythian triad" (Scythian animal-style decorations, arms and horse- harnesses) which prove that Tuva was one of the centres where the development of cultures of the Scytho-Siberian cluster took place. From the kurgan 13 of Sagly-Bazhi II in the Ovur region, Tuva, a low-relief horn plaque (Plate 76) in the form of a recumbent horse[110] with head cast down, has been found. Although the horse was an essential feature of nomadic culture, it is unusual as a subject, as most animals represented are wild rather than domesticated. The mane is indicated by rows of curving, leaf-like shapes. Curved designs including scrolls emphasise the horse's musculature. The typical almond-shaped eyes are noticed there.

Gold earrings (Plate 77) from the central Aldy-Bel' burial barrow I, of the Saryg-Bulun burial site, are reminiscent of the Taxila type.[111] They consist of conic pendants decorated with granules and comma-shaped insets. So far the Arzhan barrow remains the only completely excavated monument among the great barrows of Tuva, though there are several other great barrows similar in appearance in the centre of the Ujuk basin. Gold garment decorations (Plates 78 and 79) representing birds of prey and an iron figurine inlayed with gold representing a predatory animal[112] have been found from the burial site of Kosh-Pej, barrow 2, in Tuva. The gold garment-decorations representing birds of prey are very much similar to the birds of prey found in the western section specially at Litoy kurgan (Plate 44)[113] of the seventh century B.C. Kosh-Pej has also revealed gold garment-decorations (Plate 80) in the posture of reposing panthers[114] and a gold *svastika*-shaped decoration and iron buckles covered with gold leaf (Plate 81).[115] It is interesting to note that

Chiliktin-type gold cornelian and turquoise beads and gold hemispheric plaques with loops soldered on to their back were found from Kosh-Pej. The garments of the dead buried in the Ujuk barrows were covered with numerous decorations of gold. Eagles and other birds of prey carved out of gold leaf are widely represented and they were attached to a headdress. The belt of garments had various belt-clasps of bronze or iron covered with gold leaf, and "butterfly"-shaped plaques[116] were found. These plaques are similar to those found in Altai, Tillya-tepe, the Minusinsk basin and the Baikal region dated in the fifth to fourth centuries B.C. Kosh-Pej 2 has images of ibexes and boars carved out of gold leaf.

In the burials of Suglug-khem dated in the second century B.C., typical Śaka/ Scythian bronze buckles and belt decorations (Plate 82) were found.[117] The garments of a noble warrior from the same burial, decorated with more than a hundred golden figurines,[118] were found. The belt was inlaid with gold leaf, decorated with twenty cowrie shells which were also covered with gold leaf. In three of the female burials of Suglug-Khem high caps were found along with gold earrings, wooden combs, gold pins, gold torques, bronze cauldrons and mirrors, some of which have zoomorphic side-handles (one representing an ibex) (Plate 83).[119] L. R. Kyzlasov thinks that the barrow of Suglug-Khem was erected by the Śakas migrating from central Kazkhstan.[120] The findings are similar in style to those found from Ptichata Mogila in Bulgaria: two rich burials in the Vysokaya Mogila on the Dniepr and the kurgan of Arzhan in Tuva (all dated in the eighth to seventh century B.C.).The kurgan of Arzhan-2 in Tuva valley poses a major question about the authorship of the splendid gold pieces discovered there. The ornaments depicting a workmanship of the highest quality confirms the fact that the Scythians in the eastern section were well acquainted with gold techniques. Several thin gold disks, imprinted with coiled feline images near the Mayemir kurgan in the Altay Republic, Issyk kurgan in the East Kazakhstan, and the recently excavated burial on the Ukok plateau in the Altay Republic have also revealed much richness. From the Golden Barrow at Chilktin in East Kazakhstan were recovered twenty-nine gold foil images of felines and several foil images of deer with inlaid turquoise eyes. As in the case of the Mayemir finds, these foil images had been pressed over more sturdy forms carved from wood or leather. The coiled felines from Chiliktin are similar to the coiled feline shaped bridle ornament (Plate 2) from Temir-Gora.[121]

The early Scythian gold reindeer (Plate 84) from Chilikta, [122] and the gold deer (Plate 63) from the royal Scythian burial at Kostromskaya, in the Caucasus[123] for instance, have a typically Scythian folded pose. From kurgan 5, Chilikta burial ground (south of Lake Zaysan), Kazakhstan, two reindeer-shaped plaques have been found. They have been dated to the early Scythian period, from the second half of the eighth century B.C. to the first half of the seventh century B.C. Gold and turquoise have been cleverly used. On each of these flat, gold-sheet plaques, probably used to decorate a leather quiver, the reindeer faces right, with legs folded under the body. The head is raised, with nostrils, mouth, and eye indicated by hollows; the pointed ear is inlaid with turquoise which was generally found in Siberia; and the large antlers have one branch in the front and four to the rear, a more naturalistic rendering, characteristic of this eastern region, than the more stylized depictions of stags in the Scythian art of the Pontic steppes. Both plaques were hammered over a mold in low relief. From the same burial several hundred gold objects have been found. Among them were small reliefs of a typically early Scythian and Siberian animal style, especially the stags with feet crouched beneath the body, and the stylized antlers. Arresting bronze arrowheads were found in a sheath adorned with golden stags dated in the seventh to sixth century B.C. The fourteen figures of gold reindeer from Chilikta were found with remnants of a leather quiver and arrows and gold plating decorated with 24 figures of deer in separately stamped compartments like the one from Kelermes (Plate 50) in the Caucacus.[124]

The Issyk kurgan reveals extensive use of gold. But whether the Issyk burial was that of a man or a woman is a mystery[125] as new evidence suggests that the one buried in the Issyk kurgan was a woman. The body had been attired in boots, trousers, and a leather tunic decorated with some 2,400 arrow-shaped gold plaques. Thirteen gold deer heads flanked by three gold plaques of moose with unusual twisted torsos (Plates 85 and 86) had been sewn on to a belt.[126] Snow leopards with gaping mouths decorated on a gold torque was found around the neck of the skeleton. Plaques of horses were found with twisted torsos decorated scabbards that held an iron dagger and a sword. These ceremonial weapons, both embellished with gold animals, lay beside the remains. A short sword or dagger like the akinakes from Filippovka (Plate 67)[127] has also been found. The hilt is composed of opposed griffins' heads. Near the head was a gold-bound whip handle. Ceramic, silver and bronze vessel, as well as flat wooden dishes and beaters for koumiss (fermented mare's milk) were also found in the tomb. The most spectacular object in the burial was a conical headdress elaborately decorated in gold.[128] The intact burial at Issyk and other Śaka burials establish the existence of a tradition at least as early as the fifth century B.C. of using gold plaques to so ornament a garment as to acquire the appearance of gold cloth. The same can be said about the Tillya-tepe burial. The headdress from Issyk was probably made of felt with a flap extending down over the neck. Its base consisted of pairs of winged mountain goats carved out of wood and sheathed in gold. Two gold foil strips painted black and red were set vertically on the centre of the hat. On each side of these strips were what some scholars have called a pair of gold feathers or wings and a pair of upright gold arrows or miniature spears. On a felt carpet from kurgan 5 at Pazyryk in southern Siberia, of about the same date as the Issyk burial, a similar motif is found.[129] Gold-foil depictions of mountains, birds, snow leopards with twisted torsos, winged tigers, and mountain goats were attached to the sides of the headdress, and a small gold ram was set on its point. Although the burial was said to be of a man, the headdress reminded the Kazakh excavators of the hats worn by brides in traditional wedding ceremonies. Artifacts in the Issyk burial are so similar to those found in burials of women warriors and priestesses at Pokrovka in the southern Ural steppe that one cannot help speculating that this person was actually a young woman. Three earrings adorned with turquoise, carnelian and white beads suggest more elaborate jewellery than is usually associated with male Śaka warriors. A gilded bronze mirror is placed to the body's left and above the head. Such mirrors are associated with priestesses in archaeological contexts at Pokrovka, Tuva, in southern Siberia west of Lake Baikal and the Altai mountains. Both male and female shamans in Tuva still use mirrors in curing rituals.[130] From the Altai culture, eighth to the seventh century B.C., a bronze mirror (Plate 87) with figures of a standing stag and a mountain goat has been found.[131] The cast, round mirror, once brightly polished, is now corroded. The reverse has a high rim; the loop handle in the centre was broken off in antiquity. Five raised-outline figures of stags and one of a mountain goat, arranged around the handle, decorate the surface. The animals are shown in profile, their heads raised high and surmounted by spiraliform antlers or horns. Each has four thin, elongated legs ending in pointed hooves, as if it were standing on tiptoe. The style is similar to that found on the earlier so-called deer stones and on petroglyphs in the Sayan and Altai mountains and in Mongolia. In antiquity, mirrors were not simply objects of daily use but were thought to possess magical powers.

The Issyk burial is also similar to that of a fifth century B.C. burial of a woman in Ukok in the Altai Mountains excavated in 1993.[132] Among the objects found at Ukok were a silver mirror with an incised deer on its reverse, wooden trays and bowls. The Ukok woman wore a short kaftan, leather boots and an elaborate coiffure resembling a conical hat. Tattoos of animals with twisted torsos on the Ukok female are paralleled in the gold ornaments from Issyk. Similar to the golden ram figurine surmounting the headdress from Issyk burial are the wooden ibex heads found from Kuturguntas, Siberia. It is not clear, however, to which object the ibex heads (Plate 88) from the Kuturguntas barrow have been attached.[133]

Since the Scythians did not have palaces, they carried their wealth on their own bodies and on the regalia of their horses, their weapons and their utensils. This extreme display of wealth and status seems to have been acquired during their Near Eastern sojourn.

Excavations in the old Nisa area in Turkmenistan (primarily a Parthian site) shows sculptures made of unfired painted clay, and some of them are dressed in nomadic Scythian costume.[134]

The Mongolian steppe excavations have yielded "deer stones" dated in the eighth century B.C. These stones are discribed as stylized portrayals of nomad warriors.[135] Many such stones have been found in Mongolia, the Tuva Autonomous Republic of the former U.S.S.R. beyond Lake Baikal and the mountainous Altai and in a slightly different form in the Urals.[136] During the eighth century B.C. similar cultures of Scytho-Siberian type emerged and developed simultaneously as there was the gradual emergence of an economy based on nomadic cattle-breeding.

The revival of the Karasuk tradition may be seen in the figures of standing animals, even while a flourishing production of Scythian—derived rampant and galloping animals simultaneously developed. The animals are found on knives and small belts most frequently, but also on brooches and belt plaques, all covered with skillfully elaborated ornament. Certain clasps, or round fibulas, envelope the silhouette of the animals in concentric circles; others twist them in the form of an 'S', and in some we find the hooves transformed into circles. It is noteworthy that, from the beginning of the Bronze Age, the Chinese artist liked to contort his animals into an 'S' shape. In the eighth century B.C., Ordos art had its origins in the confluence of the Chinese art with that of Tagar, and subsequently constituting with the latter and with the Scythian Art, the triad of the steppes. The art of the Ordos itself was a powerful evolutionary factor in the passage of the Scythian Art into Scytho-Sarmatian art. Pazyryk, Shibe, Noin-ula could be the possible centres of Scytho-Sarmatian art. Here again, spirals, palmettes, roundels and other floral shapes were the most popular of the purely non-representational patterns. The saddles, which are represented on Scythian metal-work, seem to follow closely the lines of the actual saddles found at Pazyryk.

From kurgan 1 Tuekta, in the Altai Mountains, many bridle ornaments have been found. A cedar bridle ornament (Plate 89) in the form of two griffin's heads[137] is noteworthy. The head of a griffin with a long neck merges into a stylized body, ending in what appears to be a tail but is actually another head, smaller but identical. Depictions of serpents' or birds' heads at the end of the tail of a mythical beast were known in southern Mesopotamia and later in Assyria. The style in which the eyes, beak, and tufts are fashioned has much similarity to the traditional manner in which griffins were stylised in the Altai during the sixth century B.C.[138] This object, laterally pieced through the base, may have been a horse's bridle ornament. Similar carved wooden objects have been found by Polosmak in excavated graves in the Altai Mountains (1991).[139] The pieces seem to be small replicas of the monstrous stag figures that decorate the belt of the buried in the Issyk kurgan in eastern Kazakhastan. From the same grave (Tuekta) a bridle ornament (Plate 90) in the form of a head combining the features of a predator, a camel, and a griffin has been found.[140] The upper jaw is like a bird's beak. Similar composite creatures (Plate 91) are found from Filippovka.[141] A unique bridle ornament consisting of the full-face head of a tiger (Plate 92) from Tuekta shows a new style in crafting the larch tiger.[142] The vertical wood grain is slightly incised to create strips down the head and the body is in the form of two addorsed profile heads of predatory bird's or griffins. The technique of joining two bodies as found in the Scythian art of the western section (Kul-oba) is also in use in the eastern nomadic art. A similar plaque consisting of two elk-heads in relief is found at Tuekta. This highly ornamental design (Plate 93) is like one frontal animal's head or two in profile.[143] A cedar bridle ornament at Tuekta (Plate 94) shows torsional, triskele composition.[144] Such compositions are perhaps symbolic of circular movement and are common in the Śaka/Scythian art. The tradition of fabricating psalias with references to different parts of the same animal was an established and creative tradition as found in the burials of Tuekta and Pazyryk. Similar psalias were found from Zhurovka and Axjutintsy. Appliquê work from Tuekta and Pazyryk represent a different visual perspective of the Scythian art. They are in most cases made of leather. The appliquê tiger work (Plate 95) from Tuekta[145] has comparable representations on southern Siberian and Central Asian petroglyphs and on Tuva metal work from the eighth to the fifth century B.C. The appliquê of two roosters from Pazyryk (Plate 96)[146] reminds us of the leather silhouettes used in shadow puppetry in Orissa and Southeast Asia.

Regarding the "frozen grave" barrows of the Scythian period, Ak-Alakh deserves special mention after Bashadar and Tuekte. The barrow's location is in the Kosh-Agach region of the Gorno-Altai autonomous district, about 14 kms. from the present Chinese border. Ak-Alakh is the largest of a group consisting of six mounds which form an irregular chain stretching along a North— South axis (a feature characteristic of the Pazyryk culture burial monuments).[147] Several horses were buried at Ak-Alakh, and four of them were probably bridled. Among the finds were seven complete sets of wooden harness decorations (Plate 97).[148] Saddles made of felt were decorated with polychrome appliquê work and some pieces of a compound bow. Ak-Alakh was a burial of the "middle-level" nobility, standing somewhere between the common people burials (as found at Ulandryk, Justyd, Tashanty) and the elite burials (the great barrows of Pazyryk, Bashadar, Tuekte, Berel and Koltandyk).[149] Elite burials had richly adorned horses. Decorations of horse harness (Plates 98 and 99) in the shape of griffins[150] attest to the Scythian identity of the grave. The Ak-Alakh griffins considerably enriched the iconography of them and they were very popular among the Pazyryk people. Many of the objects of wood discovered in the barrow belong to the well-known types which occur in the royal as well as common burials of the Pazyryk culture. It is interesting that the griffin decoration of a horse harness from Ak-Alakh is stylistically similar to the eagle-shaped larch bridle ornament (Plate 100),[151] dated in the sixth century B.C. and belonging to the Altai culture. The eagle, like the griffin, is depicted frontally with lowered spread wings (as at Ak-Alakh). Both the bridle ornaments have a minimum of detail on the head, and the elaboration of the body is limited to two gracefully bent parallel lines in relief, indicating the wing feathers, and a fanlike tail consisting of a three-lobed palmette. The motif was also known in Central Asia and India[152] and appeared on the Eurasian steppes in the first millennium B.C. A similar eagle-shaped plaque (Plate 101)[153] as the Ak-Alakh griffin, is found from the Altai culture. It is dated in the sixth century B.C. and is made of gold.

However, there are several objects, which have rare themes on them, like that of a wild boar attacked by panthers. The boar's proportions and its static figure remind us above all of the animal represented on the famous Kelermes mirror.[154] Noteworthy is the number of fish cut in felt to decorate horse harnesses at Pazyryk.

This technique of attaching pieces of decoration could be clearly seen in the terracotta art of the Saka/Scythian/Pahlava/Satavahana strata in the context of Indian archaeology. Two wooden shields display a simplified decorative technique: rhombic figures set one into another (Plate 102).[155] Ak-Alakh, excavated in 1990, is also important for its high sharp-pointed hats of thick felt.

From 1993 to 1997, fifty kurgans have been excavated near the town of Pokrovka in the Kazakhstan border. These kurgans reveal women buried with bronze daggers and arrowheads. The find from Pokrovka is very much similar to that found in the burial mounds on the steppes of southern Ukraine. Many of the Ukrainian graves had female burials yielding swords, spears, daggers, arrowheads and armour. It is significant that Herodotus in his travels north of the Black Sea in and about 450 B.C. had reported hearing tales of warrior women who rode the steppes of southern Russia. Herodotus called them Amazons, but the neighbouring Scythians called them Oiorpata or killers of men. In time the Scythians and Amazons joined and formed a common group. Then they left the northern Black Sea region towards the eastern steppes between the Don and Volga rivers. They also went south to southern Kazakhstan or northern Uzbekistan.[156] Pokrovka yields reveal a definite Scythian influence, thereby indicating that their creators might have come from the regions situated on one of the great east-west trade routes, perhaps somewhere in southern Kazakstan. These finds include a bronze belt buckle from northern China and a set of hammered and chased gold plaques probably depicting snow leopards, which inhabit the Tien-Shan mountains of Kyrgyzstan and Western China.[157]

Archaeological excavations at the Bulak-Bashi Koshrabad site yielded Kaunchi I/II culture artifacts, which are believed to be indicative of the massive waves of migrating tribes of the Śaka and Kaunchi cultures from beyond the Syr Darya River. They fused with the sedentary crop-farming population of the oases in southern Central Asia, which resulted in a syncretic culture.[158]

In a site 50 km. east of Almaty, in Kazakhstan, was found the burial chamber of a tribal leader, comparable to the European Scythian burial sites. It is the first and only burial complex of such a high-ranking person to have been excavated in Central Asia. The burial (mid-first millennium B.C) was established by Śaka tribes, and both the costumes and burial rites were similar to those used at Tillya-tepe in Northern Afghanistan in the first century A.D. Gold leaf objects were used to decorate the clothing of the buried. Weapons, a circular gilt bronze mirror with handles at the sides and two concentric circles on the back and a headgear including a diadem attached to its base were found. The man's gold jewellery comprised an earring, a pendant and two rings. Metal plaques with a tiger's head *en face* were sewn on to the fabric of the tribal leader's clothing between fifty-nine horizontal and fifty-nine vertical slats. They included geometric patterns such as 2411 small triangles, 30 small rectangles, 488 rectangles, 162 squares, 30 circles, 108 crescents and 113 rhomboids. The belt was made of massive rectangular plates on to which were affixed smaller plates in the shape of reclining deer heads. An iron dagger, its upper side shaped like the head of two facing griffins and its handle and sheath decorated with gold plates depicting an elk and a horse, and a sword, the upper side and cross of which is encrusted with small gold plaques and gold thread twisted, around the handle, were hung from the belt. 31 vessels were found. Two silver bowls, a large one, the outside engraved with thirty-two rings and the inside decorated with two concentric circles, and a small one, the outside decorated with twenty-six signs resembling Aramaic letters but still undeciphered, a bronze bowl, two dishes, one large and one small, made from a single piece of birch, were also found. Ten ceramic ewers and six basins were found, together with silver forks with the upper part of the handle in the shape of a bird's neck and head with a sharp beak.[159]

There has been much controversy regarding the chronology of the Pazyryk burials. The bearers of the Pazyryk culture may have migrated to eastern Kazakhstan from the west Siberian steppes at the end of the first millennium B.C.[160] Pazyryk headdresses included four statuettes of horses discovered at Katanda. All show reclining creatures with griffin's heads set upon the horse's bodies. Stamped gold plaques were also found at Katanda. The latter has also yielded a silk band decorated with carved wooden figures of horses, fabulous beasts, monsters, stags and bears in a row. The pieces of furniture recall examples from Pazyryk. Bukhtarna tombs reveal sixteen horses in four rows with heads pointing to the east. Fully caparisoned, they had iron bits, leather bridles adorned with ornaments of carved wood and birch bark covered with thin sheets of gold. The coffins of human burials were adorned with copper birds resembling those in the Scythian tombs of the Volga and Ural regions. Weapons similar to those of the Scythian nomads were found. Further burials resembling Pazyryk were found at Bashadar where the wooden coffin sides were decorated with a carved row of four tigers advancing from left to right. The coffin lids had stags, wild boars, mountain goats, in a more flexible style than that of

Pazyryk. Sixteen horses interned there must have belonged to a tribe similar to that of Pazyryk. Pazyryk horse representations display trimmed manes (there are a felt carpet and a bone saddle-inlay to illustrate this) which, according to V.B Kovalevskaya, is one of the characteristic features of a saddle horse. V.O. Vitt presumed that the practice of trimming equine mane had most probably developed among the Śaka and Scythian tribesmen who were skilled archers.[161]

In 1991 excavation was made of the larger barrow of a complex at Kuturguntas in Pazyryk. Extant grave goods included fragments of fur clothings, felt appliqués, and metal and wooden objects which are parallel to those found in other Pazyryk graves. The wooden bridle decorations of the principal horse show the popularity of the griffin motif in Pazyryk art.[162] The lid of the main coffin at Kuturguntas was fixed with large copper nails reminiscent of the fish-representations so characteristic of the Pazyryk culture. Among the surviving grave goods were stamped bronze griffin heads (Plate 103), obviously used to decorate garments.[163] Pieces of thin woolen cloth, leather appliqué works shaped like griffins, two rams' heads in wood, probably from a torque or a headdress, a small iron plaque covered with gold leaf which decorated a quiver, several beads, two schematized figurines representing fantastic birds carved from thick leather and a woolen cord woven of two thick threads were also found. Incidentally, carpet making in central Asia from the third century B.C. onwards, used such woolen cords woven of two thick threads. The Kuturguntas grave goods are similar to those discovered in the Ak-Alakh barrow and Tashanta-2 burial complex, all at Pazyryk. Fur garments found at Kuturguntas were made of numerous small pieces of fur sown together. Garments made of numerous pieces were believed to possess certain magic protective qualities.[164] Similar beliefs are still widespread among the Tajik, Uzbek, Karakalpak, Kazakh, Kirghiz and some other peoples.[165] Horse harness decorations of the Kuturguntas barrow are very similar to the fantastic creatures decorating horse harness from the Ak-Alakh barrow and Tuekte barrows. Tuekte was an important centre of nomadic art in the eastern section. Bridle plaques from the Tuekte barrow had square cavities covered with pieces of red leather. This technique probably aimed to imitate metal objects inlaid with precious stones or some polychrome appliqué work.

In Azerbaijan, the region of pre-Pazyryk Hanlar is important for the Scytho-Siberian connection. On excavation of three burials south-west of Hanlar, one burial has yielded a "sledge" drawn by two stags.[166] It reminds one of the later Pazyryk burials of the Altai dating from the early Scythian period, where the horses supposed to draw the chariots had stag marks covering their heads. This tradition survived at Tillya-Tepe in Northern Afghanistan.

The design of many objects such as pots from Śaka burials in the Pamir Mountains and brazier altars showing winged lions from Semirechye (the Northwest foothills of the Tien Shan Range) can be seen as representational. During the last twenty-five years, several new items have been added to the collection of bronze lamps due to chance finds in Semirechye,[167] near Almaty. An interesting lamp (Plate 104) from Alatau[168] had as its attachments two camels (Plate 105),[169] with typical Śaka/Scythian style of big eyes, round pupils, plump cheeks, and oblong holes as ear cavities. Among the cult bronzes, a tiger-griffin (Plates 106 and 107)[170] representation has also been found. Another lamp from Samal in the Semirechye area has fifteen animal figurines set clockwise along the rim. With ears bulging out, they have S-shaped horns, almond-like eyes and twisted tails. The lamp has a vertically set hollow tube for a wick with two figurines of mounted archers set symmetrically by the sides of the tube. The rider holds a composite Scythian bow.[171] A graceful figurine of a bronze winged panther represents a fantastic animal with its twisted forepart. It (Plates 106 and 107) has narrow almond-shaped eyes and between its shoulder-blades, it has a convex circle formed by two 'commas'.[172]

Two principal areas where Śaka bronzes were widespread are Sinkiang and Semirechye. Two finds made beyond the Semirechye area include a fragment of an incense-burner and a figurine of a warrior found near Dzhambul in South Kazakhstan. They, along with a lamp excavated from a barrow by the village of Bukon near Zaysan in East Kazakhstan,[173] are definitely closer to the northern Semirechye Śaka style. There are already over 20 Śaka cult bronzes from Kazakhstan and Kirgizia, and probably even more from Chinese Turkestan.

Excavations at the Ili river sites have yielded bronze ornaments and jewels with early indications of the animal style. Many objects have been found, the majority of which can be attributed to the Śakas, Wu-sun and the Turks. Bes-Shatyr, on the right bank of the Ili river is a major Śaka site. In Kirgizya, covering the basins of the Issyk-kul and Balkhash Lake, a number of kurgans have yielded objects, the majority belonging to the nomadic tribes from the seventh century B.C. to the fourth century A.D. The Śakas inhabited the Tyan-Shan, Talas, and Alay mountains as well as the Issyk-kul region. Figures of animals in an early "Scythian style" were found in the Semirechye, near Lake Issyk-Kul and near the Chu and Talas rivers and at Sokuluk, west of Frunze.[174] It is not always possible, however, to draw a sharp line between the Śaka period and the following period of the Wu-sun. Ritual bronze utensils, discovered on the northern shores of Lake Issyk-Kul, included sacrificial tables, lamps, a cauldron, and a bronze figure of a recumbent yak. In Central Tyan-Shan, Śaka tombs were found, and some belonged to the Wu-Sun. Kara-Nulak in Alay valley in Kirghiziya yielded iron knives, arms, various kinds of potteries, bronze articles such as mirrors, bracelets, inlaid ear-rings, jewels and other ornaments belonging to a female skeleton, all showing Śaka/Scythian affiliations.

From the ninth to the third century B.C. in Uzbekistan, a typical agricultural culture called the Burgulyuk culture developed in the oasis of Shash (Tashkent region), situated to the north near the nomadic steppe-zone. The material culture has a clear similarity to the culture of the Śaka/Scythians.[175]

A process of urbanization started, and this was directly connected with a strengthening of state power and probably the irrigation of fertile river valleys (as archaeology has shown) of Amudarya, Kashkadarya, Zeravshan, Chirchik and Syr-Darya. A coiled feline motif from Uigarak cemetery in the lower Syr Darya region is inevitably a Śaka variation bridle plaque (Plate 108)[176] from Kulakovsky dated in the early fifth century B.C.

We come to the excavation of a rural settlement of Kundzhulitepa, 1.5 km east of the site of Erkurgan (in the district of Kashkadarya). The remains of the settlement are visible as a small circular mound and is dated in the second half of the sixth century B.C.[177] An oval intaglio found there shows a triumphal procession. The man in the centre is shown in full detail. He has a moustache, and is clad in a long-sleeved shirt, tight trousers and soft leather boots, undoubtedly the attire of the Śaka/Scythian nomads or Śaka/Parthian nomads. The gem has a Sogdian inscription. A very close parallel can be found on a relief kept in the Toronto Museum, representing Śaka warriors.[178] Not only their garments but their hairstyles have much in common with those depicted on the Kashkadarya gem. The same hairstyle often appears on Parthian coins bearing portraits of Arsacid rulers.[179] At the same time there is one more feature often seen on the Indo—Scythian coins which offers another parallel with the gem, namely, the equestrian representations of kings holding various symbols of power. Similar representations occur on the coins of Azilises, Azes, Gondophares and Soter Megas.[180] The equestrian figure on Gondophares' coins is crowned by a Nike who is flying behind him and is holding a wreath above the rider's head in a manner very similar to the composition of the gem.[181] The gem, thus, supplements our notions about the art of the Śakas, Parthians or Śaka-Parthian tribes on their route to India.

In the eastern section, finally, we come to a territory near the Indian borderlands, the Pamirs. The Śaka graves in the Pamirs, very near the Afghan border, have yielded several objects in the animal style. Archaeological evidence from the Pamirs and its comparison with other materials confirm the evidence of written sources that, in migrating to India, the Śakas passed through this mountain region. A small bronze cauldron (Plate 109) with two circular handles and an additional handle in the form of a horse head, [182] was found from Imit in Ishkoman, Punyal (second century B.C. to first century B.C.) south of the Hindukush range. A bronze cauldron from Alicur II, kurgan 3, on the left bank of the Gunt river, Southern Pamirs, with two circular handles was similar to the Imit cauldron. The knob (Plate 110) at Alicur II, kurgan 3, has an eagle-griffin.[183] A rhyton (Plate 111) from Imit is an artifact rooted in the artistic heritage of the nomads.[184]

Bronze plaques acquired in the Kandia valley dated in the first to the second centuries A.D. include an ibex (Plate 112) to whose horns the head of a bird is attached.[185] The body of the animal is worked out as an S-spiral in relief with two circular cells in it. The piece is now in the National Museum, Karachi. A petroglyph made with a metal implement from the site of Thalpan Bridge, on the so-called Altar Rock,[186] shows a stag followed by a beast of prey with two tails. The peculiarity of the two tails also occurs in the dêcor of narrative bronzes in China. A pommel (Plate 113) topping the hilt of an akinakes[187] (the hilt is of bronze with an iron blade) was found from Akbeit, kurgan 3 in the easternmost Pamirs, very near to the Afghan and Chinese borders. A plaque (Plate 114) depicting a stag has been found from Termansy, near Akbeit, with the typical spiralled Scythian antlers.[188] The S-spiral decorating the body of the Kandia plaque is used as an 'abstract' design covering a clasp. A similar bronze was found in Pamirskaja (Plate 115).[189]

The enormous amount of gold as found from the Pattan hoard in Kohistan district is remarkable. The gold ring (Plates 116 117 and 118) of Pattan[190] dated in the second to late first century B.C. has a series of engraved animals, most of them in a crouching pose, in a remarkable composition. The tigers depicted frequently are reminiscent of the Ordos bronzes.

Śaka tombs in the Eastern Pamirs have yielded various utility objects. There were bronze objects, ornaments, bronze jewellery with semi-precious stones and bronze figures of animals, similar to the Scythian animal art style of the sixth to the second centuries B.C. Objects from Vakhsh have yielded a collection of seals, clay vessels with human and animal heads on the sides and handles, as well as a steatite tray of the Taxila type with a person riding a hippocampus dragon. The treasure of the Oxus contains a similar relief.[191]

C. DIFFERENCES IN (1) STYLE, (2) TECHNIQUE AND (3) CHARACTER OF ART BETWEEN THE WESTERN AND EASTERN SECTIONS

In this section an attempt has been made to delineate the differences in style, technique and character between the western and eastern sections of the Scythian/Śaka art. The Scythian/Śaka art of the western and eastern sections (or vice versa), despite their differences, can be regarded as a single great phenomenon. But a detailed churning of the archaeological data reveals that the primary motifs of the Scythian nomadic animal art originated from the eastern section. Therefore, the problem arises of equating the artifacts of the western section and the later art of the eastern section with the parent art form. Apart from this fundamental criteria of chronology, some other factors are to be considered. The vast stretch of Scythian/Śaka art from the Danube to the borders of China comprising the western and eastern boundaries of the western and eastern sections had to encounter the art of other great civilizations at different times. The literary sources of different nationalities had much to say about this. Thus, in spite of being a single great phenomenon, this art had definite regional innovations and the tenacity of the original (core) animal art style, in spite of its peripheral blending, never gave the feeling of being exhausted. However, the units of the 'cone' and the 'periphery' are constantly blurring. The sojourn of the Scythian art between the two sections is a wonderful history of the evolution, growth and development of the nomadic animal art forms.

The broad terms- "Scythian", "Sauromation", "Sarmatian", and "Śaka" have emerged to characterize the material culture of the Eurasian nomads. These terms were derived from the descriptions of ancient authors, who utilized these labels to convey a variety of meanings. They were employed both as general references to the horse-riding peoples and as specific tribal, cultural, and geographical designations. Archaeological evidences more or less suggested a tripartized society of herder-cultivators, warriors and priests. Archaeological investigations have led to the further definition of these terms as markers of particular aspects of cultural groups that flourished at a particular time, or displayed individuating genetic or linguistic traits. Certain stylistic features both differentiate the nomadic arts of the Pontic steppes, the Caucasus, the Don-Volga-Urals, the southern Siberia, Central Asia, and China and also interrelate them within a broad cultural continuum. This unity has been conveyed by the use of the terms "animal style" and "Scytho-Siberian animal style".

The deer is probably the most common motif in the so-called animal- style art of the steppe nomads. The deer motif in the Scythian art is generally associated with the reindeer which is native to northern Siberia and the forest steppes as far west as Eastern Europe. The early Scythian gold reindeer (Plate 84) from Chilikta, in eastern Kazakhstan, [192] and the gold deer (Plate 63) from the royal Scythian burial at Kostromskaia,[193] in the Caucasus, for instance, have a typically Scythian folded pose. Both have a balanced composition and smooth gold surfaces. The Kazakhstan deer plaque dated in the second half of the eighth century B.C.- the first half of the seventh century B.C., was hammered over a mould in low relief. Its large antlers have one branch to the front and four to the rear, and they bear a more naturalistic rendering. This was more of a characteristic of the eastern region, than the more stylized depictions of stags in the Scythian art of the Pontic steppes. The Kostromskaia deer plaque dated in the end of the seventh century B.C. is typical of the Scythian artistic tradition of combining realism and abstraction, and complemented by additional ornamental antlers, which appear as a row of rhythmically repeated S-spirals. The musculature of the neck is emphasized, definitely more than its Kazakhstan counterpart. The famous Kelermes deer plaque (Plate 50)[194] from a gorytus (dated in the second half of the seventh century B.C.) was a formalized version (in stance and modulation of the anatomical parts) of the Chilikta deer. The Filippovka deer dated in the fourth century B.C. have top-heavy antlers and bodies covered with decorations. Its stylistic affinity lay to the east, in the Altai Mountains, where the earlier kurgans (eighth to seventh centuries B.C.) of Bashadar, Tuekta and Pazyryk yielded objects with similar over-all ornaments on the bodies of animals. Such ornamentations may have arisen, in part, from the ease with which decorative spirals can be produced in wood carving. This decorative tradition was common on the eastern steppes not only in wood carving, but also in gold-work (as in the stag-shaped gold belt ornaments from the Issyk Kurgan, in eastern Kazakhstan, dated in the fourth century B.C.). Although the monstrous Issyk stags (Plates 85-86) are in a folded pose, their bodies are decorated with incisions and spirals, and there are spiral ornaments beneath the chins.[195] The carved horn belt plaque (Plate 76) in the shape of a horse, from Sagly-Bazhi II, in Tuva,[196] shows the same elaborately decorated surfaces as the Filippovka deer. A gold belt plaque (Plate 119) said to have been found at Verkhneudinsk (modern Ulan-Ude), east of Lake Baikal, in Mongolia,[197] probably represents the eastern most extension of the style. The bird's heads on the antlers of the five deer[198] placed in the corridor of the Filippovka tomb may symbolize an aspect of a tribal deity, the bird of prey. Similar birds of prey were found on the headdress decorations, and a gold epaulet from Ziwiye (late eighth to seventh century B.C.) in the Near East. But the antler-with-bird's-head motifs widely used in the western section during the fourth century B.C. were more aggressive in appearance.

Beginning in the sixth century B.C., the repertoire of images in the art of the Altai expanded to include mythical creatures, such as the griffin. In no other ancient culture does the griffin motif appear in such a multiplicity of renderings. The Altai artists treated the griffin (Plate 89) in an original way. The tuft feathers were delineated with relief lines and the eyes were either round or almond-shaped. The curling beak was worked in relief, and the ear, leaf-shaped with a spiral at the base.[199] But the griffins of the western section were more formidable in appearance and were more slender and agile in form (as depicted in the detail of two griffins savaging a horse from the lower frieze of the Tolstaya Mogila pectoral).

The stylized zoomorphic style, which laid the foundation for the Scythian art, gradually became dominant in the fifth and fourth centuries B.C. New subject-matter began to infiltrate the Scythian art during this period. From the Sarmatians, the Scythians borrowed the image of the wolf, and from the nomads of southern Siberia the image of the elk. Zhurovka, in the Dnepropetrovsk region, testifies to this development. A plaque from Zhurovka exhibits two non-antlered elk's heads (Plate 120) with ears and snouts touching each other.[200] The wooden plaque (Plate 93) from Tuekta, in the Altai,[201] is comparable to the Zhurovka ornament but it is one hundred years older.

In the fourth century B.C. the dominant art form was exquisitely designed decorative objects in which ornamentation was more important than representation. The animal figures lost their former three-dimensionality and became flat and oversimplified. Relief was replaced by engraving. Some bridle decorations (Plate 121) were in the form of flowers made from birds' heads.[202] In many cases the image of the animal vanished among the intricate spirals (Plate 122).[203] Thus the animal style, having forfeited its elegant simplicity, gained something new in both the sections. The eastern section, which had originally started with decorative compositions in its animal style, was not that fast in changing the dynamic animal style to a new phase. In the western section, the changes into rhythmical forms and original, exuberant decorative compositions were apparent from the fourth century B.C. onwards.

In Scythian art, we find small representations of beasts skillfully juxtaposed upon spaces on the bodies of large figures like the Kul-Oba deer (Plate 64),[204] dated in the fifth century B.C., and the Kelermes panther (Plate 62)[205] (dated in the seventh century B.C.) This style is rare in the Scythian art of the eastern section.

In the western section, the narrative traits were more significant. Many objects in the western section have narrative scenes, which have been analyzed by scholars as depictions of Scythian myths. The nomadic art of both the sections strove after a decorative compactness; however, the organic animal form is the original element in the eastern section and has superceded the decorative details. Here the purely ornamented shapes are secondary and generally arises out of the degeneration of animal forms which we may call transmutation. The compactness lost much of its significance in the eastern section, where animal art was a tool for ornamentation in the micro. The macro aspect in the west lost much of its relevance, as there were further changes in mediums. Significantly, gold was not much used. The narrative aspect, as seen from the vessels of silver gilt found at Chastyye Mogily and Solokha, has not been seen in the eastern section. Objects from the Solokha barrow revealed the disappearance of archaic elements and there was somehow a vital Hellenization of virtually all the motifs. The panther is altogether replaced by the lion, the eagle by the griffin. Horses and boars appear with deer as prey; all are treated with the same idealized realism apparent in the handling of the predators. Graceful tendrils interwoven with flowers emerge as significant ornamental motifs. They and the birds and insects that adorn them represent the closest Scythian art which comes to a deliberate reference to a landscape. Most important, however, is the appearance of human representation: idealized, vigorous, and apparently narrative in import.

Some Scythian art objects in the western section indicate an amalgamation of Hellenic and Scythian elements and an appropriate and justifiable use of Hellenized form to Scythianized themes (Plate 198).[206] The best of Scythian art is based on a number of qualities which are integrated and presented as a whole especially in gold technology. Of these qualities, monumentality is well demonstrated by the Kelermes griffin-headed poletop (Plate 6),[207] bridle ornaments (Plates 123-124), also from Kelermes,[208] a torque with spiralled rope from Solokha,[209] and the massive spiralled-rope bracelet (Plate 41) with sphinx terminals, from Kul-Oba.[210] Another distinctive quality is the use of plain gold surface to enhance the inner vitality of an animal or an animal confrontation. At Scythian sites, when bronze and gold works of art were cast, the craftsmen used the lost wax method involving wooden models. Wooden matrices were also widely used for metal repoussê work.

R. M. Minasyan believes that the whole of Scythian decorative metal work had been very much influenced by the carving technique, echoes of which can be traced in the most famous examples of Scythian animal style metal artifacts.[211] There was a basic understanding of the plastic qualities of wood as is so charmingly expressed in the carved wooden objects found from the sixth century burials at Tuekta, and in the objects from fifth and fourth century burials at Pazyryk. In the eastern section, monumentality was not that important. Perhaps the survival economy had changed to a more settled way of life. The monumentality of the Kostromskaya stag and the Kelermes panther has been almost phenomenal but this milestone had not been achieved in the eastern section.

Also, in the western section the understanding of the power of empty areas and the spacing of figures were more developed, as in the spacing of figures on the Kul-Oba vessel (Plates9-12),[212] the Chertomlyk amphora (Plate 16),[213] in the Solokha comb (Plate 43)[214] and the spacing of animals on the Bolshaya Bliznitsa pectoral (Plate 32).[215] In the eastern section the ornamentation of the whole available space was important.

In the later Śaka/Scythian art, the respect for monumental and simple forms was somehow threatened, if not overwhelmed by, elaborations as clearly reflected in the Kul-Oba phiale.[216] In it, the only Scythian elements (aside from its find site), are the rather caricatured images of Scythian males depicted amidst Gorgon-Medusas, boar heads and bees. Significantly, the cauldrons of the western section (whether they had any magico-religious purpose is uncertain) lost much of their significance. They were hardly found in Śaka burials. Thus, archaeologically, one common cultural substratum has led to diverse yet common features, with a scope for changes. The animal style followed remarkably different lines of development according to the areas concerned. While the Scythian art passed from stylized linear figures to a more elaborate style, on the other hand, the art of the Siberian area passed from rigid forms to geometric combinations i.e., animals twisted into the shape of a circle with legs forming an openwork circle or contorted in a horizontal S (some of which are of nomadic origin and others, Chinese).

Amazingly, the clothing plaques found in the Scythian burials of the western section are appreciatively representational and one does find examples of more geometric renderings. Clothing plaques from the eastern section have a greater geometrical understanding, as at Issyk.

In the case of ornaments, the eastern section examples are more simple in technique. Precious-metal techniques had originated in the east, but on the ornaments of the western section, the surfaces of particular examples were an amalgamation of braided threads, notched threads, granulation and even tiny, sheet-gold figures. Individually, these elements can be traced in the eastern section. An interesting Achaemenid vase (Plate 125)[217] has been found from the kurgan of Filippovka. It has made use of both gold and silver. Gold is inlaid in horizontal strips around the silver body. Cast gold was essentially a Persian tradition and it occured in Scythian art. It is noteworthy to consider whether Achaemenising gave a new lease of life to the Scythian art. The advanced techniques of filigree and granulation in contrast to the rudimentary technique of hammering gold had all been practised before the time of the Scythians. Embedding in gold of coloured substances, usually turquoises, first became popular in those parts of Scytho-Siberian areas adjoining the Persian frontier and then passed into west Siberia and South Russia. Earlier the Scythians did not use this technique to a great extent. The Sarmatians, however, made extensive use, in not only embedding the stones, but also setting them in cloisons.

The great development of orfevrerie cloisonee took place in Achaemenid Persia. The Scytho-Siberian objects in the Oxus Treasure link the gold-smith's craft of Achaemenid Persia and that of western Siberia of the ancient Scythic art. Among the Scythians, the bracelets were usually formed from a twisted or smooth gold rope terminating in a modelled element. In the western section the bracelets are rounded, while those of the eastern section are characteristically bow-shaped.

The ancient Near Eastern tradition of overlaying objects made from baser materials with gold sheets or foil [218] was continued by Hellenistic gold workers and the Saka-Pahlavas and Kushans.

A gold neck ornament (Plate 126)[219] from the Siberian collection of Peter I, dated in the fifth to the fourth century B.C., is significantly different from the neck ornaments of the western section. This ornament is made of three smooth tubes and is divided by hinges into two unequal parts. This division of a large front and a smaller back is a peculiarity of the eastern section. The animal figures, attached to the upper tube, are hollow and made from two halves soldered together and are similar to those from Siberia and from Central Asia. Between the tubes are two ornamental strips with rhomboid and circular hollows (again a Śaka/Scythian characteristic) for turquoise and coral inlays.

Cylindrical beads with gold caps (Plate 127)[220] are unique to the eastern section. Gold caps were used on handles of utility objects and weapons found from the barrows of the western section. Granulation on the gold caps created beautiful triangular forms. These forms were transmitted to the ornaments found from the eastern section including India, as will be seen below.

Although zoomorphic images dominated the Scythian art, depictions of people are also significant. Representations of mounted horsemen are a special category. These were usually found on metal utility objects, or ornaments belonging to both the eastern and western sections. But the representation of mounted horsemen on colourful felt rugs (Plate 128) was a characteristic of the eastern section as found from kurgan 5 at Pazyryk.[221]

In the eastern section, comparatively, there are lesser female images than in the western section. Scythian males are represented in direct relationship with animals: riding horses, shooting rabbits, or milking animals and preparing their skins. Mundane female representations are almost absent. They are more often associated with animals, and the animals are either fantastic, such as griffins or hippocampi; or fearful, such as lions or snakes; or the human female becomes fused with snakes or birds. Most of the Saka/Scthian female depictions are associated with the terrible and one is shifted to the world of death, magic and unnaturals. Some of the important images depict the brotherhood scenes and animal representations also reveal scenes of dual relationships. The materials drawn from the burials of the eastern section contemporary to the Pontic burials of the Scythians in the western section, appear to confirm that human imagery hardly dwelled within the subject-matter of early nomadic art.

Just as a comparison between materials from the Śaka, Pazyryk, and Tagar traditions with analogous materials from the Scythians lead to the inescapable conclusion that the style and subjects of the latter derive from the culture that characterized the former, so the rock carvings of northern Central Asia promise to provide source materials for understanding the origins and possibly the implications of Scythian visual imagery. Traditions always experience changes along with the birth and death of new traditions that signify elements added, subtracted or merged into new forms. The combination, interplay and interchange of significant elements form the dynamics for the pattern of creativity. As a result the whole is created and each object in the Śaka/Scythian repertoire goes well beyond simplistic designations and vocabulary.

It may therefore be surmised that

1. The Scythian/Śaka art originated in the eastern section, then traversed to the western section. Cross currents and isolated developments are found there. The eastern section had its own evolution, developments and continuity with its detours.

2. With the later Śakas and later Scythians we find the formation of "states" as in Bactria or India, which were capable of dealing more or less effectively with the nations by which they were threatened or with whom they traded. Not surprisingly, perhaps, the very formation of "statehood" brought an end to the distinctive early nomadic way of life by the 1st century B.C. but art forms obviously continued.

3. This continuation of art forms oscillated between the 'animal style' and the 'nomadic animal style' and the relationship between these two were quite astute.

The style, technique and character of art of the Śaka/Scythian artifacts in the borderlands of India and India itself have been discussed in the next two chapters.

References

1. *Scy. Art.*, p.23, Pl.1.
2. *Ibid.*, p.25, Pl.7.
3. *En. Wor. Art.*, Vol.2, p.22.
4. Roger Cribb, *Nomads In Archaeology,* Cambridge, 1993, p.68.
5. Madina Tesieva, 'Koban Bronzes in Tli', *Aleksandravskii prospect,* No.7 Sept. Oct. 1999, Vladikavkaz, p.3. The table, however, shows a time gap of some six hundred years (2000B.C.-1400B.C.) which might have been due to overlapping of archaeological findings.
6. G. Borovka, *Scythian Art*, New York, 1928, p.41.
7. E.H.Minns, *Scythians And Greeks*, New York, 1913, Fig. 85.
8. *Art. Scy.*, p.183.
9. *Scy.Art.*, Pl.47.
10. E.H. Minns, *op. cit.*, Fig. 281.
11. *Ibid.*, Figs. 279-280.
12. *Art. Scy.*,p.186.
13. *Ibid.*, p.190.
14. *Ibid.*, p.218.
15. *Ibid.*, p. 221.
16. *Ibid.*, Fig. 112.
17. *Ibid.*, p. 249.

18. *Ibid.*, Fig. 113.
19. *Ibid.*, Fig. 115.
20. *Ibid.*, Fig.116.
21. V.D. Blavatskiy, *Art Of The Northern Black Sea In Antiquity*, Moscow, 1947, p.71.
22. *Art.Scy.*, Figs. 82,83.
23. See his paper 'Skifskiy Mifologicheskiy Syuzhet v Iskusstve i ideologii Tsarstva Ateya' in *Sov. Arkh.*, 1970, No.3, pp.90 to 101.
24. *Scy. Art.*, p.5.
25. *Ibid.*, Pls. 171-173.
26. *Art. Scy.*, Figs.85-86.
27. *Scy. Art.*, Pls.265-268.
28. *Art. Scy.*, Fig.18.
29. M.Vickers, 'Golden Greece; Relative Values, Minae, and Temple Inventories', *Am. Journ. Arch.*, Vol. 94,1990, pp.613-625.
30. *Scy. Art.*, Pls.162-163.
31. *Ibid.*, Pls. 164-165.
32. E.H. Minns, *op.cit.*, Fig. 318.
33. *Scy. Art.*, Pls.115-116.
34. *Ibid.*, Pls. 247-248.
35. R.Higgins, *Greek and Roman Jewellery*, Berkeley and Los Angeles, 1980, Pl.24 D.
36. R. Ghirshman, *The Arts of Ancient Iran*, New York, 1964, Pl. 137.
37. *Scy. Art.*, Pls. 45, 46.
38. *Art. Scy.*,p.146.
39. *Scy. Art.*, Pl.223.
40. *Ibid.*, Pl. 135.
41. *Ibid.*, Pls. 226-228.
42. *Ibid.*, Pl. 232.
43. *Ibid.*, Pl. 229.
44. *Ibid.*, Pl. 134.
45. R. Higgins, *op.cit.*,p.130.
46. *Scy. Art.*, Pl.251.
47. E. H. Minns, *op.cit.*, Fig. 119.
48. *Scy. Art.*, Pls. 118 — 121.
49. *Ibid.*, Pls. 255,256.
50. *Ibid.*, Pls. 122,123.
51. *Ibid.*, Pls. 126, 127.
52. *Ibid.*, Pls. 236, 237.
53. *Art. Scy.*, p. 122.
54. *Scy. Art.*, Pl. 125.

55. *Ibid.*, Pl. 240.
56. *Ibid.*, Pl. 239.
57. V.D. Kubarev, *Kurgany Ulandryka,* Novosibirsk, 1987, Pl.XXVII/10.
58. *Scy. Art.*, Pl.124.
59. V.D. Kubarev, *op.cit.,* Pl.LXIX/9.
60. *Scy. Art.,* Pl.235.
61. K.A. Akishev, *Kurgan Issyk,* Moscow,1978,Figs.74,75.
62. *Scy.Art.,* Pl.234.
63. *Ibid.,* Pl.182.
64. *Scy. Art.,*Pl.250.
65. E.H. Minns, *op.cit.,*Fig.42.
66. V. Schiltz, *Les Scythes et les Nomades des Steppes,* Paris, 1994, pp.359, 414 and Pl.359.
67. S.I. Kaposhina, 'Pamyiatniki zverinogo stilya iz O'lbii',*K.S.I.I.M.K*, XXXIV, 1950, Fig.9.
68. *Scy. Art.,* Pl.19.
69. *Ibid.,* Pl.142.
70. *Ibid.,* Pl.196.
71. *Ibid.,* Pls.208,209.
72. *Bac. Gol.,* Pl.78.
73. *Scy. Art.,* Pl.23.
74. R. Ghirshman, *op.cit.,*Pl.147.
75. *Scy. Art.*, Pls.224,225.
76. E.H. Minns, *op.cit.*, Figs.124,125.
77. *Scy. Art.*, Pls.32-35.
78. *Art. Scy.*, p.233.
79. *Scy. Art.*, Pls.37-40.
80. *Ibid.*, Pls.66,67.
81. *Ibid.,* Pls.155,156.
82. *Ibid.*, Pls.150-154.
83. *Ibid.*, Pl.17.
84. *Ibid.*, Pl.16.
85. *Ibid.*, Pl.213.
86. *Gol. De. Eur.*, Pl.153.
87. *Ibid.*, p.6.
88. *Ibid.*, p.7.
89. *Ibid.*, p.8.
90. *Ibid.*, p.80,Pl.5.
91. *Ibid.*, Pl.6.
92. *Ibid.*, Pl.7.
93. *Ibid.*, Pl.8.

94. *Ibid.*, Pls.9,10,11.
95. *Ibid.*, Pl.13.
96. *Hist. Civ. Cen. As.*, Vol.II,p.160.
97. *Ibid.*, p.161.
98. *Ibid.*, p.210.
99. M. Aurel Stein, *Ancient Khotan,* p.210.
100. *Ibid.*, p.211.
101. *Ibid.*, p.213.
102. *Scy. Art.*, Pls.36,37.
103. *I.B.I.A.S.C.C.*, Issue 5, p.71.
104. *Gol. De. Eur.*, Pl.174.
105. M. Edwards, 'Unearthing Siberian Gold', *National Geographic*, June 2003, p.129.
106. *Ibid.*, p.123.
107. V. Semenov, K.Chugunov, 'New evidence of the Scythian-type culture of Tuva', *Anc. Civ. Scy. Sib.*, Vol.2, p.311.
108. *Ibid.*, p.312.
109. *Ibid.*, p.315, Fig.4.
110. *Gol. De. Eur.*, Pl.197.
111. V. Semenov, K. Chugunov, *op.cit.*, p.318, Fig.6.
112. *Ibid.*, pp.322, 323, Figs.9,10.
113. V. Schiltz, *op.cit.*, p.88, Pl.64.
114. V. Semenov, K.Chugunov, *op.cit.*, p.324, Fig.11.
115. *Ibid.*, p.325, Fig.12.
116. *Ibid.*, p.327.
117. *Ibid.*, p.332, Fig.18.
118. *Ibid.*, p.333.
119. *Ibid.*, p.331, Fig.17.
120. *Ibid.*, p.333.
121. *Scy. Art.*, Pl.7.
122. *Gol. De. Eur.*, Pl. 170.
123. *Gol. De. Eur.*, Pl. 170.
124. *Ibid.*, Pl.142.
125. J. Davis-Kimball, 'Chieftain or Warrior Priestess ?', *Archaeology*, Sept.-Oct. 1997, p.41.
126. *Gol. De. Eur.*, p.7, Figs.4,5.
127. *Gol. De. Eur.*, p.7, Figs.4,5.
128. J.Davis-Kimball, *op.cit.*, p.40.
129. *Ibid.*, p.40.
130. *Ibid.*, p.41.
131. *Gol.De.Eur.*, Pl.169.

132. J.Davis-Kimball, *op.cit.*, p.41.
133. M.V.Polosmak, 'Investigations of a Pazyryk Barrow at Kuturguntas', *Anc. Civ. Scy. Sib.*, vol.2, p.100, Fig.7.
134. G.A.Koshelenko, A.M.Bader, V.A.Gaibov, 'Archaeological Studies in Turkmenistan', *Anc. Civ. Scy. Sib.*, Vol.1, p.273.
135. *Gol. De. Eur.*, p.245.
136. *Ibid.*, p.248.
137. *Ibid.*, Pl.177.
138. *Ibid.*, p.254.
139. *Ibid.*, p.254.
140. *Ibid.*, Pl.178.
141. *Ibid.*, Pl.67.
142. *Ibid.*, Pl.180.
143. *Ibid.*, Pl.183.
144. *Ibid.*, Pl.184.
145. *Ibid.*, Pl.185.
146. *Ibid.*, Pl.187.
147. N.V.Polosmak, 'The Ak-Alakh Frozen Grave Barrow', *Anc. Civ. Scy.Sib.*, Vol.1, p.347.
148. *Ibid.*, p.348, Fig.1.
149. *Ibid.*, p.353.
150. *Ibid.*, p.352, Figs.4,5.
151. *Gol. De. Eur.*, Pl.179.
152. *Ibid.*, p.256.
153. *Ibid.*, Pl.175.
154. N.V. Polosmak, *op.cit.*, p.354.
155. *Ibid.*, p.353, Fig.6.
156. J. Davis-Kimball, *op.cit.*, p.46.
157. *Ibid.*, p.46, Pl.47.
158. *I.B.I.A.S.C.C.*, Issue 5, p.51.
159. J.Turner ed., *Dictionary of Art*, Cambridge, 1994, Vol.16, p.577.
160. Yu. S. Khudyakov, 'Problems of the Genesis of Culture of the Hunnic Period in the Altai Mountains', *Anc .Civ. Scy. Sib.*, Vol.3, p.329.
161. V.O. Vitt, Loshadi, 'Pazyrykskikh Kurganov', *Sov. Arkh.*, No.XVI, Leningrad, 1952, p.198.
162. Cf. N.V.Polosmak's paper cited above, (Note 154) p.92.
163. *Ibid.*, p.96, Fig. 3.
164. *Ibid.*, p.99.
165. N.L.Zhukovskaya, *Kategorii I Synvolika Traditsionnoi Kulturi Mongolov*, Moscow, 1988, p.93.
166. Ya.I.Gummel, 'Excavations to the south-west of Hanlar in 1941', *Anc. Civ. Scy. Sib.*, Vol.2, p.225.

167. F.P. Grigorev, R. Ismagil, 'The Cult Bronzes of Semirechye of the Saka Period', *Anc. Civ. Scy. Sib.*, Vol.3, p.241.
168. *Ibid.*, p.242, Fig.1.
169. *Ibid.*, p.243, Fig.2.
170. *Ibid.*, p.243, Figs.5,6.
171. *Ibid.*, p.246.
172. *Ibid.*, p.243, Figs.5,6.
173. M.I. Artamonov, *Sokrovischa Sakov*, Moscow, 1973 p.40, Fig.47.
174. G. Frumkin, 'Archaeology in Soviet Central Asia. III-Kirghiziya and the Fergana Valley', *Central Asian Review,* Vol.12, p.18.
175. G.A. Pugachenkova, 'The Antiquities of Transoxiana in the light of Investigations in Uzbekistan (1985-1990)', *Anc. Civ. Scy. Sib.*, Vol.2, p.8.
176. *Scy. Art.,* Pl.61.
177. K. Abdullaev, S. Raimkulov, 'A Triumph Scene on an engraved gem from Kundzhulitepe (Kashkadarya)',*Anc. Civ. Scy. Sib.*, Vol.2, p.221.
178. *Dyn.Art.Kus.*, Fig.59.
179. D. Sellwood, *An Introduction to the Coinage of Parthia*, London,1980, Pl.3(1).
180. A.K. Srivastava, *Catalogue of Śaka-Pahlava Coins of North India*, Lucknow,1972, Pl.IV.1-5, 7, 9, 11; V.4; V.6-8; VII.1-4.
181. B.N. Mukherjee, *Kushāna Silver Coinage,* Calcutta, 1982, p.22, Pl.V.25.
182. K. Jettmar, 'The Art of the Northern Nomads in the Upper Indus valley', *South Asian Studies*, No.7,London 1991, p.2, Fig.1.
183. *Ibid.*, p.3,Fig.2.
184. *Ibid.*, p.10,Fig.14.
185. *Ibid.*, Pl.3.
186. *Ibid.*, Pl.6.
187. *Ibid.*, p.6, Fig.5.
188. *Ibid.*, p.6, Fig.7.
189. *Ibid.*, p.6, Fig.6.
190. *Ibid.*, pp.14, 15, Figs.20, 21, 22.
191. B.A. Litvinsky, Igor R.Pichikjan, 'Gold Plaques from the Oxus Temple', *Anc. Civ. Scy. Sib.*, Vol.2, p.219.
192. *Gol. De. Eur.*, Pl.170.
193. *Ibid.*, Pl.140.
194. *Ibid.*, Pl.142.
195. *Ibid.*, p.7, Figs.4, 5.
196. *Ibid.*, Pl.197.
197. *Ibid.*, Pl.210.
198. *Ibid.*, p.14.
199. *Ibid.*, Pl.177.

200. *Ibid.*, Pl.155.
201. *Ibid.*, Pl.183.
202. *Ibid.*, Pl.152.
203. *Ibid.*, Pl.154.
204. V. Schiltz, *op.cit.*, p.159, Pl.116.
205. *Ibid.*, pp.20, 21, Pl.8.
206. *Art. Scy.*, p.66.
207. *Scy. Art.*, Pl.15.
208. *Ibid.*, Pls.4, 5.
209. *Ibid.*, Pls.122, 123.
210. *Ibid.*, Pl.182.
211. R.S.Minasyan, 'The Origin of the Distinctive Features of the Animal Style', *A.S.G.E.*, Issue 29,1988; Issue 30, 1990, pp.74, 75.
212. V.Schiltz, *op.cit.*,pp.173-175, Pls.125-127.
213. *Ibid.*, p.195, Pl.144.
214. *Ibid.*, p.414, Pl.359.
215. *Ibid.*, pp.384-385, Pl.310.
216. *Scy. Art.*, Pls.164,165.
217. *Gol. De. Eur.*, Pl.19.
218. R. Higgins, *op.cit.*, pp.33,34.
219. *Gol. De. Eur.*, Pl.208.
220. *Ibid.*, Pl.17.
221. *Ibid.*, p.14, Fig.14.

5 Śaka-Scythian and Indian Art : Beginnings

A. IN THE BORDERLANDS

So far as the borderlands are concerned, the prine focus is on the area from the south of the southern section of eastern Scythia.[1] Between the river Oxus in the borderlands and North-Western India there were Bactria (in northern Afghanistan), Aria (West Afghanistan including Herat), Drangiana or Śakastāna[2] (South-West Afghanistan including the Seistan region), Arachosia (south-eastern Afghanistan including the Kandahar area) and Paropanisadae (the area to the east of the Hindu Kush in North-East Afghanistan).

Thus, the regions which were incorporated in Afghanistan in the late pre-Christian and early Christian centuries, were Bactria, Paropanisadai, Arachosia, Gedrosia and Drangiana. Bactria[3] (in Northern Afghanistan) was bounded on the north and also on the east by Sogdiana (situated in Uzbekistan), on the west by Margiana (part of modern Turkmenistan), and on the south or south-west by a part of Aria (modern Herat region in Afghanistan). Below it was Drangiana[4] (or Śakastāna, modern Seistan). According to Ptolemy, India Intra Gangem[5] (Indian subcontinent minus the area to the north and north-east of the Ganges) lay on the east of Paropanisadai[6] (modern Kabul-Begram region to the south-east of the Hindu

Kush was within its limit), Arachosia[7] (the south-eastern Afghanistan around Ghazni and Kandahar) and Gedrosia[8] (in a part of Baluchistan). The territory of Afghanistan outside the Hindu Kush was generally called Ariana.

Of these areas, the most important site yielding Śaka/Scythian artifacts is Tillya-Tepe in northern Afghanistan, dated in the first century B.C. to first century A.D. Tillya-Tepe's connections with North-West India is shown by the evidence of, *inter alia*, a gold medallion (Plate 129 A) displaying on one side a lion with a Kharoshtī inscription.[9] The inscription reads *siho vigato bhayo* meaning the 'lion who is devoid of fear'. This attribute indicates the lion as a theriomorphic representation of Śākyasimha (Gautama Buddha). On the other side of the medallion (Plate 129 B) appears a naked and bearded man turning a wheel. He is identified with Heracles-Krishna.[10] The evidence of the medallion[11] thus establishes an Indian connection with the Tillya-Tepe site of the first century A.D. This Indian connection is of key significance as it indicats the percolation of Śaka/Scythian elements in early Indian art. The repetition of styles, motifs of the Śaka/Scythian repertoire at Tillya-Tepe have been revealed as a result of excavations. The discoveries of the Afghan-Soviet Archaeological Expedition in 1978-79 in the town of Shibargan in northern Afghanistan, show various artifacts in the ancient burials dated in the first century B.C. to the first century A.D. They impress us by reflecting the Śaka/ Scythian elements in varying degrees.

Excavations at Tillya-Tepe have yielded more gold ornamental plaques and ornaments than utility objects, weapons and horse trappings. It is noteworthy that these had a fair distribution in the Scythian burials of the western section. Of key significance at Tillya-Tepe are the Parthian coins with local overstrikes found along with a coin of Tiberius.[12] The Parthian coins have substantially shown that the Parthians had much trade in the Indian borderlands specially with the semi-nomadic cattle-raising pastoralists on the Parthian empire's borders.[13] The Śaka/Scythians had to collaborate with the Parthians, unlike the Kushānas, who successfully controlled several channels of the Silk Roads that led along the Indus Valley to the port of Barygaza (modern Broach) from where ships sailed for North Africa, thus affording to bypass Parthia and the Parthians.[14] The formation of these routes was to a considerable extent associated with the natural resources of certain regions. Therefore, the case of bypassing or avoiding the Parthians was not applicable to the Śaka / Scythians, and this is important in the cultural context.

The animal style, as apparent from the Tillya-Tepe objects, was an essential part of the art of the Eurasian nomads. We have come across it during the course of our study of objects belonging to the Eastern and Western sections of the Scythian/Śaka art in Chapter 4. It appeared again at Tillya-Tepe, in the ornamentation of utility objects, ornaments, weapons, horse trappings and other burial goods, as well as in tattoos. Animals were depicted singly or in complex compositions in this animal style. Details were accentuated by means of coloured inlays, curvilinear ornamentations, additional zoomorphic elements, and exaggerations of the animal bodies. Gold phials (Plate 130) from burial 4, Tillya-Tepe,[15] have a close parallel in the gold phial from Gonio.[16] These gold phials are in the form of cast dishes fluted with grooves furring out from the central circlet. The massive gold phial from Gonio is similar to the silver bowls widespread in Georgia in the first century A.D. A gold pyxis from burial 3, Tillya-Tepe, has similar parallels in the later Śaka complexes. The gold pyxis[17] consists of three segments, having a bottom, a cylindrical body and a lid with a handle. The whole cast body is embellished along the waist with a horizontal band of laurels, each of which is bounded at the base by a curved thong. The separately cast bottom has been soldered on to the body. The lid is embellished with the same ornamental design as the body of the vessel. The protruding handle is topped by a finial or pommel whose shape is reminiscent of a pomegranate. It carries an embossed ornamental design along the rim. The round loop, one of which is soldered on to the lid and the other on to the body, are linked by a braided gold chain. The abundant use of loops soldered on to various artifacts is a characteristic feature of Tillya-Tepe art. From Burial 3 has also been found a gold bowl, cast of a thin sheet and subsequently embossed. The bottom of the bowl is strongly concave.[18] The techniques of soldering, casting of thin sheets of metal and embossing were in use from the early Scythian period. Another interesting utility object, found from Burial 3, is a cast flat-bottomed pot (Plate 131) with a lid and an upright lip. Soldered on to its shoulders are two loops, one on either side and they are made of twisted wire with coiled ends. Passed through both loops are two chains, which are attached to the soldered-on ring-shaped handle of the pot's flat lid.[19] Attached to the rim of another cast gold bowl found from burial 4, Tillya-Tepe, is a gold scale model of a tree (Plate 190).[20] This type of scale model of a tree along with a gold figurine of an ibex had been incorporated into a ceremonial headdress akin to a diadem or crown as attested to by the celebrated gold diadem from the Khokhlach barrow (Novocherkassk Treasure) of early second century A.D. Thus the skilfully crafted diadem from the Khokhlach tumulus has parallels among Tillya-Tepe ornaments. The Khokhlach style has also been revealed in the contemporary Kobyakovo diadem and analogous adornments were found from barrow

46 near the village of Ust'-Labinskaya of early second century A.D.[21] It is interesting that the techniques used at Khokhlach were also apparent in ornaments found at Nogaichik and Taxila. Brooch-plates in the shape of rams have been encountered both at Nogaichik-Sokolova Mogila and Tillya-Tepe.[22] Thus, an overall compositional analogy is seen not only by an identical choice of subject-matter such as tree and ibexes, but also by such purely technical elements as the tiny pillars or rings in which the legs of the animals terminate. The Scythian repertoire includes similar gold scale models of trees with similar branches of wire and leaf-like disks dangling from them.

The rim of a pear-shaped silver utensil from Tillya-Tepe carries a fillet in relief of high grade silver. This is again ornamented with a chain-like design of impressed half-moons or crescents. Chains with dangling crescents have been frequently used in Śaka/Scythian objects from the early period.[23]

A particular mirror (Plate 132)[24] from Burial 3 has a massive ivory handle ornamented with a plain scratched design. The obverse is smooth whereas the reverse is edged with a raised rim embellished with barely marked bosses and with a cone-shaped prunt in the middle. This mirror is similar to a round mirror having an identical ivory handle from Taxila (Plate 133).[25]

Whatever the source of the tradition of securing gold ornaments onto clothing, the Eurasian nomads carried that preference to extraordinary lengths, as is well documented by the rich burial at Tillya-Tepe. Hundreds of ornamental plaques have been found in the Tillya-Tepe burials, whose exact positioning enables us to reconstruct the ornamental décor of such parts of clothing as cuffs, sleeves and hems. The reconstruction of the entire apparel would be like the typical Scythian close—fitting tunic, as depicted on numerous Scythian utility objects.[26] Also the garb of a king on a pendant from Tillya-Tepe is typically Scythian. Even the annular, curl-tipped horns of dragons with their backward contorted quarters as depicted on this pendant, are peculiar to the Scytho—Siberian animal style. Similarly executed dragons have been found from Gonur stone amulets. The site of Gonur has been recently excavated and is dated near about the first century A.D.[27] Also, the motif of the horned and winged horse on this pendant is very much similar to the winged and horned horse motif found on a cap from Issyk barrow in Kazakhstan.[28] Burial 1 at Tillya-Tepe has remains of a gold threaded apparel, showing the gold threads with a multitude of pearls on them and some intricate designs edged with gold plaques. These gold plaques (Plate 134) have an identical repoussê ornamentation of the 'man with a dolphin'.[29] The representation of the dolphin is fairly realistic except in its body scales. Perhaps the goldsmith had a hazy notion of the creature or he had tried to create a stylistic counterpart. A similar dolphin (Plate 135) has been found from the burial mound at Nogaichik.[30]

The treatment of the dolphin's scales was also applicable to the griffin plaque and the griffin's-head handle from Ufa, dated in the fourth century B.C. (Plate 136).[31] The image of the dolphin could be of local Bactrian provenance, the latter having an association with Graeco-Roman art, in which the dolphin representation holds a leading place. Similar dolphins are stylistically represented on handles from Taxila. Also from Tillya-Tepe are sewn-on six-petal rosette plaques. They are arranged in a checker-board pattern in two rows recalling the well-known Scytho-Siberian form. This checker-board pattern could be an individual collation in the eastern section of the Scythian art.[32] Within the Scythian tradition of clothing plaques, the earlier plaques, dating to the seventh, sixth and fifth centuries B.C. tend to be made of more solid metal and are larger than those of the fourth century B.C. By the end of the first century B.C. many of the plaques were small in size and extremely thin. Perhaps the demand for such plaques led to mass production by means of stamping metal sheets. Ornamental bands at Tillya-Tepe recall the ornamental bands found from Scythian burials of South Russia of fifth and fourth centuries B.C. Thus, the ornamental band at Tillya-Tepe attests to the continuation of the techniques in ornamental works, such as minute granulation, inset work with turquoise, and repoussê rosettes, from a very early period.[33] A necklace of gold beads (Plate 137) from burial 6 is made of slightly elongated beads secured by a pair of cone-shaped clasps. The surface of each bead is articulated into 109 eight facets, with the ribs marked by minute granulation.[34] Tillya-Tepe gold rings are embellished with a simple ornamental design of circles and almond shapes (eyes). These gold rings are similar in technique and embellishments to the Oxus ring, the flat hoop of which expands into a circular bezel, with a lion embossed. Its legs extend round the hoop on either side. The bronze ornament from the fourth tumulus of Seven Brothers barrow was similarly executed. Pendants in the shape of circles (Plate 138) have been found in the cemetery at Tillya—Tepe,[35] and in Scythian barrows dating from the second century B.C. to the first century A.D. in the Kuban region. Also, heart-shaped leaf pendants have been found in Tillya-Tepe barrows.[36] The treatment of the ivy motif on the Kul-Oba Athena pendant had again revisited Tillya-Tepe.

Tillya-Tepe has also yielded brooch-plaques in the shape of ram horns. Analogies of rectangular brooch-plaques with four-petal rosettes (Plate 139) have been found in burial 1 at Tillya-Tepe.[37] Bracelets with widening ends have been found on the left arm of the buried man. Similar bracelets on the left arm of the buried man have been found from Porogi, dated in the first century B.C. to first century A.D.[38] Bracelets with antelope terminals are cast with open-ended terminals. These bracelets (Plate 140) from Tillya-Tepe[39] have petal-like ears and coiled horns, which are encrusted with convex and highly polished turquoise beads.

An interesting imagery of the Scythian repertoire was figures of goddesses with furies or with other wild animals. The plaques with images of females seated on a panther and a lion-griffin were found from Bolshaya Bliznitsa. Represented on large gold pendants from burial 2 at Tillya-Tepe was the type 'Mistress of Animals' (Plate 141).[40] She wears a high calathus, a long skirt under a belted jacket, and holds in either outstretched hand a twisted animal of syncretic form. The same imagery was found on the earrings from Tolstaya Mogila, each in the form of a female standing against two lions.[41] From burial 4 at Tillya-Tepe, comes a superb belt with nine plaques representing a figure seated on a large feline. The figure (Plate 142) is probably that of a male, in quasi-nomadic attire.[42] Thus, from the sixth century B.C. down to the first century A.D., plaques depicting men/women or animals were an integral part of Śaka/Scythian imagery. Like the robed woman on a panther, and another on a griffin,[43] both from Bolshaya Bliznitsa, similar couples on mythical lions have been found from burial 6 at Tillya-Tepe. The clasp disks (Plate 143) found at Tillya-Tepe[44] have massive convex forms, made in the cast technique. These are similar to the ones found at Taxila. Clasp disks have three massive rings soldered on to the back for purposes of fastening. Soldered on to one is a hook, and on to the other, a loop that terminates in inward-turned scrolls. These inward-turned scrolls were widely used in Śaka art forms in India including architectural decors. These inward-turned scrolls so beautifully displayed on cauldrons of Raskopana Mogila (Plate 144), Ukraine,[45] revisit as motifs quite popular in the *āyāgapatas* found from Mathurā, dated in the first century A.D. onwards. Hairpins found at Tillya-Tepe show the usage of thin gold sheet shaped like quadrefoils (Plate 145)[46] in such a manner, that two of the lobes are horizontally aligned, and the other two are bent downwards. It also has crescent-shaped plaquettes. These crescent-shaped plaquettes are also found in the famous hair ornament (Plate 146) from Ufa,[47] of fourth century B.C. Cut from gold sheets are flowerlet plaques in the form of rosettes, and these were quite popular in Tillya-Tepe burials. The rosettes comprise of four heart-shaped lobes, each of which, in turn, is impressed with a straight and deep line down the middle and a curved line along the rim. Another interesting find is a five-lobed brooch partitioned by small lozenges, with rim curved inwards. Each of the five heart-shaped lobes is embellished with a pair of pear-shaped turquoise inlays. Several techniques of incrustation of metal objects were in use in Śaka/Scythian art. One of them is the insertion of precious or semi-precious stones or glass fragments. Another is the insertion of enamels, both combined to form the cloisonnê technique. The six-petalled rosettes, found from Tillya-Tepe burials were cut from gold sheets. On the reverse of each rosette is a loop for attachment. Five and six-petalled rosettes (Plates 147,191,192) were also found from Taxila.[48] Similar rosettes were also found in the Pavlovsky Barrow[49] of the fourth century B.C. and on the disc pendant (Plates 148,149, 27) from Kul-Oba.[50] The Tillya-Tepe rosettes are also similar to the rosettes bordering the lower edge of the boat-shaped pendants of Kul-Oba (Plates 148,149,27).[51] Hollow and boat-shaped earring clips (Plate 150) with two soldered halves are yet another fascinating group from Tillya-Tepe[52] ornaments. The terminals of the clips are embellished with an identical ornamental design. There is the distinguished motif of a chain row of equilateral triangles, and further down, a chain of lozenges. This boat-shaped form was frequently used in the Scythian jewellery, especially in the Kul-Oba ear ornament, Novoselitsy gold earrings,[53] and those from Krasnoye Znamya, Novozavedennoe, Kabardino-Balkariya[54] and Volkovtsy (Plates 17,18).[55]

Another Scythian motif of the ram horn continued in the Śaka/Scythian period. Brooch-plates in the shape of ram horns (Plates 151,152) have been encountered at Tillya-Tepe, burials 5 and 3,[56] and they are similar to those found from Tulkhar, Sokolova Mogila and Nogaichik.[57] Plaques of different shapes, geometrical and otherwise seem to have carried the Scythian legacy at Tillya-Tepe, and from Tillya-Tepe elsewhere. Thus, the Śaka/Scythian repertoire branched out into various categories without losing its focus. Seen from a surveying distance, they seem to be the living images, which had carried their tradition, with an interest and an inwardness across the vast expanse of space and time.

The 'bow with bosses' plaques (Plate 153)[58] from Tillya-Tepe have their parallels at Taxila (Plates 154,155).[59] Encrusted trefoil plaques (Plate 156) from Tillya-Tepe[60] are very much similar in shape to the copper, bronze and lead trefoils (Plate 157) from Taxila.[61] The pear-shaped plaques (Plate 158) from Tillya-Tepe[62] have further variations at Taxila (Plate 159).[63] Trident-shaped plaques with circlets have been found both at Taxila and Tillya-Tepe. At Tillya-Tepe both trident-shaped plaques and eye-pupil plaques are found (Plate 193).[64] Plaques with elongated insets and flowerlet plaques (Plate 194)[65] were important motifs in Tillya-Tepe art. These were encrusted with turquoise. Encrusted trefoil patterns of motifs, pear-shaped motifs and trident-shaped motifs have been used extensively in the jewellery found from Scythian barrows.[66] Especially noteworthy are the large horned and small horned plaquettes (Plates 151,152)[67] from burial 3, Tillya-Tepe. These plaquettes were cast in the shape of curved horns with two raised vertical stripes on the front. The rims have been perforated twice in both the types. Similar ones (Plates 160,161) have been found from Taxila.[68] The Taxila plaquettes were made of copper, bronze and lead.

The horse accoutrements from Tillya-Tepe have definite Śaka/Scythian affinities. Noteworthy are the temple pendants, which formed a striking part of the ornamentation of these horse accoutrements. The temple pendant from Tillya-Tepe have two identical protomas or foreparts of a horse turned in opposite directions, with almond-or 'eye'-shaped turquoise insets (Plate 195).[69] Similar protomas of two horses were also found in the Luristan bronzes.[70] Burial 4 at Tillya-Tepe has yielded a bridle embellished with gold phalerae and arched plaques with repoussê designs executed in the Scytho-Siberian style.[71]

Weapons belonging to the Tillya-Tepe burials stylistically support their Śaka/ Scythian heritage. Depictions of stags, however, become rare. The images and motifs of animal combat, fantastic monsters, floral patterns resembling *nandipadas* (Plate 196)[72] and hunting scenes are prevalent, as these may be linked symbolically to the world of the dead. They may be also linked to Herodotus's accounts of signs of valour. The iconography of the griffin on the scabbard covering from burial 4 of Tillya-Tepe is similar and almost identical to the Porogi griffin . Porogi is in the Yanpol District of the Vinnitsa region.[73] The male and female burials of Porogi are dated in the last century B.C. to the first century A.D. Again, the Tillya-Tepe scabbard (Plates 162,163)[74] coverings are stylistically similar to the gold toilet phial from Khokhlach.[75] The clasps of the sword-belt of Porogi (Plate 164)[76] are technologically and typologically similar to the openwork clasps from some of the burials of Tillya-Tepe . Certain parallels with the Tillya-Tepe gold can be observed in the scenes as well, like the plaques from burial 2 portraying the hero as holding two dragons by the paws. Articles of a sword-belt set from the Kosika burial, north of Astrakhan, have analogies in both burial 4 of Tillya-Tepe and Porogi.[77] The Kosika findings can be dated in the middle of the first century A.D. The style can be related to that of the Siberian-Altai nomadic world, on the wooden scabbards found at Borotab, Ulandryk, Barbugazy barrows of the fourth and the third century B.C.[78] The treatment of the monsters on the Tillya-Tepe scabbard is also apparent on the Kobyakovo torque. The beards and manes of the wolf-headed dragons of the Kobyakovo torque are executed in the same manner by interwoven braids and notches, as the monsters on the Tillya-Tepe scabbard (Plate 165).[79] A number of stylistic details of the Kobyakovo torque are reminiscent of the gold decorations of the necropolis in Tillya-Tepe at the threshold of the Christian era. Rich with diverse turquoise inlays, the seven main shapes used in the Kobyakovo torque were almond, rectangle, parallelogram, comma, etc., and were found practically in the same combinations on the earrings, clasps and sword scabbards from Northern Afghanistan (Plates 162,163,165).[80] The mythical creatures with human bodies and animal heads of the Kobyakovo torque wear armour which are similar to that depicted on the coins of Azes, and on a relief found from Khalchayan in Uzbekistan.[81] The figurines of musicians from Tillya-Tepe[82] all sitting with legs crossed are similar to the sitting male character depicted on the Kobyakovo torque. The figure of a warrior from Koy-Krygankala[83] attests to the same pose. Perhaps, as an iconographical canon, the seated pose of persons with their legs crossed became ingrained in the Central Asian regions at the threshold of the Christian era. Hinged bracelets similar to the open work gold bracelet, near the left wrist of the skeleton at Kobyakovo, and decorated in the animal style, also originate from Kazakhstan and Northern Pakistan.[84] As to the shape of the cup held by the central figure of the torque Kobyakovo, it is similar to that of the vessels from the Sarmatian barrows of the first century A.D. These cups were made of gold and silver and have realistically executed zoomorphic handles. The sword of the hero is similar to those found in Gandhāra reliefs.[85] The costumes of the zooanthropomorphic creatures are similar to those of the Kushāna armour consisting of a plated cuirass with a tight-fitting upper part and a widening short skirt. The elongated version of the Kushāna armour appears on the coins of the Indo-Śaka rulers of Gandhāra at the threshold of the Christian era[86] and is shown in detail on the bone plaque with a battle scene from the Orlat necropolis in Uzbekistan[87] dated, probably, to the same time. Thus, the objects from Tillya-Tepe suggest many shared features of the Śaka/Scythian repertoire in their animal style. The characteristic of this site was the use of coloured inlays for accentuating ornamentation. Precious stones were also used specially in curvilinear ornamentation. The animal style of Tillya-Tepe often used additional zoomorphic elements and exaggeration of parts of the animal's body. The maintenance of such a vast repertoire obviously implied that the nomads had an intimate economic relationship with the agriculturists of the oases and river plains, and both of them had a definite part in the formation of the nomadic art.

B. IN THE NORTH-WESTERN PART OF INDIA

The early art of the north-western part of India displays Śaka/Scythian elements to a significant extent. The north-western part of the subcontinent, now mainly in Pakistan, and a part of Afghanistan, formed the so-called 'base' of India's contacts with early Central Asia. In this region, Taxila was a major stronghold of Śaka occupation.[88]

The north-western part of the Indian subcontinent mainly embraced the territories of Gandhāra, Uddiyāna (Swat), Kāúmïra, Sindhu-Sauvïra (mentioned in the Junāgadh inscription of Rudra-dāman I dated in the year, 150 A.D. were situated on the west and east of the lower Indus) and also the areas in between them. Geographically, Gandhāra denoted an area which lay on both sides of the Indus and contained two great cities viz. Pushkalāvatï (Charsadda in the Peshwar District) and Takshaúïlā (Taxila in the Rawalpindi District). To the north of Gandhāra lay Uddiyāna or the Udyāna, identifiable with modern Swat (in Northern Pakistan). To the east of Uddiyāna lay the country of Chi-pin. The name denoted a large territory in the north-western section of the Indian subcontinent including Kāśmīra. From the *Ch'ien Han-shu*[89] (composed in 54 A.D.), it is evident that Chi-pin was an ideal region for commerce with a variety of merchandise. An important trading centre in the north-western section of the Indian subcontinent was Taxila. The Taxilans might have participated in transit trade, buying only what they actually used and not having there any important distributing centre. Thus, it appears that Bactria, Kabul-Begram region (Paropanisadai), North-western India including Taxila and Chi-pin, and the lower Indus area, etc., formed a commercial zone. The Indo-Greeks were in possession of this zone or parts of it from the middle of the 3rd century B.C. to the late 1st century B.C. The economic importance of the territory, once ruled by the Indo-Greeks, continued in the ages of the Scytho-Parthians. The same trend continued under the Kushānas. Nomadic art manifests itself on Kushāna art; however, nomadic elements in Kushāna art are not dealt with in this study.

Prior to the coming of the Śaka-Pahlavas, Taxila had a rich tradition of art due to the amalgamation of indigenous and foreign art traditions. This was revealed by the excavated stratas at Taxila. The archaeological records show the cultural changes, and also indicate an influx of Śaka/Scythian art forms, as apparent from the findings in the early Śaka and Śaka-Parthian strata at Taxila. Taxila did not have burials. Therefore the utility objects, ornaments, weapons and horse trappings were found from the Śaka—Parthian strata. Taxilan potteries from Scytho-Parthian levels have typical Śaka/Scythian and Scytho-Siberian motifs of simple parallel bands, chequered triangles, chevrons, loops, quatrefoil crosses, trees and birds, zigzags and wavy lines.[90] Ovoid-shaped store-jars[91] were also common. Bell-shaped[92] carinated vessels in bronze and copper have also shown Scythian affinities. Jugs with two handles like the amphoraes were fairly present in the Scytho-Parthian levels. Beakers with deep flared mouths became popular under the Śakas and Parthians. These beakers had the *svastika* motifs. The usage of deep flared mouths was commonly practised by the Śaka/Scythians in their inventory of utility objects. Vessels of copper and bronze with projecting nail heads[93] were also common in Taxila. Such nail heads were similarly seen in metal utility vessels of the Scythian barrows in the western section. The Śaka-Parthian strata at Taxila also yielded clay vessels with nail head imitations of metal originals. Interestingly, inkpots in the form of small vases with wide mouths, and usually with two lug-ears,[94] have been found. These are reminiscent of the Gaimanova Mogila vessels' lug ears (Plate 8).[95] Śaka and Parthian influences, yet again, manifest themselves in shapes and decorative motifs on stoppers which were surmounted by grotesque heads of animals, parts of animals, and even by recumbent forms. Some variations were there at Taxila regarding utility objects. There was some sort of mass usage of utility vessels of the Śaka/Scythian style. Earlier, from Tillya-Tepe and other burials of the western section, or for that matter, from the Issyk barrow (where the burials were of chieftains, or of royal personages) there were specific forms of utility vessels. But at Taxila, the Śaka/Scythian motifs spread to a wider range of objects of daily use, whatever be their dimensions. Vessels with animal-headed handles were also found from the Śaka/Parthian strata at Taxila. These vessels are similar to those found from the kurgan of Khokhlach (Plate 166)[96] and Tillya-Tepe, both dated in the first century A.D. Such zoomorphic handles are typical of Scytho-Siberian productions from an earlier period and continued in the Śaka/Scythian productions in India in the first century A.D. The Taxila vessels[97] with animal-headed handles have several analogies in Scythian vessels (Plates 167,168) belonging to the western section.[98] The meaning, form and function of the vessels and the animal motifs and the disposition of the zoomorphic ornaments, must have deep roots in antiquity. They took the utilitarian role of attachments on vessels. Such continuity of form and ornamentation can be explained only by their cultural significance. Similar vessels with zoomorphic handles (Plate 169) have been found from the Amirtyuba burial of Azerbaijan dated in the first century B.C. to the first century A.D.[99] Other vessels common to the Scythian burials like rhytons and amphorae, have also been found from Sirkap, Taxila. They have typical Śaka/Scythian motifs executed in bands. The incised, embossed and appliquê ware from Sirkap, also shows the Scythian influence. A squat flask of unique shape from Bhir Mound, Taxila, shows the decoration of incised chevrons and cross-patterns. Lamps found in the Śaka-Parthian strata were made of schist and other soft stones. The commonest shape was of a leaf or heart-shaped vessel, sometimes provided with a handle projecting from the back, sometimes with pierced lugs for suspension. In the bowl-shaped lamp of green steatite from the Mahal site in Sirkap,[100] (dated in the middle or later part of the first century A.D.), the Śaka/Scythian nomadic art form seems to have left its mark. The lamp has a spout and three lugs pierced, perhaps, for suspension. Between the lugs are acanthus leaves, and on the spout, an elephant's head is carved in low relief. Elephants are noticed in the Śaka art of India. Other lamps found from Taxila similarly attest to the Śaka/Scythian influence, as displayed in parts of vessels and attachments. Another utility object common to the Scythian burials was the tripod stand. From Sirkap, Taxila has been found an iron tripod stand for cauldrons. It consisted of a ring supported on three legs.[101] Iron hinges of double-leaf pattern have also been found from Taxila. Bronze and copper hinges of double-leaf pattern dated in the first century A.D., have also been found. Allied to the leaf motif, but with a variation, was the leaf-and-knob motif. From Sirkap were found copper spoons, dated in the first century A.D., with leaf-and-knob motif attached to the handles.[102] Spatulas with heart-shaped blades and some with *nandipada* handles have also been found from Sirkap.[103] Shallow bowls of silver, reminiscent of the Scythian silver bowls, have been found from Taxila.[104] Two circular concave lids of silver (Plates 170,171) have been detected from Sirkap. In the middle of the concave upper sides are looped handles in the form of fish soldered to the lids.[105] Both the technique and the motif remind one of the nomadic toreutics.

Votive or ritual tanks assignable to the third and second centuries B.C. were found from Taxila in the Bhir and Sirkap sites. These were in the form of round bowls with a number of miniature saucer-shaped lamps around their rims. The later ones found from Sirkap had square forms, and perched midway between the lamps were birds with outspread wings.[106] The later votive tanks are assignable to the first centuries A.D. The inclusion of the birds could be due to the Śaka/Scythian influence, as bowls with rams or birds perched on the rims were common in Scythian and Scytho-Siberian utility objects.

The base of a bowl from the Dharmarājikā *stûpa* is stamped with a medallion of a lion and elephant in relief. A similar medallion is in the Sānchi *stûpa* III railings. Stone trays (Plate 172) found from Taxila are reminiscent of the Śaka/ Scythian repertoire, especially in the treatment of leogryphs, winged stags, hippocamps and fish-tailed monsters.[107] The geometric and floral designs, and the use of quatrefoil rosette motifs on the stone trays are all very much affiliated to the nomadic tradition. The designs on the stone trays are similar to the floral, geometric, abstract and animal designs on stone discs and ringstones (Plate 173).[108] The hippocamps of Taxila remind us of the hippocamps of the Oxus Treasure, and also the gold plaque from Kul-Oba.[109] The leogryphs of Taxila are similar to those from the Seven Brothers barrow (Plate 174).[110] A hippocampus with a horseman is shown on a steatite toilet disk from Garavkala in Tajikistan dated in the first century A.D.[111] Similar ones are found on stone tablets from Taxila, and on reliefs from Gandhāra, as well as on Han mirrors from China. The stone reliquaries from Taxila are similar to those discovered from Airtam, Ushturmulla, and Kara-Tepe,[112] the latter on the bank of Amu Darya in present southern Uzbekistan. Terracotta male heads with conical caps (Plate 175)[113] from Taxila strengthen our view of Taxila as a Śaka-Parthian site. The seals and sealings in Sirkap, along with the coins, firmly establish the Śaka/Scythian, Śaka-Parthian antecedents of Taxila. There were numerous Śaka coin types from Taxila, the commonest of Maues' types was his 'Elephant head and Caduceus' coins. Coins of both Azes I and Azes II were prolific at Sirkap.

Other than utility objects, the Śaka/Scythian elements of art in Taxila were also manifested in horse accoutrements, weapons and jewellery. Jewellery moulds from Ter and dated in the Sātavāhana period are similar to some Taxila moulds. Rosettes with beaded margins found at Prabhas Patan were actually covered with gold foil (this usage of gold foil was very much prevalent on the rosette plaques of the Scythian period). Horse trappings made of iron, copper, bronze and lead have been found from Taxila. The iron bits found at Taxila date from the first century A.D. The S-shaped cheek bars[114] definitely show the nomadic influence. The cheek bars made of bone and ivory with incised parallel lines and chevron motif, recall Scythic types. Copper, bronze and lead buckles and clasps are found from the Śaka-Parthian period. Ornamental clasps with dot-and-comma cloisons[115] and bronze ornamental buckles in the form of modified *nandipadas* with three pear-shaped cloisons (Plate 176) in the middle for inlay-work,[116] revisit Taxila. In fact, both in the Taxilan horse-trappings and jewellery, there is a special feeling of revisiting the Scythian and Scytho-Siberian art. Some of the Taxilan bronze buckles and other horse trappings are similar to the trappings (Plate 82) found from the Suglug-Khem burial.[117] Again, the horse trappings from Aldy-bel, Arzhan and even from Tagar are similar to those from Suglug-khem. This is an indication of the eastern origin of Scythian art, and since horses were important, therefore their trappings were to be given priority. The iron horse-bits (Plate 177) from Taxila[118] reveal a remarkable similarity with the horses' bits (Plate 178) found from Filippovka kurgan 6.[119] The horse-bit terminals of bone from Taxila are reminiscent of those from the Zhurovka Barrow (Plate 179).[120] Buckle-plates are comparable to those from the Otonkon hoard (Plate 180).[121] Horse-bits having stylized heads of animals[122] have Taxilan counter-parts. The propeller-type cheek pieces on the bone plates from the Orlatsky barrow in the Samarkand region, of first century A.D. have also been found at Ai-Khanum and in the layer of the first century A.D. in Sirkap.[123] Iron and bronze arrowheads and other weapons from Taxila reveal Śaka/Scythian influence. Bone weapon handles found from Scythian sites have similar counter-parts at Taxila.

Leaf-shaped spear tips[124] are abundant in the Śaka—Parthian strata at Taxila. Similar leaf-shaped spear tips (Plate 181) were found from the Filippovka kurgan.[125] A kneeling warrior on the pyxis from Kosika[126] has distinctive arrowheads with three points belonging to the fork type. The earliest finds of this kind of arrowheads in the adjacent areas are the arrowheads from the complexes of the first century A.D. in Taxila.[127]

Ornaments like torques, pendants, earrings and necklaces from the Śaka-Parthian strata in Taxila, show Śaka/Scythian elements but compared to Tillya-Tepe there was less use of gold. Necklaces (Plates 182,183) from Bhir mound[128] were made of beads similar to the beads from Tillya-Tepe. The necklaces from Taxila (Plates 199, 200, 201) reveal the beautiful interplay of beads, plaques and pendants.[129] The plaques in the Taxilan necklaces had spaces for encrustations. Similar intermingling of beads, plaques and pendants had been found in a necklace from Karagodeuashkh barrow (Plate 184). In the latter example,[130] dated in the late fourth century B.C., the plaques are filigreed. It is worth noting that the different shapes of the plaques persisted in the Śaka/Scythian art of later period as found from Taxila, Tillya-Tepe and other areas. Even shell ornaments show motifs of heart patterns, chevrons, and conventionalised bird-head patterns. Fragments of shell bangles show incised chevron patterns[131] and 'dot and comma' motifs.[132] Beads of Tillya-Tepe type continue to be found mainly in the Śaka-Parthian strata at Taxila. Animal beads were mostly found from Śaka-Parthian level in Sirkap. The animals represented are lions, birds, frogs, tortoises, elephants, rams, monkey and bull. The lion,of which five specimens were found from Sirkap, was symbolical of the Buddha, the 'lion of the Úākyas' and likely, therefore, to be popular in a stronghold of Buddhism such as Taxila.[133] Finger-rings with flat almond-shaped bezels recall Scythic types with Hellenistic influence. It is evident from the designs themselves that the jewellery found at Taxila, the manner in which the gems are applied, and the style of incrustation which arose at Taxila in the first century A.D. were the direct outcome of the Śaka-Parthian occupation .We have already seen that in the Scythian jewellery, incrustation was very much popular. Hairpins from Taxila have bird-on-tree motifs, which have definite Scythian connections. Gold ear-pendants of 'disk-and pendant' types have been found from Śaka-Parthian strata in Sirkap, dated in the first century A.D. (Plate 185) An interesting gold ear pendant from Taxila[134] has motifs of rosettes and leaves which were inlaid with turquoise paste. The ornament consists of two pieces joined by a hook. The lower piece consists of an amphora in the centre, and on either side of it is an infant Eros riding on a winged sea-lion. Four plaited chains hang from the latter and end in a pearl and leaf terminal. The motif of Eros on the winged sea-lion is reminiscent of the motif of 'Cupids astride dolphins' as found from Tillya-Tepe. Another gold earring from Taxila[135] consists of a six-petalled blossom with a circular centre of applied wire enclosed by granules of regular size. The inner petals (cut from sheet gold) are plain and the outer petals (of stamped sheet gold) are filled with granules of different sizes. Twisted wires are attached to the back and appear as loops from the front, adorned with granulated rosettes. Beneath the blossom is a turquoise vase mounted with granulated sheet gold. Stylised dolphins of sheet gold link the vase and rosette. When viewed aerially, the image occupying the space, i.e., the linking portion, seems like a *nandipada*. Several Scythian-Siberian-Śakan techniques are manifest in this earring, namely, the 1) use of applied wire, 2) use of granulated gold mounts, 3) images worked in the round and subsequently chased (as the dolphins), and 4) use of sheet gold trefoils with applied wire and granulated borders. Also from Sirkap were found gold bracelets with square clasps encrusted with gems. A Taxilan bracelet has much similarity with the Kul-Oba bracelet. Lion-head shaped terminals of gold bracelets (Plate 186) from Taxila[136] are similar to a pair of identical cast gold bracelets from burial 6, Tillya-Tepe.[137]

Bracelets with hinged joints as found from Taxila were also represented on friezes on the Kosika cup, and on the high relief with horsemen from Khalchayan. Several gold bracelets from Sirkap dating from the first century A.D., having rectangular clasps are similar to the golden bracelets from Olbia (Plate 187).[138] The rectangular clasps, as well as the scheme of decoration put them close to the Olbian ones, although the bracelets from Taxila have hoops made of a single piece. The piece originating from Taxila includes both flat lamellar hoops[139] and open-worked hoops, decorated with S-shaped figures.[140] These bracelets from Taxila are close to the Olbian pieces (given their geometric designs, use of gems and their use of cabochon inlays, in this case, amber, rock crystal, and glass paste). Given their construction, a pair of bracelets from the first century A.D. Sarmatian burial of Sokolova Mogila in the South Bug basin stand close to the pieces from Taxila. A medallion from Taxila depicting Eros and Psyche[141] is very much similar to a medallion decorating a silver cup from the Nogaichik female burial mound,[142] dated in the first century A.D. In the Taxila medallion, the figure of Eros is on the left and he is embracing Psyche with his left arm, and the faces of the figures are depicted strictly *en face*. The quality of the workmanship and its oversimplification reflects what is undoubtedly an imitation of a Hellenistic prototype produced by a not particularly competent craftsman. It is, however, worth noting that the motif of Eros and Psyche was quite widespread, above all in terracottas starting with the Hellenistic era. In a gold repoussê plaque dated in the first-second century A.D. and from the Taxila-Punjab area (formerly in the collection of Col. D. H. Gordon) shows Hāriti and Panchika (Kubera) seated, surrounded by the typical beaded border. The dress of the god reveals nomadic influence.[143] The gold protome of a dolphin from the fibula[144] found from Nogaichik is reminiscent of the dolphin handles from Taxila.[145] A Taxilan gold brooch in the form of a repoussê figure of winged Aphrodite (Plate 188)[146] is similar to the Aphrodite figurine, from Tillya-Tepe.

Mirrors have been found from Taxila, Adichanallur, Basarh, Brahmapuri and Rairh. Of these, the Taxila[1] (Sir John Marshall, *Taxila*, Cambridge 1951, Vol. III, Pl. 182b.) mirror had an intact ivory handle. The Rairh[2] (K. N. Puri, *Excavations at Rairh*, Jaipur 1940, p.43, Pls. XX,15 and XXI,14.) bronze mirrors (found from

Sunga-Kushana levels) are fitted with a tang having a flat circular rim all around. All the mirrors at Taxila come from Saka-Parthian levels at Sirkap, datable to c. 100 B.C.-A.D.100. The Taxilan mirror with a wavy rim has its counterpart at Bulandibagh, Patna. Handles of bone and ivory decorated with incised bands, hatchings and mouldings have been found from Taxila. They were probably meant for mirrors. Bronze mirrors from a hoard at Brahmapuri[147] are similar to that found from Basarh but belonging to the early historic period.

The Kalwan monastic establishment at Taxila had yielded a casket of schist from its relic chamber. The casket is covered with gold-leaf, a technique followed by the Scythians and Sakas for a long time. The schist casket contained another spherical casket covered with gold-leaf and twelve rosettes of thin gold sheet, fragments of bone, different beads and other objects, including a copper plate inscription of the year 134 of Azes engraved in Kharoshti.

Excavations at Shaikhan Dheri, about 22 miles north of Peshawar, have yielded Scytho-Parthian artifacts in phase I (stratographically). It is important to note here that there was no indication at all to distinguish the Scythian period from that of the Parthians. However, the range of the objects are fascinating and they continue to confirm and elaborate the Śaka/Scythian elements. The head of a lady, richly decorated and having the triangular headdress with rosettes at the corners, has been found from Shaikhan Dheri. The lady wears roundels at the ears and has a decorated forehead band,[148] similar to the one from Khokhlach. The emblemata figurines on bowls from Shaikhan Dheri create a distinctive style, as these figurines are embossed on the inside of the bowls by a mould. The technique appears to be peculiar .Out of six such bowls, five came from the late Parthian levels, along with coins of Maues, Azes I, Azilises, and Gondophares.[149] The major element in Indo-Parthian numismatic iconography is the central figure in Śaka/Scythian costume, holding an object over the head of the elephant rider and probably it was the branch of a tree. This motif was also seen in the Hellenistic art.[150] Another feature of the Indo-Parthian numismatic iconography and also of the Indo-Scythian repertoire was the equestrian representations of kings holding various symbols of power, among which is a short stick ending in a hook and looking like an *ancus*, as seen on the coins of Azilises, Azes, Gondophares, and Soter Megas.[151] Some coins from Shaikhan Dheri are similar to the motifs on the gem engraving found from Kundzhulitepe in Kashkadarya, southern Sogdiana. The triumph scene on an engraved gem from Kundzhulitepe, excavated in 1988, shows familiarity with Śaka-Parthian numismatic iconography.

The Kundzhulitepe gem[152] is dated in about the first century B.C. to the early part of the second century A.D. i.e., prior to Shaikhan Dheri. Thus, the coin iconography was in transit from Kashkadarya to the North-West India. Male heads with the typical Scythian pointed caps have been found from Shaikhan Dheri. One of the trenches yielded a female head with an elaborate headdress with a tricorn over the head and rosettes at the ears.[153] A horse's head from Shaikhan Dheri shows the typical Scythian horse's head collar, chin strap, and face strap with circular eyes.[154] Shaikhan Dheri has also yielded gold leaf shaped pendants[155] with soldered loops for suspension. Such pendants have been prolific at Tillya-Tepe. Artifacts, therefore, from various regions of North-West India, show the gradual assimilation of Śaka/ Scythian and Parthian, as well as Hellenistic elements into their traditions. This process was intensified from about the middle of the first century B.C. onwards. A similar assimilation had occurred earlier in South Russia, between the Cimmerians, the Scythians and the Pontic Greek settlers.

The Śaka/Scythian elements are also discernible in Gandhāran art. A Gandhāra panel shows men wearing the Scythian costume. Similarly, one of the reliefs from Buner (Plate 189)[156] shows a series of musicians in Scythian costume. The scale-armoured figure[157] besides Pancika-Kubera from Takal, shows Scythian affiliation. Scale armoured figures have been frequently depicted on friezes of utility objects, and on weapons in Scythian art. The neck ornament of Pancika—Kubera[158] reflects nomadic affiliations. The Scythian costume is also seen on reliefs of Sahri-Bahlol, Rokhri, Jamalgarhi, Ranighat, Swat, Khair Khanch and at Hadda and Begram. It is noteworthy that, as found from Timargarha and Gandhāra Grave cultures dated sixth century B.C. onwards, the main anthropological element of the population could be linked to those from the Caspian region. It is important to note that the image of a hippocampus with a horseman as shown on a steatite toilet disk from Garavkala in Tajikistan of first century A.D.[159] has Indian parallels. The image has also been found on Gandhāran reliefs, on stone tablets from Taxila, and also on Han mirrors. The characteristic sculptures of Gandhāra during the first three or four centuries A.D. were produced in vast quantities for the Buddhists and their monasteries. The figures of Bodhisattvas are noted for their adornments as they were decked in the finery of local magnates.[160] The figures have massive earrings, armlets and torques, often incorporating bird or animal forms. On their diadems and armlets can sometimes be seen the high-haunched animals of the 'animal style' of the Scythians and Sarmatians.[161] The techniques of carving stone or moulding terracottas, do not favour the reproduction of lighter, more delicate creations such as have been found in numerous Śaka/Scythian artifacts from the north-west. Therefore, the sculptured jewelleries no longer represent the real jewelleries (in use) but have become conventionalized.

The Śaka/Scythian elements in later Indian art as found in the regions east of the north-western part of the subcontinent which had undergone Śaka rule, will be discussed in the next chapter. But there were some sites like Māt near Mathurā which flourished parallel with Taxila and other north-western sites during the first century A.D. Māt, incidentally, has yielded figures with pointed caps. These pointed caps have been repeatedly identified with the Śaka/Scythian pointed caps. But the Māt cap is very much similar to the depiction of the coiffure of the Buddha as found from the Kolkhozabad region, again dated in the first century A.D.[162] The large, intricately carved stone plaques, called '*āyāgapatas*' have been understood as Jain votive tablets of homage, which were produced in Mathurā during the first century B.C. and first century A.D. It is interesting to note that in the symbolic relief carving of the ā*yāgapatas*, we see Śaka/Scythian elements and Śaka/Parthian motifs. These motifs have composite anthropomorphic and theriomorphic features. It seems that Parthian art forms with their Iranian background had well mingled with the Śaka/Scythian nomadic animal art.

References

1. The Śaka/Scythian elements in early art of India as witnessed in, C. East of the north-western part of the subcontinent, and D. Other areas in India, which had experienced Śaka-Pahlava rule, have been dealt with in the next chapter as in the first place they experienced lesser penetration of Śaka/Scythian elements and secondly they belonged to later periods, i.e. after the Śaka-Pahlava rule.
2. Śakastāna, has been discussed in chapters II, III, IV above.
3. *Geog. Cla. Pt.*, p.142.
4. *Ibid.*, p.147.
5. *Ibid.*, p.147.
6. *Agr. So. Imp. Par. Hist.*, p.2
7. *Geog. Cla. Pt.*, p.147.
8. *Ibid.*, p.148.
9. *Bac. Gol.*, Pl.131.
10. *Ibid.*, Pl.131.
11. B.N. Mukherjee, 'A Note on a Gold Coin or Medal found at Tillya-Tepe (Afghanistan)', *Mudrā,* Calcutta, 1989, pp.37-39.

12. G. A. Pugachenkova, 'The Antiquities of Transoxiana in the light of Investigations in Uzbekistan (1985-1990)', *Anc. Civ. Scy. Sib.*, Vol. 2, p.35.
13. Koshelenko and Pilipko, 'Parthia', *Hist. Civ. Cen. As.*, Vol. II, pp.36-137.
14. David Christian, *A History of Russia, Central Asia and Mongolia: Inner Eurasia from Prehistory to the Mongol Empire*, Blackwell Publishers, Oxford, 1998, Vol. I, p.121.
15. *Bac. Gol.*, Pl. 139.
16. O.D. Lordkipanidze, T.K. Mikeladze, *Le trêsor de Gonio*, Tbilisi, 1980, pp.35, 59.
17. M.Treister, 'New Discoveries of Sarmatian Complexes of the 1st Century A.D.', *Anc. Civ. Scy. Sib.*, Vol. 4, p.41.
18. *Bac. Gol.*, pp.238-239, Fig.22.
19. *Ibid.*, Pl.141.
20. *Ibid.*, Pl.121.
21. I. P. Zasetskaya, *Zolotye ukrasheniya gunnskoi epokhi,* Leningrad, 1975, p.17, Fig.3.
22. M.Y. Treister, 'Concerning the Jewellery Items from the Burial Mound at Nogaichik', *Anc. Civ.Scy. Sib.*, Vol. 4, p.154.
23. *Bac. Gol.*, p.34.
24. *Bac. Gol.*, Pl.144.
25. *Taxila,* Vol. 3, Pl.182, b=no. 211.
26. The typical Scythian costume is discussed in Chapter IV above.
27. V. Sarianidi, 'New Discoveries at Ancient Gonur', *Anc. Civ. Scy. Sib.*, Vol.2, Fig.16.
28. K. A. Akishev, *Kurgan Issyk,* Moscow, 1978.
29. *Bac. Gol.*, Pl.86.
30. Cf. M.Y.Treister's article cited in Footnote No.26 above, p.138, Figs.10-11.
31. *Gol. De. Eur.*, Pl.70.
32. The checker-board pattern is discussed in Chapter IV above.
33. *Bac. Gol.*, p.20.
34. *Bac. Gol.*, Pls.66, 67.
35. *Ibid.*, p.234, Fig.24.
36. *Ibid.*, p.235, Fig.36.
37. *Ibid.*, Pl.27.
38. Cf. M. Y. Treister's article cited in Footnote No.21 above, p.39.
39. *Bac. Gol.*, Pl.105.
40. *Ibid.*, Pls.44-47.
41. *Art. Scy.*, p.97.
42. *Bac. Gol.*, Pl.97.
43. *Art. Scy.*, p.181.
44. *Bac. Gol.*, p.226. Fig.2.
45. *Gol. De. Eur.*, Pl.168.
46. *Bac. Gol.*, Pl.18.

47. Gol. De. Eur., Pl.14.
48. *Taxila*, Vol. III, Pl.179, nos. 83, 84, 93.
49. *Art. Scy.*, p.99.
50. *Ibid.*, Figs.4-7.
51. *Scy. Art.*, Pls.130, 133, 134.
52. *Bac. Gol.*, Pl.32.
53. *Scy. Art*, Pls. 247,248.
54. S.V. Makhortykh, 'Scythians and Sarmatians of the Northern Caucasus; Recent Archaeological Finds', *Anc. Civ. Scy Sib.*,Vol.1, p.60, Fig.1.
55. *Scy. Art.*, Pls. 115, 116.
56. *Bac. Gol.,* p.255. Fig.12; p.239, Figs.30-31.
57. Cf. M. Y. Treister's article cited in Footnote No.26 above, pp.154, 155.
58. *Bac. Gol.*, p.227, Fig.10.
59. *Taxila,* Pl.179, b=no.23; Pl.179, =no. 88; Pl.136, o=nos. 144, 145.
60. *Bac. Gol.*, p.108, Pl.51.
61. *Taxila*, Pl.179, no. 63.
62. *Bac. Gol.*, p.234, Fig.27.
63. *Taxila*, Pl.180, no. 151-160.
64. *Bac. Gol.*, Pl.23,24.
65. *Bac. Gol.,* Pl.25, 26.
66. Scythian jewellery of the western section has been discussed in Chapter IV above.
67. *Bac. Gol.*, p.239, Figs.30, 31.
68. *Taxila,* Pl.179, nos.37-41; Pl.181, nos.168-176.
69. *Bac. Gol.*, Pl.40.
70. R.Ghirshman, 'Notes Iraniennes IV : Le Trêsor De Sakkaez. Les Origines De L'art Mêde Et Les Bronzes Du Luristan', *Artibus Asiae*, Vol. X, 1950, pp.181-206.
71. Scytho-Siberian art style has been discussed in Chapter IV above.
72. *Bac. Gol.*, Pl.158.
73. Cf. M. Y. Treister's article cited in Footnote No.21 above, p.37.
74. *Bac. Gol.*, p.222, Pl.164.
75. I. I. Tolstoi, N.P.Kondakov, 'Russkie Drevnosti v Panyatnikakh Iskusstva', *Collected Publications ,* Moscow, 1990, Vol. 3, p.140.
76. Cf. M. Y. Treister's article cited in Footnote No.21 above, p.75, Fig.2.
77. *Ibid.*, p.51.
78. V.I. Sarainidi, *Khram and Necropol' Tillya-tepe,* Moscow 1989, p.98.
79. *Bac. Gol.*, Pl.160.
80. *Ibid.*, Pls. 160—166.
81. M. Treister, 'Sarmatian Treasure of South Russia', *Archaeology*, Jan/Feb 1997, p.49.
82. V.I. Sarianidi, *op.cit.*, p.66, Fig.23.

83. Yu.A.Rapoport. 'Khorezmiiskie Ossuarii', *Iz Istorii Religii Drevnego Khorezma,* Moscow, 1971, Fig.23f.
84. Cf. M. Y. Treister's article cited in Footnote No.21 above, p.43.
85. G. A. Pugachenkova, *Iskusstvo Gandkhary,* Moscow, 1982, p.123, Fig.129; p.130, Fig.136; p.145, Fig.153.
86. M. V. Gorelik, 'Sakski dospekh', *Tsentral Aziya : Novye pamyatniki pis'mennosti I iskusstva,* Moscow, 1987, p.368, Figs.2, 6.
87. G. A. Pugachenkova, *Drevnosti Miankalya,* Tashkent, 1989, p.149, Fig.71.
88. *Taxila*, as a Śaka site has been discussed in Chapter III above.
89. *C.H.S,* Ch 96 A, 10 B.
90. *Taxila*, Pls. 130, 131.
91. *Ibid.*, Pl.121, no. 3.
92. *Ibid.*, Pl.123, no. 6.
93. *Ibid.*, Pl.174, nos. 255-258.
94. *Ibid.*, Pl.125, no. 142.
95. *Scy. Art.*, Pl.166.
96. *Gol. De. Eur.*, Pl.132.
97. *Taxila,* Pl.123, no.80.
98. *Scy. Art* , Pls, 102, 103, 104.
99. I. Aliev And G.Goshgarli, 'Archaeological Investigations In Azerbaijan (1986-1990)', *Anc. Civ. Scy. Sib.*, Vol. 1, p.267, Fig.3.
100. *Taxila,* Vol. III, Pl.146, no.114.
101. *Ibid.*, Pl.162 e.
102. *Ibid.*, Vol. II, p.594.
103. *Ibid.*, Vol. III, Pl.177.
104. *Ibid.*, Vol. II, p.612.
105. *Ibid.*, Vol. III, Pl.189, nos.20, a,b.
106. *Ibid.*, Pl.136, no. 156=u=no. 155
107. *Ibid.*, Pls. 144, 145, no. 81.
108. *Ear. Orn. Anc. Ind.*, p.135, Fig.VI.6; p.139, Fig.VI.14; p.139, Fig.VI.16.
109. *Scy. Art.*, Pl.207.
110. *Ibid.*, Pl.76, 77.
111. Cf. M. Y. Treister's article cited in Footnote No.21 above, p.63.
112. B. Yu. Stavisky, 'A Buddhist cult centre on the right bank of the Oxus,Excavations at Kara-tepe in Termez in 1983-1992', *Anc. Civ. Scy. Sib.*, Vol. 3, p.292.
113. *Taxila,* Vol. III, Pl.134, nos. 51.
114. *Ibid.*, Vol. II , p.551.
115. *Taxila,* Vol. III, Pl.172, m=no. 30.
116. *Ibid.*,Pl.172, n=no.31.

117. V. Semenov, 'New Evidence Of The Scythian Type Culture Of Tuva', *Anc. Civ.Scy. Sib.*, Vol.2, p.332, Fig.18.
118. *Taxila,* Vol. III, Pl.165, nos. 96—98.
119. *Gol. De. Eur.,* Pls.118, 119.
120. *Art. Scy.,* Fig.145.
121. N.L. Tchlenova, 'Objects Of The Scythian "Animal Style" From The Taiga Zone Of Siberia', *Anc. Civ. Scy. Sib.,* Vol. 3, p.322, Fig.2.
122. *Scy. Art.*, Pl.275.
123. O.Guillaume, 'Contribution à l' etude d'un artisant bactrien prê-hellenistique', in : *Actes de colloque franco-soviêtique* 'L'archaeologie de la Bactriane ancienne', Dushanbe, 1982, Figs.7, 8 .cf. also *Taxila ,* Vol. III, Pl.165, no. 100, a, b.
124. *Taxila,* Vol. III, Pl.164, no. 68.
125. *Gol. De. Eur,*, Pl.120.
126. Cf. M. Y. Treister's article cited in Footnote No.21 above, p.6.
127. *Taxila* , Vol. II, p.560, Vol. III, Pl.169, 200—202 .
128. *Ibid.,* Vol.III, Pl.136 , f=no.145, o=nos. 144, 145.
129. *Ibid.,* Vol.III, Pl.193, nos. 56, 57, 58.
130. *Scy. Art.*, Pl.254.
131. *Taxila,* Vol. II, Pl.201, no. 13.
132. *Ibid.,* Vol.III, Pl.201, no. 18.
133. *Ibid.,* Vol.II, p.748.
134. *Ibid.,* Vol.III, Pl.190 c.
135. *Gol. Tre. Jew. Ind.*, p.17, Pl.3.
136. *Taxila,* Vol. III, Pl.195, i=nos.133—136.
137. *Bac. Gol.*, p.52.
138. M.Yu.Treister , 'Two Golden Bracelets From Olbia In The Walters Art Gallery', *Anc. Civ. Scy. Sib.*, Vol. 8, p.25 , Fig.9.
139. *Taxila,* Vol. III, Pl.196, a, b.
140. *Ibid.,* Pl.196 c,d,e .
141. *Ibid.,* Pl.207, 11.
142. Cf. M. Y. Treister's article cited in Footnote No.26 above p.131.
143. *Gol. Tre. Jew. Ind.,* p.16, Pl.1.
144. Cf. M. Y. Treister's article cited in Footnote No.26 above, p.131.
145. *Taxila,* Vol. III, Pl.189, nos. 20, a, b.
146. *Ibid.,* Vol.III, Pl.191,s=no.96.
147. Karl Khandalawala, 'Brahmapuri', *Lalit Kala*,No.7, 1960, pp.62-63 and Pl.XVI 14, 15 and 17.
148. A.H.Dani, 'Shaikhan Dheri Excavation, 1963 — 64 , In search of the second city of Pushkalavati' , *Ancient Pakistan* ,1965/66, Vol. II, p.57. 149 *Ibid.,* p.65.
150. M. Mitchiner, *Indo— Greek and Indo—Scythian Coinage ,* London , 1975, Vol. 1, p. 88.

151. A. K. Srivastava , *Catalogue of Śaka—Pahlava Coins of North India,* Lucknow, 1972, Pl.IV, 1—5 , 7, 9, 11; Pl.V, 4; Pl.V, 6—8; Pl.VII, 1—4.
152. K. Abdullaev , S. Raimkulov, A Triumph Scene On An Engraved Gem From Kundzhulitepe, Kashkadarya, *Anc. Civ. Scy. Sib.*, Vol. 2, p.
153. A.H. Dani, 'Shaikhan Dheri Excavation 1963/64', *Ancient Pakistan,* 1965/66,Vol II, p.70.
154. *Ibid.,* p.85.
155. *Ibid.,* Pl.XLIX.
156. *Dyn. Art. Kus.*, Pl.58.
157. *Ibid.,* Pl.62 a.
158. *Ibid.,* Pl.62.
159. *Drevnosti Tajikistana* (Antiquities of Tajikistan), No. 364. pp.138—9.
160. *Gol. Tre. Jew. Ind.*, p.13.
161. M.I. Rostovtsev, *Animal Style in South Russia and China,* Princeton, 1929, Pl.XVIII, 5.
162. B. A. Litvinsky, 'Ancient Tajikistan', *Anc. Civ. Scy. Sib.*, Vol.1, p.301, Fig.5.

6 Influences on Later Indian Art

This chapter is an attempt to trace the Śaka/Scythian elements in Indian art from about the middle of the first century A.D. onwards with reference to various contexts. In the preceding chapter we have discussed the Śaka/Scythian elements in Indian art in the major areas of Indo-Scythian rule, i.e., the borderlands and in the north-western part of the subcontinent, till the middle of the first century A.D.

The major areas once under the Śaka/Scythian or Śaka-Pahlava rule continued to experience the impact of nomadic art styles. Unfortunately, we do not have enough data in several sites to be able to examine in more detail the Śaka/Scythian and Śaka-Pahlava elements. Nevertheless, we continue to regard several sites in the Indian sub-continent for providing evidence for the assimilation of Śaka/Scythian and Śaka-Pahlava elements with the indigenous art styles. The published data exhibits the settlement structure related to the period concerned along with the source materials for the subject. This is evident from the objects unearthed at the sites of Shotorak, Paitāva and Kham Zargar. As we shall see below, these sites have yielded various utility objects, weapons, horse trappings, ornaments and sculptured reliefs which indicate Śaka/Scythian and Śaka-Pahlava art elements.

Some minor regions of Śaka/Scythian and Śaka-Pahlava rule, from the first century A.D. onwards, have been discussed in Chapter 2. Among the minor areas, mention may be made of modern Kashmir, Haryana, Mathura, Saurashtra, Rajasthan and the western part of Madhya Pradesh, from where various artifacts dated in the first century A.D. onwards reveal the impact of the Śaka/Scythian and Śaka-Pahlava or Scytho-Parthian art styles. Regions other than the areas ever ruled by the Śaka/ Scythians or Śaka-Pahlavas also received the impact of the Śaka/Scythian and Śaka-Pahlava styles in the formation of their art objects, as in Maharashtra, upper Tamil Nadu, Andhra Pradesh and West Bengal. Perhaps these areas experienced the diffusion of the Śaka/Scythian and Śaka-Pahlava styles due to their proximity or linkages via trade routes. Another factor could be the expansion of these areas as a result of trade with the Andhra kingdoms,[1] which fact seems to have strengthened the stylistic factor.

We go back to the three sites of Shotorak, Paitāva and Kham Zargar, located in the heart of the major areas of Śaka/Scythian rule, i.e., between the borderlands of India and the north-western part of the subcontinent, in search of Śaka/Scythian and Śaka-Parthian art elements. The three sites can be broadly located in the Kapiśâ region in the eastern part of Afghanistan, to the south of the Hindu Kush mountains and adjacent to ancient Gandhâra. Various vessels having utilitarian purposes as is evident from the Gandhara reliefs reveal Graeco-Parthian influence, especially in the wine cup besides others. In Indian art, wine cups are found in abundance in Sunga, Satavahana and the Kushana period. In search of Saka/Scythian elements in Indian art tradition, it is interesting to note the survival of Graeco-Parthian style in the Gandharan context. For example the style of the depiction of mugs in Gandhara reliefs continues till now in the metal tankards of Kashmir and North-West India.[2] Here, the nomadic cultural evolution was set in motion by the presence of the Úakas, subsequently by the Parthians, and then of course by the Kushânas, after the latter crossed the Hindu Kush mountains. Under the Kushâna rule, Kapiśâ became the first important political centre outside Bactria, and Shotorak lies five km east of Kapiśâ-Begram. Shotorak's proximity with Kapiśâ is important, as Kapiśâ already had an established urban centre supported by fertile lands and a good irrigation system, which had been in existence since Achaemenid times. Akra, an Achaemenian site is also important in this context. Meuniê excavated Shotorak and dated the site from the second to the third century A.D. on the basis of a coin of Vāsudeva, which had been discovered beside the votive *stūpa* D4.[3] From the remains of a large standing Buddha image and pedestal from Shotorak, we see two images on the left side of the Buddha.[4] These two images are wearing the typical

Scythian costume and are similar to the attire of the donors in the relief of the Buddha flanked by Kāśyapas, also from Shotorak (Plate 202).[5] The figures of Trapuśa and Bhallika, flanking the Śākyamuni (Plate 203),[6] at Shotorak are depicted as wearing the Scythian type tunic, baggy trousers, and both are sporting long beards. Similarly, in the relief of the worship of Śākyamuni's alms bowl (Plate 204),[7] from Shotorak, the flanking figures protecting the bowl are wearing the typical Scythian tunics with belts or girdles and close—fitting trousers. Similar costumes are also seen to be depicted on several sculptures of Indo-Scythian devotees (Plate 205) from Takal.[8] A Śaka/Scythian devotee from Jaulian, Taxila, wears a similar belted tunic reaching below the knee, as at Shotorak. In a relief (Plate 206), found from Paitāva[9] comprising an image pedestal with Maitreya flanked by figures, some are wearing belted tunics, up to the knee and their trousers are tucked in boots, while others are wearing tunics below the knee, and baggy trousers. A fragmented relief with Śaka/Scythian devotees and another relief fragment with garlands borne by Śaka/Scythian men have been found from Shotorak. It seems that nomadic art had traversed a long way and was in the service of the spread of Buddhist religion.

An interesting gold amulet case (Plate 233)[10] has been found from Ahin Posh, near Jalalabad, Afghanistan. It is dated in the second, third century A.D. The openings on this eight-sided cylinder are backed with garnets, as are those on the two ends, one of which can be opened. The motifs on the gold amulet case have garnet incrustations and they are similar to the Śaka/ Scythian motifs. Such cylindrical amulet cases, designed to be worn on a cord, can be seen on the chests of the bejewelled Bodhisattvas of the Gandhara period.

Two gold *tatankacakras* or discal ear ornaments (Plate 234) from Gandhara of circa third century A.D. are preserved in the Metropolitan Museum of Art.[11] They depict a goose with floriating feathers, in the typical Scythian 'curved inwards' style. The central motif is encircled by a double border.

A terracotta tray probably from Bannu (the Bannu Basin lies about 150 miles southwest of Peshawar in the North-West Frontier Province of Pakistan), now in the Ashmolean Museum, consists of a central compartment framed by four surrounding compartments. The depiction of the archer[12] and the stylized couchant lion in the compartments show the nomadic influence. The dress of the archer is typically Scythian.

We go further east and find at the head of the Doab of the Indus and Jhelum rivers, the great centre of Taxila. We have already seen that Taxila occupied a major meeting point of the trade routes coming from Kabul, from Kashmir, and from eastern India. Kashmir was again linked with western Tibet and Tibet was linked with Nepal and Bengal. In the last decades of the first century B.C. there were political changes taking place in the west-Punjab region around Taxila. The Greeks under the leadership of Apollodotus II were subsequently able to regain the territories of the Punjab which they had earlier lost to the Indo-Scythian Maues. However, they were finally expelled from this region around c. 55 B.C. by another Scythian prince, Azes I, who dethroned Hippostratus (the last Greek king to reign in the west Punjab, including Taxila and Pushkalâvatī). A *tetradrachm* of Apollodotus II from the Sarai Saleh hoard found on the North-West Frontier, in the Abbotabad region, with two combined monograms, suggests that Apollodotus II was the immediate successor of Maues, and both reigned within a short lapse of time in the same region.[13] Thus,it was Azes I himself who definitively established the Indo-Scythian dynasty in the region of the West Punjab. It is noteworthy that stylistically the portrait of the king on the Apollodotus's *drachm* is similar to the one issued in the west-Punjab mints. The hoard found in the Malakand region, not far away from the ancient cities of Pushkalāvatī (near Peshawar) and Taxila is similar to the Peshawar hoard containing coins of Azes I, Azilises, Azes II and Gondophares.[14] Again, it is to be noted that trade between upper Mesopotamia and North-West India, both overland and by way of Mesene and the Persian Gulf was frequent during the first century A.D.[15]

Taxila and its surrounding sites have yielded utility objects, ornaments, weapons, coins and horse-trappings, dated in the middle of the first century A.D. onwards. Most of them betray the Śaka/Scythian, Śaka-Pahlava or Scytho-Parthian styles. The style of these objects can hardly be distinguished as belonging prior to the first century A.D. or after the first century A.D. The Taxila valley had access to diverse kinds of raw materials from regions as far removed as Mirzapur and Mathura.

A. EAST OF THE NORTH-WESTERN PART OF INDIA

For our present study, the region east of the north-western part of India may be broadly divided into the Upper Ganga Valley or the Ganga Jamuna Doab, Middle and Lower Ganga Valley, the Malwa plateau and its adjoining plain, the Deccan, coastal Gujarat, Maharashtra and Western and Eastern Ghats.

The region east of the north-western part of India was noted for the extensive working of iron in the neighbourhood of Sof, east of Achabal. It is noteworthy that the *Periplus* informs us that during the first century A.D. Indian iron used to be exported from Ariaca on the Gulf of Cambay area.[16] Again, a diagnostic feature of Scythian culture was the adoption of iron metallurgy.[17] It may be presumed that the Śaka-Pahlava areas of rule generally followed the geographical directions of the trade routes. With Śaka-Pahlava rule, it may also be assumed that Śaka-Pahlava elements would be present in their art forms. Perhaps, the Śaka-Pahlavas were involved in the iron working, a craft which no doubt conferred a magical prestige on its practitioners, and in the iron trade, as they were ruling over the peripheral areas of Kashmir, during the middle of the first century A.D. The Semathan excavation in Kashmir has yielded various objects expressing the impact of Śaka/Scythian and Śaka-Pahlava styles. These are mainly found from period IV and period III strata. Period IV of the excavated area has yielded bowls with incurved rims, vases, ink-pot type lids, all dating from the first to the fifth century A.D. If we consider carefully, we find that the inkpot type lids from Kashmir are stylistically similar to the inkpot type lids found from Taxila. Also found from period IV stratum are bowls with footed bases, and some terracotta figures. One terracotta figure has a bearded and moustached head, with chubby cheeks and protruding elongated eyes, reminiscent of the Śaka-Pahlava style. This style continued in the Early Kushâna period. Another seated terracotta figure[18] from Kashmir (Period IV of the Semathan excavation) has folded drapery and a scarf covering the back of the head in the typical Central Asian style. The figure has prominent eyes, a long beard and hairdo. It is carrying something in his left hand, and iconographically it recalls the nomadic style. This cross-legged seated figure, bearded and with the Scythian costume is also seen in the Śaka-Sarmatian burial complexes, as in the central character of the Kobyakovo torque (Plate 207)[19] dated in the first and second centuries A.D. Tillya-tepe has also yielded a similar cross-legged seated and bearded figure wearing the Scythian costume.[20] It was therefore a common iconographic type practised throughout the region, from Central Asia to the east.

Excavations at Harwan, Kashmir, have revealed a large number of terracotta figures, along the periphery of the *stūpa* remains, and they are dated in the early centuries of the Christian era.[21] The pavement of the courtyard of the Harwan *stūpa* consists of large moulded brick tiles, and the favourite pattern seems to have been a large disc consisting of several concentric circles within a single central unit. Other motifs include wavy lines, fish-bone patterns, flower designs, geese in rows, cocks, rams fighting, deer looking with their heads turned backwards, archers on horsebacks and men in armour hunting deer with bows and arrows. One is reminded of the *âyâgapatas* of Mathura. Thus, the geometrical and animal motifs suggest a probable Śaka/Scythian affiliation, more so as Kashmir was within the Śaka-Pahlava territories. Another factor possibly hints that the tiles were made of Śaka-Scythian, Śaka-Pahlava and Kushâna patronage. This assumption is based on the fact that each tile bears a number in Kharoshtī script. The Kharoshtī script flourished principally in the third to the fourth centuries A.D. in north-western India. Two scripts of Indian origin i.e., Brāhmī and the Kharoshtī were used in early Central Asia. Kharoshī seems to have been introduced earlier than Brāhmī. Legends in the Prākrit language and the Kharoshī script can be noticed on the coins of a group of rulers (possibly Indo-Parthian or Indo-Scythian origin) struck in or near Khotan in circa. first century A.D. or rather in first century B.C. to first century A.D. This ruling dynasty, hailing probably from the north-western section of the Indian subcontinent, might have been responsible for the official use of the above language and script in Central Asia. The continuation of the use of Prākrit and Kharoshī in Khotan is suggested by a record found at Endere (no.661) dated in the third to the fourth century A.D.[22] It follows therefore that the Harwan tiles belong to a period prior to the fourth century A.D. and they represented Indian imagery in a Central Asian nomadic rendering. Not only the designs stamped on the tiles, but also the style of the human figures depicted, show heavy features, prominent cheekbones, slanting eyes, receding foreheads, and some were dressed in trousers and caps. The heads are shown in profile with their bodies facing front. Impressions on a rectangle (found on a tile) containing a dragon *(makara)* with foliate tail and crest, and upraised trunk—like snout, similarly, betray elements of nomadic art (Plate 208).[23] Ancient Buddhist settelements having pavements of baked terracotta files resembling those found from Harwan have been found from Gurwait-Yarikhan in the Badgaon district of cenral Kashmir. Other sites from Kashmir yielding terracotta files include Hoinar (Liddru), Dardkote (Hut mura) and Doni-Pather (Pahalgan). This diffusion of nomadic art into the Kashmir area was probably due also from Western Tibet. A lion image cast in leaded copper-zinc-tin alloy[24] has been found from Kashmir and it has been dated by P.Pal in the first century A.D. It is similar in style to the Taxilan representations of lions (found in strata dated in the first century A.D.) in their prominently curved chests, hairy manes and curling tails. Similar representations of lions belonging to the Kushana period were found from Mathura.[25] The Avatāra Frame from Kashmir[26] now in the Sri Pratap Singh Museum, Srinagar, is extraordinary for the complexity of its design and is a masterpiece of Kashmiri metalwork. At the apex of the arch stands a multi-headed Vishnu and immediately below him is the figure of Śiva. The remaining figures, each framed by a medallion (which is reminiscent of the individual motif of the crouching stag) formed by the continuously joined lotus tendrils, represent the different heroic as well as placid aspects of Vishnu. This Avatāra frame belongs to the tenth century A.D. and somewhere in the technique the metal-smith uses animal imagery with their convolutions as found earlier in the nomadic metal style (toreutics). It is significant to note here that if any group of artisans who might have retained Hellenising tendencies among a new barbarian clientele (such as the Śaka and Yueh-chih,) it would have been the Bactrian metal-smiths who produced articles of luxury in precious metals and dazzling gold jewellery for their new masters. Within this tradition, elements of a recherchê transmuting oriental Hellenism (including the nomadic elements) persisted up to the Islamic era. History made it certain that it would of course spread to India. We go back to the Avatāra frame and its metalwork that depict the continuously joined lotus tendrils and the animal imagery, so striking to the eye with all their convolutions. In this context, we must mention Tibet and its metalwork. Pre-Buddhist Tibet had connections with the various nomadic groups (through China of course), as is apparent from the animal style on various brass plaques from Miang, bronze belt buckles from Tsaparang, bronze amulets with figures of stylized animals from Tholing, similar to the objects of sacred significance as found from Luristan[27] bronze objects (Plate 209) from the Lake Manasarovar area, and those from Yarlung. A handle or terminal in the form of a stylized ram's head from Shigatse, also amulets depicting four linked birds (a version of this can be seen in the votive tank found from Taxila), bronze figurines of felines, pendants having bell shapes, all reflect Scytho-Siberian forms. From the ninth century onwards, Tibetan metalwork had definite linkages with Kashmiri metalwork, as attested to by various sculptures. The wavy scrolls and convolutions of the animal imagery of Kashmir are also found in Tibetan works like the Bodhisattva Avalokiteshvara image[28] and in another bronze image of Avalokiteshvara dated in the eleventh and twelvth centuries A.D.[29] It therefore seems that Kashmir, Tibet and Nepal were entangled in the Śaka/Scythia and Scytho-Siberian network of art forms.

Excavation work in the post-independent period in Kashmir unfolded fascinating cultural material detected as belonging to diverse cultural assimilations linked with different routes. The excavation at the site of Ambaran has a special interest for the deliberation of multi-cultural interaction particularly during the period of the present study. In the following pages we have tried to highlight the basic element which signified the process and development of the Saka/Scythian art tradition in the Kashmir region. The Saka/Scythian element is discernible in the spouted vessels including the one with a grotesque animal head, a pot lug bearing the head of a lion, two small terracotta grotesque heads, terracotta moulds of ornaments and iron and copper objects. The terracotta heads of horses from Akhnur are well-known. The sites at Ushkur, Harwan and Ambaran (Akhnur) are located outside the area of Gandhara.[30] The Taxilan *stupas* of the Saka-Parthian and Kushan periods like those at Dharmarajika, Kalwan and Jandial monastic establishments have their construction pattern and decorative mouldings at the stupa bases similar to the *stupas* at Ambaran. From the heavily encrusted reliquary with a broken lid were found thin circular gold sheets as found from Kalwan, Taxila. Thirty circular thin sheets of gold and with two circular rimmed thin sheets of silver were found along with 150 pearl micro-beads, 12 cylindrical coral beads, two metallic micro-beads, an oval-shaped silver casket and a circular gold casket. The reliquary spot also yielded four full and six broken circular thin sheets of gold, an amethyst bead and three encrusted copper coins.

Jewelleries from Kashmir and Ladakh and the surrounding regions reflect the Scytho-Siberian-Śaka tradition. Gold is still highly valued because of its inalterability and its adaptability to all sorts of uses. As we all know, it is the only metal found in a usable form in its natural state. In Kashmir, the rural women till now have intricately worked silver necklaces with embossed almond-shaped and round pendants fixed to it at intervals.[31] This type of Kashmiri silver necklace attests to the continuation and innovations of techniques and forms of the Śaka-Scythian-Sarmatian tradition. Gulubands[32] (as are commonly known) are necklaces from Ladakh. They consist of silver ornaments set with turquoises strung together with two rows of coral beads and silver pendants on two threads. They have a striking compositional similarity with the Śaka/Scythian jewellery, like the necklace (Plate 212) from Tillya-tepe.[33]

Not only in Kashmiri metal-work and jewellery, but also in carpet making in Kashmir, we are grateful to the Śaka/Scythians for their influence. Carpets made in the knot—system in Kashmir seem to continue the Śaka/Scythian and Scytho—Siberian techniques of rug making. This is evident from the similarity of Kashmiri rugs with the ancient rugs of the Pazyryk burials. Horses buried at Pazyryk had plaited tails, sometimes knotted at half length instead. Carpets found at Pazyryk and later in Kashmir have often used plaited ends, and this style is still in use not only in Kashmir, but also in Tibet and Nepal. The excavation of tombs at Pazyryk in Siberia and at Noin-ula in Mongolia has shown that both leather and felt were in use in the fourth century B.C. for the manufacture of everyday items such as carpets and saddle covers, as well as magnificent hangings commissioned by the elite. Leather appliqué-work was also popular. Leather has a naturally integrated structure so it can be cut without fear of fraying. This makes it ideal for use in appliquê and especially for the making of hard—wearing clothes and covers. Animal and baggage covers in the same technique are widely used in Northern India and Pakistan.[34]

Bronzes in Nepal also reflect the Śaka/Scythian and Śaka—Pahlava styles. In the image of the Nāksal Sūrya, dated about 1159 A.D., we find Sūrya dressed in the nomadic costume[35] and the local people refer to the image as 'Śāka Sūrya'. The image wears a double-breasted jacket open at the neck and high boots. Round metal plaques, called *manda* in Newari, are inset in the ground next to the Buddhist *stūpas* in Nepal (one is reminded of the tiled courtyard adjacent to the Harwan *Stūpa*), and they are revered, even to this day. These *mandas a*s are very much similar to the Indian *âyâgapatas*.

Ritual vessels from Chamba, having animal-headed handles, and another having a ribbed surface, are presently in the collection of the Bhuri Singh Museum, Chamba. The ritual vessels are similar to the Scythian utility objects. These are still used in Chamba. Water pots from contemporary Kinnaur are noteworthy for their shapes and the spouts which are in the form of fish,[36] betray nomadic designs. The stylized vegetal scroll seems to have been taken directly from a Scythian relief panel. The iconography of Ganeśa images in Himachal Pradesh, during the pre-Pratihara and Pratihāra period (tenth century A.D.) has some interesting features. The long receptacle of the *modak*, the conical crown and the garland of bells remind us of the nomadic influence which had been truly embedded in the folk elements. These features were automatically incorporated in the Pratihāra art style.[37]

Earrings from Chamba region, locally known as Charka Bunda Bali[38] are similar to the Śaka/ Scythian earrings in their technique and form. Significantly, the lower portion of a silver earring (locally known as Dhedu Jhumka)[39] worn by the women of Chamba is similar to that of the Śaka/Scythian tradition. From the region of Simla Hills, Himachal Pradesh, various ornaments (used daily) reflect the nomadic tradition. Tiny floral rosettes,[40] decorating head jewels, reveal the continuation of the earlier traditions. A lovely necklace from the Simla hills shows trellises of diamond-shaped pieces, barrel-shaped beads and triangles.[41] This popular ornament reveals nomadic influence. The trefoil pattern, so common in the Śaka/Scythian style revisits in the modern nose rings[42] from Himachal. They are an integral part of the whole composition. Silver earrings from Himachal Pradesh with numerous small silver balls hanging from a crescent[43] reflect the Scytho-Siberian form. The famous Vaikunthanatha[44] deity of Himachal Pradesh is wearing the lozenge type of earrings probably because of Kashmiri influence.[45] Actually, the root lies in the nomadic tradition, as we may humbly point out.

Devendra Handa, in his recent work[46] has contributed a chapter on the sculptural specimens of the Saka-Kushana period related to the Buddhist remains from Haryana. He has pointed out the presence of Mauryan Buddhist assemblage as the foundation of the Saka-Kushan art tradition. The influence of non-Indian elements found in the images of Buddha and Bodhisattva recorded from Mahmudpur, Jhajjar, Lalpur, Bhuna, Rohtak besides the classic specimens of terracotta *Asvamukhi* from Sugh and a Bodhisattva from Sirsa qualify the whole artistic trait of the Saka/Scythian type.

Excavations at Naurangabad, Haryana, 2000-01 has yielded a large number of coins of the Yaudheyas. Some of these coins exhibit certain elements of the Indo-Scythian coinage.

Archaeological excavations in the district of Sonipat in Haryana have revealed the emergence and continuous evolution of settlements from the early Harappan to the early historical period of the Kushânas.[47] The occurrence of a large hoard of 1200 *hemidrachms* of Graeco-Bactrians and about 10000 coins of the Yaudheyas, Kushânas and later Kushânas speak of its significance in the early historical and historical periods. The Harsana Kalan site dated in the first century A.D. yielded bevelled rims of bowls and the shard of a lid with a conical central knob.[48] Similar utility objects have been unearthed from the Śaka/Scythian stratum at Taxila. The nomadic ornamental tradition of Taxila had certainly spread to the adjoining Punjab. Throughout the medieval age and till the modern period, several nomadic traditions persist in the Punjab area. This is noticeable in the Punjabi jewellery comprising earrings, bracelets and head ornaments.[49] Enamelled gold necklaces (called Champâ-kali) from Amritsar also attest to the continuation of the nomadic tradition. These necklaces are set with gems and strung on red silk covered with gold wires.[50] Excavation at Brass, district Fateh Garh Sahib, Punjab, shows the cultural sequences of late Harappan culture, PGW, black-slipped and grey ware cultures, Sunga-Kushan and Medieval. The pottery of Sunga-Kushan period is marked by stamp designs showing *nandipada*, pipal leaf, *triratna* motifs reminiscent of the Saka/Scythian style. Vessels were designed with painted bands, zig-zag and wavy lines. Incurved bowls, basins, lids, votive tanks, basins with spout and iron spear-heads reveal the latter style. Excavation at Rohira, Punjab, exposed a coin of Gondophares of the first century A.D. from Period III. Stamped pottery were also found from this period.

Sites of the early historical period have also been excavated at Muhammadnagar, district Gurgaon under the direction of B. R.Mani. A 4m deposit of Period V at the site belongs to the Kushana period but the assemblages of the Pre-Kushana and Kushana phases reveal the influence of the occupation of the Indo-Scythians. The cultural sequence of the site is quite similar to that noticed at Harnol, another site in the neighbourhood. The minor antiquities are noted for their nomadic affiliations. Muhammadnagar also yielded structures of the Kushana period and a few specimens of Kushan copper coins. Explorations in Mewat Area, district Gurgaon, have revealed several sites of the early historical period whose antiquity and assemblages are similar to those of Muhammadnagar. These cluster of sites are Autha, Muhammadnagar, Bhadas, Malab, Gohana, Hathin, Ata, Mundheta (Mundehta), Mamlika, Gokalpur, Luhinga, Papra, Harnol, Mandikhera, Gangwani, Jamalgarh and Paimakhera. Jamalgarh displays Sunga-Kushan red ware and bricks.

A hoard of Jaina bronzes from Hansi in the Hisar District was excavated in February 1982, and the presence of such bronzes attests to the prevalence of Jainism in Haryana during the eighth to the tenth centuries A.D.[51] Images of Mahāvidyā Achchhuptā have been found. She is wearing full boots and riding a horse bedecked with saddle and trappings. She is seen holding a sword and arrow in the normal and extra right hands and a bow and shield in the corresponding left hands. The entire image of Mahāvidyā, consisting of individual elements like boots, sitting astride a horse, the trappings, sword and arrow, conjures up a nomadic imagery.[52] In an ancient mound in Kangra fort, there is an apparently ruined temple with remains of a decorated stone block having two reasonably stylized animal riders.[53] We cannot definitely ascertain any Śaka/Scythian influence at work, but the coins found at Kangra are similar to the Indo-Parthian ones with the obverse having a horseman and Śrī and the reverse showing recumbent bulls.[54] The Nurpur Temple at Kangra has a peculiar ornamentation consisting of projected figures of grotesque animals and geometrical motifs,[55] including the comma motifs and the stylized antlers or S-shaped motifs. The motifs make one think in terms of the influence of Śaka/Scythian art. The Śaka/Scythian motifs are not new in the architectural dêcor of India. The individual components of Kīrttimukha, where both human and animal motifs are fused together, have been frequently used in Hindu temples.[56] These are similar in style to the horned Kïrttimukha as found from Sirkap, Taxila. A head of a Śiva image from Mathurā dated in the third-fourth century A.D. has a Kīrttimukha as a headdress. A similar one is depicted on the headdress of Śiva of the Daśāvatāra cave, Ellora. The Śaka/Scythian influence can also be traced in the *āmalaka* of the temple. Its solid shape is that of a ring stone. The naturally perforated ring stone is the prototype of the many carved stone discs found in various sites of Taxila[57], Śankisa, Kosam and Patna. Kīrttimukhas have been abundantly used in Khajuraho temples, and in other temples of Northern Gujarat and Rajasthan even in the eleventh century A.D.

The ancient site of Atranjikhera is located in district Etah in Uttar Pradesh. Other than Sankisa, Ahichchhatra and Kausambi, the Atranjikhera mound is one of the four largest sites in Uttar Pradesh. Two circular and thin gold foils have been found from Period IV, Phase D, Atranjikhera. Both pieces are decorated with granulated designs.[58] One of the gold foils has triangular motifs of granulated pattern. The same Phase has also yielded a Kshatrapa coin. Two artifacts found from Period IV deserve special mention. One is a terracotta openwork plaque or design block[59] having a geometrical pattern on one side and the other is a terracotta lid[60] bearing a floral-cum-geometric pattern. Terracotta amulets also reveal the Saka-Parthian motifs. Though Period IV signified the N.B.P.W. culture, (Atranjikhera revealed a continuity of occupation from about the second millennium B.C. till the Mughal period with short-time habitational break between Periods I and II and V and VI) the assimilation of Saka-Parthian elements had begun. The same may be said regarding other sites in Northern India including Taxila.

A terracotta medallion from Shahabad, district Hardoi, Uttar Pradesh,[61] has been found in an ancient mound called Angai Khera. The obverse of the grey coloured medallion depicts a confrontation between a male figure trying to overpower an animal figure. The head of the animal is turned backwards and the left fore-leg is raised to the back. It reminds one of the Scythian deer's posture especially the body curvature, movement and modelling. A somewhat similar plaque has been reported by J. Marshall from Bhita and is published in the Annual Report of the Archaeological

Survey of India for the year 1911-12, (Pl. XXIV). According to M.C.Joshi, the said medallion, on stylistic considerations, appears to belong to the 3rd century A.D. The animal figure is that of a composite animal with the head of *makara* and the body of a lion with anklets. The tight-fitting cap on the head of the male figure is of Saka/Scythian origin. His large rounded eyes attest to its affinity to the Saka/ Scythian atelier. The auspicious symbols and designs on the reverse of the medallion were common in the Saka/Scythian repertoire. These symbols and designs are also found on the images and tribal coins of 2nd-3rd centuries A.D.

With due emphasis on the artifacts obtained from various areas of Sanghol it will be seen that its remains can be dated from the Late Harappan to the Kushana period. Sanghol is a significant site with reference to the development of settlements in the upper Ganga valley. Its settlement history since the Harappan time displays a proliferation of economic base, basically agrarian. At the same time it has a tremendous artistic tradition clearly visible in the forms of sculptural art as well as other forms. The Hathiwara Mound in Sanghol contains the habitational deposit and cultural material of the Kushana period (also treated by some as Sunga-Kushana period). Beads of semi-precious stones, bowls with incurved rim, use of stamped and incised decoration, are noteworthy. The motifs include *swastika*, *triratna* leaves, loops, circles, and other geometrical patterns. Copper coins of the Indo-Parthians were found in abundance. An ivory comb (recalling the one from Taxila) has been found.

Excavations at Narhan (on the left bank of the river Ghaghara in Bansgaon Tehsil of district Gorakhpur) have yielded pottery (Period IV) constituting essentially the same types commonly associated with the Kushan sites.

Excavation at Jhusi, district Allahabad, Uttar Pradesh revealed cultural deposits ranging from the early medieval to the Kushan period. The Sunga-Kushan level yielded typical stamped pottery, beads fashioned on semi-precious stones attesting to the Saka/Scythian style. The ancient mound at Durvasa south-east of Allahabad city has yielded numerous vestiges of the Kushan period. Durvasa was a part of the ancient trade route from Sravasti (Sahet-Mahet). Sringaverapura, district Allahabad, has provided a sequence of cultures starting from about the early first millennium B.C. to the early medieval times. Period IV has yielded seals and sealings, one of them reading *Dhankasa*, and another *Gosalakasa* in characters of the 1st century B.C.-A.D. In one of the areas excavated at Harsh-Ka-Tila, Thanesar, Kurukshetra, more than thirty terracotta tablets having in most cases three oblique, vertical or curved lines have been found and these are similar to the ones found from Rangmahal, Sanghol and Sringaverapura.

Siswania in the Basti district of Uttar Pradesh has yielded various artifacts displaying the nomadic influence. Two handmade figurines with pointed headdress in the style of warrior figures having goat-like faces, a male head with moustaches and crown with circular jewel ornamentation, one male terracotta head with typical Scytho-Kushan ethnic features and terracotta ornamented horses are some of the finds expressing foreign elements. Archaeologists have identified the remains found from the excavation at Siswania, district Basti, as belonging to the late NBPW phase, Sunga and Kushan phases. A careful analysis of the remains attest to the presence of the Saka/Scythian element. The incurved bowls, basins, cooking pots, ink-pot lids, spouted pots, terracotta plaques depicting horses and horse-rider give an overall picture of the assimilation of the nomadic element. Amongst the important antiquities, mention may be made of *gaja-Lakshmi* plaques, gold plated earrings and a ring with a lion figure.

Khairadih, district Ballia, has yielded among other antiquities a large number of stamps, seals, stoppers, pendants, crucibles and copper and iron objects displaying typical animal and geometric motifs of the Saka/Scythians[62] .

Exploration in the Mid-Ganga Valley, districts Allahabad, Kausambi, Pratapgarh, Jaunpur and Bhadohi has revealed a number of sites like Dharampur, Hetapatti Sirohi, Nibhapur-Piprahi,Channapur Dih, Matethu, Bhiski, Handia, Neebi, Pathsala, Badara, Kala Kaserua, Mahmudabad, Ramnathpura(Dihwa), Sudanipur, Ummedpur,Malak Payagi, Unch Dih, Soraon, Nadar, Nibhapur Baban, Bairi-Bisa, Cherapur/Tikari and Unjh all yielding Kushana pottery. It would be better to classify these artifacts under Kushana art although it is very difficult to draw a line between artifacts showing Saka/Scythian/Saka-Pahlava style and artifacts displaying the Kushana style. The same may be said of the artifacts unearthed from Bhagwas, district Sonbhadra, Uttar Pradesh, Nai-Dih, district Sonbhadra, Uttar Pradesh and Kandbhari Gate and Chirenath Temple sites in Sravasti, district Sravasti.

The excavation at Ramasare Purwa, district Lucknow[63], exposed three settlement periods. The earliest is the late Kushan period. Significantly, the stamped designs on the ceramics continue with the patterns of the Saka/Scythian period. The stamped designs include sigmas, concentric circles, horizontal lines and triangles with dots. A potter's stamp with criss-cross design and concentric circles was also found. Knobbed-lids and ink-pot type lids were found in abundance. A pot with an animal-headed spout having lozenge-shaped eyes has also been found. Excavations at Sankisa, district Farrukhabad-witnessed continuous activities from NBPW period to the Gupta period, having brick structures of Gupta, Kushan and Sunga periods.

The excavation at Kopia, Uttar Pradesh, has yielded artifacts betraying Saka/ Scythian elements. A unique decorated pot having stamped motifs of *nandipada* has been found from Kopia. Kopia is located on the Khalilabad-Bakhira road, 12 kms north of Khalilabad town in Sant Kabir Nagar district (erstwhile part of district Basti) and has an extensive Kushan settlement strata. Terracotta figurines having goblin-like bulging eyes have been found[64] from Kopia.

Sanchankot, district Unnao, Uttar Pradesh has yielded Indo-Scythian coins. The site was excavated in 2004-2005.[65] The richest Sunga-Kushana deposit yielded various artifacts betraying Saka/Scythian elements. Over a vast area of central Uttar Pradesh covering the districts of Unnao, Hardoi, Kanauj, Farrukhabad, Shahjahanpur, Pilibhit, Keri-Lakhimpur and Sitapur, various sites have yielded continuous stratigraphy from NBPW to the Medieval period. The site of Saunphari may be noted for its terracottas, copper and iron objects belonging to the Pre-Kushana phase.

Excavations at Ahichchhatra show continuous levels of occupation from Stratum VIII, dated in the 300-200 B.C. to Stratum IV, dated in the 100-350 A.D. Pottery shards from Stratum IV show certain motifs, which could be equated with the Śaka/Scythian motifs. These motifs include twin fish, rosettes, *nandipadas* (which were also found from Taxila) and snakes flanking a central pillar.[66] Votive tanks found at Ahichchhatra[67] are similar to those from Taxila. According to some scholars, these votive tanks could be of indigenous origin.

Kauśâmbï was an important urban centre during the first centuries of the Christian era. Terracotta figures (Plate 210),[68] from Śaka-Parthian levels have the typical conical caps. Also goblets with flat and footed bases were found. A terracotta drummer (Plate 211) with a peaked cap[69] definitely displays Śaka/Scythian influence. Other terracotta figures, with their dresses and decorations, somehow reflect the Śaka-Pahlava style of Seleucia and Dura. Stratigraphically, they all belong to the first and second centuries A.D., a period when the Śaka-Pahlavas, through trade and conquests, had penetrated not only north-west India but also the plains of northern India. Many names of Śaka origin have been found in the inscriptions excavated in the Ghoshitarāma area of Kausambi. Votive tanks of Kausâmbi were similar to those found from Taxila and Ahichchhatra. In the votive tanks of Kausambi were found seated figures, usually drummers, dressed in trousers and belted tunics reaching up to the knees, thereby revealing the nomadic attire. Excavations at Narhan[70] , near Gorakhpur, have revealed similar votive tanks with lamps and birds on the rim of the tanks, and musicians squatting against the walls of the tanks.

From the first century A.D. onwards, Mathura and its surrounding regions have yielded various artifacts, clearly betraying the continuation of the nomadiac style. Two fragments from Mathura, of the a Śaka and Kushāna period, and now in the Patna Museum, show remnants of the silver and gold with which they were coated, or else the gold was employed in the polychromy of the plaque.[71] Another artifact[72] from Bulandibagh show definite recrudescence due to the Scythian origin.

Excavations at Sonkh have proved rewarding for the Śaka/ Scythian factor. The levels 23 and 24 contained structural remains and instructive finds of the Kshatrapa period of Mathura. They represent a culture which is a mixture of indigenous (India) and foreign (Śaka) elements, best shown by the appearance of Kshatrapa coins along with those of Rāmadatta of the Datta dynasty of Mathụra.[73] A round plaque depicting on the obverse a ferocious lion standing over its prey is found from Sonkh.[74] The lion stretches across the whole width of the plaque with the head turned backwards. Under its legs are two crouching wild boars, and on the lower edge, an iguana is depicted.

An interesting sculpture of Baladeva[75] (now in a Private Collection, Switzerland) is curved on both sides. Dated in the 100-300 A.D., it is made of mottled red sandstone, characteristic of the Mathura region of U.P. It depicts a splendid figure of *makara* (in a stylistic manner) on one side, and a regally attired seated figure on the other. Two Śvetambara monks are depicted against the lotus seat, and a third figure, dressed in a tunic and trousers in the Scythian mode, is shown in front of the club. He could be a Scythian or a Kushâna convert, donor, or a native who had adopted the foreign attire.

Early Gupta gold and silver coinage had evolved from Hellenistic and Śaka-Kushâna coinage, not only in design but also in treatment and execution. In some of the imperial coins up to Skandagupta, the costume of the kings and its treatment retain Scytho-Kushâna characteristics.[76] The coins of the Western Kshatrapas express quite consistently the Saka-Kushana style. The excavation at Mansar, district Nagpur, has shown a continuous settlement pattern from the Middle Stone Age to the historical period. In the Satavahana-Vakataka strata a coin of Western Kshatrapa king showing Swami Rudrasena III's bust on the obverse and on the reverse a *chaitya* with inscriptions reading *Maha Kshatrapasa Swami Rudradaman Putasa Raja Maha Kshatrapa Swami Rudrasena* 21 Saka (A.D. 348-378) has been discovered.

The large number of pottery spouts assignable to the Gupta period and found from Ahichchhatra, Râjghât, Śâkambharï and other sites are indeed remarkable. They are mostly designed in the form of heads of animals such as boars, elephant, lions, *makaras* etc. There can be no doubt that such utilitarian devices, like spouts and lug-handles or lug-ears of cooking and drinking vessels, etc., had evolved from earlier models, with modifications.[77] The Śaka-Scythian tradition of using animal heads as motifs on utilitarian objects must have had an indirect influence on later Indian models.

A stone disc (Plate 216) from Rājghāt is presently in a private collection at Varanasi. This example[78] was carved from chocolate soapstone having a prominent grey streak running across the centre. The carved obverse is in an excellent state of preservation while on the reverse may be noted a deep groove and a roughly incised check pattern. A circular protuberance at the centre forms the core of a full-blown lotus having 23 petals. Around the lotus in a clock-wise direction moves a file of nine quadrupeds comprising a lion, three hares, a mole, a ram, a dog, one goat and an antelope. The zone remains redefined by a double band of cable-moulding. Beyond this richly carved central depression there may be found three concentric bands of 'notch like design' or 'beaded bands' on the sloping edge. This particular stone disc clearly betrays Achaemenid and nomadic styles.

A general structural sameness marks both the ring-stones and stone-discs, yet discovered sporadically from distant early historical sites of northern India, namely, Taxila, Ropar, Mathura, Sankisā and Kosam, Rājghāt, Patna, Murtaziganj, Ujjain, and Vaisali. These were characterized by jewel-like workmanship and exquisite finish. These specimens of early Indian lithic art were crafted from various materials like alabaster, soapstone, sandstone, steatite and diorite. It may be mentioned here that Ropar, like Taxila, has adequate evidences to have witnessed a developed, prosperous phase of near urban character from the beginning of the early historical period, built up over some long periods of time. The main red ware shapes from Ropar in the period concerned are bowls, basins with and without lug or loop handles, vases, pear-shaped jars, carinated handis and lids of different shapes and sizes. Among them there are many shapes which along with their variants, occur at Hastinapur, Ahichchhatra, Kausambi, Prakash, Vaisali and Taxila.

We have found terracotta models of foreigners wearing the typical Scythian attire (with their distinctive facial type) from Harwan, Rajghat, Kosam, Bhita and other sites including those of the Punjab and the North-West India.[79] A particular back—rest of a Nalanda Buddha image introduces some novelty in the usual decorative scheme of the art of Nalanda.[80] It belongs to the fifth century A.D. Instead of the customary leogryph of the classical Gupta steles, we find in our sculpture that the vertical space between the *makara*—headed crossbar and the rectangular seat is filled by a queer animal. From a perusal of the royal seat painted in Cave I at Ajantâ,[81] the creature seems to be a deer or perhaps a goat. The habit of filling up an available space (with an animal motif) is somehow reminiscent of the Śaka/Scythian influence. The use of buckled girdle, as found on an image of Bodhisattva Padmapâni, from Nalanda may have been a popular style which continued from the Śaka—Parthian period to the Gupta period.[82] Other than the buckled girdle, another utility object, the ringtopped mendicant's staff (*khakkhara*) held by monks as found in the stucco reliefs of Nalanda is reminiscent of the Scythian pole-top.[8]

Exploration and subsequently excavation in district Raipur have brought to light the remains of two different monastic-complexes belonging to a period between the first century A.D. to the third-fourth century A.D. An iron helmet and a javelin were discovered from one of the cells of the complex. A few Saka-Kshatrapa coins were found along with sem-precious stones and terracotta beads and wheels, iron implements and bone points.

The archaeological site of Amilkoni, district Rewa has yielded NBPW sherds along with Kushan pottery. The dimension of the mound indicated that the site has witnessed continuous habitation for a substantial time. Various types of bowls, dishes, basins, medium sized vases, iron and copper objects and beads of semi-precious stones were found. The exposed cultural levels from mid NBPW phase to Kushan period obviously takes into account the influence of the Saka style. Under the banner of nomadic style it is sometimes very difficult to distinguish the Saka and the Kushan level. The Kushan period at this site was characterized by brick structures including the typical Kushan brick flooring.

Ornaments of Rajasthan and Maharashtra[84] show the partial continuation of the Śaka/Scythian jewellery forms and techniques. These include spiked silver bracelets from Rajasthan and armlets of silver and dyed cotton threads, known as *bâjubandh* which are still worn by the women of the Meena and Jat communities of

Rajasthan. Boat-shaped earrings transformed into traditional Jaipuri and Punjabi 'Makris', are still a popular type of ear ornaments. Lunate,[85] crescent and boat-shaped earrings are still in use in Rajasthan and they all reflect the ancient nomadic forms. Hanging gold earrings[86] are still in use in Barmer, Jaisalmer. In modern Rajasthani jewellery, several items continue the nomadic tradition. Stylised elephants and mythical animals are still depicted on Rajasthani bracelets. Geometrical motifs, such as triangles, dotted lines, dots and circular bands continue to decorate bangles and head jewellery from Rajasthan.[87] Rajasthani pendants enameled with stylised birds[88] and necklets with flower, almond, leaf, and lemon-shaped designs[89] reveal the Śaka/Scythian influence. Individual units of motifs[90] of the Jaipur enamelled jewellery again are reminiscent of the nomadic style. Gold enamelled phalas[91] or ornaments worn on the side of the head, from Jaipur show the Śaka/Scythian influence. A head of Śiva from Kalyanpur, Udaypur District, Rajasthan, preserved in the Pratap Museum, Udaypur, has an interesting ear ornament. The sculpture is of black schist and belongs to the sixth century A.D. On the right ear the obverse face of the earring depicts a young woman, probably a princess with attendant figures. One of them include a dwarfish man with a bent staff and peaked cap[92] recalling the nomadic cap.

Explorations along the Banganga river, district Bharatpur, Rajasthan have exposed about thirty sites.[93] Sites like Santruk, Rarh, Ahar, Sogar, Bori, Bhandor, Nagla Tuhiram, Sewar, Bagdhari, Jheelra, Par, Dharsnoi (Tehsil Wer), Rahimgarh, Halena, Sarsena and Bachhrain have yielded Kushan artifacts. We are already well acquainted with the so-called 'dynastic art' and its prototypes as defining and classifying the art of the Kushan period but Kushan art is unthinkable without its preceding Scythian/ Saka/Scythian/ Saka-Pahlava art forms. One has to be cautious in defining an art object as 'Kushana' as Bharatpur is geographically close to that great centre of 'Kushan art', Mathura. I suppose the magnitude of 'Kushanness' should be clearly explained by scholars of the Kushan idiom. I am sure the above sites should expose the Scythian/Saka/Scythian/ Saka-Pahlava art styles and their assimilation in Indian art. In this context, it is worth mentioning that archaeologically the region i.e. Bharatpur, shows numerous settlement remains since the arrival of Black-and Red Ware (BRW) using people. The site of Noh not only has the bearing of early settlement but also it could be treated as a nucleus area for the spread of metal bearing settlement. In all probability, the region played an important role for the growth of village farming communities along the Ganga valley. All these sites reveal the cultural continuity till the Saka-Parthian period and the economic factor was important for the assimilation of non-Indian art tradition including the proliferation of intermixing artistic activities.

B. OTHER AREAS OF INFLUNCE OF THE ŚAKA-PAHLAVA ART

Not only through trade routes, but the areas of Śaka/Scythian and Śaka—Pahlava influence were also connected through the spread of Buddhism. Inscriptions from Nagarjunakonda mention a lady named Cāmtisiri as a major donatrix, requesting for *nirvâna* in return for charitable acts. This was a Mahâyâna practice also known from some early inscriptions from Taxila. A composite animal[94] from a Nagarjunakonda frieze reveals Śaka/Scythian influence as also the well-known Scythian type guardian figure on a pillar[95] from Nagarjunakonda.

The excavation at Hampi, district Bellary revealed six metres of habitational deposit having seventeen different layers belonging to four distinctive periods— Period I—grey ware, Period II—early historical, Period III—Kushan and Period IV—medieval periods. Assemblages of Periods II and III show Saka/Scythian influence.

Not only at Nagarjunakonda but the terracotta art of Chandraketugarh also reflects Śaka/Scythian influences in some of its forms and motifs.[96] It is very tempting to suggest that the stone moulds found from Champa, Bihar, had a definite Saka/ Scythian element in their subject and style but nothing definite cannot be said about this. The moulds reveal various shapes and designs of ornaments, chains of varied designs (namely, bead-shaped, circular leaf-shaped, elongated leaf-shaped and makara-shaped necklaces) pendants (especially a crescent shaped pendant), earring and talismans. On the reverse side of the moulds can be seen a rider on horseback, charging with a spear in front. The stone moulds reflect the development of goldsmith industry of the period concerned. In this context it may be mentioned, that Chirand, a site in Bihar, has yielded many antiquities of the Sunga, Kushan and Pala periods. It is well-known that the Chirand mounds have given us a continuous historic sequence from the Neolithic to the Pala period. Chirand is famous for its double-faced-female and male mask. It may be noted that from Nevasa a big pot looking like a mask has been found and the latter is datable to the 1st or 2nd century A.D. Taradih, Bihar, has yielded various antiquities of the Kushan period from Period III. They include beads of semi-precious stones, conical objects, dabbers and discs. Like Chirand the site continued till the Pāla period.

Three rock shelters containing prehistoric rock paintings were discovered at South Bihar, around the forested hills of Ranigadar.[97] Geographically, this region lies in the northern extension of the Vindhyan ranges. The rock art of this region has been classified into several styles on the basis of styles, superimpositions, subject matter and patination. Paintings in dark red, white outline and in wash depicting horse riders, warriors and other persons in the typical Scythian dress constitute Style-9 representing the Saka-Kushan period.

Excavations at Peddavegi, 12 km north of Eluru town in district West Godavari had yielded a carnelian intaglio among other finds. The area around the village formed part of ancient Vengi. Vengi was the capital city of the Salankayanas, Vishnukundins and the Chalukyas that ruled Andhradesa from the middle of the fourth to the eleventh century A.D. Panini had mentioned *Salankayanka*, the country of the Salankayanas and Ptolemy (first century A.D.) had mentioned the *Salakenoi* of Vengi. Plano-convex in section, the intaglio depicts a female figure carved centrally. She has a bejeweled turreted crown, wide eyes, bulbous cheeks and wears an upper tunic and a lower trousers like robe. The dress and crown are reminiscent of the female deities depicted on Indo-Scythian and Kushan coins and seals. It is obvious that the specimen was brought to the Vengi region. Intaglios formed an important part of Hellenistic and Central Asian art. Peddavegi had also yielded a plaque depicting Mahishamardini having round eye balls and bulbous cheeks. Among the minor antiquities mention has to be made of the cubical dice of terracotta, ear ornaments and combs of ivory recalling the Kshatrapa-Satavahana examples. Another limestone plaque depicts a *Srivatsa Sri* with *Sakti* or spearhead retaining the characteristic features of the earliest *Srivatsa* form as found in the Saka/Scythian/Saka-Pahlava sites and on the early Satavahana coins.

The Western Kshatrapas of Śaka-Pahlava descent ruled Gujarat for some time during the first to fourth centuries A.D. The excavations at Hathab, district Bhavnagar, Gujarat has yielded iron objects in huge quantity including axes, sickles, knives and other decorative objects belonging to the period of Kshatrapas.[98] According to the Periplus (1st century A.D.) Indian iron was exported from Ariaca (Gulf of Cambay) to Abyssinia. Hathab is about 1½ km from the Gulf of Cambay and as it yielded a profusion of iron objects datable to the 1st-2nd century A.D., it seems that Hathab played an important role in the iron trade. Two sites namely Astakapra and Khadsliya, both near Hathab yielded large quantities of slags in various shapes and at various stages of working.[99]

Present Gujarat is not only geographically a compact unit but the settlements and material culture are also distinct from other areas of India.[100] Some modern day handicrafts of this area show traces of the nomadic influence. The nomadic style had left its influence on the folk idiom. In Gujarat, Gujra is a ceremonial pottery used at the time of marriage. At least three types of Gujras are found. They are about 6 to 9 cms long conical objects and look like the Saka/Scythian conical caps.[101] It is difficult to trace the antiquity of the Gujras. In Kashmir a similar type of object known as '*sani-patul*' is used in marriages and worshipped by the people as '*siva-linga*'.

Kutch is noted for its fine gold craft. Kutch workshops still fabricate ornaments using the ancient methods of granulation (also practised by the Scythians) and encrustation. A pair of gold hanging earrings (Plate 228)[102] from Kutch of rather large dimensions, continues the nomadic form of crescents decorated with gold globules and wire. The horned-plquette design revisits Gujarati earrings. The Gujarati specimen closes on hinges[103], but when the hinge is opened, the entire earring spreads in the form of the typical Scythian horned-plaquette. A striking pair of silver discal earrings (Plate 229)[104] from Gujarat depicts four birds around the central disc and is reminiscent of the animal style. The intricate jewellery of the various semi-nomadic herders like the Kanbe farming caste and also the Muslim herders called the Barri Kutch made use of the above techniques. They still wear the hansli torque made of coiled spring like wire. Also similar to the Śaka/Scythian jewellery are the silver 'tiger' anklets (Plate 213) worn by the Bharhard herder women of Saurashtra,[105] either made locally or in Mumbai.

A fragmentary pottery found from Vallabhipur, district Bhavnagar, Gujarat, depicts a bust probably of a Western Kshatrapa king. The bust is depicted within a dotted circle in low relief. The use of a dotted circle in ornaments, seals, plaques, coins and sculptured panels was typically nomadic in origin and had been incorporated in later styles with whom it had confronted.

Necklaces (Plate 214) of linked silver chains, with bells from Maharashtra,[106] and bracelets (Plate 215) of linked silver repoussê work from South India[107] all reflect Śaka/Scythian elements as found from both the western and eastern sections of the Scythian art. Specimens of soapstone rosettes with a beaded margin found in Prabhas Patan (Somnath, Junagadh District, Gujarat) were actually covered with gold foil reminiscent of the Tillya-tepe gold rosette plaques.[108] Gold plated earrings from Prabhas Patan Period III and a pulley-shaped jasper ear-stud having a gold plate with a repoussê pattern[109] are reminiscent of the Śaka/Scythian technology. During the Śaka-Satavahana period of ancient Indian history, the variety and amount of jewellery found on deities was at its peak.[110] A few Satavahana jewellery moulds (Plates 237 and 238) from Ter[111] are stylistically similar to those found at Taxila.[112] In the early eighties of the last century some beautiful oval-shaped terracotta earrings were found at Ter (Osmanabad District). They are now kept at the State Museum, Ter. A round pendant (probably part of an earring) in beige- terracotta shows a herd of elephants in different postures around a big tusker (facing the viewer). The style of the pendant (Plate 232)[113] is reminiscent of the animal style. The elephants have been shown in a vivid manner in all sorts of positions in two concentric rows around the tusker. Small terracotta plaques having a similar subject (i.e. elephants at Ter) have been found at Ahichchhatra from the Sâtavâhana period.[114] Two crescent type earrings (Plate 231)[115] from Ter attest to the nomadic influence. The cubic stone moulds[116] from Ter show the carving 'en creux', into which crescent earrings were made either of thin repoussê metal, or perhaps terracotta. The moulds (Plate 230) are presently in the Ter Museum. These Satavahana moulds are similar to some of the single moulds found at Taxila. Both the Taxilan and Satavahana moulds catered to the same technique of pressing a thin sheet of gold or silver into the fissures of the design or intended pattern (as in the mould). Once the impression is obtained, the final workings are manually done, of course, with the help of punchers and gravers.

Terracotta conical earrings[117] are found from the site at Bhokardan, Maharashtra. They belong to the post-Sâtavâhana period. Whether these conical earrings can be associated with the nomadic conical caps is a matter of conjecture. G. B. Deglurkar classifies some of the hollow cones[118] (similar to the conical earrings) without a hole as gamesmen. He reports that seven gamesmen were excavated in Period IA (second to third century B.C.), 24 in IB (first century B.C. to the second/third century A.D.), and 12 in Period II (post-Sâtavâhana till the third century A.D. onwards) while all the other earrings (cones with holes) were excavated during Period II. Reel or amphora type terracotta earrings could be a development from the conical shaped earrings. The former type of earrings can be still seen in Himachal Pradesh. Interestingly, crescent-shaped terracotta earrings were found from Bhokardan (Aurangabad District), recording the largest findings.[119] They belong to the Sâtavâhana period and perhaps Bhokardan was a manufacturing site.

During the early centuries of the Christian era, the coastal region of Western India became the focus of two major political powers the Satavahanas and the Śaka-Kshatrapas of Western India.[120] One of the dynasties of the Śaka-Kshatrapas of Western India, known by their coins and inscriptions, displaced the Satavahana for some time between the first and second centuries A.D. These Śakas are known as the Ksaharâtas. We know that during the period between 1st century B.C. and 2nd century A.D. the Kushanas were ruling in north India, the Kshatrapas in Gujarat, the Satavahanas in the Deccan, and the Cholas and Pandyas in the south. Apart from these centralized regional power bases and their administrative network ,this period also witnessed a significant trade economy based on Roman trade and contacts wih China via the silk route. There was a large inflow of gold and silver bullion into the subcontinent from the Roman empire in return for luxury commodities like ivory, silk, precious stones, perfume, pearl, indigo, etc. It was a sea-trade from several ports on the western and eastern coast and the Satavahanas and Kshatrapas, the then powerful rulers in this region, seemed to have controlled, to a large extent, the trade. Ports like Bharuch, Sopara and Kalyan on the western coast, Tamralipta, Masulipatnam and others on the east coast all testify to the archaeological evidence of the Roman trade. Guardian sculptures (Plate 239) flanking one of the cave entrances at Pitalkhora, Maharashtra, wear tunics with frilled edges and probably top boots[121] and probably they were Saka/Scythians employed by the Indian kings. The Posheri bronze cornucopia[122] (Plate 236) is stylistically very close to the Saka/Scythian artifacts, especially, the beaded bands below the upper scalloped edge, the vertical ribbings of the lower half, and the depiction of a terrible face having bulging eyes, snub nose and thick handle-bar moustache.

Archaeological excavations (November 2002) at Kasba Peth (Pune, Maharashtra) has yielded finds belonging to the early to late Satavahana (200 B.C. to 200 A.D.) and Vakataka (4-5th century A.D.) periods. The circumstantial evidence gives enough clue to the process of absorption in artistic activity between the indigenous and Saka-Scythian styles.Though the actual rescue excavation was carried out at Ashtekar Wada, the remains of an early habitation deposit were first identified at Lavalekar Wada. Both the sites[123] yielded pottery similar to that of the Satavahana period, which has also been found at sites around Pune, like at Bhosari. The detailed survey of the Kasba Peth area yielded similar ceramic types like varieties of globular pots with different rim forms like out-turned, beaded and constricted neck, carinated handis, shallow bowls, storage jars with heavy rounded or beaded rims, conical and dome-shaped lids with grooved rims. The pottery and the objects found are similar to those found in the Satavahana levels at Shirwal, Nevasa, Ter and Nasik. During the first century A.D., Bharuch in Gujarat and Kalyan in Maharashtra were two of the largest ports from where the external trade was conducted between India and Rome. Goods moved both towards the north via Ujjain, Mathura into the east to Pataliputra and north to Taxila and the south from Kalyan to Bhaja on the Western Ghats into Paithan which was the Satavahana capital and other regions of the Deccan. We were discussing the Kasba Peth area of Pune. Now, Pune is close to Bhaja. This external trade gave a boost to the internal crafts and led to a flourishing economy with social stability. This economic and social stability is reflected in the large religious donations that were made by trading families and craftsmen to the religious organizations as is seen from the inscriptions at cave sites like Karla, Bhaja, Nasik, etc.

Arambha, an excavated site in Maharashtra, has some amount of assemblage throwing light on the presence of non-Indian elements of art at Period III designated as Saka-Satavahana phase. A terracotta coin mould found from this site has been assigned to the Sakas.[124] However the specific information related to Scythian art requires separate investigation. Excavators pointed out that during the early historic period the occupants had exploited local resources including semi-precious stones and shells for the production of luxury objects for the supply of trading materials to the urban centres like Kaundinyapur, Adam and Pauni. We have already encountered art objects recorded from the said settlements revealing close association with the Saka/Scythian/Saka-Pahlava elements. Adam in the Wardha Wainganga divide, district Nagpur, has yielded (Period V) enough artifacts[125] betraying the nomadic influence. The ceramics include bowls, basins, dishes, lids and lid-cum-bowls. Techniques like stamping, incision, cording and appliquê were adopted for the decoration of the pottery. The motifs include *triratna* of different types, rosettes, swastikas, birds, hollow roundels and herring-bone patterns. Spouts of plain and decorated varieties were also found. Beads of semi-precious stones, copper and iron objects, and about 263 coins (including a significant number of Satavahana coins) were also found.

The contextual evidence related to the Saka/Scythian presence at the cultural assemblage recorded at Pauni could be realized in different ways. Firstly, the direct evidence justifies the assimilation of Indian and non-Indian cultural intercourse. The 'Indian' part had already assimilated enough Central Asian elements prior to its encounter with the nomadic influences (our main concern here). Excavations at

Pauni show that the site was habitated from pre-Mauryan to late medieval periods.[126] Secondly, the circumstantial evidence at Pauni gives enough clue (showing contemporary usages) about the process of absorption in artistic activity between the two (Indian/non-Indian). It may be stated that the contemporary Indian art emerged as a potential receptor for the absorption and feedback. Pauni, district Bhandara, Maharashtra, is 82 kms. due south-east of Nagpur and is about three kms south-west of Wainaganga, one of the most sacred rivers of the Vidarbha region. The location of Pauni and its close association with other Saka-Satavahana settlements like Ter give us an idea of the consistency of assimilation and the emergence of Scythian representation in the art of the sub-continent. A unique coin of the Saka Kshatrapas bearing the royal bust on the obverse has been found from Jagannatha Tekdi, Pauni. The palaeography of some of the epigraphic evidence can be put between 1st century B. C. and 2nd century A. D. With regard to pottery the circumstantial evidence included spouts and bowls with bevelled rims from Phase III at Pauni. This Phase is characterized by Red Polished Ware. R. P. W. is found from various sites in India in levels datable to 1st century B. C. to 4th-5th century A. D.[127] Excavations at Amreli, a Kshatrapa site in Saurashtra, has yielded much R.P.W. Artifacts from Chandakapur Tekdi, Pauni, may be put in a later time bracket than those from Jagannatha Tekdi (around circa 1st century B.C. to 2nd century A.D.). A copper punch-marked coin belonging to the early Satavahanas depicts a new variety of Taxila symbol comprising of a central boss with a crescent on either side and a fish or double-barbed arrowhead on the two remaining sides on the reverse.[128] The obverse of the same coin has *nandipada* motifs.

Paunar, district Wardha, Maharashtra, is a small village situated on the right bank of the river Dham, a tributary of Wardha. The Saka-Kshatrapas (during 2nd-3rd centuries A.D.) seem to have held sway over the Vidarbha region. At Paunar itself, a Kshatrapa coin has been found. Excavations[129] have revealed that the antiquity of Paunar goes back to the beginning of the first millennium B.C. and the site continued till the late medieval period. Carinated bowls, globular pots, lids, spouted pots, sprinklers and sherds of amphora-shaped vessels are significant yields of the ceramic assemblage of 2nd-3rd century A.D. Beads are more vocal in representing the Saka/Scythian element. Other than agate beads (biconical short cylinder, truncated barrel and octagonal faceted)[130], the triangular barrel-shaped carnelian beads have already been encountered in several northern sites in strata datable to 1st century B.C.-2nd century A.D. Terracotta lid-cum-covers having animal headed knobs and a *triratna* amulet[131] have also been found from the concerned strata. A votive tank, similar to those found from Taxila(in the Indo-Parthian levels) and Ahichchhatra(in A.D. 100-200 levels) has been found from Period IIA, Paunar. A fragmentary terracotta lion-mask (also found from Taxila and Nevasa) somehow attaches Paunar to the nomadic exposure.

The excavations at Benagutti, Sannati, district Gulbarga have brought to light a single culture deposit (1.05m) of Satavahana period. It consists of a large vihara-complex. Among the antiquarian remains are some sculptural fragments, some bearing inscriptions in Brahmi characters of third century B.C.[132] The red ware comprises of vessels of various sizes in shapes of globular pots, carinated handis, lid-cum-bowls, bowls and large storage vessels. Among the stamped motifs were noticed different varieties of *triratna* symbols of which a unique, highly stylised *triratna* with two *makara/matsya mukhas*, floral and geometric designs, is noteworthy. The latter example displayed a clear nomadic influence or its absorption in Indian style. What is interesting is that the appliquê designs were mostly confined to floral and finger pressed bands and cord impressions were restricted to loop designs. Loop designs held an important place both in the western and eastern sections of Scythian/Saka art. Some of the sculptured panels found during excavation at Kanaganahalli, Sannati, district Gulbarga are inscribed in Brahmi characters of first to third century A.D. recording donations made by common men, traders, kings and even a mendicant hailing from the Himalayas. The panels contain the portrait sculptures of Satavahana kings.

At Sambhar a plaque depicting a mythological scene and a Kïrttimukha made in gold leaf were found.[133] Brahmapuri hoards have yielded the largest number of copper and bronze objects revealing a highly advanced technique of metal work.[134] Among the objects, a wine jug with a trefoil rim and a lion-face handle has been found. The disc on which the lion's paw rests has traces of silver inlay in the pattern of tendrils surrounding the paw. It was originally soldered to the jug. A small vessel and its cover at Brahmapuri[135] has been engraved with the motif of galloping horse, panther and a bear, a lion, a winged mythical creature with eagle's beak, acquatic birds like geese and strange fish-shaped motifs. . The above carinated handi having thinly incised pattern of running animals in two bands recalls the famous torques discussed earlier.

A repoussê plaque of a mythical lion with beaked eagle's head (perhaps a decorative piece) was also found from the Brahmapuri hoard. Spouted pots with and without handles and having animal-shaped spouts were found from Sisupalgarh, Paunar and Maheshwar dated in the second century A.D.[136] Spouts in the form of bird's beaks were also found. Devnimori and Rangmahal have also yielded similar utility vessels. May be they were of specialized use on certain occasions.[137]. The Brahmapuri hoard has yielded a bronze piece, probably, a mace head consisting of a ring over which are four mythical creatures. It is almost Scythian in style. A smaller but similar piece was also found from the hoard. Another bronze attachment consisting of a griffin, mythical lion, standing with the right front paw lifted up may be surely associated with the Saka/Scythian atelier.

Decorative timberwork of Punjab and Kangra manufactured in the form of doors, door-surrounds, carved beams reflect nomadic traits. The brackets (Plate 217) supporting the projecting balconies have intricately interwoven struggling animal forms.[138] They belong to the medieval period or just earlier. These wooden brackets betray the nomadic influence. In Rajasthan, in the Shekhawati region and in some parts of Gujarat, wooden brackets (similar to the wooden reliefs of Pazyryk and Kuturguntas) are still used as architectural elements, and are strikingly similar to those found from Tibet (fragments of wooden doorways dated in the eleventh to twelvth centuries A.D.) Carved wooden pillars[139] from Gujarat with floral, animal and curving tendril designs somehow enmesh the nomadic style. Also wooden architectural elements (Plate 218) carved in the form of a horse and a lion (especially the lion in a square niche,[140] with curled tails) from Saurashtra, Gujarat, reflect the nomadic style.

Recent archaeological excavations in the Narmada valley, at the sites of Maruchichli and Chhalpakala have revealed some artifacts of the Kshatrapa and Satavahana periods.

A bidri-ware (bowl with a silver inlay) made in Bidar in the nineteenth century shows the design of concentric circles with swarming fishes around a central floral disc.[141] It is reminiscent of the bowl designs from Scythia. The manufacture of bidri-ware in Bidar was a local tradition during the 15th century; it is known that local rulers summoned metal workers from Persia (from where some nomadic elements or strains communicated). Incidentally, in Hyderabad, there is an Irani *gali* (lane of the Irânis), where workers beat the basic shape out of brass sheets and then decorate them with repoussê designs.

Ornaments manufactured at Mumbai (earlier known as Bombay) and Kolkata (earlier known as Calcutta) also depict the ancient nomadic motifs and techniques.

Bonding minute spheres of gold to a gold surface or simply granulation is still a favourite technique of the gold-smiths. On the other hand, repoussé (from the French "thrust back") in relief on thin metal beaten up from the reverse side, is another favourite. Necklaces made in Kolkata and Mumbai, still contain motifs which have been earlier encountered at Taxila (Plate 219)[142] and elsewhere in the nomadic world. This is apparent in the manufacture of gold necklaces (*jalli*) at Mumbai. The latter is characterized by square gold plaques, chased and ornamented with fine granulated work and united to the other by gold links and open-work pendants at the bottom.[143] The nomadic style is also apparent in the silver anklets and bracelets of open work design (and a ring of ball ornaments round the perimeter), from Mumbai.[144] Ornaments manufactured at Kolkata continue to reflect the nomadic tradition and style. Nepali Har,[145] a type of necklace, consists of inter-linked gold beads of various shapes (Plate 220) recalling the Śaka/Scythian types. Gold bracelets with *makara* head terminals (Plate 221)[146] obviously attest to the nomadic style. Small gold plaques (Plate 222) of various shapes[147] are used by the gold-smiths of Kolkata for the manufacture of small ornaments and parts of ornaments. Most of these motifs have been found in both the western and eastern sections of the Śaka/Scythian art. A type of bracelet (known as *chur* in Kolkata) has the trefoil[148] pattern framed (Plate 223A) in a row. Various arm ornaments from Kolkata continue reflecting (Plate 223B) the popular nomadic motifs. The trefoil plaques have been extensively found at Tillya-tepe. A jeweller's mould[149] of cast brass (Plate 224) is an interesting specimen depicting various motifs which have been deeply incised. It belongs to the twentieth century India. When a gold-smith needs to produce endless identical repetitions of small motifs, he may use a mould, hammering sheet gold or silver into a preformed depression on the metal block. This mould is probably as attractive as the jewellery it produced.

On careful consideration the Śaka/Scythian motifs are thus found to have been embedded in Indian culture. Even the popular apparel of *salwar-kâmeez* (this type of costume is popular throughout India and among the Indians living abroad), with its tunic and baggy pant, reflect the nomadic attire. As seen, jewellery of various forms and style continue to reflect the usages of the ancient nomadic motifs. Throughout the medieval and early modern period the nomadic motifs continued in Indian jewellery and metal craft. The motifs still continue in the modern period. Not only in jewellery but also in Indian textiles (produced from various states) the nomadic motifs percolate. An interesting brass lamp shade from Uttar Pradesh

(Plate 227) shows nomadic affiliations. It is similar to the openwork cone-shaped head-dress from Ak-Burun barrow.[150]

Going back to the north-west, (the region of transit of so many 'Indian' idioms) various objects still in use in the Swat valley, reflect the animal style. Some specimens are kept in the Linden Museum and they attest to the continuation and perhaps the re-creation of the Scythian art. These consist of wooden livestock amulets,[151] bells, simple everyday objects, and tools, like a drumstick, a catapult, a spindle, and a hammer. These are decorated by the carvers as if in homage to the Śaka/Scythian art of the eighth century B.C. to the fourth century A.D. The small selection of medicine spoons[152] from Swat are impressive evidences (Plate 225) that such items need not be boring; the individuality and creativity in the treatments of the handles is notable.

Large wooden ladles, with floral and geometric decorations,[153] also reflect the nomadic style. Ornaments like wrought silver neck rings with engraved and punched geometric decorations, earrings, arm-rings from Swat reveal the Śaka/Scythian elements. The component parts of pectoral ornaments (Plate 226)[154] found from the Swat valley echo the Śaka/Scythian elements.

Thus, these objects and tools were decorated by the carvers with the imagery of the Śaka/Scythian art of the eighth century B.C. to the fourth century A.D. The treatment of the individual tools, and their handles are an object lesson for designers. Their technique was steeped in the nomadic tradition, and at the same time it suited their practical functions. Animal amulets with geometric and simple plant motifs, rosettes and stylized ram's horns still continue. In other areas of the subcontinent the ram's heads gradually disappears, as it loses its shamanistic symbolism and sêance.[155] In India, ram's horns or stags are less common in the later period. In the early Scythian period, Siberian shamanism dominated. There the shamanistic seance was a symbolic journey in which the shaman becomes a horned animal (a deer or a reindeer) in order to restrain his animal wife, the daughter of the spirit of the forest.[156] This deer motif therefore ceased to be irrelevant in the Indian context.

Thus, we are seeing new phenomena or simply seeing the ancient Śaka/Scythian repertoire with a new vision. The obvious courage of treatment that so delights us and which only the large perception of the nomadic world can inspire, continues to be felt fairly strongly indeed in Indian art. More information for tracing the nomadic tradition in Indian art is encouraging us to extend our understanding about the influence of the Saka/Scythian element. The scope of further elaboration in this issue is amazing and requires refinement of assemblage, analysis and interpretation of the stylistic factors in search of a more coherent picture.

References

1. *Hist. Civ. Cen. As.*, Vol. II, p.203.
2. K. Krishna Murthy, 'The Domestic Art Delineated in the Gandhara Reliefs', *Puratattva*, No.7, 1976-77, pp.96-103.
3. Haruko Tsuchiya , 'An Iconographical Study Of The Buddhist Art Of Shotorak, Paitâva And Khan Zargar', *Silk Road Art And Archaeology,* 2000, Vol. 6, p.100.
4. *Dyn. Art. Kus.* Pl.99a
5. *Ibid.,* Pl.98a.
6. *Ibid.,* Pl.102.
7. *Ibid.,* Pl.103.
8. *Ibid.,* Pl.62a.
9. *Ibid.,* Pl.104.
10. *Gol. Tre. Jew. Ind.*, p.20, Pl.17. cf. also Hugh Tait (ed.), *Seven Thousand Years of Jewellery,* British Museum, London, 1986, No. 535.
11. *Ear. Orn. Anc. Ind.*, p.37, Fig.I. 45.
12. J. C. Harle, 'Artefacts of the Historical Period from Bannu', *South Asian Archaeology* 1987 *Part 2*, Rome, 1990, p.649.
13. Osmund Bopearachchi, 'The Arsacid Empire : Sources and Documentation', *Das Partherreich Und Seine Zeugnisse,* Stuttgart, 1998, p.396.
14. *Ibid.,* p.399.
15. G. Huxley, 'Geography in the Acts of Thomas', *Greek, Roman and Byzantine Studies,* 24, 1983, p.75.
16. W.H.Schoff, *Periplus of The Erythraean Sea,* New York, 1912, p.60.
17. *Hist. Rus. Cen. Asi. Mon.*, Vol. I, p.127.
18. G.S.Gaur, 'Semathan Excavation; A Step Towards Bridging the gap between the Neolithic and the Kushâna Period in Kashmir', *Archaeology and History,* Vol. 1, 1987, p.133.
19. Cf. M.Y.Treister's article cited in Footnote No. 21 in Chapter V, p.80, Fig.9.
20. V.Sarianidi, *Khram i Nekropol' Tillya-tepe,*Moscow, 1989, p.66, Fig.23.
21. R.C.Kak, *Ancient Monuments of Kashmir,* p.107.
22. B.N.Mukherjee, *India in Early Central Asia,* New Delhi, 1966, p.11.
23. R.C.Kak, *op. cit.*, Pls. XX. VIII, Figs.17, 18.
24. Catalogue No. M. 81. 153. 2, Indian Art Special Purposes Fund; The Los Angeles County Museum of Art.
25. Chandra L. Reedy, *Himalayan Bronzes: Technology, Style And Choices,* 1997, p.151, Pl.k 32.
26. P.Pal, *Bronzes of Kashmir,* p.70, Pl.II. abc.
27. Giuseppe Tucci, *TransHimalaya* , Archaeologia Mundi, Geneva, 1973, Pl.8.

28. *Ibid.,* Pl.151.
29. *Ibid.,* Pl.154.
30. B. R. Mani, 'Excavations at Ambaran 1999-2001: Akhnur Terracotta and Discovery of Buddhist Reliquary in Exposed Stupa', H. P. Ray and C. Sinopoli ed., *Archaeology as History in early South Asia*, New Delhi, 2004, p.392.
31. *Fol. Tri. Des. Ind.*, p.25.
32. *Ind. Jew.*, Pl.XLIII, No. 6.
33. *Bac. Gol.*, Pl.64.
34. John Gillow, Bryan Sentance, *A Visual Guide to Traditional Techniques. World Textile*, London, 1999, p.156.
35. P. Pal, *The Arts of Nepal*, Vol. 1, p.142, Fig.34.
36. Subhasini Aryan, *Crafts of Himachal Pradesh,* 1993, pp.88, 24.
37. Arun Kumar Singh, 'Ganesha Images in Himachal Pradesh. An Iconographical Study', *Purâtattva* , 33, Nov.-Dec., 2003, New Delhi, pp.150, 151.
38. *Ind. Jew.*, Pl.XII, No. 1.
39. Rustam J. Mehta, *Handicrafts and Industrial Arts of India*, Bombay, 1960, Pl.XI, No. 2.
40. *Fol. Tri. Des. Ind.*, Pl.59.
41. *Ibid.*, Pl.59.
42. *Ear. Orn. Anc. Ind.*, p.318, Fig.A 12.51
43. *Ibid.*, p.315, Fig.A 12.42.
44. M. Postel, A.Neven, K.Mankodi, *Antiquities of Himachal,* 1985, p.99.
45. *Ibid.*, pp.82-86.
46. D. Handa, *Buddhist Remains from Haryana*, New Delhi, 2004.
47. R.C. Thakran, *Dynamics of Settlement Archaeology,* New Delhi, 2000, p.23.
48. *Ibid.*, p.281.
49. *Ind. Jew.*, Pl.XXXIX.
50. *Ibid.*, Pl.XVI, No. 1.
51. D. Handa, *Jaina Brozes from Hansi,* Simla, New Delhi, 2002, p.29.
52. *Ibid.*, Pls. 44a, 43a, b.
53. Dilip K. Chakrabarti, S.J.Hasan, *Antiquities of Kangra,* New Delhi, 1982, pp.28-29.
54. *Ibid.*, p.58.
55. *Ibid.*, Pl.20.
56. Stella Kramrisch, *The Hindu Temple*, New Delhi, 1976, Vol. II, p.323.
57. *Ibid.*, Vol. II, p.323.
58. R. C. Gaur, *Excavations at Atranjikhera*, Delhi, 1983, p.447.
59. *Ibid.*, Pl.CI A.
60. *Ibid.*, Pl.CVI B.
61. *Purātattva*, No. 6, 1972-73, Plate V (a).
62. *Indian Archaeology 1996-97-A Review*, p.111, fig.9.

63. *Ibid.*, p.151
64. A. K. Kanungo and V. S. Shinde, 'Excavation at Kopia 2005: A Preliminary Report', *Purātattva*, No. 35, 2004-2005, Pl.8.
65. D. P. Tewari and D. K. Srivastava, 'Excavations at Sanchankot, District Unnao, U.P. (2004-05), *Purātattva*, No 35, 2004-2005, p.186.
66. A. Ghosh, K.C.Panigrahi, 'Pottery of Ahichchhatra', *Ancient India* , 1946, No. 1, p.46.
67. V.S.Agrawala, 'Terracotta figurines of Ahichchhatra', *Ancient India* , No. 4. 1947- 48, pp. 125-126.
68. G.R.Sharma, 'Excavations at Kausambi, 1949-50', *Memoirs of The Archaeological Survey of India* , No. 74, Fig.34.
69. G.R.Sharma, '*Excavations at Kausambi, 1957-59*', Pl.XXXB.
70. P.Singh, *Exacavations at Narhan 1984-89,* 1994, p.209.
71. Barbara Stoler Miller, *Exploring India's Sacred Art*, New Delhi,1994, p.78.
72. *Ibid.*, p.83, Pl.3-2. II.
73. Herbert Härtel, *Excavations at Sonkh,* Berlin, 1993, p.112.
74. *Ibid.*, p.140, Pl.148.
75. Pratapaditya Pal, *The Peaceful Liberators : Jain Art from India,* Los Angeles County Museum of Art, 1994, p.169.
76. *Hist. Cul. Ind. Peo.,Clas. Ag.*, p.559.
77. *Ibid.*, p.557.
78. Anjan Chakravarty, 'A Mauryan Stone-Disc from Râjghât', *Kalâ.*,Vol. VIII, New Delhi, 2003, p.137.
79. *Hist. Cul. Ind. Peo.,Clas. Ag.*, p.555.
80. Debjani Paul, *The Art of Nâlandâ,* Enschede,1987, Pl.2.
81. Madanjeet Singh, *Ajanta : Painting of the Sacred and the Secular,* New York, 1965, p.43, Pl.20.
82. Debjani Paul, *op.cit.*, Pl.7.
83. *Ibid.*, p.46.
84. *Ibid.*, p.84, Pls. 65-68.
85. *Ear. Orn. Anc. Ind.*, p.311, Fig.A 12.35.
86. *Ibid.*, p.316, Fig.A 12.46.
87. *Fol. Tri. Des. Ind.*, Pl.54.
88. *Ibid.*, Pl.55.
89. *Ibid.*, Pl.58.
90. *Ind. Jew.*, p.92, Fig.1; p.98, Figs. 1-13.
91. *Ibid.*, p.101, Figs. 1-5.
92. *Ear. Orn. Anc. Ind.*, p.118, Fig.V.49; p.119, Figs. V.50, V.51.
93. Baldev Singh Negi, "Explorations along the Banganga River, District Bharatpur, Rajasthan", *Purātattva*, No. 17, 1986-87, p.5.
94. Elizabeth Rosen Stone, *The Buddhist Art of Nagarjunakonda,* New Delhi, 1994, p.69.

95. *Ibid.*, Fig.232.
96. E.Haque, *Chandraketugarh,* Studies in Bengal Art Series, No. 4, Dhaka, 2001, p.88.
97. A. K. Prasad, 'Important Discoveries of Prehistoric Rock Paintigs, Ancient Inscriptions and Stone Age Tools in Southern Bihar and Adjoining Jharkhand', *Purātattva*, No.34, 2003-2004, p.68.
98. R. N. Kumaran, M. K. Dwivedi and V. D. Jadhav, 'Iron Objects from Hathab', *Purātattva*, No. 34, 2003-2004, p.91.
99. *Ibid.*, p.93.
100. A.G.Irani, 'Archaeology of the Settlement of the Kshatrapa Period',*Purâtattva,* 1997-98, No. 28, p.77.
101. Syed Anis Hashim, 'Ethno-Archaeology of the Traditional Ceremonial Pottery of Gujarat', *Purātattva*, No. 19, 1988-89, p.61, Figs. a, b and c.
102. *Ear. Orn. Anc. Ind.*, p.317, Fig.A 12.57.
103. *Ibid.*, p.310, Fig.A 12.33, the 2nd example.
104. *Ibid.*, p.307, Fig.A 12.24, the 2nd example.
105. Ilay Cooper, John Gillow, *Arts and Crafts of India,* Thames and Hudson, 2001 , p.84, Pl.64.
106. *Ibid.*, p.84, Pl.67.
107. *Ibid.*, p.84, Pl.68.
108. M.K.Dhavalikar, *Sâtavâhana Art,* New Delhi, 2004, p.103.
109. *Indian Archaeology,* 1956-57, p.17, Pl.XVIIIA.
110. *Ear. Orn. Anc. Ind.*, p.2.
111. M.K.Dhavalikar, *op.cit.*, Pl.LIX, LX.
112. *Taxila,* Vol. II, p.507.
113. *Ear. Orn. Anc. Ind.*, p.18, Fig.I.19.
114. V.S.Agrawala, *op.cit.*, p.162.
115. *Ear. Orn. Anc. Ind.*, p.27, Fig.I.30.
116. *Ibid.*, p.27, Fig.I.28.
117. G.B.Deglurkar, *Excavations at Bhokardan*, 1973, Fig.30,Nos. 45-52.
118. *Ibid.*, p.161, Fig.32, Nos. 1-18.
119. S.B.Deo, R.S.Gupte, *Excavations at Bhokardan*, 1974, Pl.XLIII.
120. C.Margabandhu, *Archaeology of the Sâtavâhana Kshatrapa Times,* Delhi, 1985, p. 4.
121. M. K. Dhavalikar, *Satavahana Art*, New Delhi, 2004, Pl.XV.
122. *Ibid.*, Pl.XL.
123. Vasant Shinde et al., "New Light on the History of Pune City: Results of an Archaeological Rescue Excavation", *Purātattva*, No. 33, 2002-2003, p.53.
124. Amarendra Nath, 'Arambha: a Vakataka Site in Vidarbha', *Purātattva*, No.22, 1991-92, p.70.
125. Amarendra Nath, 'Archaeology of the Wardha Wainganga Divide, *Purātattva*, No.20, 1989-90, p.95.
126. S. B. Deo and J. P. Joshi, *Pauni Excavation 1969-70*, Nagpur, 1972, p.8.

127. H. D. Sankalia, B. Subbarao and S. B. Deo, *Excavations at Maheshwar and Navdatoli*, 1958, p.161.
128. Allan, *BMCAI*, Pl.III, 10, 12, 14-15.
129. S.B.Deo and M.K.Dhavalikar, *Paunar Excavation 1967*, Nagpur, 1968, p.3.
130. *Ibid.*, p.78.
131. *Ibid.*, Fig.25, No.48.
132. *Indian Archaeology 1997-98-A Review*, p.80.
133. *Ibid.*, p.77.
134. *Ibid.*, p.78.
135. Karl Khandalawala, *Lalit Kalâ,* 7, 1960, Pl.XIX, F26-31,Pl.XX,32.4.
136. C.Margabandhu, *op.cit.*, pp.126-127.
137. *Ibid.*, p.127.
138. Ilay Cooper, John Gillow, *op.cit.*, p.32.
139. *Fol. Tri. Des. Ind.*, Pl.68.
140. Ilay Cooper, John Gillow, ,*op.cit.*, p.53, Pls. 40, 41.
141. *Ibid.*, p.61.
142. *Taxila*, Vol. III, Pl.193, nos. 56, 57, 58.
143. *Ind. Jew.*, Pl.XXIV, No.2.
144. Rustam J.Mehta, *op. cit.*, Pl.XI, No.3.
145. *J.K. Das and Co. No.34,* Calcutta, Cat.No.207.
146. *Ibid.*, Cat.No. 308.
147. *Ibid.*, Cat.No. 365.
148. *Ibid.*, Cat.No. 328.
149. *Gol. Tre. Jew. Ind.*, Victoria and Albert Museum, London, 1988, Pl.125.
150. *Scy.Art.*, Pl.229.
151. Johannes Kalter, *The Arts and Crafts of the Swat Valley. Living Traditions in the Hindu Kush,* Thames and Hudson, 1991, p.12, Fig.7.
152. *Ibid.*, p.13, Fig.9.
153. *Ibid.*, p.12, Fig.6.
154. *Ibid.*, p.102.
155. Gilles Boileau, 'Wu and Shaman', *Bulletin of the School of Oriental and African Studies*, Vol.65, part 2, London, 2002, p.353.
156. *Ibid.*, p.353.

EPILOGUE

This 'interior report' tried to analyze, in a very preliminary way the Saka/Scythian elements in early Indian art.

It is around the immoveable trinity of Egypt, the Orient and the Graeco-Roman world, whether we have a clear conscience of it or not, that our well-established habits and customs of today, lead us, to organize our vision of the civilizations of antiquity. The Śaka-Siberian-Scythian art can no longer be termed 'peripheric', nor, at most be regarded as a receptacle of influences of great civilizations. It had its own measure of intellect, space and form.

To put it scientifically, the archaeological evidences do not remain silent about the impact on the vast stretches of the Eurasian steppes, of what was the nomadic life's greatest treasure, i.e., the ornamenting influence of nomadic art. The homogeneity of the vast stretches of the Eurasian steppes did not for once lead to the loss of the nomadic identity. On the other hand, their 'art' is a potent distillation of nomadic and sedentary ways of life.

The steppe nomads left behind no written testimonies to their beliefs and practices. Scholars, therefore, in their efforts to understand them depend on archaeological evidences, on royal chronicles of the Near East and China, and on

Greek and Roman authors most of whom wrote about what was interesting and relevant to them, not necessarily to art historians, historians and archaeologists today. Often, the archaeological evidence falls apart with the written evidence. The artifacts have been classified under the western and eastern sections and it is clear that the origin lay in the east, before traversing to the west. Cross currents and individual developments in both the sections finally formed the 'whole' repertoire. The differences in the style, technique and character of the nomadic animal style continued in the Śaka/Scythian elements in early Indian art. The Śaka/Scythian elements in Indian art were essentially a continuation of the "whole' repertoire, with its accompanying changes. The question of visualizing a new phenomenon or simply seeing older patterns with a new clarity did not necessarily arise. We find that the cherished Scytho-Siberian-Śaka-motifs continued to evolve, at the same time, not losing their essential animal style. However they have been quite liberal with the contours of their basic structure. Not surprisingly, perhaps, the very formation of 'statehood' brought an end to the distinctive early nomadic way of life (as archaeological evidences reveal) by the first century B.C., but art forms (the legacy of which can be visualized) obviously continued. We all are acquainted with the opinions of Peter.B.Golden and Omeljan Pritsak on 'statehood', but it is startling to find that the nomadic style continued in later periods of oriental and occidental art. Will it be too much to say that even in the present Post-Raj India, the furniture we see around us, bear the animal style in all its ornamental appendages? Of course it is a Victorian legacy. The predecessors of the British had learnt it from their 'barbarian' antecedents.

The discussions in the above chapters are basically preliminary in nature towards understanding the Śaka/Scythian elements in the early art of India. Therefore, it is very difficult to conceive all these elements in a conclusive way; they are rather suggestive. I have also tried to postulate that the Śaka/Scythian traits are still part of the living tradition of Indian art. Surely they are enmeshed in the composite Indian culture.

It is possible that there will be equally sensational finds in the future which would lead to a better understanding of the Śaka/Scythian art.

All art originates in the human mind, in our reaction to the world rather than in the visible world itself, and it is precisely because all art is 'conceptual' that all representations are recognizable by their styles.

ABBREVIATIONS

Agr. So. Imp. Par. Hist.	*An Agrippan Source-A Study in Indo-Parthian History*, by B. N. Mukherjee, Calcutta, 1970.
Am. Journ Arch.	*American Journal of Archaeology,* Chicago.
A.N.	*Akademiya Nauk* (Academy of Sciences), Leningrad, Moscow.
Anc. Civ. Scy. Sib.	*Ancient Civilizations From Scythia to Siberia*, Leiden.
A.S.G.E.	*Archaeological Collection from the State Hermitage Museum*, St.Petersburg.
A.S.I.A.R.	*Archaeological Survey of India, Annual Reports*, Calcutta and Delhi.
Art. Scy.	*The Art of The Scythians*, by E. Jacobson, Leiden, 1995.
Bac. Gol.	*Bactrian Gold*, by V. Sarianidi, Leningrad, 1985.
B.M.F.E.A.	*Bulletin of the Museum of Far Eastern Antiquities,* Stockholm, Sweden.
B.S.O.A.S.	*Bulletin of the School of Oriental and African Studies,* London.
Cat. Co. Ind. Mus.	*Catalogue of Coins in the Indian Museum,* by V. A. Smith, Calcutta, Vol. I, Oxford, 1906.
C.C.G.S.K.	*A Catalogue of Indian Coins in the British Museum, The Coins of the Greek and Scythic Kings of Bactria*

	and India In the British Museum, by P. Gardner, London, 1886.
C.H.I.	*The Cambridge History of India,* edited by E. J. Rapson, Vol.I-*Ancient India*, Cambridge, 1922.
C.H.S.	Pan Ku, *Ch'ien Han-shu,* (T'ung-wen Shu-chý edition).
Cor. Ins. Ind.	*Corpus Inscriptionum Indicarum*, Calcutta,1929.
Dyn. Art. Kus.	*The Dynastic Arts of the Kushanas,* by J. M. Rosenfield, Berkeley, 1967.
Ear. Orn. Anc. Ind.	*Ear Ornaments of Ancient India*, by M.Postel, Bombay, 1989.
En. Wor. Art.	*Encyclopaedia of World Art*, (published by the McGraw Hill Company, New York), Vol. I-XV, 1959-68.
Ep. Ind.	*Epigraphia Indica*, Calcutta and Delhi.
Epitome.	*Epitoma Historiarum Philippicarum,* Accedunt Prologi in Pompeium Trogum, (edited by Seel, Otto., Leipzig, 1935).
Fol. Tri. Des. Ind.	*Folk and Tribal Designs of India*, by E. Bhavnani, Bombay, 1974.
Geog. Cla. Pt.	*Geography of Claudius Ptolemy*, Bk. VI, edited by E. L. Stevenson, New York, 1932.
Geog. Hup.	*Geographike Huphegesis,* by Ptolemy, edited by C.F.A. Nobbe, 3 Vols., Leipzig, 1898.
Geographikon.	*Geographikon,* by Strabo, Loeb Classical Library edition, 8 Vols. Reprint, London & Cambridge, Mass., 1959-1961.
Gol. De. Eur.	*The Golden Deer of Eurasia*, edited by J. Aruz *et al.*, New York, 2000.
Gol. Tre. Jew. Ind.	*A Golden Treasury, Jewellery from the Indian Subcontinent*, by S. Stronge, N. Smith, J. C. Harle, London, 1988.
H.H.S.	Fan Yeh, *Hou Han-shu,* (Ssu-pu pie-yao edition).

His. Ad. Pag.	*Historiarum Adversum Paganos Libri VII,* by P. Orosius, edited by C. Zangemeister, Liepzig, 1889.
Hist.	*Historiae,* by Herodotus, edited by C. Huide, Oxford, 1926.
Hist. Civ. Cen. As.	*History of Civilizations of Central Asia*, Delhi, 1999.
Hist. Cul. Ind. Peo. Clas. Ag.	*The History and Culture of the Indian People,* Vol.III- *The Classical Age*, edited by R. C. Majumdar, Bharatiya Vidya Bhavan, Bombay, 1970.
Hist. Rus. Cen. Asi. Mon.	*A History of Russia, Central Asia and Mongolia.*, by D. Christian, Oxford, 1998.
I.B.I.A.S.S.C.A.	*Information Bulletin, International Association for the Study of the Cultures of Central Asia,* Moscow.
I. H. Q.	*The Indian Historical Quarterly*, Calcutta.
Ind. Jew.	*Indian Jewellery, Ornaments and Decorative Designs*, by J. B. Bhushan, Bombay, 1957.
J.A.I.	*The Journal of the Anthropological Institute of Great Britain and Ireland*, London.
J.A.S.	*Journal of the Asiatic Society*, Calcutta.
Jour. Num.Soc.Ind.	*Journal of The Numismatic Society of India*, Calcutta, Bombay and Varanasi.
J.I.S.O.A.	*Journal of the Indian Society of Oriental Art,* Baroda.
K.S.I.I.M.K.	*Kratkiye soobshcheniya Instituta istorii material'noy kul'tury,* (Brief reports from the Institute of the history of material culture, AN), Moscow.
Nat.Hist.	*Naturalis Historiae* by Pliny, Loeb Classical Library edition, 10 Vols., London and Cambridge, Mass., 1956-1963.
N.D.	*Naukova Dumka*, Moscow.
Num.Chr.	*Numismatic Chronicle* (and *Journal of the Royal Numismatic Society*), London.
Periplus	*Periplous Tes Erythras Thalasses* or *Periplus Maris Erythraei* (Frisk, H.(editor), *Le Pêriple de la Mar Ūrythrêe,* Göteborg, 1927.)

Pun.Mus.Cat.	*Catalogue of Coins in the Punjab Museum*, by R. B. Whitehead, Vol. I-*Indo-Greek Coins*, Oxford, 1914.
Scy.Art.	*Scythian Art*, by B.Piotrovsky, etc., Leningrad, 1986.
Sov.Arkh.	*Sovetskaya Arkheologiya,* (Soviet Archaeology), Moscow.
Stat.Par.	*The Parthian Stations by Isidore of Charax*, edited by W. H. Schoff, Philadelphia, 1914.
Taxila	*Taxila, An Illustrated Account of Archaeological Excavations Carried Out Under the Order of the Government of India Between the Years 1913 and 1934* ,by J.Marshall, 3 Vols.,Cambridge, 1951; Reprint, New Delhi, 1975.
V.D.I.	*Vestnik Drevnei Istorii*, Moscow.

BIBLIOGRAPHY

A. BOOKS

Adhya, G. *Early Indian Economics*, Bombay, 1966.

Agrawala, V.S. *Masterpieces of Mathura Sculpture,* Varanasi, 1965.

Akishev, K.A. *Kurgan Issyk,* Moscow, 1978.

Artamonov, M.I. *Sokrovischa Sakov,* Moscow, 1973.

Aruz, Joan; Farkas, Ann; Alekseev, Andrei; Korolkova, Elena, ed, *The Golden Deer of Eurasia,* The Metropolitan Museum of Art, New York 2000.

Aryan, Subhasini *Crafts of Himachal Pradesh* , Delhi, 1993.

Bailey, H.W. *The Culture of the Úakas in Ancient Iranian Khotān,* New York, 1982.

Basilov, V.N. (ed). *Nomads of Eurasia,* Seattle and London: Natural History Museum of Los Angeles County and The University of Washington Press, 1989.

Bhavnani, Enakshi. *Folk and Tribal Designs of India*, Bombay, 1974.

Bhushan,J.B. *Indian Jewellery, Ornaments and Decorative Designs*, Bombay,1957.

Blavatskiy, V.D. *Art of the Northern Black Sea in Antiquity*, Moscow, 1947.

Boardman, J. *Greek Sculpture: The Classical Period* , London: Thames and Hudson, 1992.

Borovka, G.I. *Scythian Art* , New York, 1967.

Chakrabarti, Dilip K. and Hasan, J., *Antiquities of Kangra,* New Delhi,1982.

Chang, K.C. *The Archaeology of Ancient China*, New Haven and London, Yale University Press, 3rd ed. 1977.

Christian, D. *A History of Russia, Central Asia and Mongolia,* Vol 1. Blackwell Publishers, Oxford, 1998.

Colledge, M.A.R., *Parthian Art,* London, 1977.

Cooper, Ilay. Gillow, J. *Arts and Crafts of India,* Thames and Hudson, London,2001.

Cribb, R. *Nomads in Archaeology,* Cambridge, 1993.

Dalton, O.M. *The Treasure of the Oxus.* London: The Trustees of the British Museum, 1964.

Das, J.K. and Co. *Catalogue, No.34*, Calcutta, 1960.

Davis-Kimball, J; Bashilov, V.A. et al., *Nomads of the Eurasian Steppes in the*

Early Iron Age, (Centre for the Study of Eurasian Nomads, Berkeley, California, Zinat Press, 1995.)

Deglurkar, G.B. *Excavations at Bhokardan,* New Delhi,1973.

Deo, S.B; Gupte, R.S. *Excavations at Bhakardan,* New Delhi, 1974.

Dhavalikar, M.K. *Sātavāhana Art* . New Delhi, 2004.

Encyclopaedia of Asian History, Collier, McMillan, London, 1988.

Encyclopaedia of World Art, McGraw Hill Co., New York, vols.I-XV, 1959-68.

Frumkin, G. *Archaeology in Soviet Central Asia,* Leiden, 1970.

Gaur, R. C. *Excavations at Atranjikhera*, Delhi, 1983.

Ghirshman, R. *The Arts of Ancient Iran,* New York 1964.

Ghirshman, R. *Iran from the Earliest Times to the Islamic Conquest*, London, 1954.

Gillow, John; Sentence, Bryan. *A Visual Guide to Traditional Techniques. World Textiles,* Thames and Hudson, London, 1999.

Grakov, B.N. *The Scythians,* Moscow, 1971.

Handa, D. *Jaina Brozes from Hansi,* Simla, New Delhi, 2002.

Handa, D. *Buddhist Remains from Haryana*, New Delhi, 2004.

Harmatta, Janos; Puri, B.N; Etemadi, G.F.(editors) *History Of Civilizations Of Central Asia,* Delhi, 1999.

Härtel, H. *Excavations at Sonkh* , Berlin, 1993.

Haque, E. *Chandraketugarh,* Studies in Bengal Art Series, No. 4, Dhaka, 2001.

Higgins, R. *Jewellery from Classical Lands*, London: The British Museum, 1965.

Higgins, R. *Greek and Roman Jewellery,* Berkeley and Los Angeles: University of California Press, 1980.

Holt, F. *Alexander the Great and Bactria: The Formation of a Greek Frontier in Central Asia,* Leiden, 1988.

Jacobson, Esther '*The Art of the Scythians', The Interpenetration of Cultures at The Edge of the Hellenic World*, E.J.Brill, Leiden, 1995.

Kak, R.C. *Ancient Monuments of Kashmir*. New Delhi, 1971.

Kalter, Johannes *The Arts and Crafts of the Swat Valley. Living Traditions in the Hindu Kush,* Thames and Hudson, 1991.

Khazanov, A.M. *Nomads and the Outside World*, Cambridge, 1984.

Khazanov, A.M. *Scythian Goldwork*, Moscow, 1975.

Koshelenko and Pilipko, 'Parthia', *History of Civilizations of Central Asia,* Vol.II, New Delhi, 1999.

Kramrisch, S. *The Hindu Temple* , New Delhi, 1976, Vol. II.

Kubarev, V.D. *Kurgany Ulandryka*, Novosibirsk, Nauka, 1987.

Litvinsky, B.A; Guang-Da, Zhang; Samghabadi, R. Shabani. *History of Civilizations of Central Asia,* Vol. III, New Delhi, 1999.

Lordkipanidze, O.D; Mikeladze, T.K. *Le trêsor de Gonio*, Tbilisi, 1980.

Majumdar, R.C. ed, *The History and Culture of the Indian People, The Age of Imperial Unity,* Bharatiya Vidya Bhaban, Bombay, 1970.

Majumdar, R.C. ed, *The History and Culture of The Indian People, The Classical Age* , Bharatiya Vidya Bhavan, Bombay, 1970.

Margabandhu, C. *Archaeology of the Sātavāhana Kshatrapa Times,* Delhi, 1985.

Marshall, J. *Taxila, An Illustrated Account of Archaeological Excavations Carried out under the Order of the Government of India Between the Years 1913 and 1934* , 3 Vols., Cambridge, 1951; Reprint, New Delhi, 1975.

Masson, M; Pugachenkova, G. *Parthian Rhytons from Nisa*, Moscow, 1956.

Mehta, Rustam J. *Handicrafts and Industrial Arts of India*, Bombay,1960.

Minns, Ellis H. *Scythians and Greeks: A Survey of Ancient History and Archaeology on the North Coast of the Euxine from the Danube to the Caucasus*, Cambridge, 1913.

Mitchiner, M. *Indo-Greek and Indo-Scythian Coinage,* London, Vol.1, 1975.

Mukherjee, B.N. *An Agrippan Source—A Study in Indo-Parthian History*, Calcutta, 1970.

Mukherjee, B.N. *India in early Central Asia*, New Delhi, 1966.

Mukherjee, B.N. *Kushāna Silver Coinage*, Indian Museum, Calcutta, 1982.

Pal, P. *The Arts of Nepal,* Vol.1. Leiden, 1974.

Pal, P. *Bronzes of Kashmir*. New York, 1975.

Pal, P. *The Peaceful Liberators: Jain Art from India,* Thames and Hudson, Los Angeles County Museum of Art, 1994.

Paul, Debjani. *The Art of Nālandā*, Enschede, 1987.

Piotrovsky, B.B; Galanina, L.K; Grach, N.L. *Scythian Art*, Leningrad, 1987.

Postel, M. *Ear Ornaments of Ancient India*, Bombay, 1989.

Postel, M; Neven, A; Mankodi, K. *Antiquities of Himachal*, 1985.

Pugachenkova, G.A. *Iskusstvo Gandkhary*, Moscow, 1982.

Pugachenkova, G.A. *Drevnosti Miankalya*, Taskent, 1989.

Ray, H. *Trade and Trade Routes Between India and China*, Calcutta, 2003.

Raychoudhuri, H.C. *Political History of Ancient India,* Delhi, 1996 (8th ed.).

Reedy, C.L. *Himalayan Bronzes: Technology, Style and Choices,* Simla, 1997.

Rosenfield, J.M. *The Dynastic Arts of the Kushans* , New Delhi, 1993.

Rostovtsev, M.I. *Animal Style in South Russia and China* , Princeton, 1929.

Rostovtsev, M.I. *Scythia and the Bosporus*, Leningrad, 1925.

Sarianidi, V. *Bactrian Gold*, Leningrad, 1985.

Sarianidi, V. *Khram i neckropol' Tillya-tepe*, Moscow, 1989.

Schaller, G. B. *Mountain Monarchs, Wild Sheep and Goats of the Himalaya*, the University of Chicago Press, London 1977.

Schiltz, V. *Les Scythes et les Nomades des Steppes*, Gallimard, Paris, 1994.

Schoff, W.H. *Periplus of The Erythraean Sea,* New York , 1912.

Schoff, W.H. *The Parthian Stations by Isidore of Charax*, Philadelphia, 1914.

Sellwood, D. *An Introduction to the Coinage of Parthia*, London, 1980.

Singh, M. *Ajanta:Painting of the Sacred and the Secular,* New York, 1965.

Singh, P. *Exacavations at Narhan 1984-89,* Department of A.I.H.C.(BHU), 1994.

Sinor, D. (ed.) *The Cambridge History of Early Inner Asia,* Cambrige, 1990.

Srivastava, A. K. *Catalogue of Saka-Pahlava Coins of North India*, Lucknow, 1972.

Stein, M.A. *Ancient Khotan.*, Oxford, 1907 (reprint; New Delhi, 1988).

Stevenson, E. L. (Translated and edited) *Geography of Claudius Ptolemy*, Bk. VI, New-York, 1932.

Stronge, S; Smith, Nima; Harle, J.C. *A Golden Treasury; Jewellery from the India subcontinent* . Victoria and Albert Museum, London,1988.

Sutherland, C.H.V. *Gold*, McGraw-Hill, New York, 1969.

Thakran, R.C. *Dynamics of Settlement Archaeology,* New Delhi, 2000.

Tucci, G. *Trans Himalaya* , Archaeologia Mundi, Geneva, 1973.

Turner, Jane. ed., *Dictionary of Art*, Cambridge, 1994.

Vainshtein, S. *Nomads of South Siberia:The Pastoral Economies of Tuva*, Cambridge, 1980.

Van Lohuizen-de Leeuw, J.E. *The Scythian Period*, Leiden, 1949.

Vogel, J. Ph. *Catalogue of the Archaeological Museum at Mathurā*, Allahabad, 1910.

Watson, B. *Records of the Grand Historian of China*, New York, 1961.

Zasetskaya, I.P. *Zolotye ukrasheniya gunnskoi epokhi*, Leningrad, 1975.

Zhebelev, S.A. *Severnoye Prichernomor'ye*, Moscow-Leningrad, A.N., 1953.

Zhukovskaya, N.L. *Kategorii i Synvolika Traditsionnoi Kulturi Mongolov*, Moscow, 1988.

Zwalf, W. *A Catalogue of the Gandhara Sculpture in the British Museum*, Vol. 1, London, 1996.

B. ARTICLES

Abdullaev, K.; Raimkulov, S. 'A Triumph Scene on an engraved gem from Kundzhulitepa (Kashkadarya).', *Ancient Civilisations from Scythia to Siberia*, Vol. 2, Leiden, 1995.

Agrawala, V.S. 'Terracotta figurines of Ahichchhatra', *Ancient India* , No. 4. 1947-48.

Aliev, I; Goshgarli, G. 'Archaeological Investigations in Azerbaijan (1986-1990)' *Ancient Civilizations from Scythia to Siberia,* Vol. 1, Leiden, 1994.

Barnett, R.D. 'The Treasure of Ziwiye,' *Iraq* , XVIII / 2, 1956.

Boileau, Gilles. 'Wu and Shaman', *B.S.O.A.S.,* Vol. 65, Part 2, London, 2002.

Bopearachchi, O.; Pieper, Wilfried. 'Ancient Indian Coins', *Indicopleustoi: Archaeologies of the Indian Ocean*, II, Turnhout, 1998.

Bopearachchi, O. The Arsacid Empire: Sources and Documentation, *Das Partherreich Und Seine Zeugnisse,* Stuttgart, 1998.

Chakravarty, A. 'A Mauryan Stone-Disc from Rājghāt', *Kalā, The Journal of Indian Art History Congress*, Vol. VIII, New Delhi, 2003.

Dani, A.H. ' Shaikhan Dheri Excavation , 1963 — 64 , In search of the second city of Pushkalavati', *Ancient Pakistan* , Vol. II, 1965-66.

Davis-Kimball, J. 'Chieftain or Warrior Priestess?', *Archaeology*, September/ October 1997.

Domansky, Y.V. 'Antiquity's Great Reporter Historian among the Scythians,'

The UNESCO Courier, December, 1976.

Drevnosti Tajikistana (Antiquities of Tajikistan).

Fairservis, W.A. 'Archaeological Studies in the Seistan Basin of South Western Afghanistan and Eastern Iran', *Anthropological Papers of the American Museum of Natural History*, No. 48, part 1, New York, 1961.

From the Lands of the Scythians. Metropolitan Museum of Art and Los Angeles County Museum of Art, 1975.

Gaur, G.S. 'Semathan Excavation; A Step Towards Bridging the gap between the Neolithic and the Kushāna Period in Kashmir', *Archaeology and History,* Vol. 1, edited by B. D. Chattopadhyaya and B. M. Pande, New Delhi,1987.

Ghosh, A; Panigrahi, K.C. 'Pottery of Ahichchhatra', *Ancient India* , 1946.

Ghirshman, R. 'Notes Iraniennes IV: Le Trêsor De Sakkaez. Les Origines De L'art Mêde Et Les Bronzes Du Luristan', *Artibus Asiae,* Vol. X 1950.

Godard, A. 'Â propos du trêsor de Ziwiyé,' *Artibus Asiae* Vol. XIV, 1951.

Gorelik, M.V. 'Sakski dospekh', *Tsentral Aziya: Novye pamyatniki pis'mennosti i iskusstva,* Moscow, 1987.

Grigorev, F.P; Ismagil, R. 'The Cult Bronzes of Semirechye of the Śaka Period,' *Ancient Civilizations from Scythia to Siberia,* Vol.3, Leiden, 1996.

Guillaume, O. 'Contribution à l'etude d'un artisant Bactrien prê-hellenistique', in: *Actes de colloque franco-soviêtique* 'L'archaeologic de la Bactriane ancienne', Dushanbe, 1982,

Gummel, Ya. I 'Excavations to the South-West of Hanlar in 1941 ", *Ancient Civilizations from Scythia to Siberia,* Vol.2, Leiden, 1995.

Huxley, G. 'Geography in the Acts of Thomas', *Greek, Roman and Byzantine Studies,* Vol. 24, 1983.

Indian Archaeology, 1956-57.

Indian Archaeology 1996-97-A Review

Indian Art Special Purposes Fund. Catalogue of the Los Angeles County Museum of Art.

Information Bulletin of the International Association for the Study of the Cultures of Central Asia, Nauka Publishers, Moscow.

Irani, A.G. 'Archaeology of the Settlement of the Kshatrapa Period', *Purātattva,* 1997-98.

Jacobson, Esther 'The Stag With Bird-Headed Antler Tines: A Study in Image Transformation and Meaning,' *B.M.F.E.A.,* No.56, 1984.

Jettmar, Karl, 'The Art of the Northern Nomads in the Upper Indus Valley', *South Asian Studies,* No. 7, London, 1991.

Kanungo A. K. and V. S. Shinde, 'Excavation at Kopia 2005: A Preliminary Report', *Purātattva*, No. 35, 2004-2005.

Kaposhina, S.I. 'Pamyiatniki zverinogo stilya iz O'lbii', *K.S.I.I.M.K.*, Vol. XXXIV, 1950.

Khandalawala, Karl. *Lalit Kalā,* Vol. 7, 1960.

Khudyakov, Yu. S. 'Problems of the Genesis of Culture of the Hunnic Period in the Altai Mountains', *Ancient Civilisations from Scythia to Siberia*, Vol. 3, Leiden, 1996.

Koshelenko, G.A; Bader, A. M; Gaibov, V. A. 'Archaelogical Studies in Turkmenistan', *Ancient Civilisations from Scythia to Siberia*, Vol. 1, Leiden, 1994.

Kubarev, V.D. 'Kinzhaly iz Gornogo Altaya' (Daggers from the Altai Mountains) in *Voennoe delo drevnikh plemyon Sibiri i tsentral'noi Azii* (Military Craft of the Ancient tribes of Siberia and Central Asia), Novosibirsk, 1971.

Kumaran, R. N. M. K. Dwivedi and V. D. Jadhav, 'Iron Objects from Hathab', *Purātattva*, No. 34, 2003-2004.

Litvinsky, B.A. 'Ancient Tajikistan', *Ancient Civilizations from Scythia to Siberia,* Leiden, 1994. Vol.1.

Litvinsky, B.A; Pichikjan, Igor R. ' Gold Plaques from the Oxus temple', *Ancient Civilisations from Scythia to Siberia*, Leiden, Vol. 2, 1995.

Makhortykh, S.V. 'Scythians And Sarmatians of The Northern Caucasus; Recent Archaeological Finds', *Ancient Civilizations From Scythia to Siberia*, Leiden, 1994.

Mantsevich, A.P. 'Sheynyye ubory Skifskogo perioda' (Necklaces of the Scythian period), *K.S.I.I.M.K.* Vol. XXII, 1948.

Miller, Barbara Stoler. *Exploring India's Sacred Art,* Indira Gandhi National Centre for Arts., New Delhi, 1994.

Minaysan, R.S. 'The Origin of the distinctive features of the Animal Style', *A.S.G.E.* (Archaeological Collection from the State Hermitage Museum), Issue 29, 1988; Issue 30, 1990.

Mukherjee, B.N. 'The Usefulness of Modern Economic-Theories for The Study of Economic History of Ancient India-An Illustration', *J.A.S.*, Vol.IX,. No. 1, 1967.

Mukherjee, B.N. *The Kushāna Genealogy*, Calcutta, 1967.

Mukherjee, B.N. 'A Note on a Gold Coin or Medal found at Tillya-tepe (Afganistan)', *Mudrā*, Calcutta, 1989.

Negi, Baldev Singh S. "Explorations along the Banganga River, District Bharatpur, Rajasthan", *Purātattva*, No. 17, 1986-87.

Parpola, A. 'Margiana and the Aryan Problem', *Information Bulletin (I.A.S.S.C.A.)*, 1993.

Polosmak, N.V. 'Investigations of a Pazyryk Barrow at Kuturguntas', *Ancient Civilisations from Scythia to Siberia,* Vol. 2, Leiden, 1995.

Polosmak, N.V. 'The Ak-Alakh Frozen Grave Barrow', *Ancient Civilisations from Scythia to Siberia*, Vol. 1, Leiden, 1994.

Prasad, A. K. 'Important Discoveries of Prehistoric Rock Paintings, Ancient Inscriptions and Stone Age Tools in Southern Bihar and Adjoining Jharkhand', *Purātattva*, No.34, 2003-2004.

Pugachenkova, G.A. S.The Antiquities of Transoxiana in the light of investigations in Uzbekistan (1985-1990), *Ancient Civilizations from Scythia to Siberia*, Vol.2 Leiden 1995.

Pinia, D.S. 'New Evidence of Pre-Kushān Sculpture from Gurgaon, District, Haryana', *East and West*, New Series, Vol.31, 1981.

Quintanilla, S.R. 'āyāgapatas', *Artibus Asiae*, Vol.52, March, No. 3, Zurich, 2001.

Rapoport, Yu.A. 'Khorezmiiskie Ossuarii', *Iz Istorii Religii Drevnego Khorezma,* Moscow, 1971.

Rayevskiy, D. S. 'Skifskiy Mifologicheskiy Syuzhet v Iskusstvei ideologi i Tsarstva Ateya', *Sov. Arkh*, No. 3,1970.

Rayevskiy, D.S. 'Kul'-obskiye luchniki', *Sov. Arkh,* 1981.

Ridgeway, B.S. 'Birds, 'Meniskoi', and Head Attributes in Archaic Greece', *Am. Journ. Arach.*, 1990.

Sarianidi, V. 'New Discoveries at Ancient Gonur', *Ancient Civilizations from Scythia to Siberia*, Vol.2, Leiden,1997.

Semenov, V. 'New Evidence of the Scythian Type Culture of Tuva', *Ancient Civilizations from Scythia to Siberia*, Vol. 2, Leiden, 1995.

Sharma, G.R. 'Excavations at Kauúāmbï, 1949-50', *Memoirs of the Archaeological Survey of India* , No. 74.

Sharma, G.R. '*Excavations at Kauúāmbï,* 1957-59,, Institute of Archaeology, Allahabad University Publication.

Sher, J.A. 'Â propos des origins du ''style animalier" ', *Arts Asiatiques,* Vol. *XLVII*, 1992.

Singh, Arun. K. 'Ganeha Images In Himachal Pradesh. An Iconographical Study', *Purātattva,* Vol. 33, Nov.-Dec., 2003, Indian Archaeological Society, New Delhi.

Stavisky, B.Y. 'A Buddhist Cult Centre on the Right Bank of The Oxus, Excavations At Kara-tepe In Termez In 1983-1992', *Ancient Civilizations From Scythia To Siberia,* Vol. 3, Leiden 1996.

Tchlenova, N.L. 'Objects Of The Scythian "Animal Style" From The Taiga Zone Of Siberia,' *Ancient Civilizations from Scythia To Siberia* , Leiden, Vol. 3, 1996.

Terenozhkin, A.I. 'Kimmeriyskiye mechi i kinzhaly' (Cimmerian swords and daggers), *Skifskiy mir, N.D.*, Kiev, 1975.

Tewari , D. P. and D. K. Srivastava, 'Excavations at Sanchankot, District Unnao, U.P. (2004-05), *Purātattva*, No. 35, 2004-2005.

Tolstoi, I.I; Kondakov, N.P. ' Russkie Drevnosti V Panyatnikakh Iskusstva', *Collected Publications ,* Vol. 3, Moscow, 1990.

Treister, M. 'New Discoveries of Sarmatian Complexes of the 1st Century A.D.', *Ancient Civilizations from Scythia to Siberia*, Vol. 4, Leiden 1997.

Treister, M. 'Concerning the Jewellery Items from the Burial Mound at Nogaichik', *Ancient Civilizations from Scythia to Siberia,* Vol. 4, Leiden, 1997.

Treister, M. 'New Discoveries Of Sarmatian Complexes', *Ancient Civilizations From Scythia To Siberia*, Vol. 4, Leiden, 1997.

Treister, M. 'Two Golden Bracelets From Olbia In The Walters Art Gallery', *Ancient Civilizations From Scythia To Siberia*, Vol.8, Leiden, 2002.

Tsuchiya, Haruko 'An Iconographical Study of the Buddhist Art of Shotorak, Paitāva And Khan Zargar', *Silk Road Art And Archaeology,* Vol.6, 2000

Tucci, G. 'Preliminary Report on an Archaeological Survey in Swat', *East and West*, N.S., Vol. 18, Nos. 3-4 (Sept-Dec), 1958.

Tyumenev, A.I. 'Khersones i mestnoye naseleniye skify', *V.D.I.*, 1950, No. 2.

Tesieva, Madina. 'Koban Bronzes in Tli', *Aleksandravskii prospect,* No.7, Sept-Oct. 1999, Vladikavkaz.

Vickers, M. 'Golden Greece; Relative Values, Minae, and Temple Inventories', *Am. Journ. Arch.*,Vol. 94, 1990.

Vitt, V. O; Loshadi, 'Pazyrykskikh Kurganov', *Sov. Arkh.*, No. XVI, Leningrad, 1952.

Vyaz'mitina, M.I. 'Ranniye pamyatniki skifskogo zverinogo stilya', *Sov. Arkh*, No. 2, 1963.

Zimmer, H. 'Some Aspects of Time in Indian Art', *J.I.S.O.A.*, Vol. I, No. 1, (June), 1933.

Select Bibliography of Original Sources

(1) ARCHAEOLOGICAL SOURCES

A. INSCRIPTIONS

Shahdaur Inscription of Damijada of the year 60, *Cor. Ins. Ind.,* Vol.II, Pt.I, p.16.

Taxila Inscription referring to Moga (Maues) and to the year 78. *Ibid.,* p.28.

Sirkap Inscription of Jihonika (= Zeionises) of the year 191. *Ibid.,* p. 82.

Mathurā Lion Capital Inscriptions of the time of Rajuvula *Ep. Ind.,* Vol. X, pp.135f; *Cor. Ins. Ind.,* Vol.II, Pt.I, pp.48-49.

Mathurā Votive Inscription of Sodasa of the year 72, *Ep. Ind.,* Vol.II, p.199; Vol.IX,pp.243-244

Takht-i-Bahi Inscription of Guduvhara (= Gondophares I) of the year 103.

Cor.Ins.Ind., Vol.II, Pt.I, pp.62-63; *I.H.Q.,* 1962,Vol.XXXVII, pp.239-241.

Basak, R.G. (editor), *Aśokan Inscriptions,* Calcutta, 1959.

Buhler, G., Āmohinī's Votive Tablet Inscription of Sodasa of the year 72',*Ep.Ind.,* Vol.II, New Delhi, 1984, p.199.

Kielhorn, F., 'Junāgadh Rock Inscription of Rudradāman, The Year 72', *Ep.Ind.,* Vol.VII, Calcutta, 1905-06, pp.36-49.

Konow, S. *Cor. Ins.Ind.,* Vol.II, Pt.I, *Kharoshthi Inscriptions With the Exception of Those of Aśoka,* Calcutta,1929.

Naqsh-i-Rustam Inscription of Shapur I., Honigmann, E. and Maricq, *Recherches sur les Res Gestae Divi Saporis,* Brussels,1953; *B.S.O.A.S.,* Vol.IX, pp.823-849; *Syria,* 1958, pp.295-360.

B. COINS

Allan, J., *A Catalogue of the Indian Coins in the British Museum, Catalogue of the Coins of Ancient India,* London, 1936.

Cunningham, A., 'Coins of the Śakas' , *Num. Chr.,* 1890, pp.103-173.

Gardner, P., *Catalogue of Indian Coins in the British Museum, The Coins of the Greek and Scythic Kings of Bactria and India in the British Museum,* London, 1886.

Jenkins, G.K., 'Indo-Scythic Mints', *Jour. Num. Soc. Ind.,* 1955, Vol.XVII, Pt.II, pp.1-26.

Newell, E.T., 'The Coinage of the Parthians', Pope, A.U. (editor), *A Survey of Persian Art,* Vol.1, reprint, London and New York, 1964, Ch.27, pp.475-492.

C. REPORTS ON ARCHAEOLOGICAL OBJECTS, EXCAVATIONS, EXPLORATIONS, etc.

Alekseev, A. Iu., 'Khoronografia Skifi vtoroi poloviny IV v. do n.e', (Chronicle of Scythia in the Second half of the fourth centuryB.C.).*Arkheologicheskii sbornik* (Gosudarstvennyi Ermitazh) 28, 1987.

Barkova, L.L., 'Reznye izobrazheniia zhivotnykh na sarkofage iz 2- go Bashadarskogo kurgana', (Carved zoomorphic images on a sarcophagus from kurgan 2 at Bashadar), *Arkheologicheskii sbornik* (Gosudarstvennyi Ermitazh) 25, 1984.

Bobrinskoi, A.A., 'Otchet o raskopkakh, proizvedennykh v 1903 godu v Chigirinskom uezde Kievskoi gub', (Rreport on the 1903 excavations in the Chigirinskii district of the Kiev region), *Izvestiia* (Arkheologicheskaia Komissia), No. 14,1905.

Dani, A.H., 'Shaikhan-Dheri Excavation, 1963 and 1964 Seasons', *Ancient Pakistan* Vol.II, 1965-66.

Ghosh, A., 'Taxila (Sirkap), 1944-45', *Ancient India,* No. 4, 1947-48.

Harle, J. C. 'Artefacts of the Historical Period from Bannu', *South Asian Archaeology 1987 Part 2*, Rome, 1990.

Ilyinskaya, V.A., 'The Feline in Early Scythian Art', *Soviet Archaeology,* No. 2, 1971.

Ilyinskaya, V.A., 'Some motifs of the Early Scythian Animal Style', *Soviet Archaeology,* No. 1, 1965.*Indian Archaeology,* 1956-57.

Kiselev, S.V., *Drevniaia istoriia iuzhnoi Sibiri* (The ancient history of southern Siberia). Materialy i issledovaniia po arkheologii SSSR (Materials and papers on the archaeology of the U.S.S.R.), No.9,Moscow and Leningrad, 1949.

Krishna Murthy, K. 'The Domestic Art Delineated in the Gandhara Reliefs', *Purātattva*, No. 7, 1976-77.

Mani, B. R. 'Excavations at Ambaran 1999-2001: Akhnur Terracotta and Discovery of Buddhist Reliquary in Exposed Stupa', H. P. Ray and C. Sinopoli ed., *Archaeology as History in early South Asia*, New Delhi, 2004.

Mantsevich, A.P., 'Dereviannye sosudy skifskoi epokhi', (Wooden vessels of the Scythian period), *Arkheologicheskii sbornik* (Gosudarstvennyi Ermitazh) 8, 1966.

Marshall.J., *Taxila, An Illustrated Account of Archaeological Excavations Carried out at Taxila under the orders of the Government of India between the years* 1913 *and 1934*, 3 Volumes, Cambridge, 1951, reprint, Delhi, 1975.

Maximova, M.I., 'A Silver Mirror from the Kelermes Barrow' , *Soviet Archaeology,* Vol. XXI, 1954.

Nanavati J.M., R.N.Mehta and S.N.Chowdhary, *Excavation at Somnath or Prabhas Patan,* M.S.University, Baroda, 1971.

Pridik, E.M., ' Novye Kavkazskie Klady', (New Caucasian treasures) *Materialy po arkheologii Rossii,* Vol. 34, 1914.

Sharma, G.R., *Exacavations at Kauśāmbī*, 1949-50, *Memoirs of the Archaeological Survey of India,* No. 74.

Shilov, V.P., 'Kalinovskii kurgannyi mogil' nik', (The Kalinovka burial ground), in *Drevnosti Nizhnego Povolzh'ia: Itogi rabot Stalingradskoi arkheologicheskoi ekspeditsii* (Antiquities from the lower Volga River region: Findings of the Stalingrad archaeological expedition), Vol I. *Materialy i issledovaniia po arkheologii SSSR* (Materials and papers on the archaeology of the U.S.S.R.), Moscow, 1959.

Stein, M.A., 'Excavations at Sahri-Bahlol', *Archaeological Survey of India, Annual Reports.*, 1911-12. *Serindia*, 5 Vols. Oxford, 1921.

Viazmitina, M.I., 'Early Relics of the Scythian Animal Style', *Soviet Archaeology,* No.2, 1963.

Yakovenko, E.V., 'The Temir-Gora Barrow', *Soviet Archaeology,* No. 3, 1972.

Young, G.M., 'A New Hoard from Taxila (Bhir Mound)', *Ancient India,* No. 1, 1946.

(2) LITERARY SOURCES

A. SANSKRIT AND PRĀKRIT

Manu, *Manusmrti* with commentary Manubhāsya by Medhātithi; edited with indexes of verses by Ganganath Jha, Calcutta, 1939.

Pānini, *Ashtādhyāyī,* edited with English translation by Sriśacandra Basu, Delhi, 1962 (reprint).

Patanjali, Mahābhāshya, edited by Kielhorn, F.R., 3 Vols., Bombay Sanskrit Series, 1980-85. The Mahābhāshya of Patanjali, Vartikā by Katyāyana, with English translation by Surendranath Dasgupta, ed. by Sibajiban Bhattacharya, New Delhi, 1991) .

Anonymus, *Kālakāchārya kathānaka,* (Brown, N., *The Story of Kālaka,* Washington, 1933; Nawab, S.M., *The Collection of the Kālaka Story,* 2 Pts.,Ahmedabad, 1959).

B. GREEK AND LATIN

Arrian, *Anabaseos Alexandrou* (Loeb Classical Library edition, 2 Vols., reprint, London and Cambridge, Mass., 1958 and 1961).

Diodorus, *Bibliothekes Historikes* (Loeb Classical Library edition, 10 Vols., London and Cambridge, Mass., 1935-1954).

Herodotus, *Historiae* (edited by Huide, C., Oxford, 1926).

Isidore of Charax, *Stathmoi Parthikoi* (Schoff, W.H.(editor), *Parthian Stations by Isidore of Charax,* Philadelphia, 1914).

Justin, *Epitoma Historiarum Philippicarum, Accedunt Prologi in Pompeium Trogum,* (edited by Seel, Otto, Leipzig, 1935).

Philostratus, *Ta Es Ton Tyanea Apollonion* (Loeb Classical Library edition, 2 Vols., London and New York, 1912).

Pliny, *Naturalis Historia* (Loeb Classical Library edition, 10 Vols., reprint, London and Cambridge, Mass., 1956-1963).

Ptolemy, C., *Geographike Huphegesis* (edited by Nobbe, C.F.A., 3 Vols., Leipzig, 1898, etc. For a translation of Ptolemy's *Geography,* see Stevenson, E.L., *Geography of Claudius Ptolemy,* New York, 1932).

Strabo, *Geographikon* (Loeb Classical Library edition, 8 Vols., reprint, London and Cambridge, Mass., 1959-1961).

Anonymous, *Periplous Tes Erythras Thalasses* or *Periplus Maris Erythraei* (Frisk, H. (editor), *Le Pêriple de la Mer Ūrythrêe,* Göteborg, 1927; for a translation, see Schoff, W.H., *The Periplus of the Erythraean Sea,* New York, 1912).

Tabula Peutingeriana (Miller, K., *Itineraria Romana,* Stuttgart, 1916; K.Miller, *Die Peutingersche Tafel,* Stuttgart, 1962).

C. CHINESE

Fan Yeh, *Hou Han-shu* (Ssu-pu pei-yao edition; for atranslation of chapter 118, see Chavannes, E., "Les Pays d'Occident d'Aprés le *Heou Han Chou,*" *TP,* 1907,).

Pan Ku, (completed by Pan Chao) *Ch'ien Han-shu* (T'ung-wen shu-chý edition; for a translation of chapter 96A see Hulsewe, F.F.P., *China in Central Asia-the Early Stage: 125 B.C.-A.D. 23,* Leiden, 1979, p.71f).

Ssu-ma Ch'ien (and also Ssu-ma T'an) *Shih-chi* (Ssu-pu pei-yao edition; for a translation of a part of the *Shih-chi,* see Watson, B., *Records of the Grand Historian of China,* 2 Vols., New York and London, 1961).

INDEX

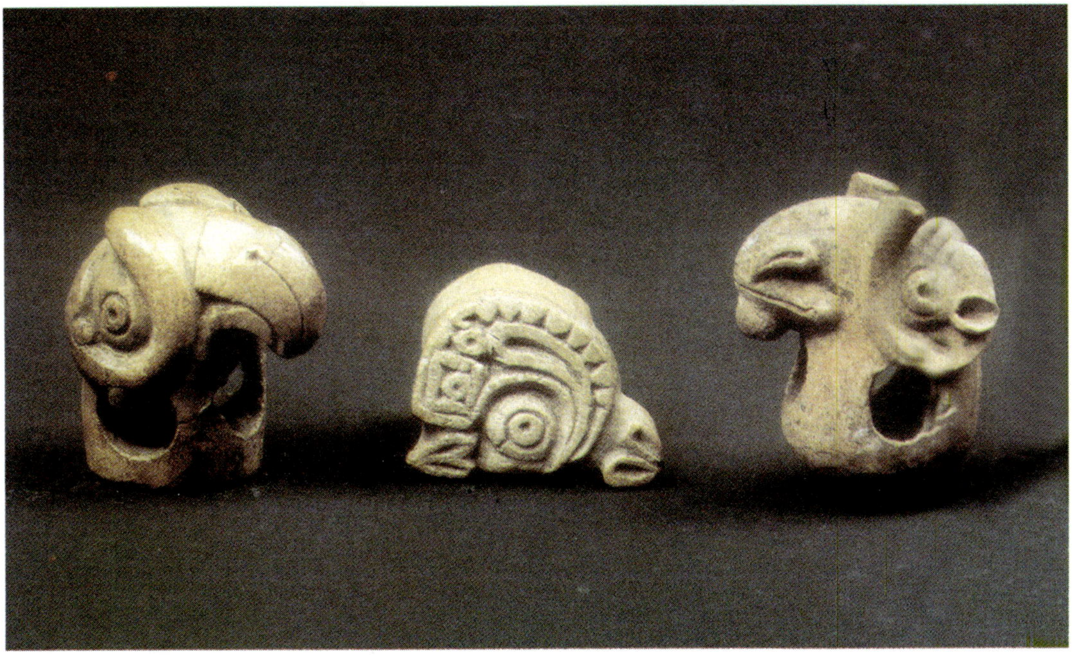

Plate: 1 Bone eye-bars for linking bridle reins in the shape of rams and ram-bird's heads, from Kelermes barrow 1. Late seventh or early sixth century B.C.

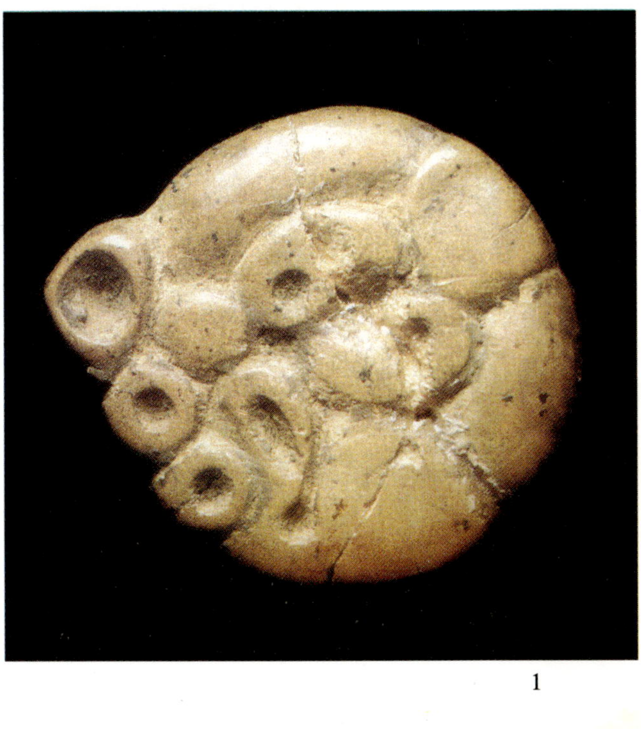

Plate 2: Bone quiver ornament of a curled-up beast of prey from Temir-Gora barrow. Mid-seventh Century B.C.

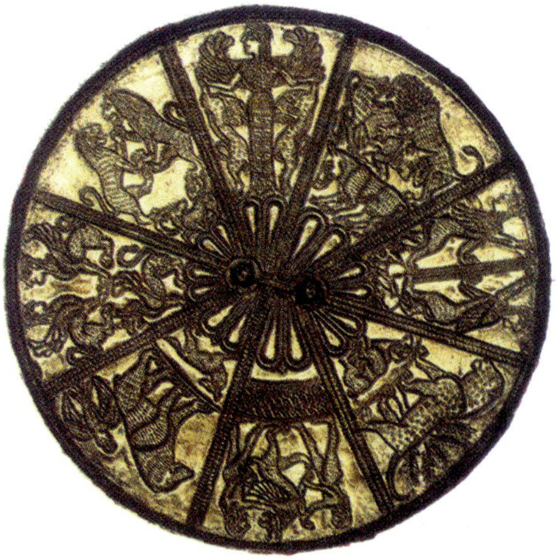

Plate 3: Reverse of a silver mirror having electrum plates with chased images of a winged goddess, animals and fantastic creatures from Kelermes, barrow 4. Late seventh or early sixth Century B.C.

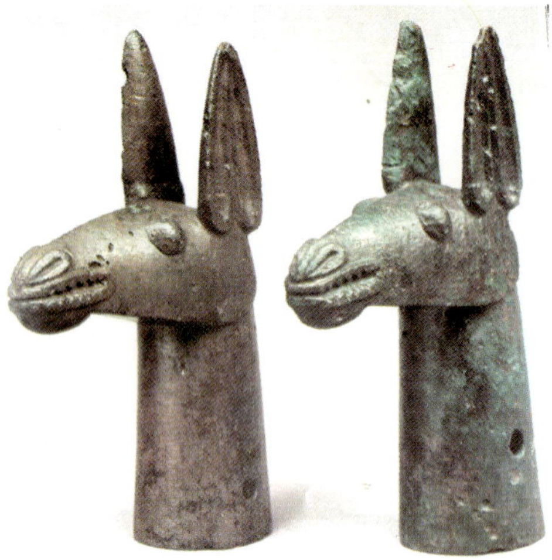

Plate 4: Bronze poletop in the shape of a horse head from Kelermes 1. Late seventh or early sixth Century B.C.

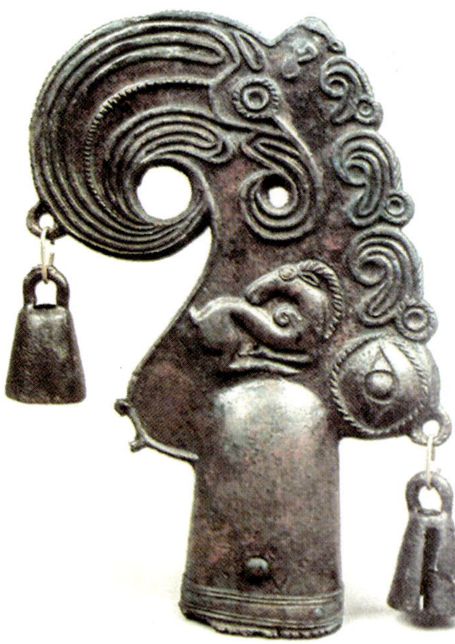

Plate 5: Bronze poletop in the shape of a large bird-head with superimposed images and hanging bells from Ulsky 2. Sixth Century B.C.

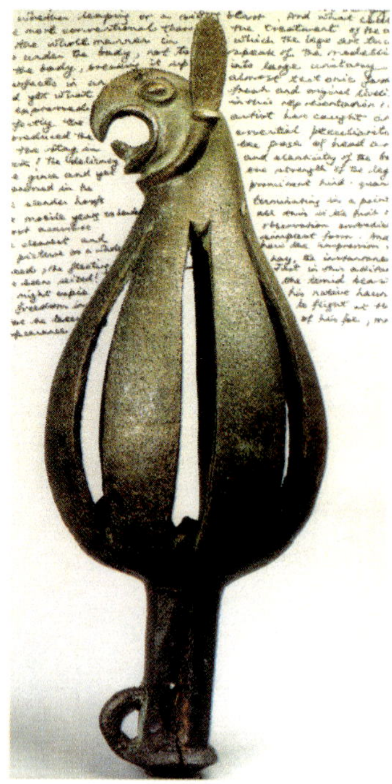

Plate 6: Bronze poletop terminating in a griffin head with openwork rattle body from Kelermes. Late seventh or early sixth century B.C.

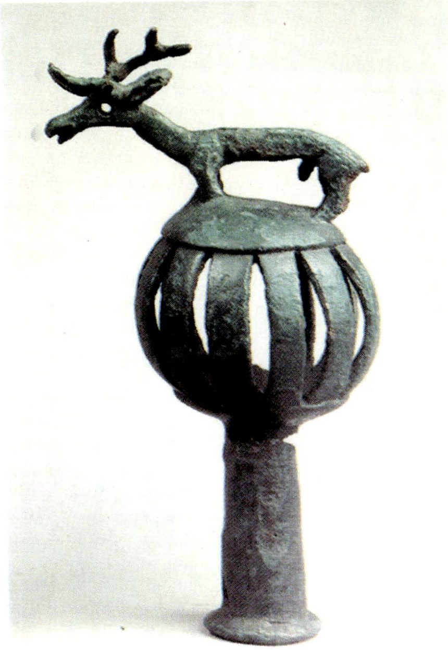

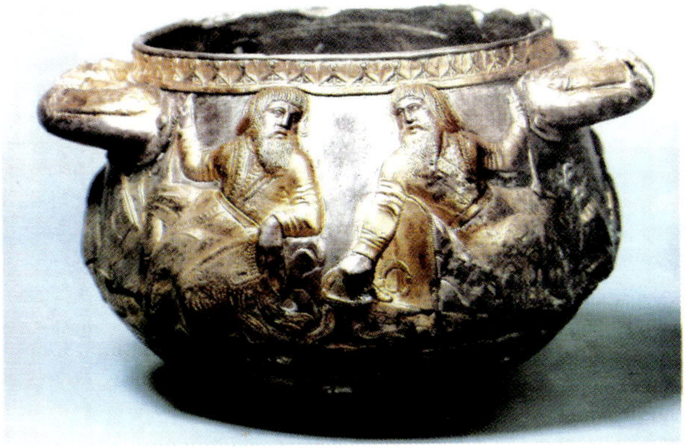

Plate 8: Silver-gilt vessel with scenes of seated Scythian warriors from Gaymanova Mogila. Fourth century B.C.

Plate 7: Bronze poletop terminating in a stag on a spherical rattle from Makhoshevsky Barrow. Late seventh century B.C.

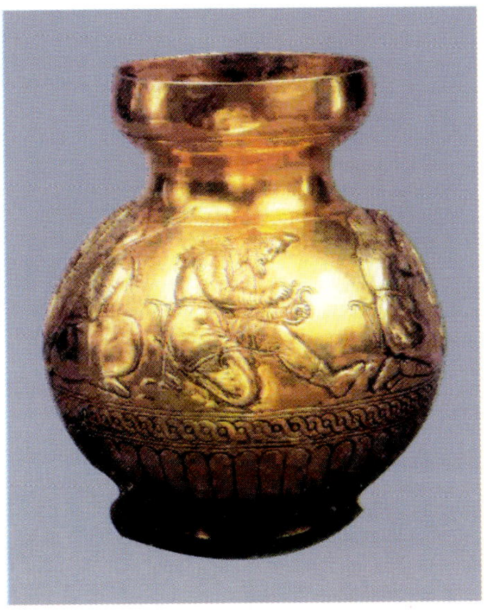

Plate 9: Gold and electrum Scythian ritual vessel with scenes of Scythian mythology and with ornaments in the lower part, from Kul-Oba. Fourth century B.C.

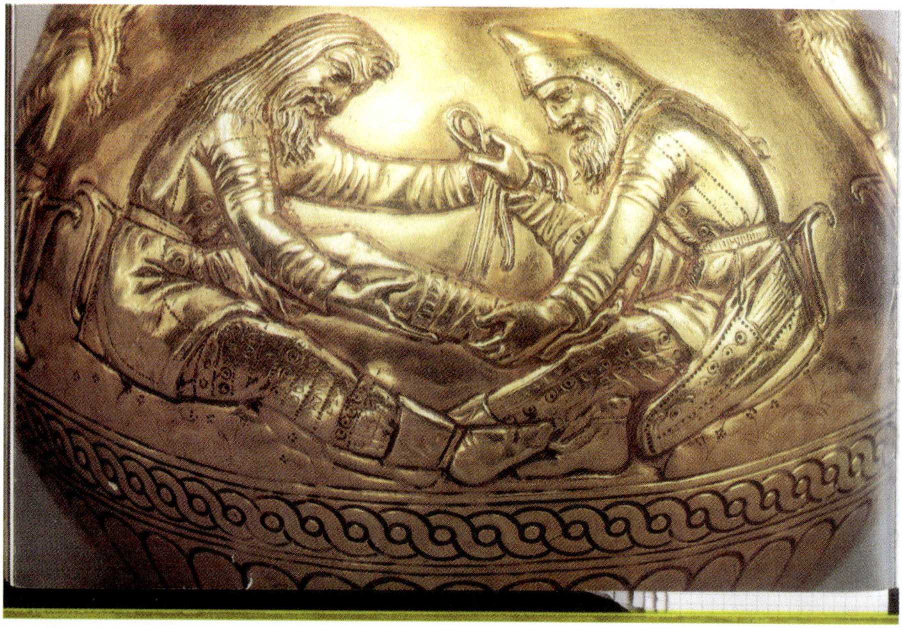

Plate 10: Details of images of Scythian males on gold and electrum ritual vessel from Kul-Oba. Fourth century B.C.

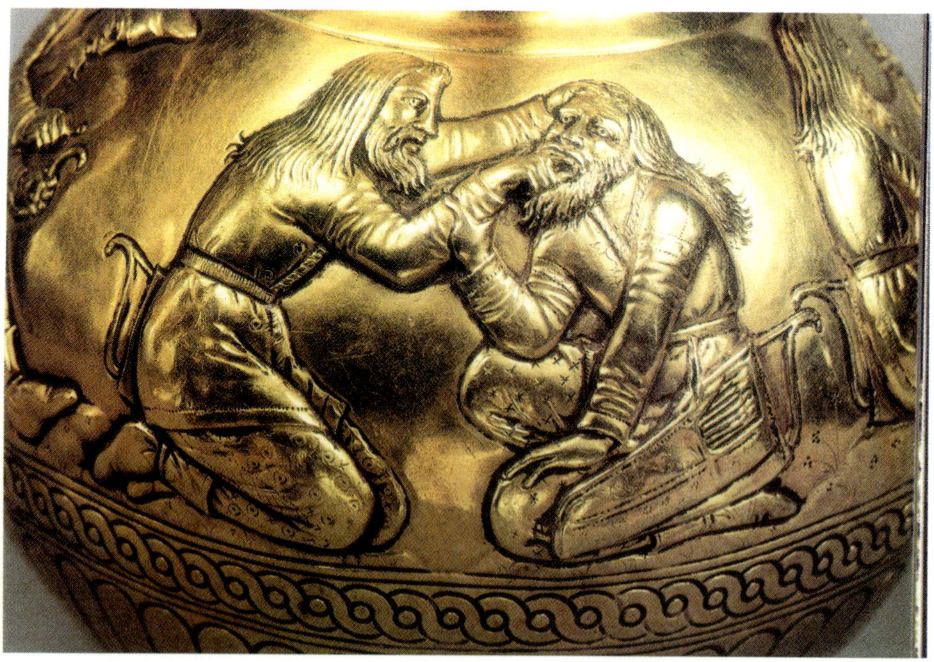

Plate 11: Details of images of Scythian males on the gold and electrum ritual vessel from Kul-Oba. Fourth century B.C.

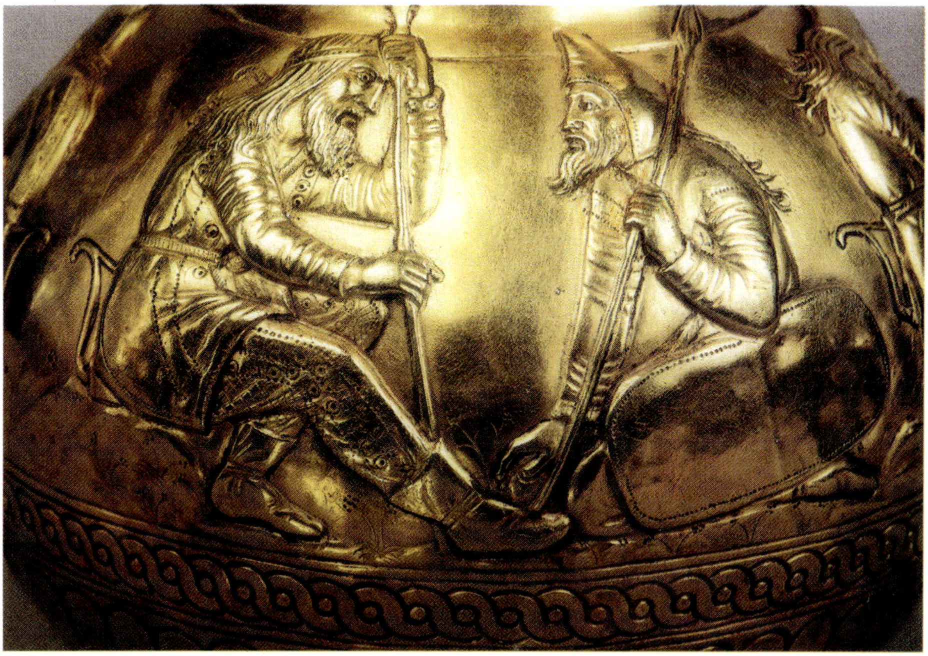

Plate 12: Details of images of Scythian males on the gold and electrum ritual vessel from Kul-Oba. Fourth century B.C.

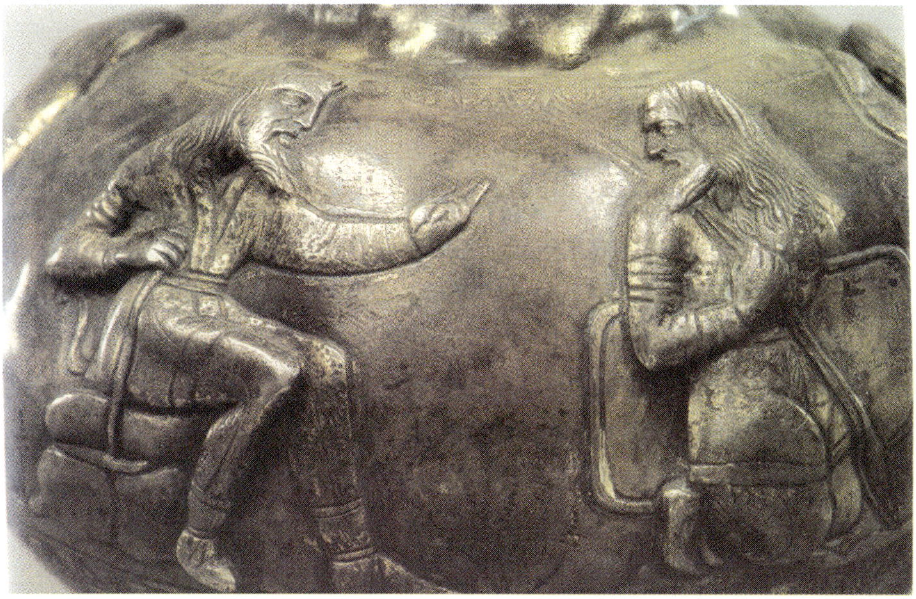

Plate 13: Silver-gilt Scythian ceremonial vessel with relief images of Scythian warriors from Chastiye barrow, tumulus 3. Fourth century B.C.

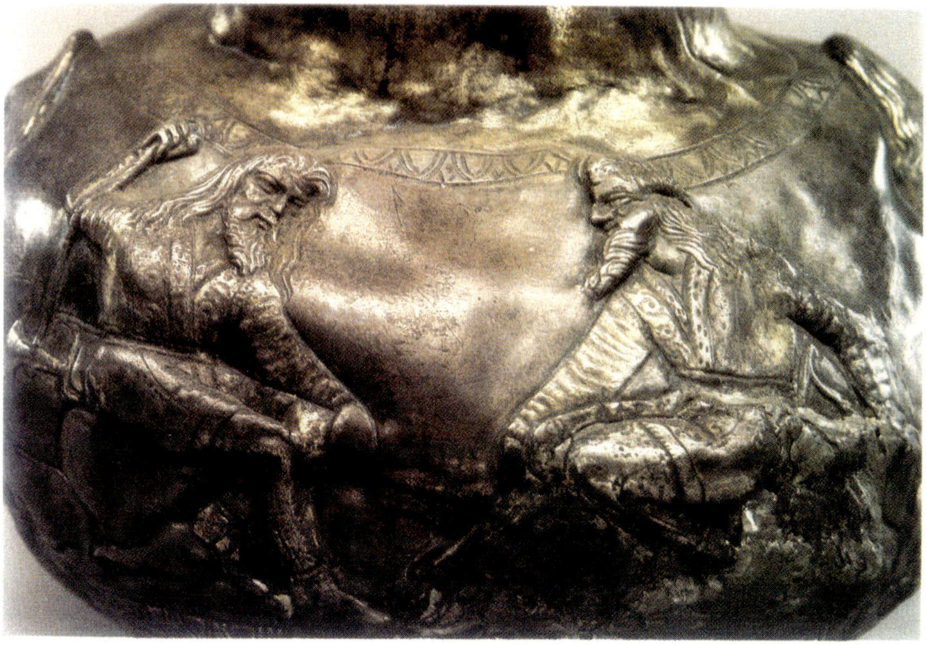

Plate 14: Details of images of Scythian males on the silver-gilt ceremonial vessel from Chastiye barrow. Fourth century B.C.

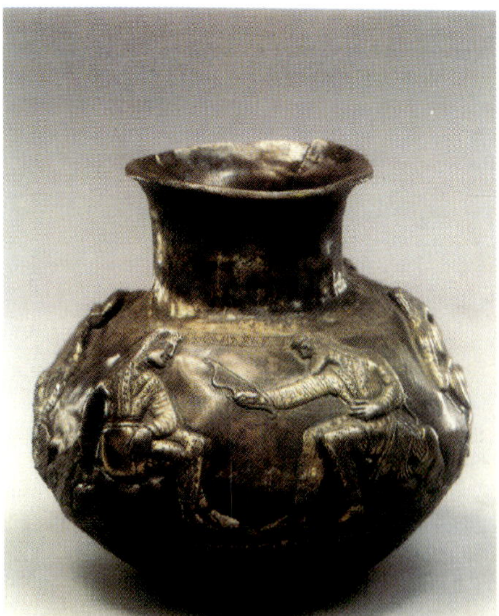

Plate 15: Details of images of Scythian males on the silver-gilt ceremonial vessel from Chastiye barrow. Fourth century B.C.

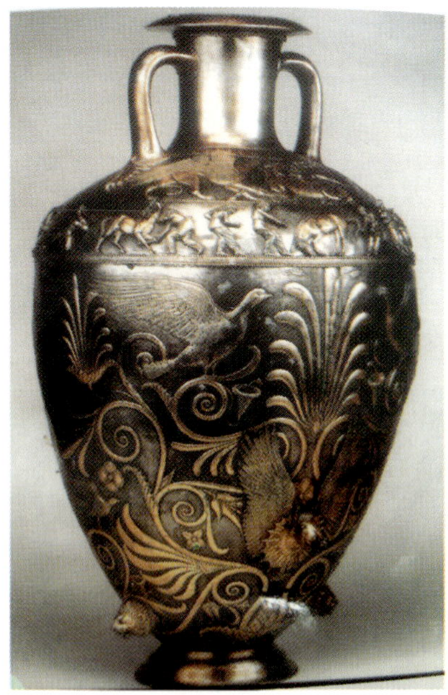

Plate 16: Silver-gilt amphora decorated with floral ornaments, birds and scenes of griffins tearing a spotted deer from Chertomlyk. Last Quarter of the Fourth century B.C.

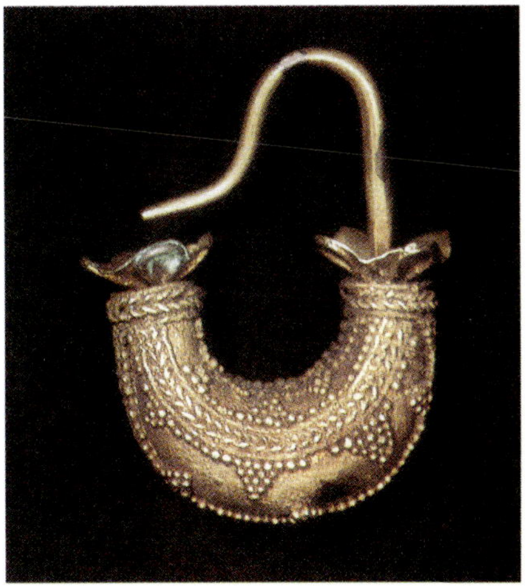

Plate 17: Gold boat-shaped earring with filigree ornament and triangles of granulated surface and rosette terminals from Volkovtsy barrow 4. Fifth century B.C.

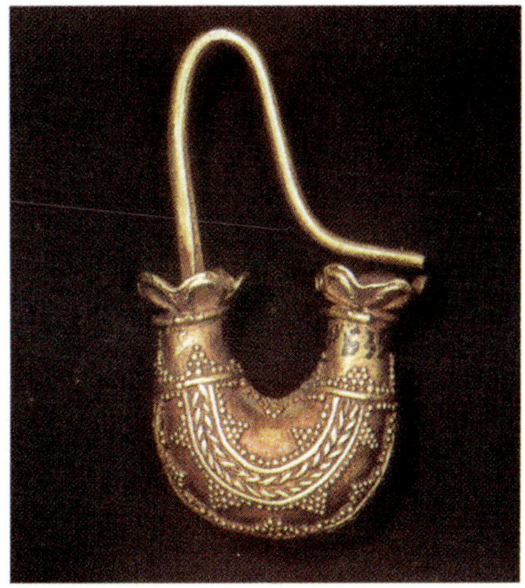

Plate 18: Gold boat-shaped earring with filigree ornament and triangles of granulated surface and rosette terminals from Volkovtsy barrow 4. Fifth century B.C.

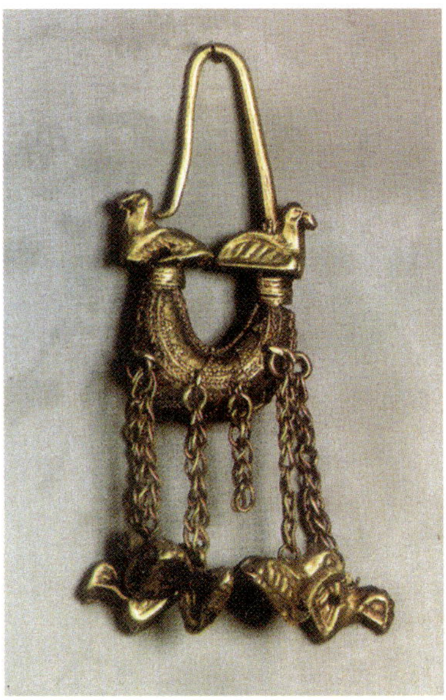

Plate 19: Gold crescent-shaped earring, decorated with granulated triangles and sculptured figurines of ducks at the ends and suspended on chains from Novoselitsy barrow 4. Fourth century B.C.

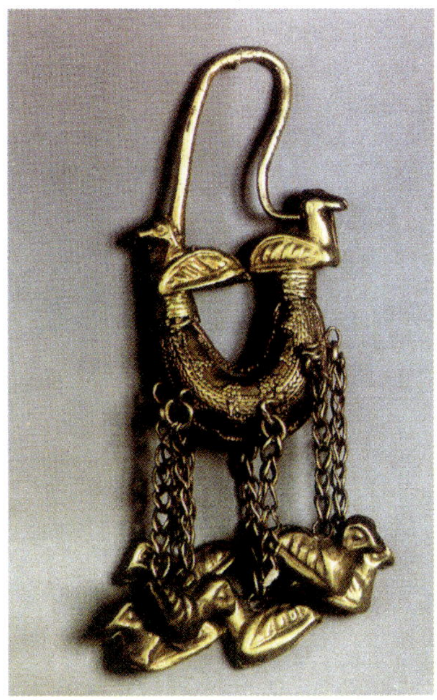

Plate 20: Gold crescent-shaped earring, decorated with granulated triangles and sculptured figurines of ducks at the ends and suspended on chains from Novoselitsy Barrow 4. Fourth century B.C.

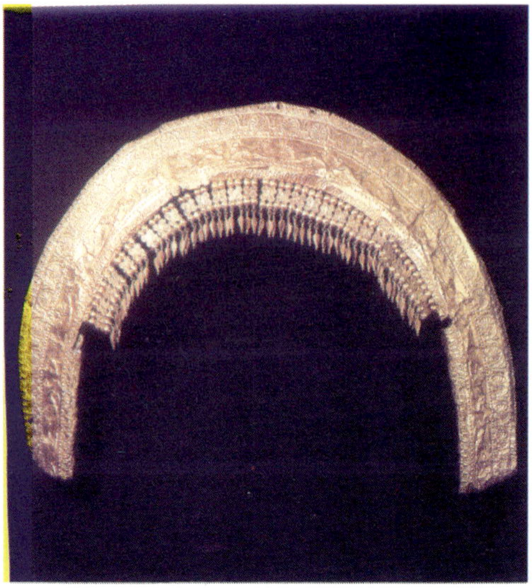

Plate 21: Gold diadem with relief figures of lions, panthers and floral ornaments from Three Brothers barrow. Attached to its lower edge are plaques with drop-like pendants. Second half of the fourth century B.C.

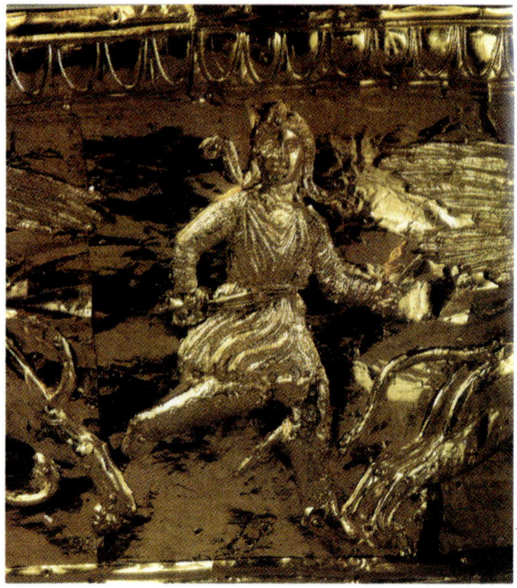

Plate 22: Details of gold and enamel calathus from Bolshaya Bliznitsa. Fourth century B.C.

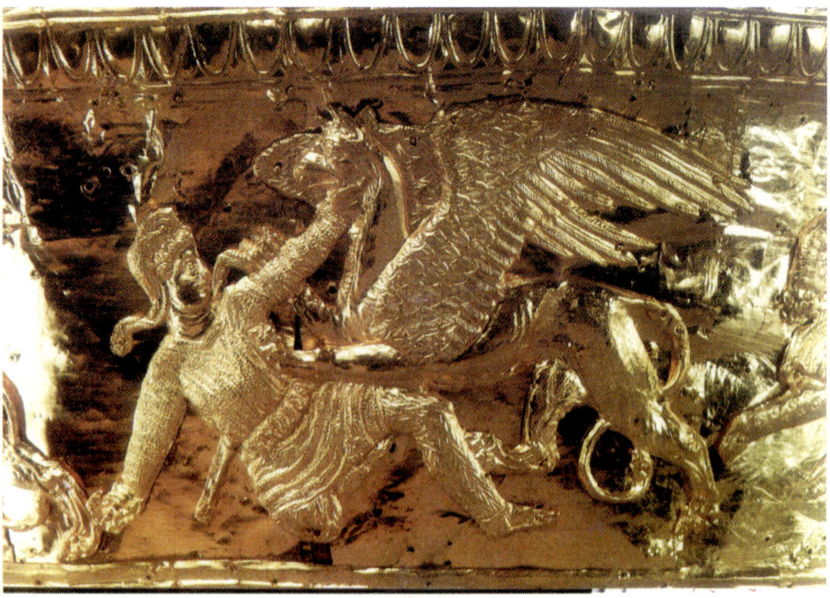

Plate 23: Details of gold and enamel calathus from Bolshaya Bliznitsa. Fourth century B.C.

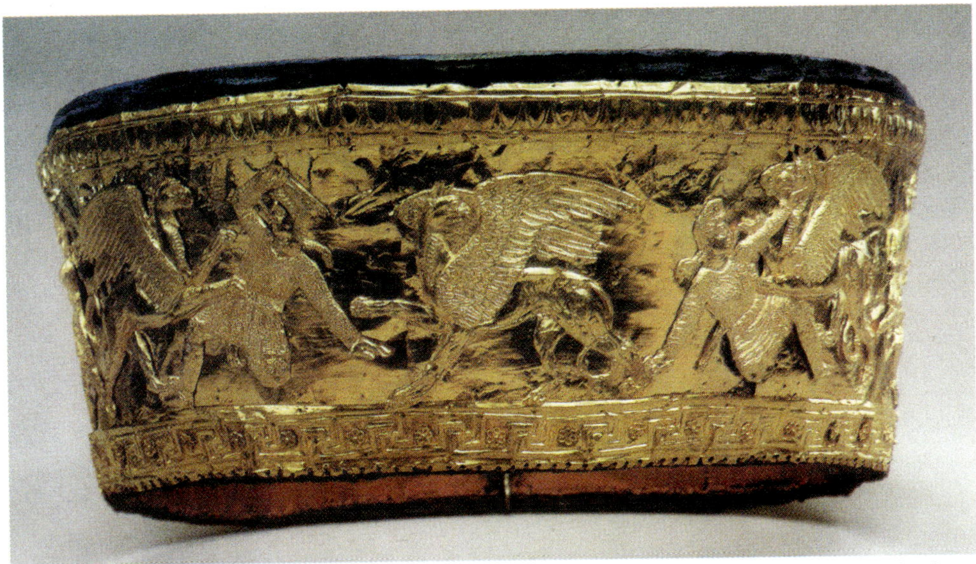

Plate 24: Gold and enamel calathus decorated with chased plates depicting Barbarians fighting griffins, from Bolshaya Bliznitsa barrow. In the upper part, egg-and-dart ornaments; lower, a meander and rosettes inlaid with blue enamel. Fourth century B.C.

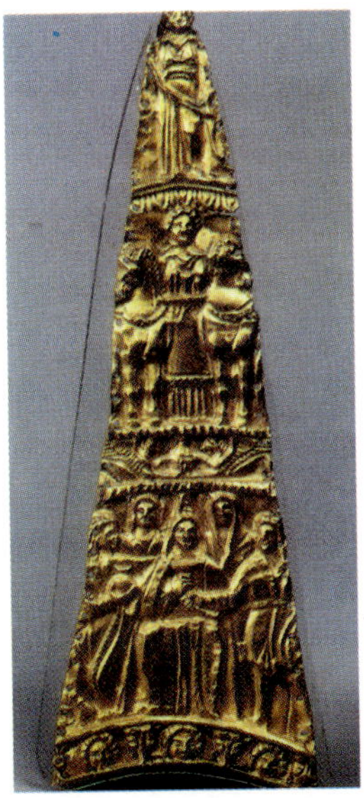

Plate 25: Gold adornment of a female ritual head-dress with relief compositions from Karagodeuashkh barrow. The upper part shows a goddess draped in a classical tunic, in the middle there is a man driving a chariot, and below, a ritual scene of libation. Late fourth century B.C.

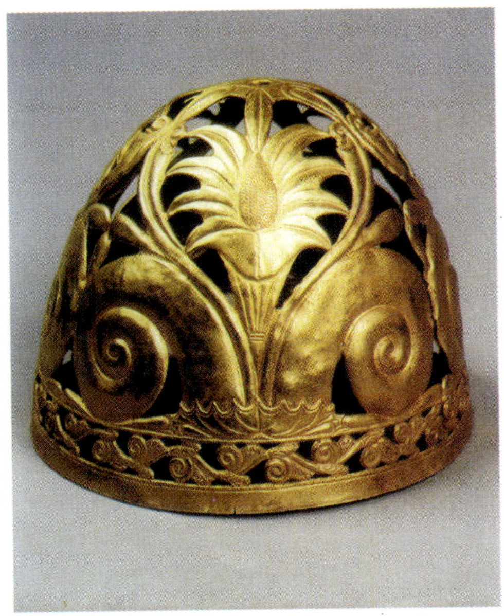

Plate 26: Gold openwork cone-shaped head-dress decorated with volutes and floral designs from Ak-Burun barrow. Fourth century B.C.

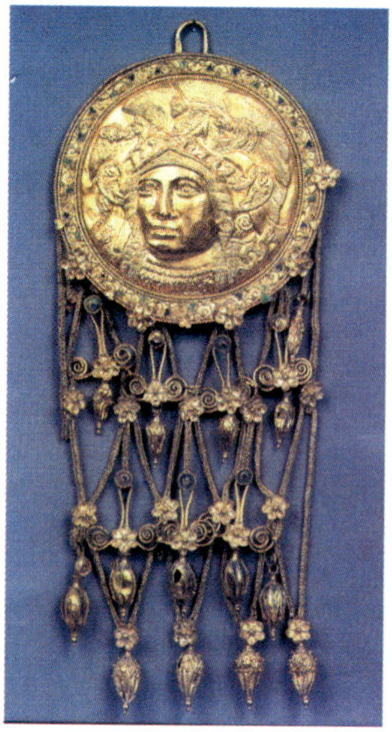

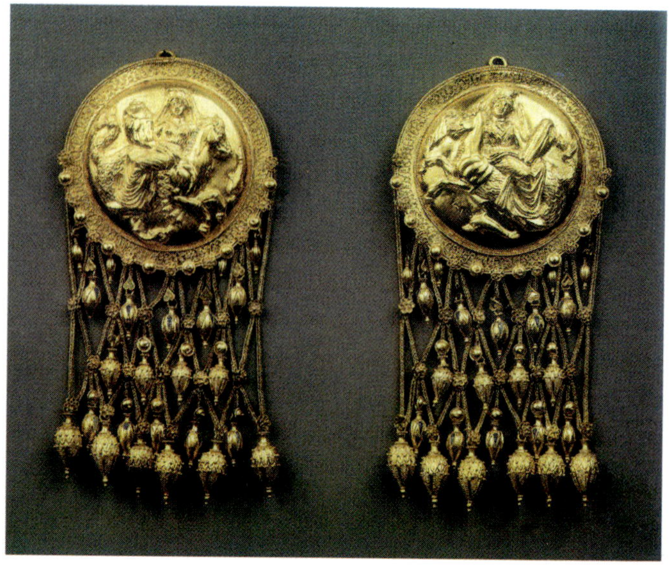

Plate 27: Gold and enamel temple pendant having a disk with relief head of Athena in a helmet with three crests supported by a sphinx and two winged horses and little griffins at its cheek pieces, from Kul-Oba barrow. Fourth century B.C.

Plate 28: Gold and enamel pair of temple ornaments, each consisting of a disk and a tracery of chains with filigree pendants from Bolshaya Bliznitsa. Fourth century B.C.

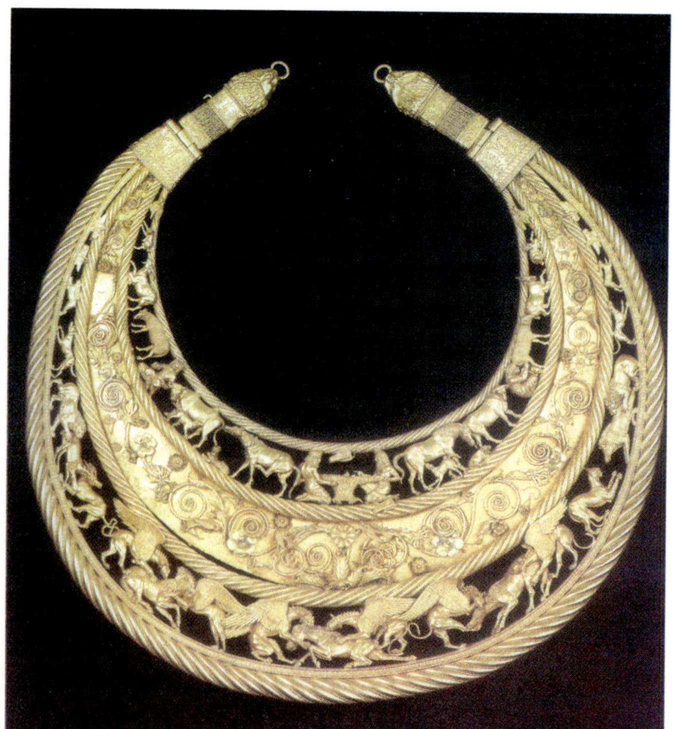

Plate 29: Gold pectoral terminating with lions heads and decorated with scenes of Scythian life in the upper frieze, fighting animals in the lower frieze and floral ornament in the middle from Tolstaya Mogila barrow. Fourth century B.C.

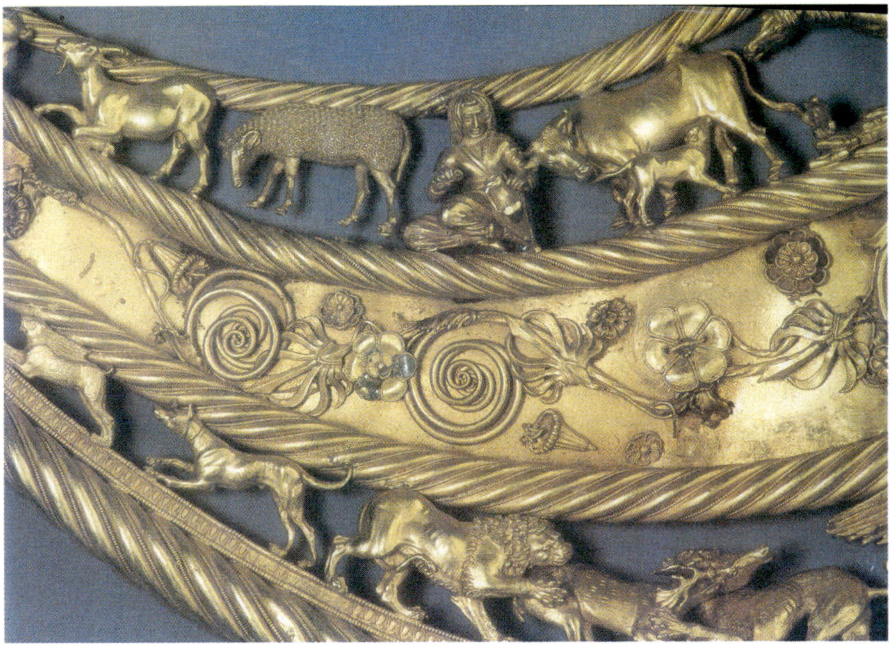

Plate 30: Details of gold pectoral from Tolstaya Mogila. Fourth century B.C.

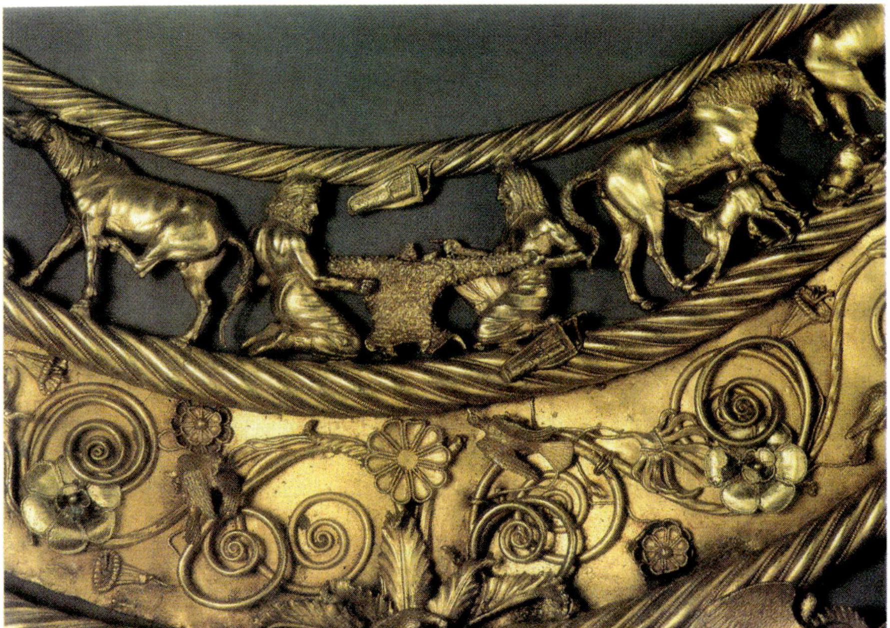

Plate 31: Details of gold pectoral from Tolstaya Mogila. Fourth century B.C.

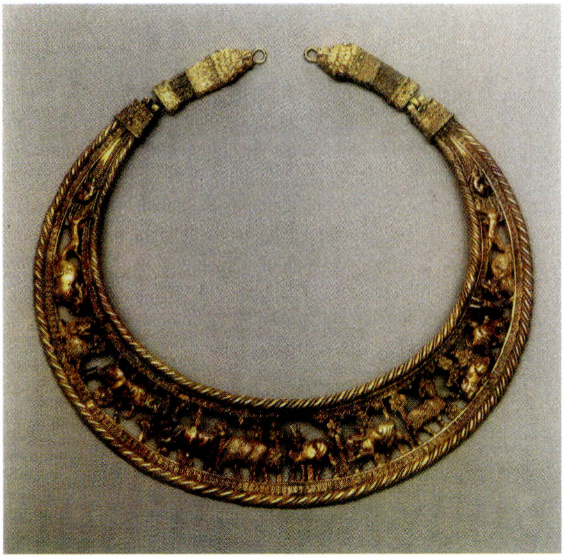

Plate 32: Gold and enamel crescent-shaped pectoral with fifteen sculptured figurines of animals (goats, rams, dogs and hares) and filigree flowers and petals between two twisted plaits from Bolshaya Bliznitsa. Fourth century B.C.

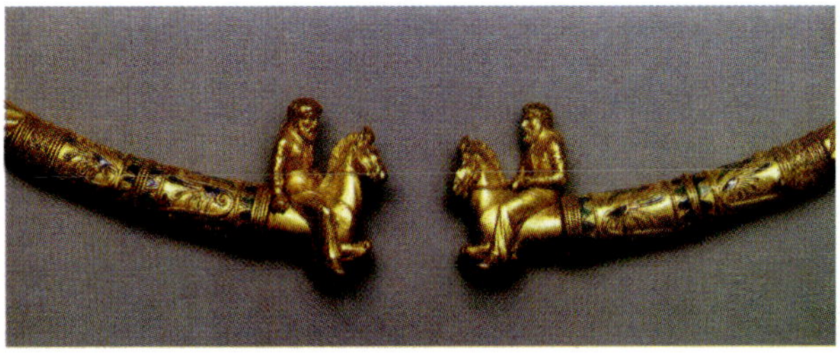

Plate 33: Gold and enamel torque of twisted gold wire with caps decorated with palmettes, lotus flowers and egg-and dart ornaments, inlaid with coloured enamels from Kul-Oba. Fourth century B.C.

Plate 34: Gold torque having smooth rope with terminals decorated with filigree ornaments and sculptured heads of lions from Talayev barrow. Fourth century B.C.

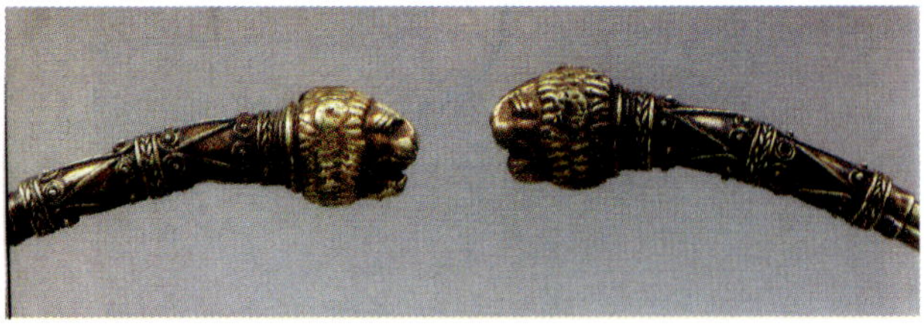

Plate 35: Gold torque with terminals in the form of recumbent lions from Kul-Oba. Fourth century B.C.

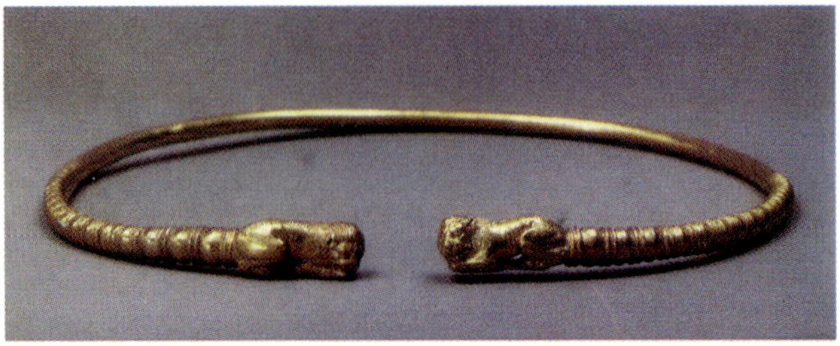

Plate 36: Gold torque decorated with ring-shaped bands, with sculptured scenes of a lion tearing Karagodeuashkh barrow. Late fourth century B.C.

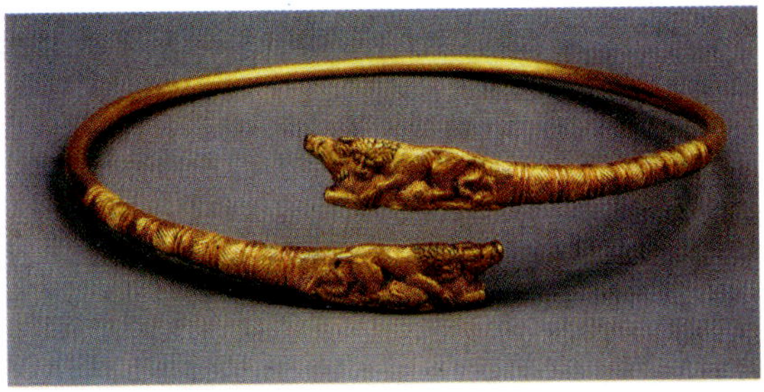

Plate 37: Gold torque with sculptured figures of lions at both ends from Chertomlyk barrow. Last quarter of the fourth century B.C.

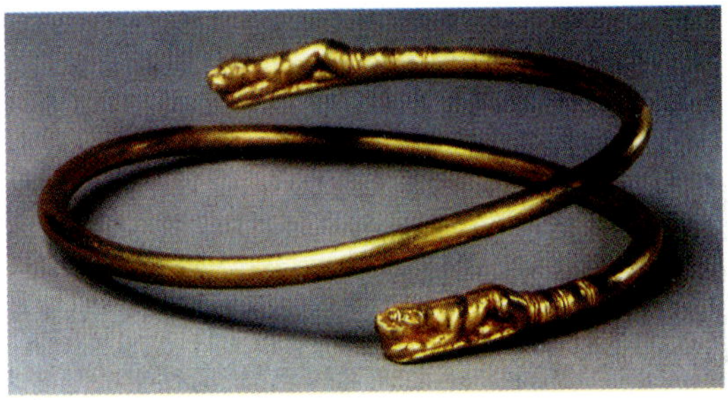

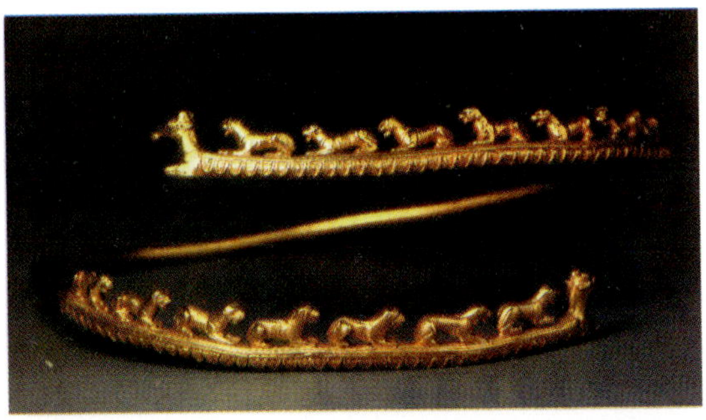

Plate 38: Gold torque with two groups of sculptured lions and terminals in the form of foreparts of deer from Tolstaya Mogila barrow. Fourth century B.C.

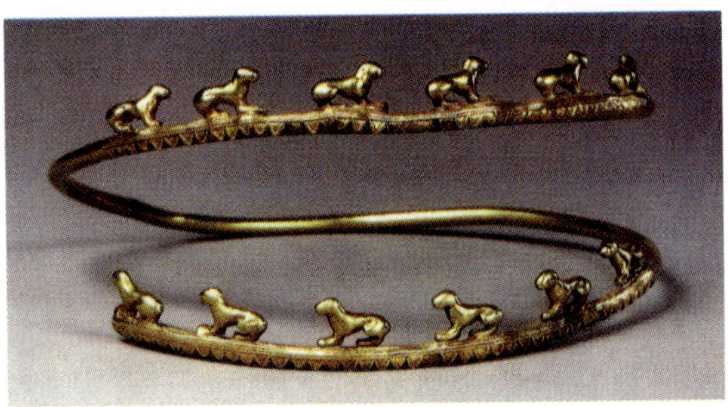

Plate 39: Gold torque decorated with sculptured figures of lions and applied jagged ornament from Chertomlyk barrow. Last quarter of the fourth century B.C.

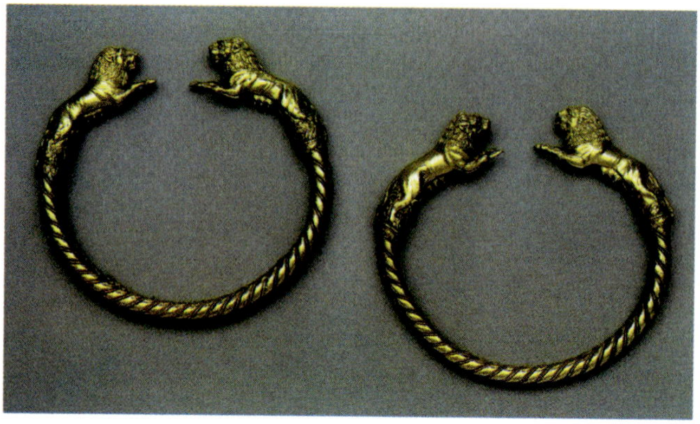

Plate 40: Gold and bronze (with traces of enamel) bracelets having bronze plaits covered by gold leaves and decorated with sculptured figures of lionesses at the ends from Bolshaya Bliznitsa. Fourth century B.C.

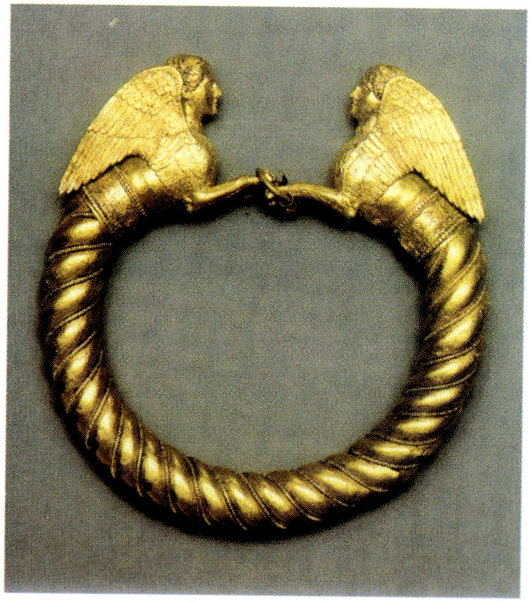

Plate 41: Gold, bronze and enamel twisted bracelet (bronze base covered with gold leaf) with terminals in the form of sculptured half-length figures of sphinxes from Kul-Oba barrow. Fourth century B.C.

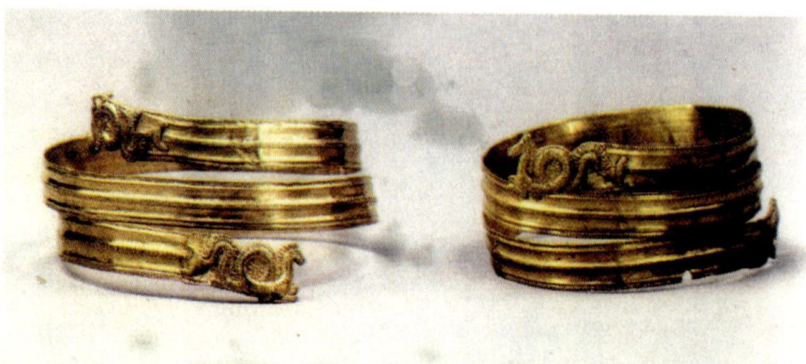

Plate 42: Gold spiral-shaped link bracelets each with relief figures of hippocampi at the ends from Karago-deuashkh barrow. Late fourth century B.C.

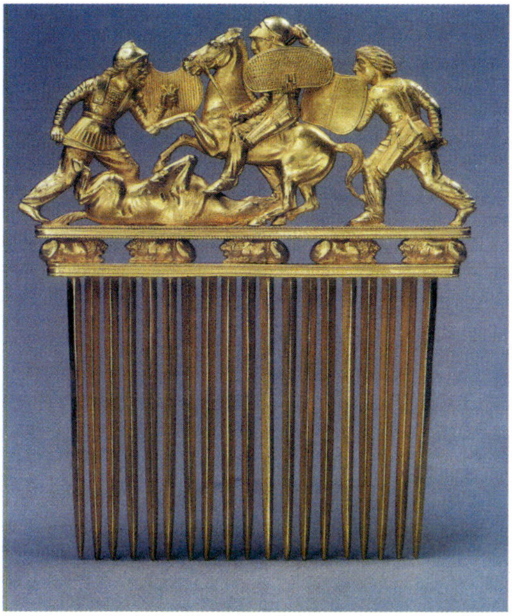

Plate 43: Gold comb with battle scene from Solokha barrow. Fifth century B.C.

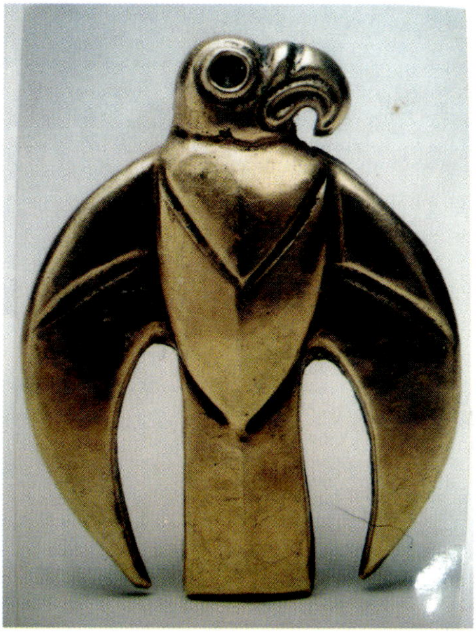

Plate 44: Gold plaque depicting a bird of prey from Litoy barrow. Late seventh or early sixth century B.C.

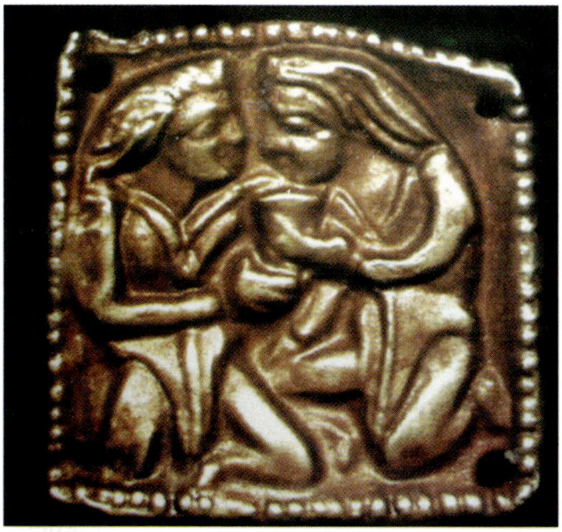

Plate 45: Gold sewn-on plaque from a vestment with a brotherhood ritual of two facing Scythians drinking from the same rhyton, from Solokha barrow. First half of the fourth century B.C.

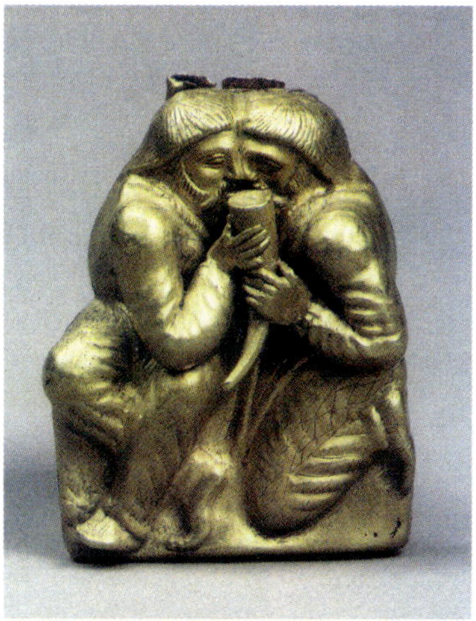

Plate 46: Gold plaque with a brotherhood ritual scene in high relief showing two Scythians drinking from the same rhyton from Kul-Oba barrow. Fourth century B.C.

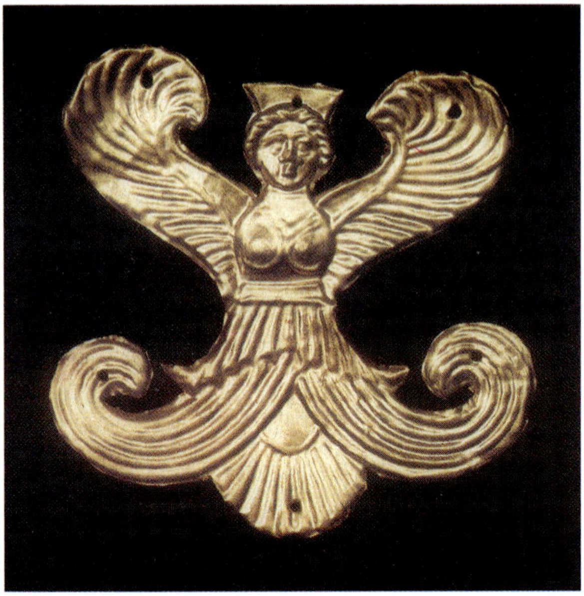

Plate 47: Gold plaque from a vestment depicting a winged goddess with branched off scrolls instead of legs and with palmettes from Bolshaya Bliznitsa. Fourth century B.C.

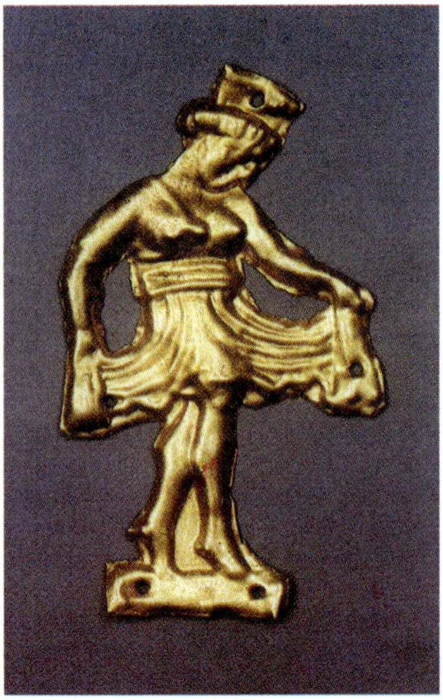

Plate 48: Gold plaque from a vestment depicting a dancing woman wearing a short tunic and holding a calathus from Bolshaya Bliznitsa. Fourth century B.C.

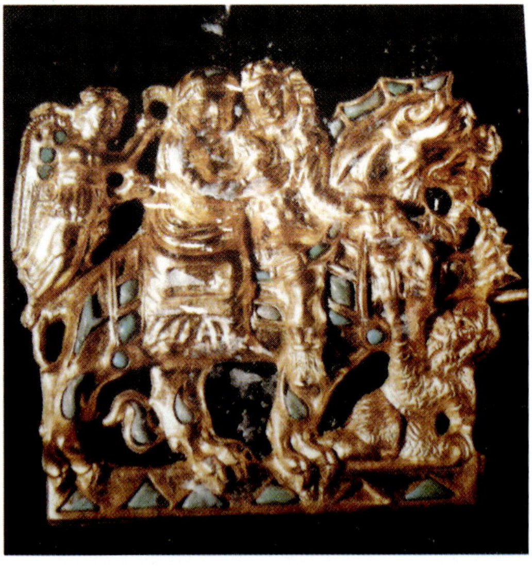

Plate 49: Clasps with amorous scene from Tillya-tepe, burial 6. First century A.D.

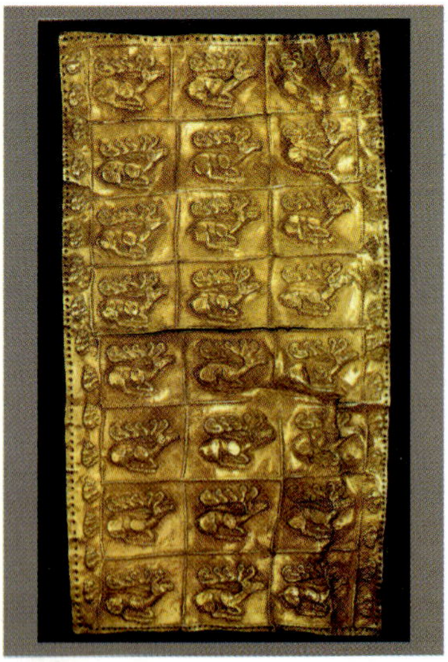

Plate 50: Gold overlay for a Scythian gorytus (case for bow and arrows) with relief figures of stags and panthers from Kelermes barrow 4. Late seventh or early sixth century B.C.

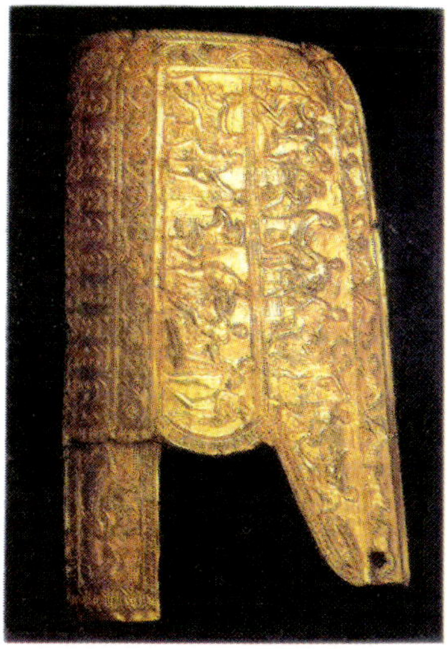

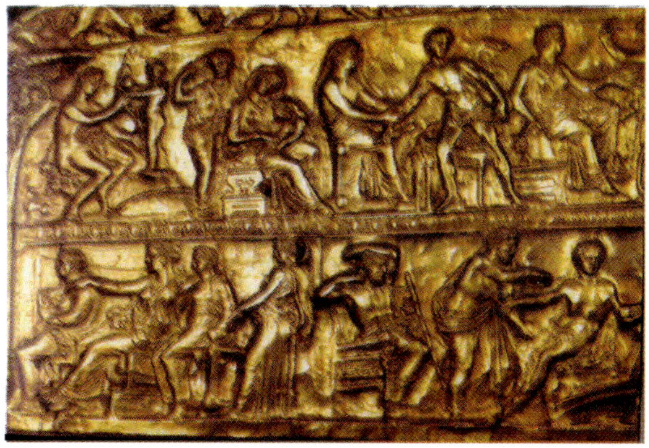

Plate 52: Details of the gold overlay from Chertomlyk barrow. Fourth century B.C.

Plate 51: Gold overlay of a Scythian gorytus with relief images of fighting animals, antique floral patterns and scenes from the life of Achilles from Chertomlyk barrow. Last Quarter of the fourth century B.C.

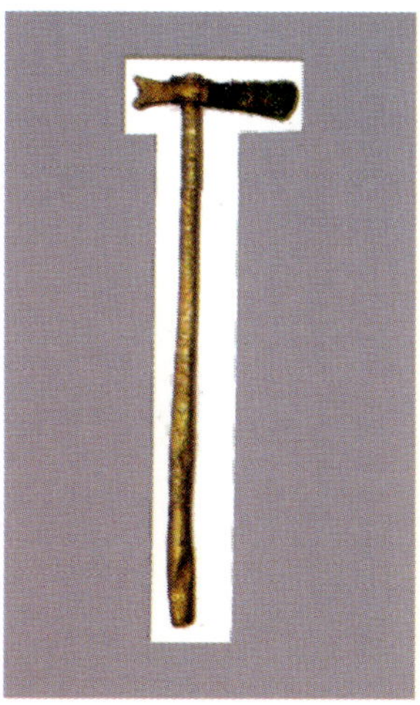

Plate 53: Gold and iron ceremonial battle-axe decorated with sculptured figures of goats and ritual scenes and animals in relief from Kelermes barrow 1. Late seventh or early sixth century B.C.

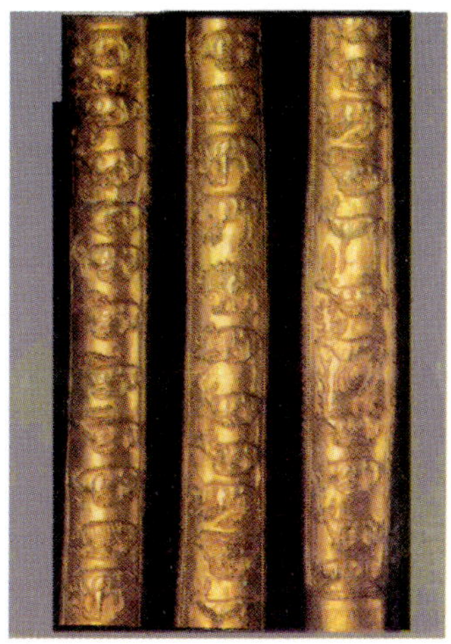

Plate 54: Details of Kelermes battle-axe. Late seventh or early sixth century B.C.

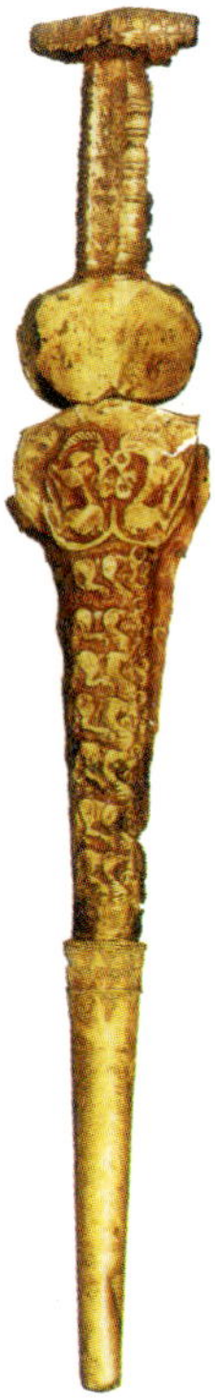

Plate 55: Gold and iron sword in a gold scabbard decorated with relief figures of ibex and panthers from Shumeiko barrow. Late sixth or early Fifth century B.C.

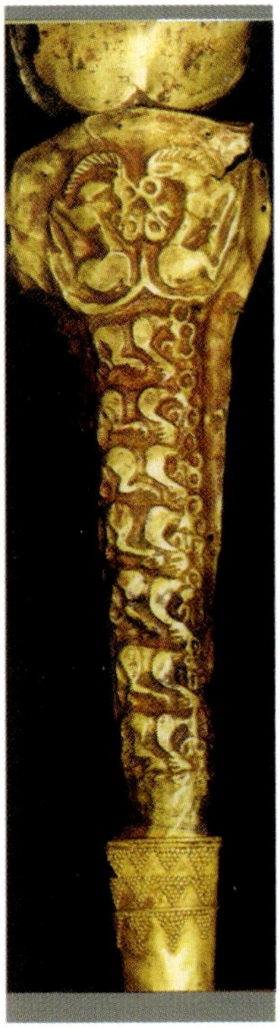

Plate 56: Details of iron sword from Shumeiko barrow. The tip of the scabbard is ornamented with granulated triangles. Late sixth or early fifth century B.C.

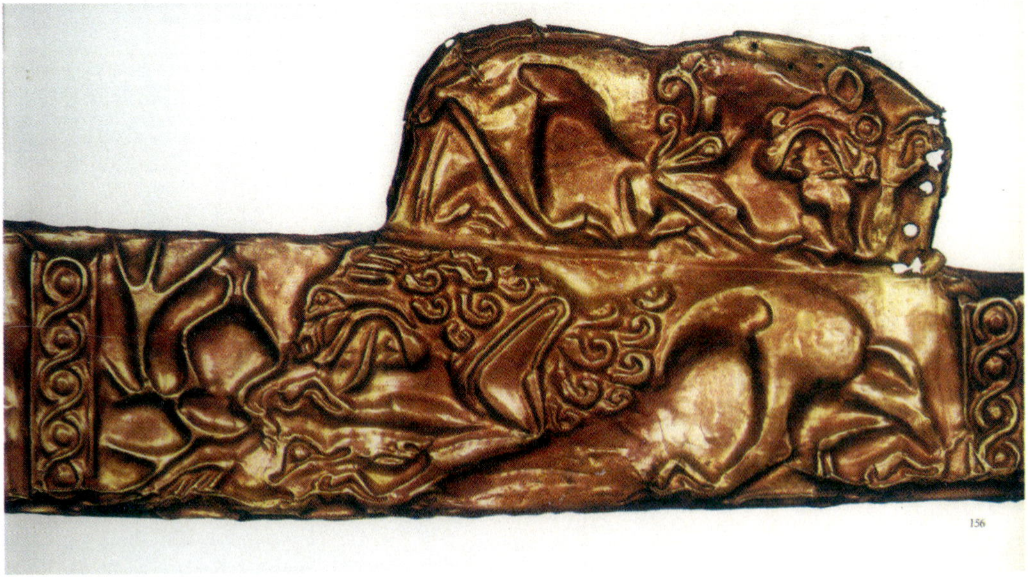

Plate 57: Details of gold scabbard with relief figures of lions tearing stag's heads from Solokha barrow. First half of the fourth century B.C.

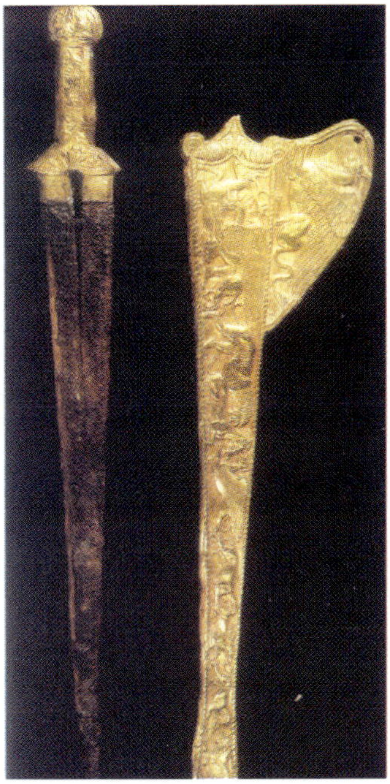

Plate 58: Iron sword and gold scabbard from Tolstaya Mogila barrow. Fourth century B.C.

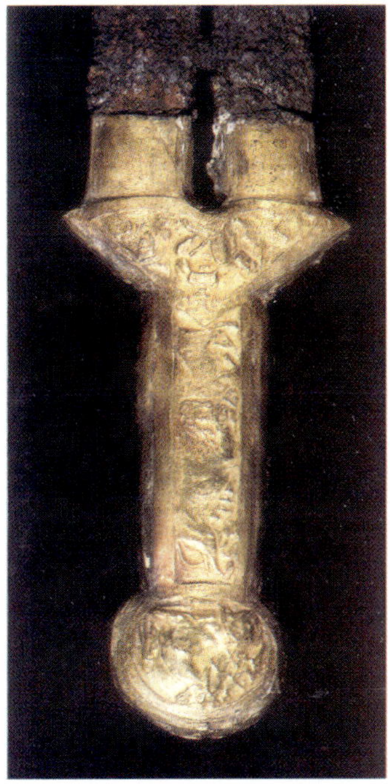

Plate 59: Details of sword hilt from Tolstaya Mogila. Fourth century B.C.

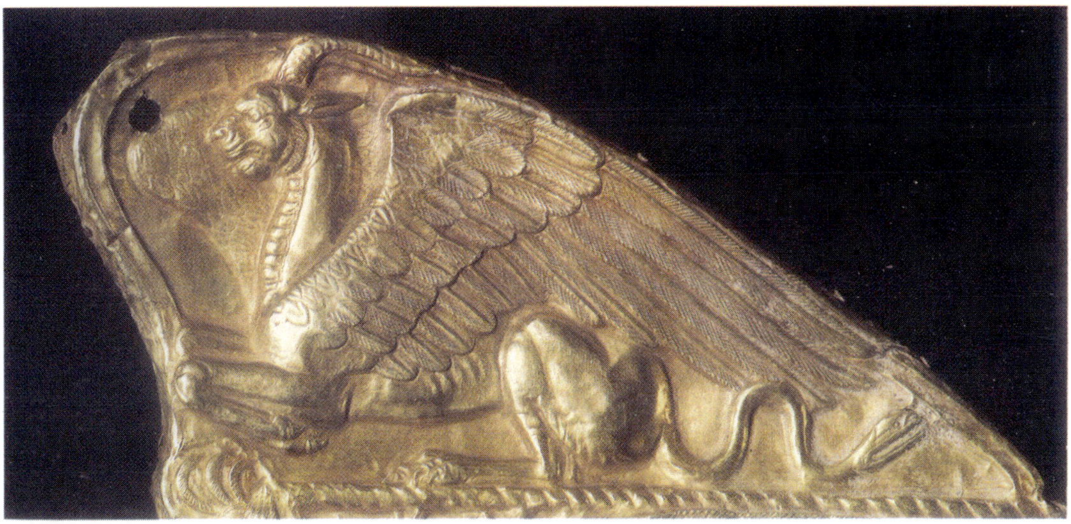

Plate 60: Details of scabbard decorated with scenes of fighting animals from Tolstaya Mogila. Fourth century B.C.

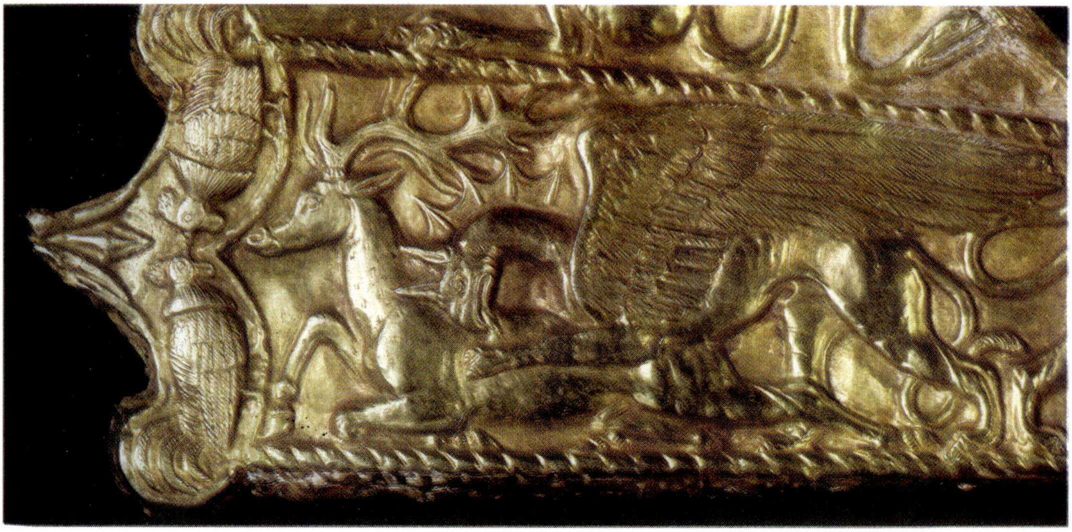

Plate 61: Details of sçabbard from Tolstaya Mogila. Fourth century B.C.

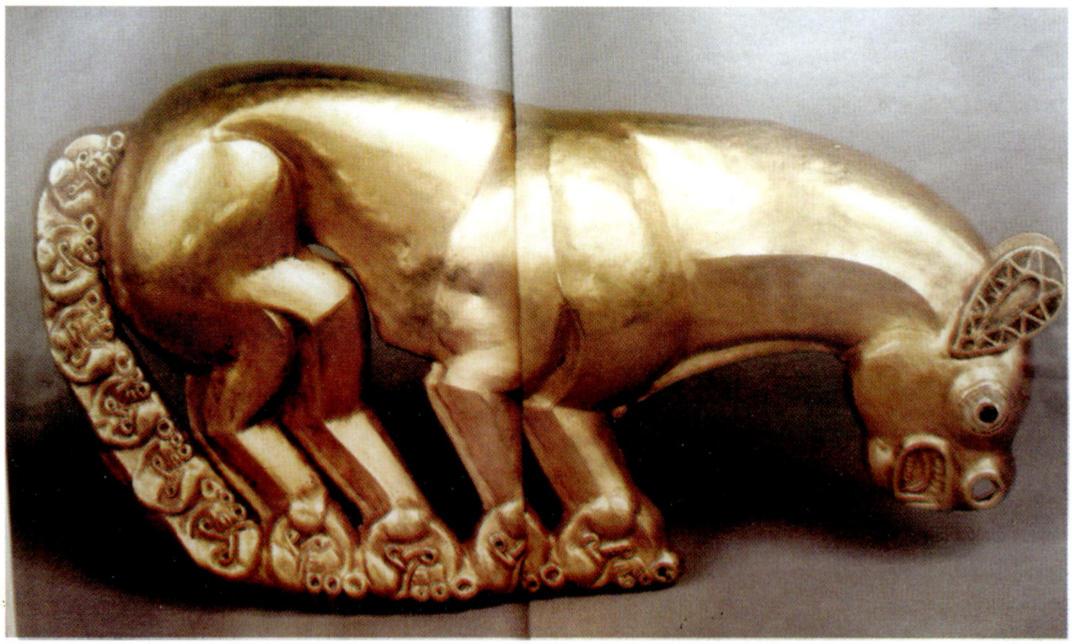

Plate 62: Gold, amber and enamel shield ornament depicting a panther from Kelermes barrow 1. Late seventh or early sixth century B.C.

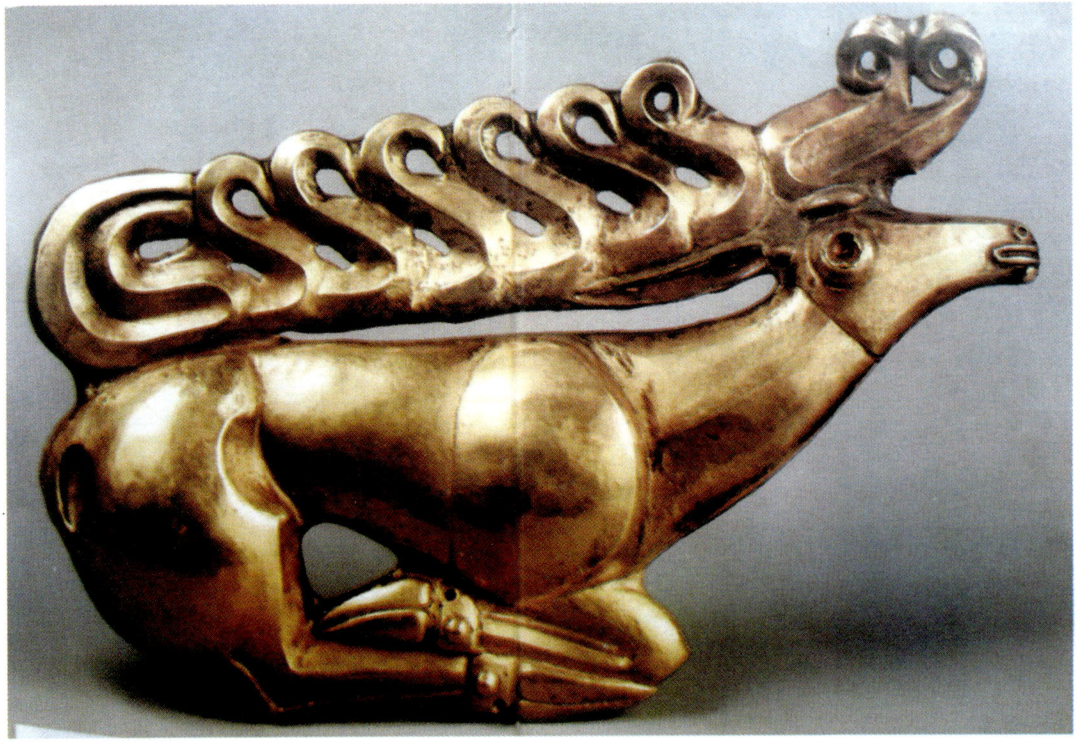

Plate 63: Gold shield plaque depicting a stag from Kostromskaya barrow. Late seventh or early sixth century B.C.

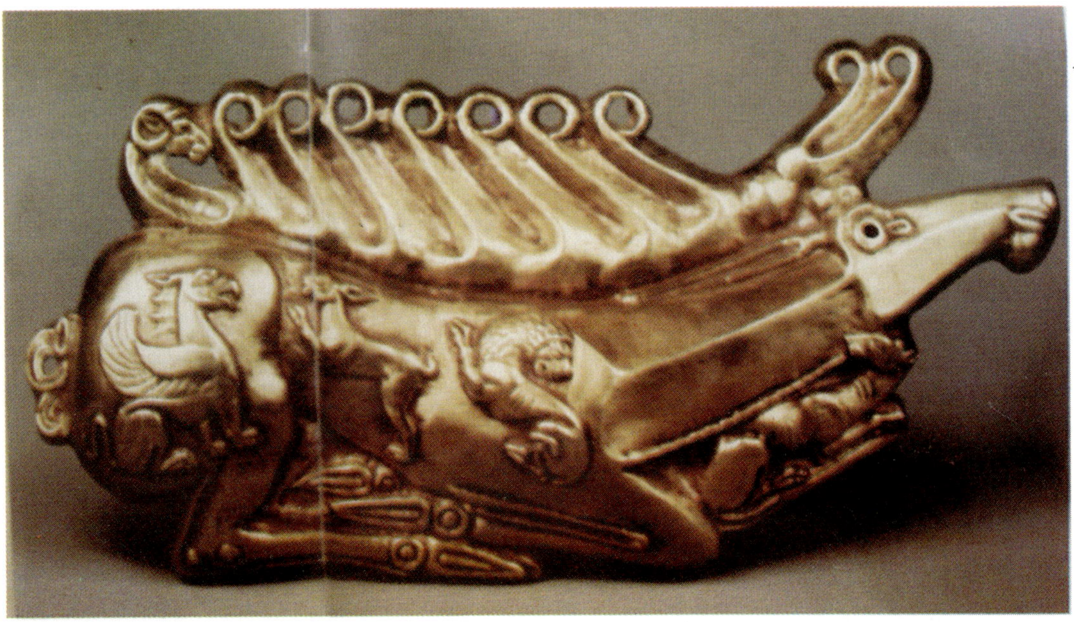

Plate 64: Gold shield plaque depicting a stag from Kul-Oba barrow. Fourth century B.C.

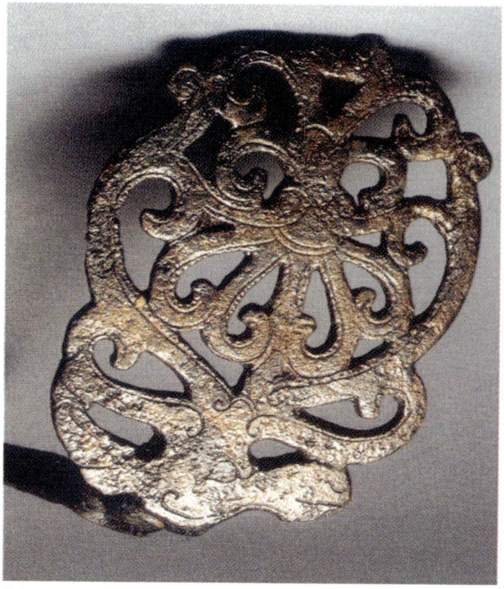

Plate 65: Bronze bridle cheekpiece depicting stylized head of a stag amid the openwork from Elizavetinskaia barrow 7. Fourth century B.C.

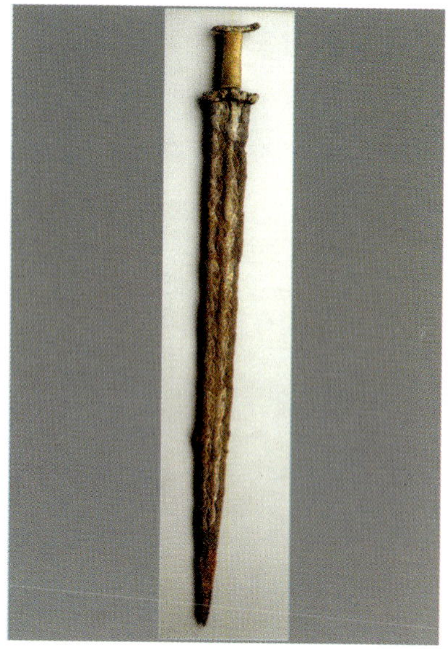

Plate 66: Iron and gold long sword from Flippovka barrow 1. Fourth century B.C.

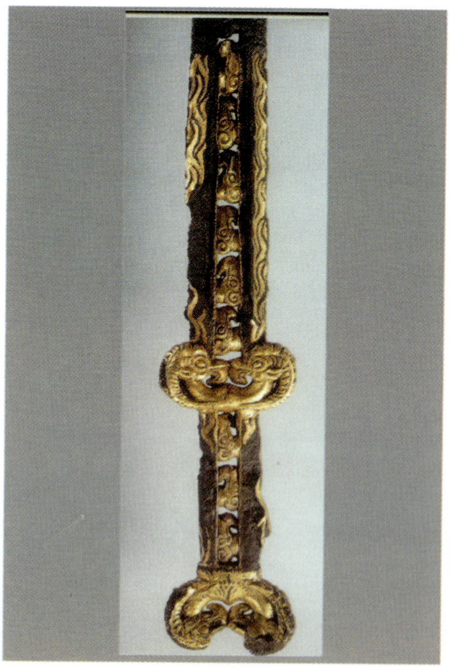

Plate 67: Iron and gold akinakes from Flippovka barrow 1. Late fifth to early fourth century B.C.

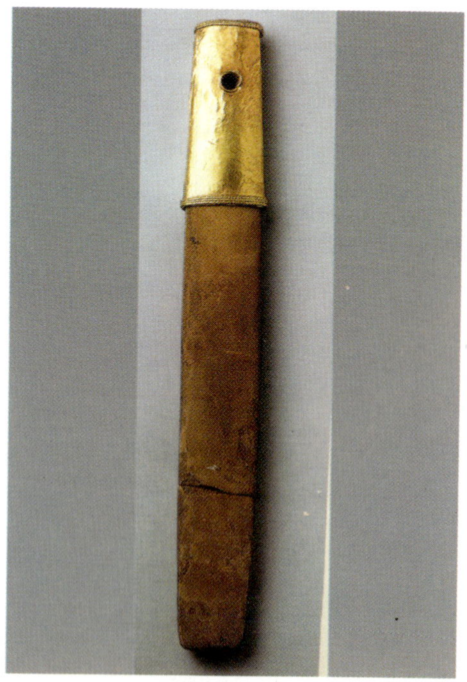

Plate 68: Sandstone and gold whetstone with decorative mounting, from Flippovka barrow 1. Fourth century B.C.

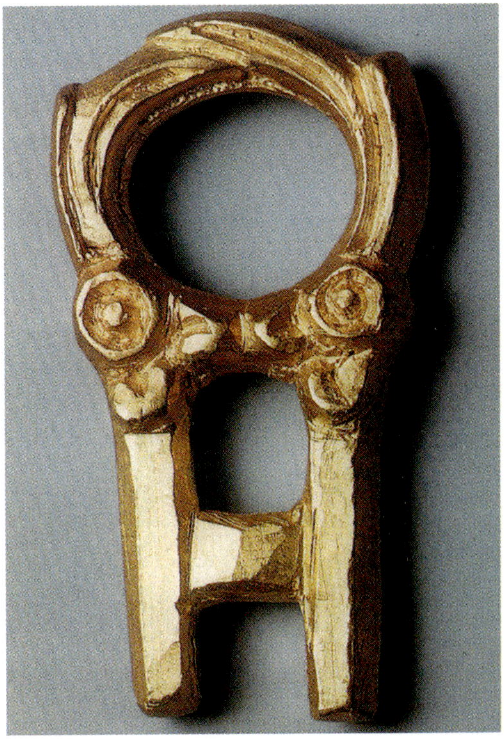

Plate 69: Gold buckle for a horse trapping from Filippovka barrow 1. Fourth century B.C.

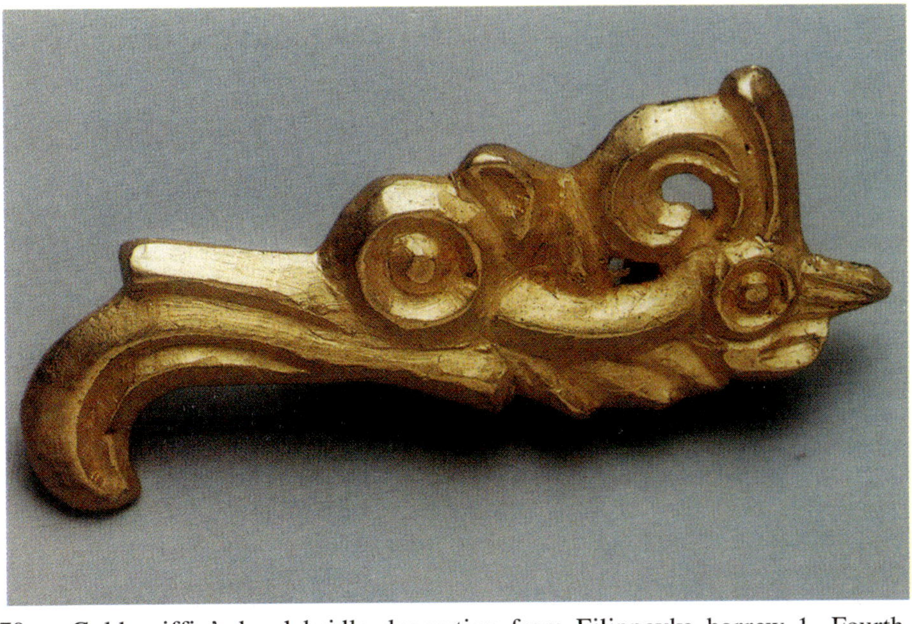

Plate 70: Gold griffin's-head bridle decoration from Filippovka barrow 1. Fourth century B.C.

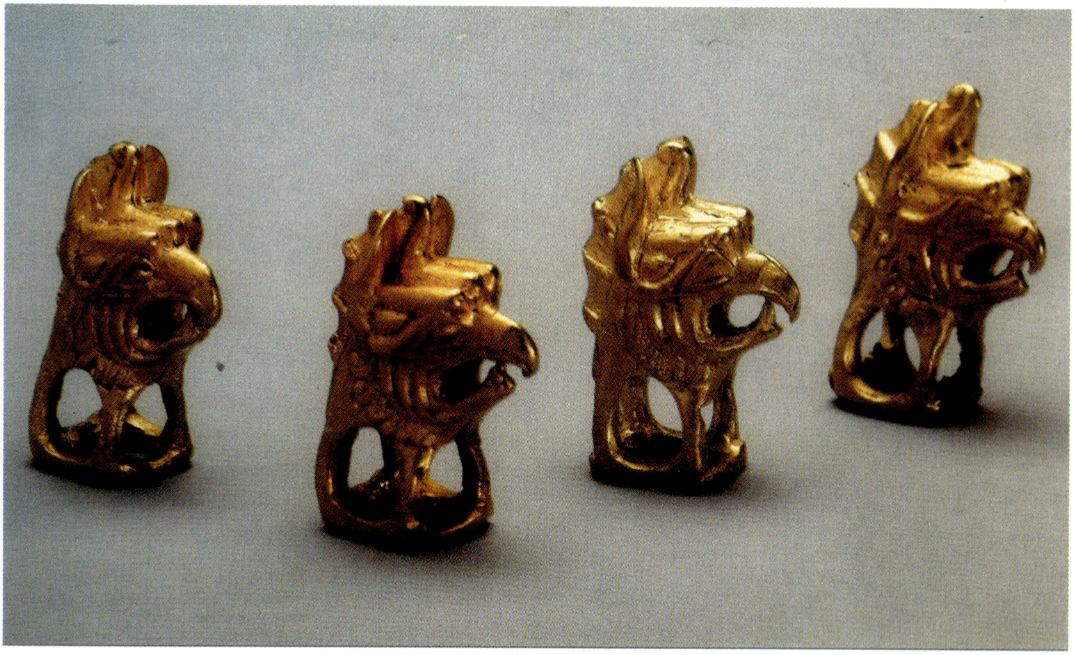

Plate 71: Four gold bridle griffin's-head decorations from Filippovka barrow 1. Fourth century B.C.

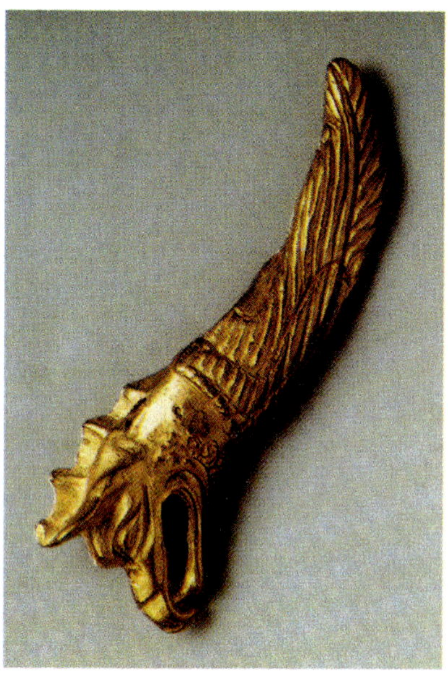

Plate 72: Gold griffin-shaped bridle decoration from Filippovka barrow 1. Fourth century B.C.

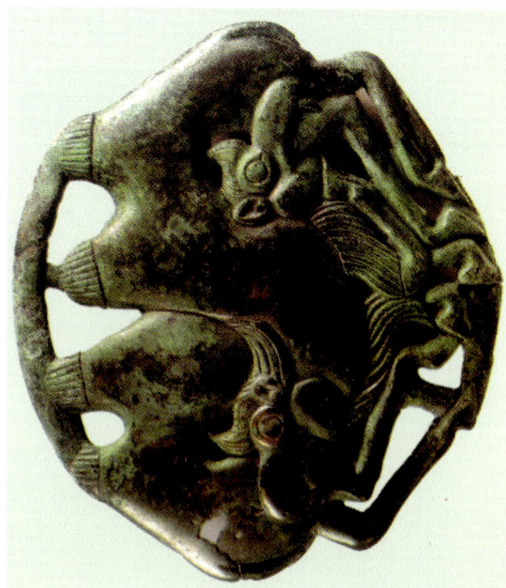

Plate 73: Bronze plaque showing a combat scene between two camels from Filippovka barrow 1. Fourth century B.C.

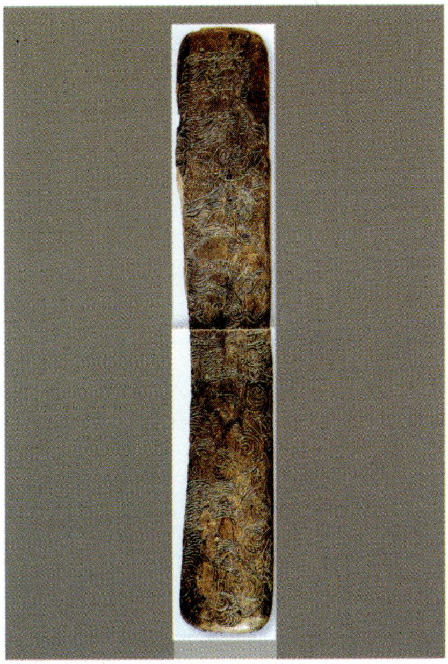

Plate 74: Cedar sarcophagus lid with zoomorphic imagery from Bashadar barrow 2. Sixth century B.C.

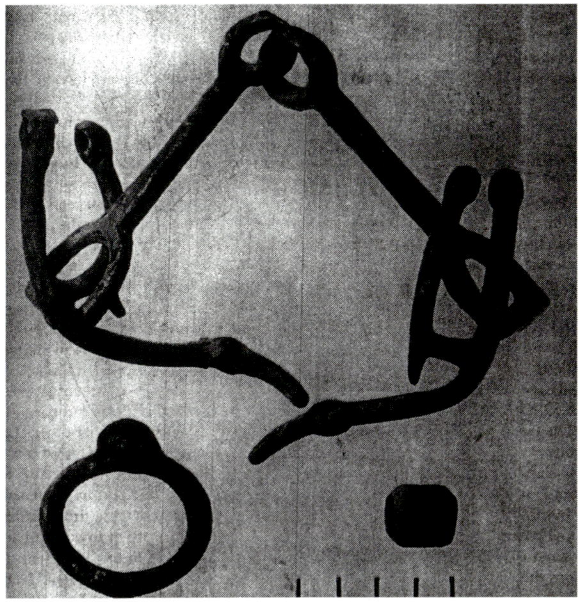

Plate 75: Bronze bridle bits with cheek-pieces, saddle-girth buckle and strap-distributor from Aldy-Bel' barrow. Eighth to sixth century B.C.

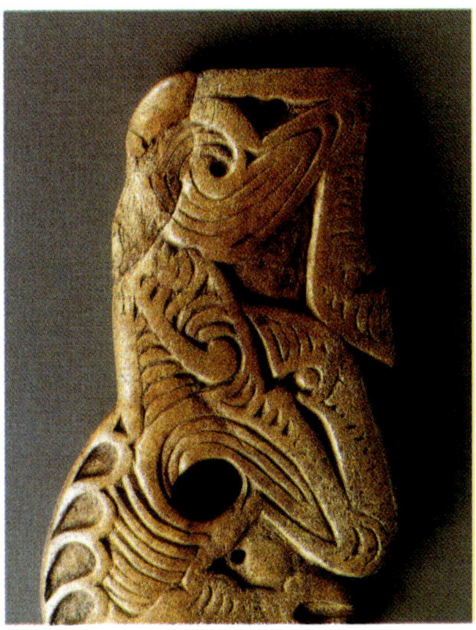

Plate 76: Horse-shaped horn plaque from Sagly-Bazhi II barrow 13. Fifth century B.C.

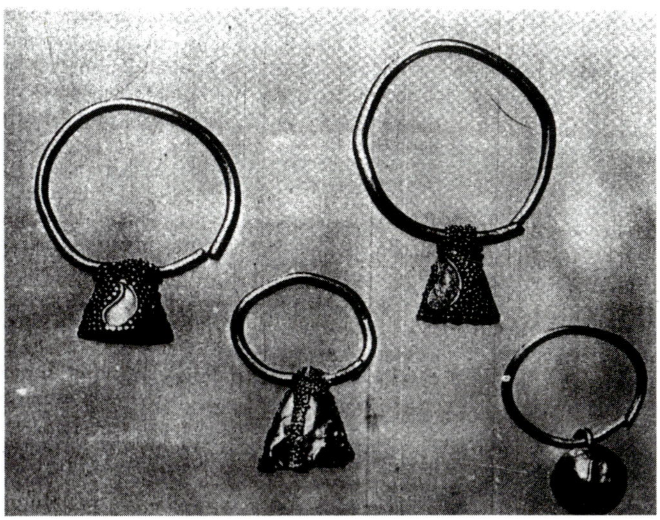

Plate 77: Gold earrings from Aldy-Bel' burial barrow 1. Fifth century B.C.

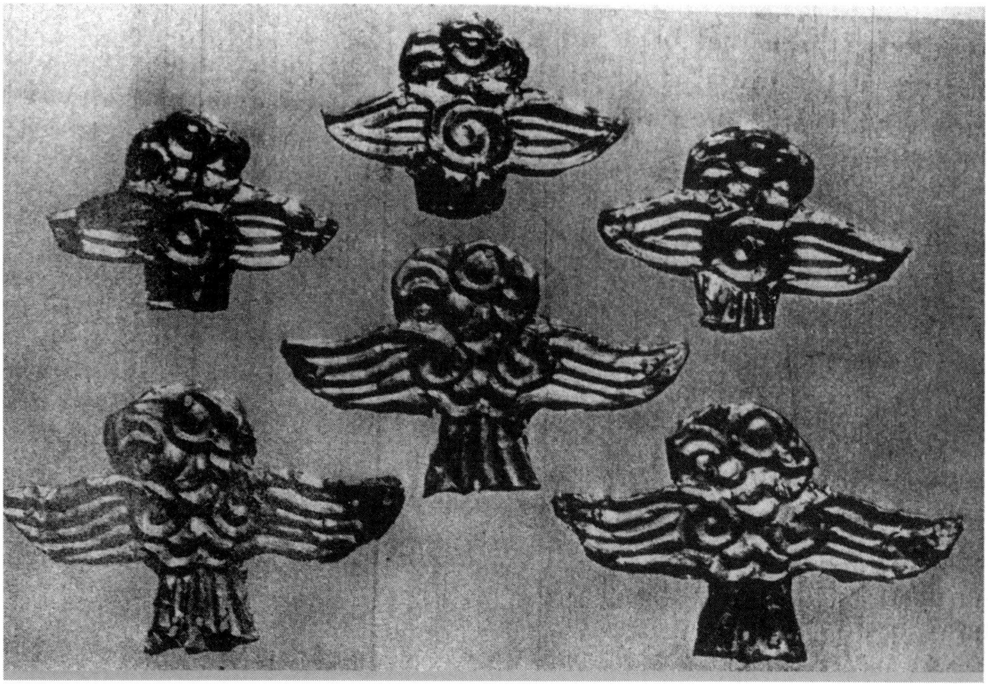

Plate 78: Gold garment-decorations representing birds of prey from Kosh-Pej barrow 2. Fifth century B.C.

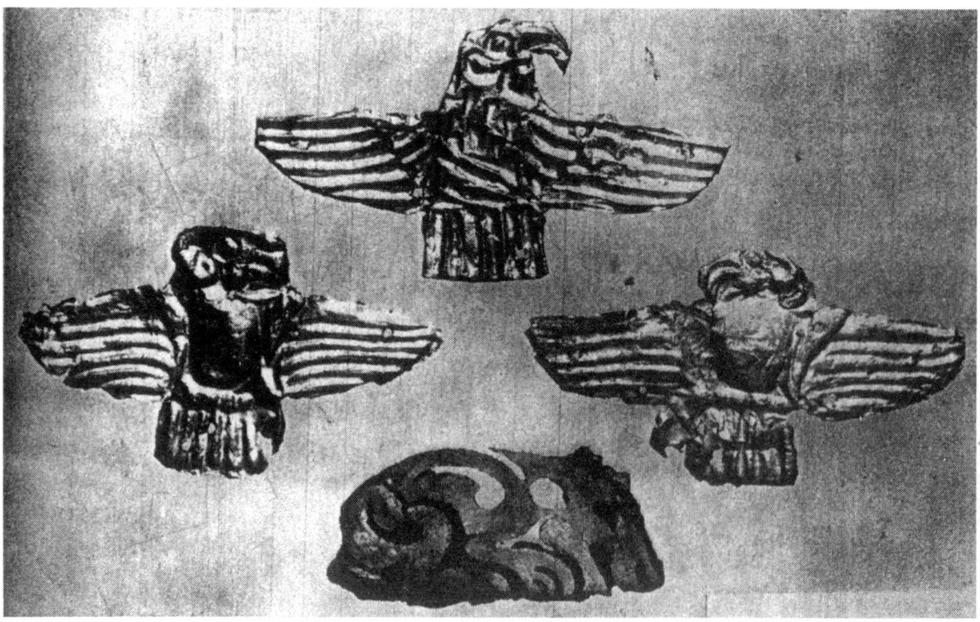

Plate 79: Gold garment-decorations representing birds of prey from Kosh-Pej barrow 1. Fifth century B.C.

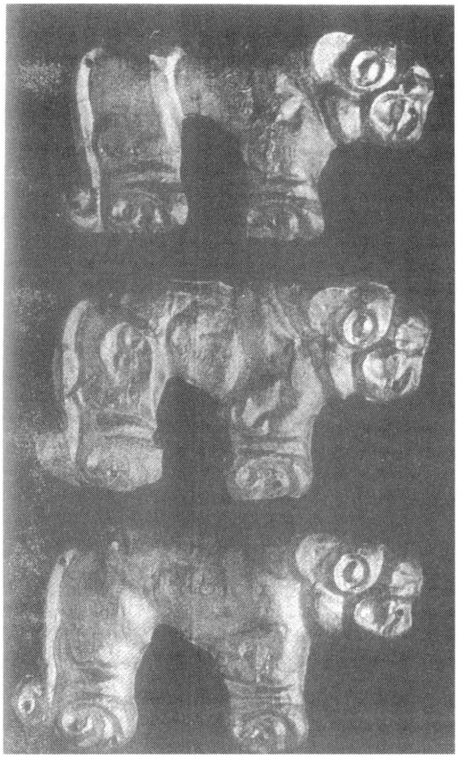

Plate 80: Gold garment-decorations shaped as panthers from Kosh-Pej. Fifth century B.C.

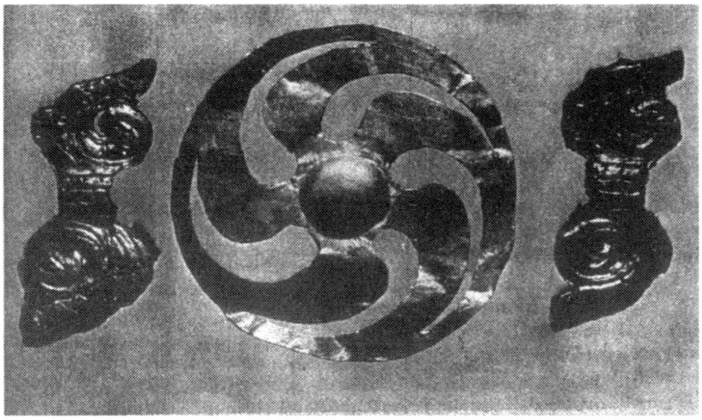

Plate 81: A gold *svastika*-shaped decoration and iron buckles covered with gold leaf from Kosh-Pej. Fifth century B.C.

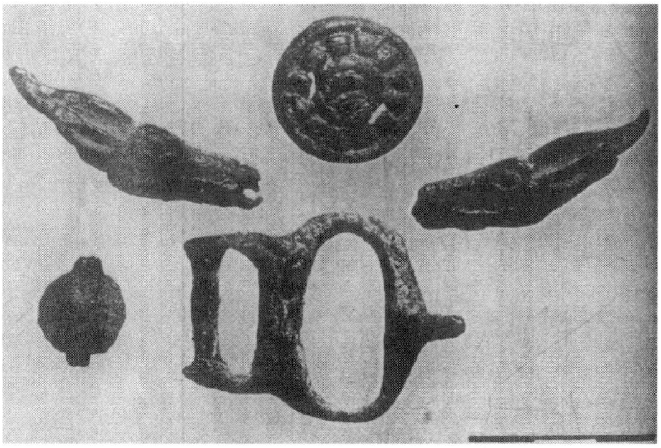

Plate 82: Bronze buckle and belt-decorations from the burial site of Suglug-Khem 1. Second century B.C.

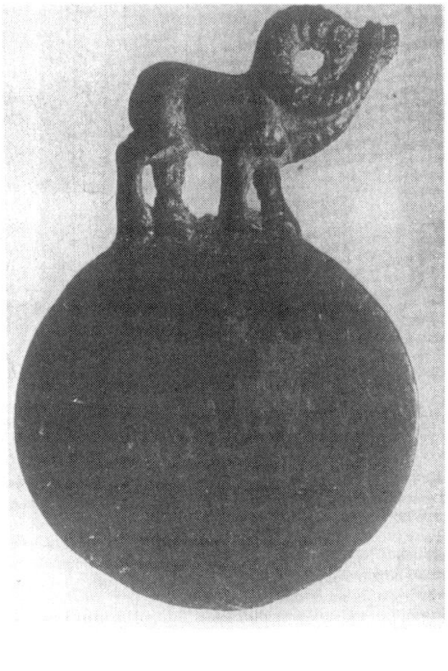

Plate 83: Bronze mirror with a zoomorphic handle from the burial site of Suglug-Khem 1. Second century B.C.

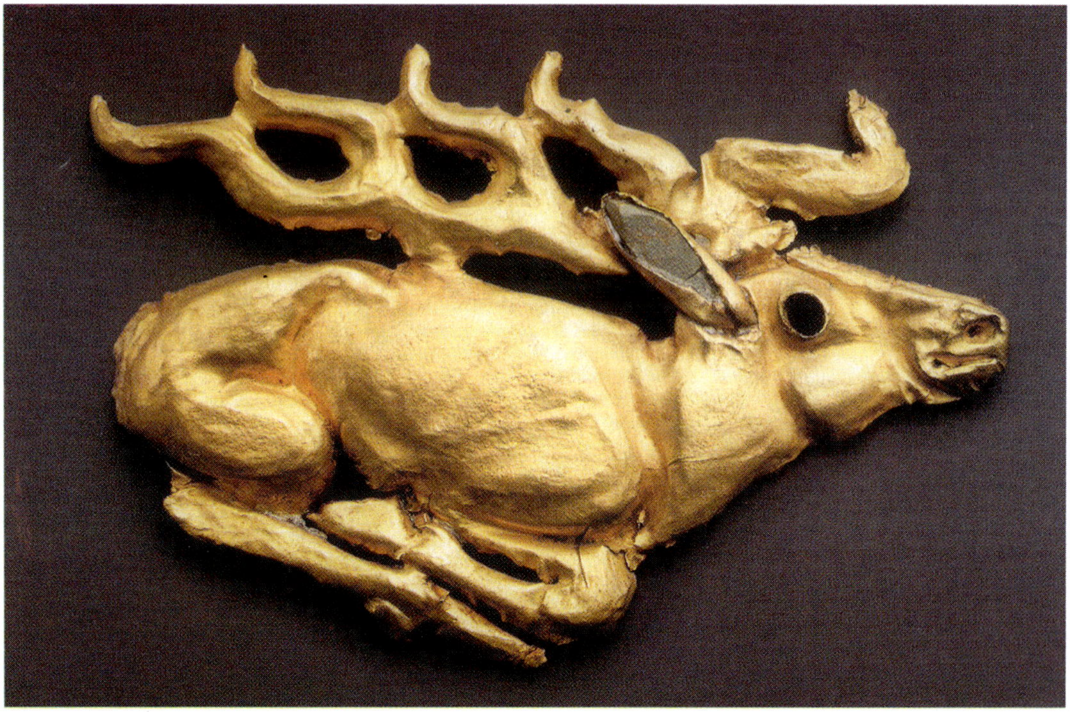

Plate 84: Gold reindeer-shaped plaques with turquoise ears from Chilikta barrow 5, Kazakhstan. Second half of the eighth century to first half of the seventh century B.C.

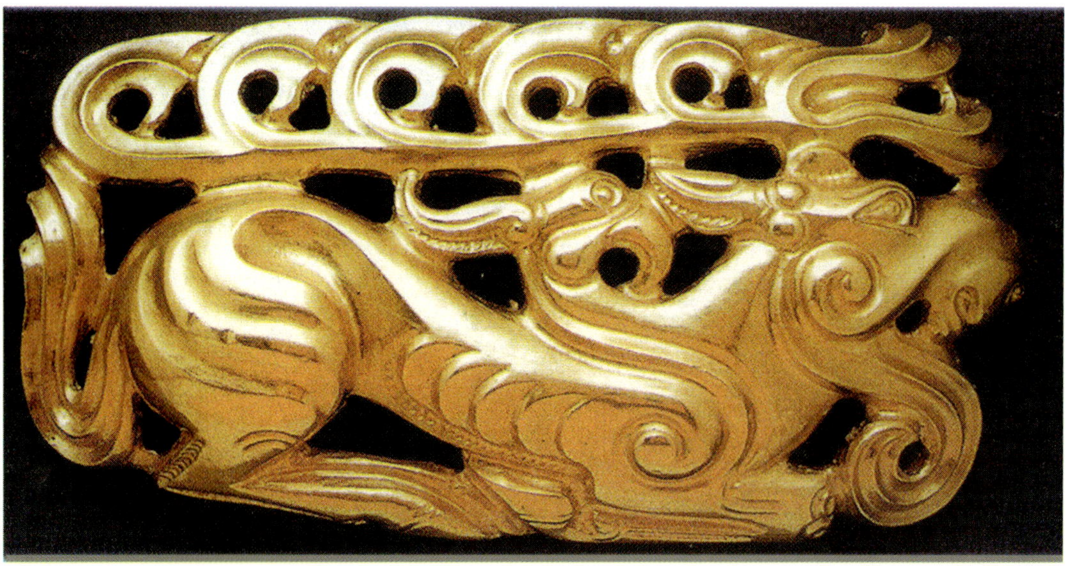

Plate 85: Gold belt plaques in the shape of a stag-chimera from Issyk barrow, Eastern Kazakhstan. Fifth to fourth century B.C.

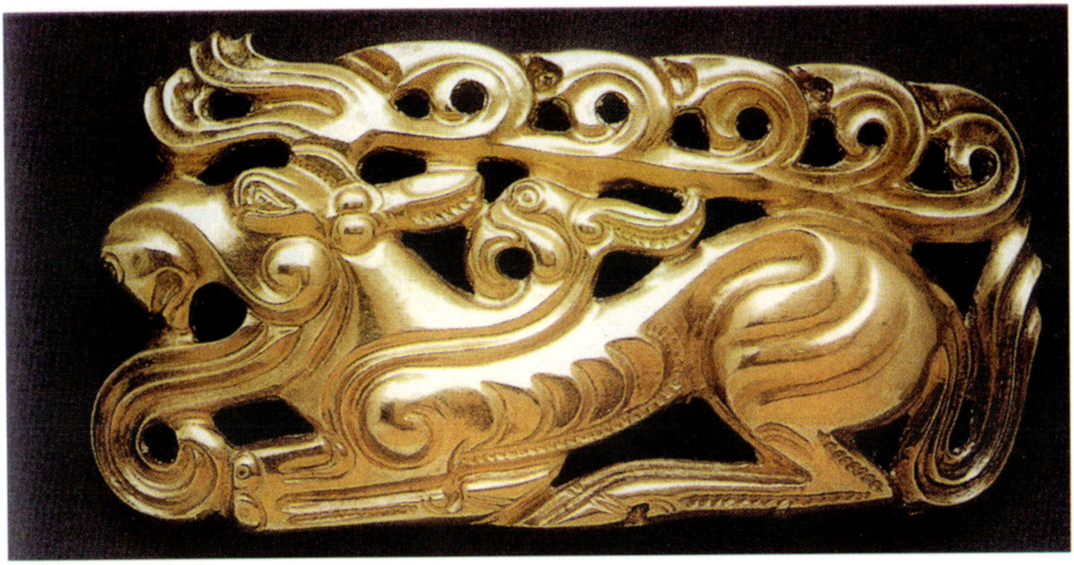

Plate 86: Gold belt plaque in the shape of a stag-chimera from Issyk barrow, Eastern Kazakhstan. Fifth to fourth century B.C.

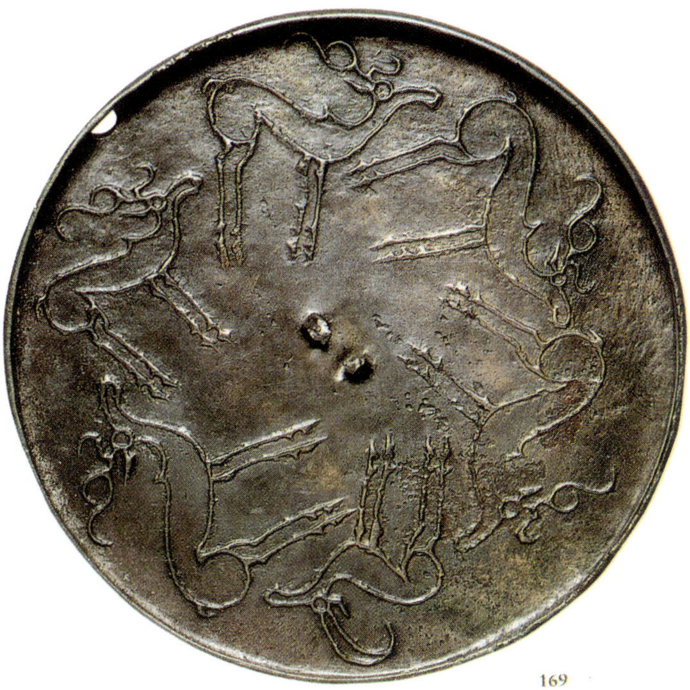

Plate 87: Bronze mirror with figures of standing stags and a mountain goat, from Ust' — Bukhtarma, Altai. Eighth to seventh century B.C.

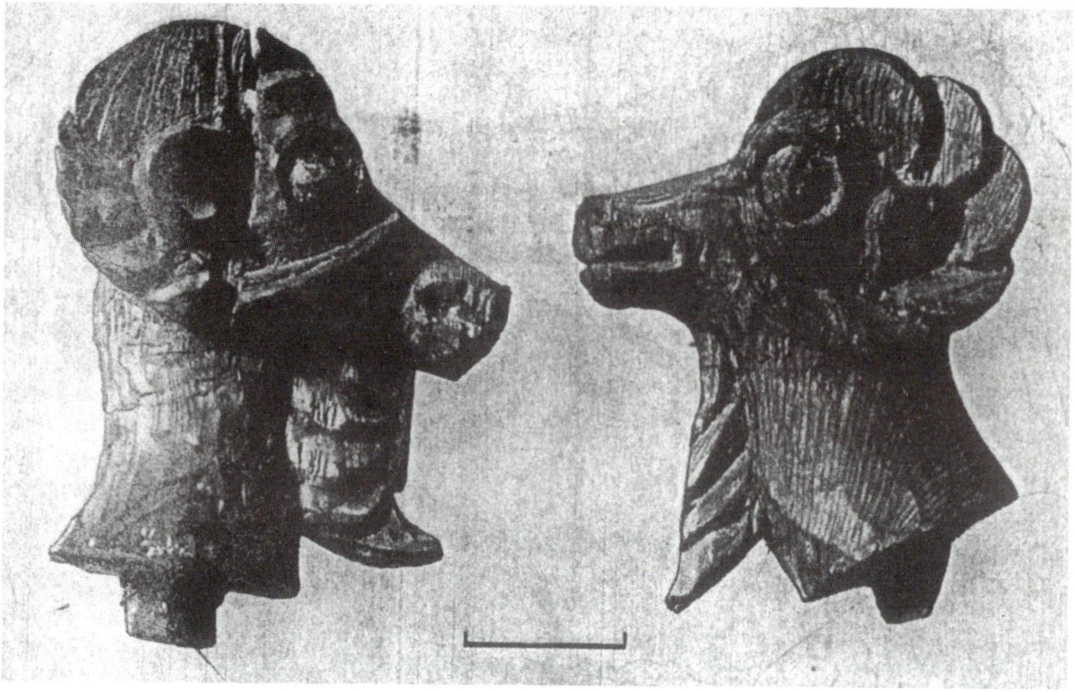

Plate 88: Wooden ibex heads from Kuturguntas barrow, Pazyryk. Fifth century B.C.

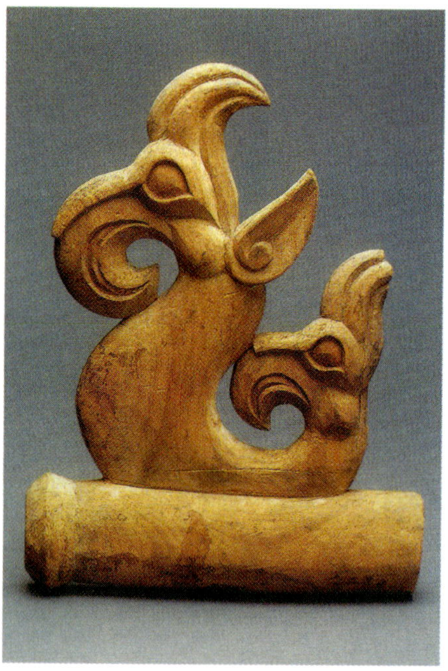

Plate 89: Cedar bridle ornament in the form of two griffins' heads from Tuekta barrow 1. Sixth century B.C.

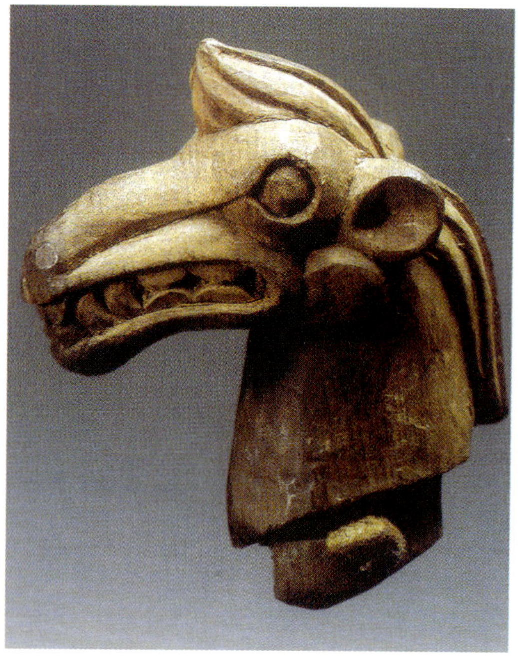

Plate 90: Larch bridle ornament from Tuekta barrow 1. Sixth century B.C.

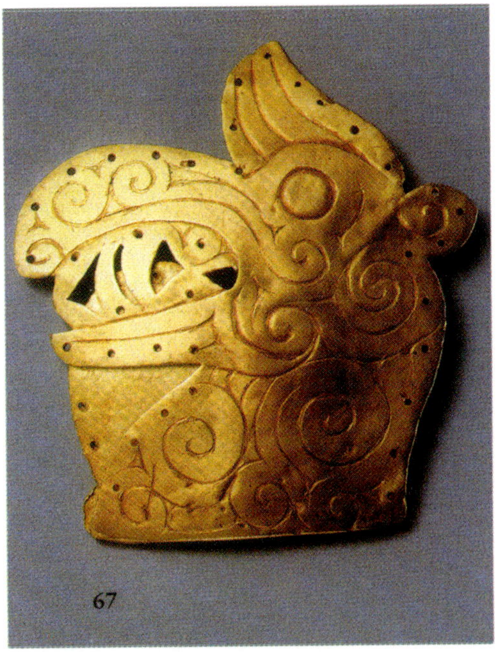

Plate 91: Gold camel-griffin's-head plaque from Filippovka barrow 1. Fourth century B.C.

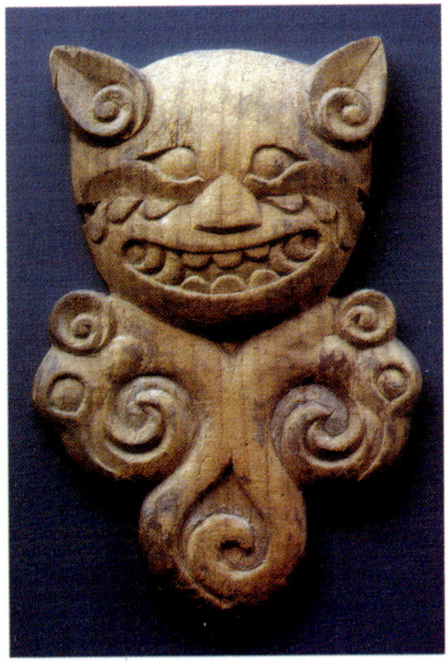

Plate 92: Larch bridle ornament from Tuekta barrow 1. Sixth century B.C.

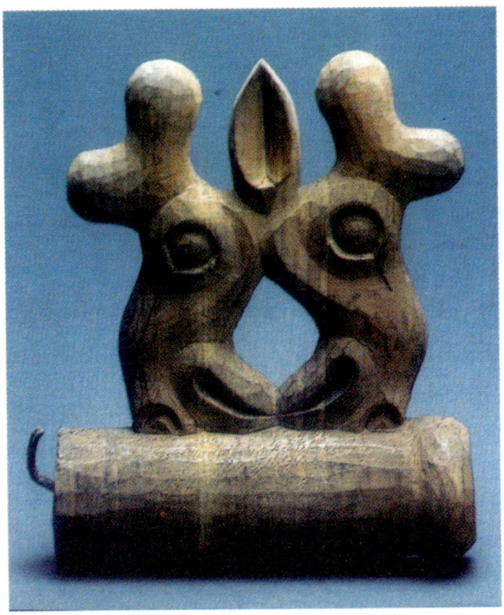

Plate 93: Cedar bridle ornament consisting of two elks' heads from Tuekta barrow 1. Sixth century B.C.

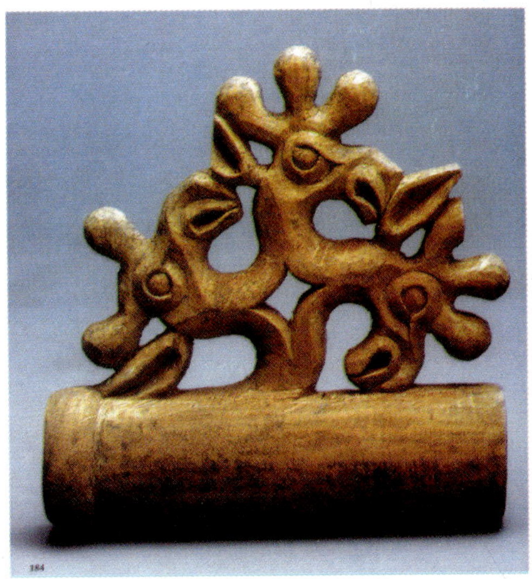

Plate 94: Cedar bridle ornament consisting of three elks' heads from Tuekta barrow 1. Sixth century B.C.

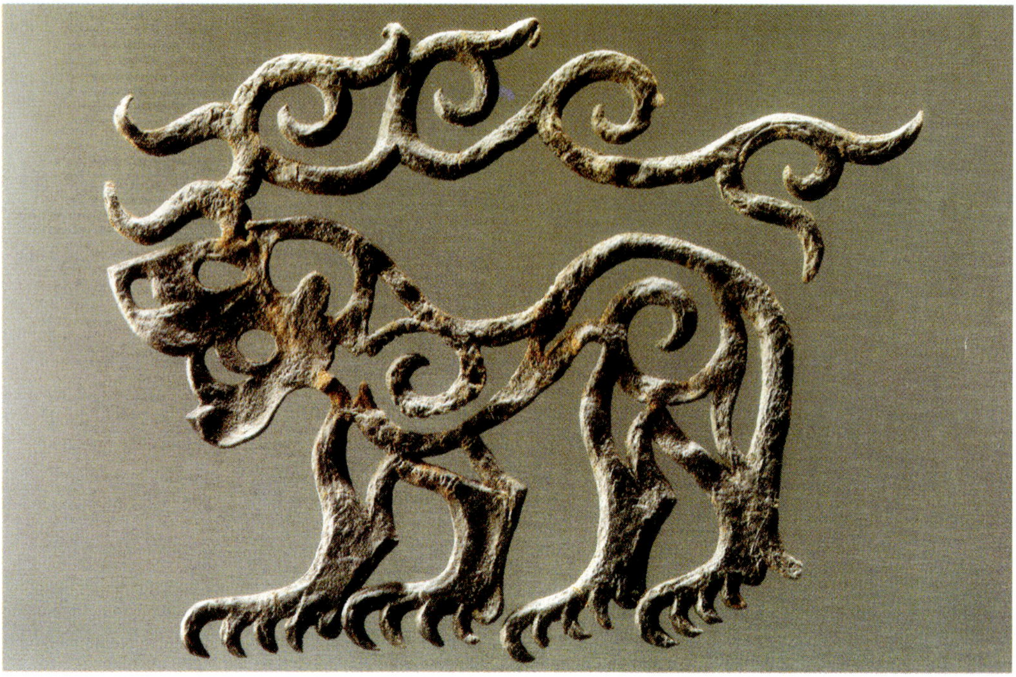

Plate 95: Leather appliquê of tiger with antlers from Tuekta barrow 1. Sixth century B.C.

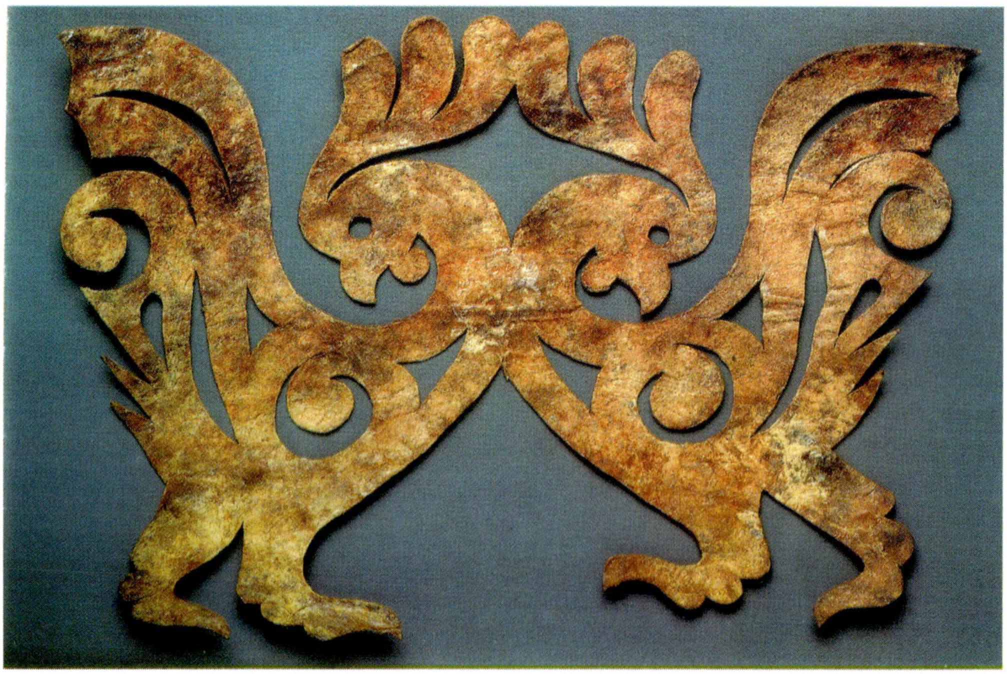

Plate 96: Leather appliquê of two roosters from Pazyryk barrow 1. Fifth century B.C.

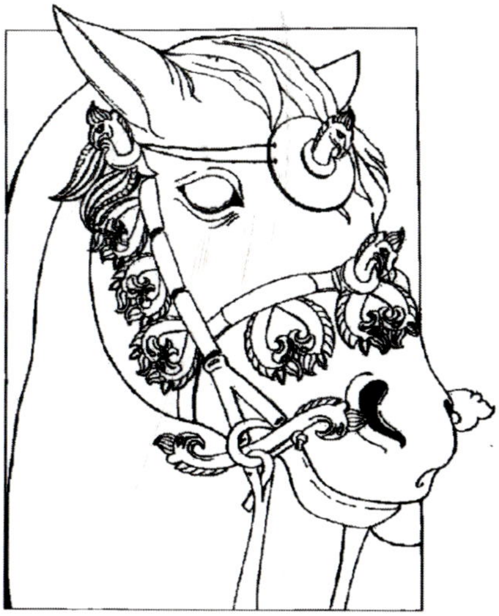

Plate 97: Wooden harness decorations from Ak-Alakh. Fourth to third century B.C.

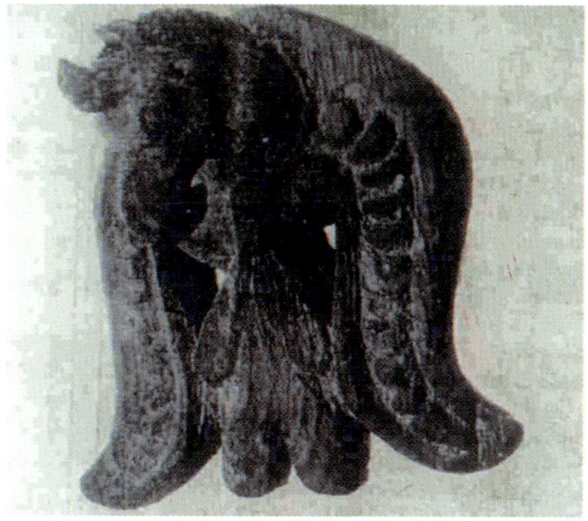

Plate 98: Horse harness in the form of a griffin from Ak-Alakh. Fourth to third century B.C.

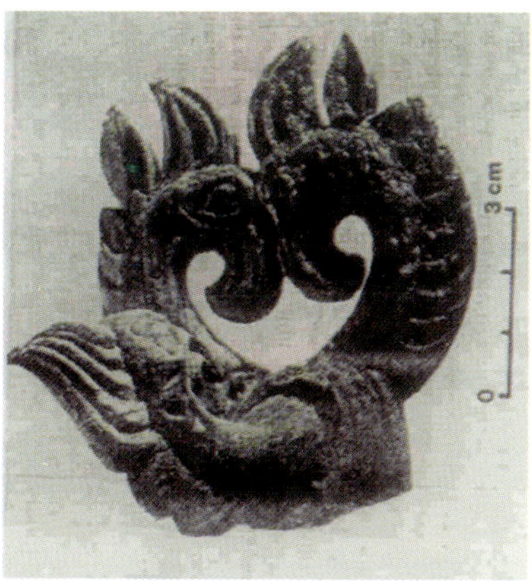

Plate 99: Horse harness in the form of a griffin from Ak-Alakh. Fourth to third century B.C.

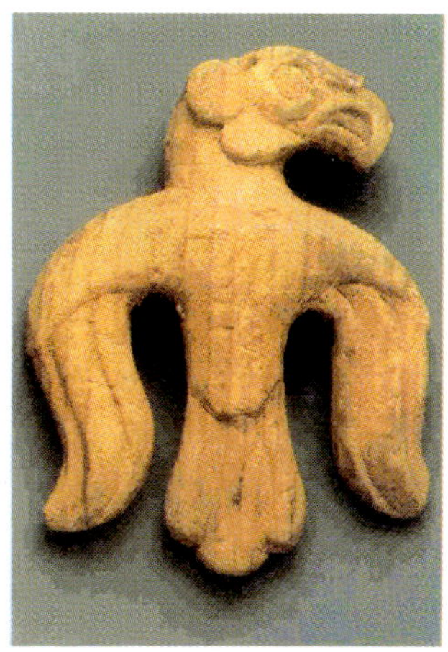

Plate 100: Larch, eagle-shaped bridle ornament from Tuekta barrow 1. Sixth century B.C.

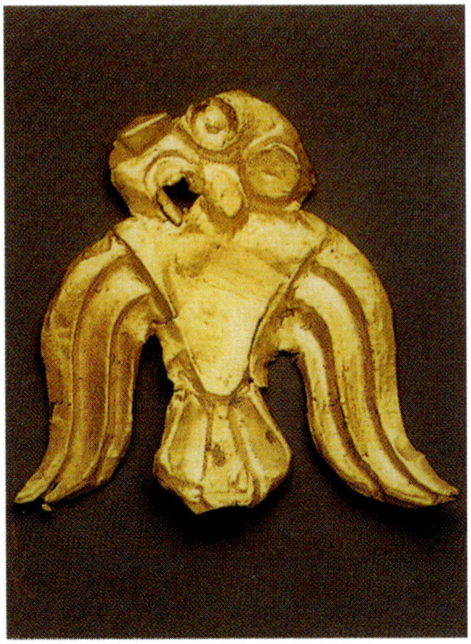

Plate 101: Gold eagle-shaped plaque from Bashadar barrow 9, Altai. Sixth century B.C.

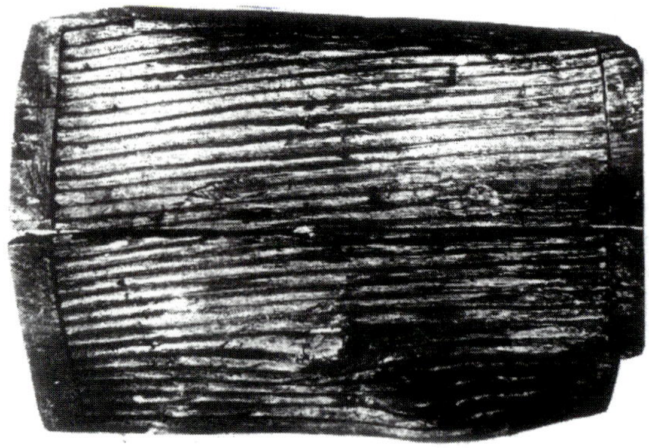

Plate 102: Wooden shield from Ak-Alakh. Fourth to third century B.C.

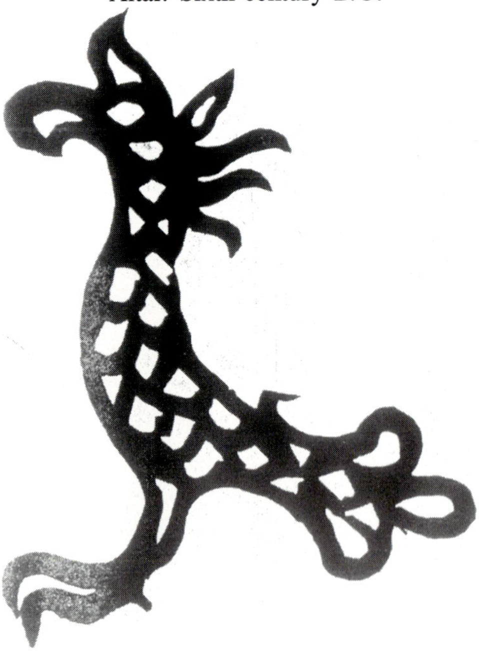

Plate 103: Leather griffin, fragment of appliquê work, from Kuturguntas. Fifth century B.C.

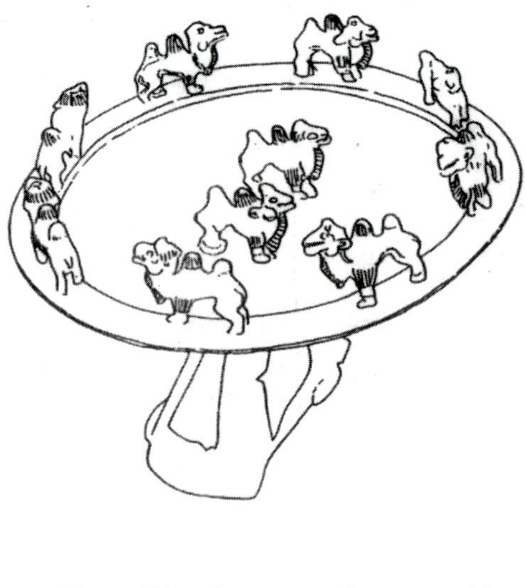

Plate 104: Lamp from Alatau, Semirechye. Fifth century B.C. to fourth century B.C.

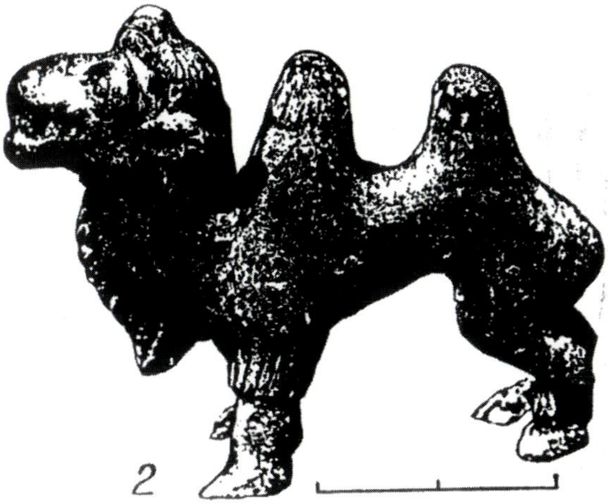

Plate 105: Camel figurine from Alatau lamp, Semirechye. Fifth century B.C. to fourth century B.C.

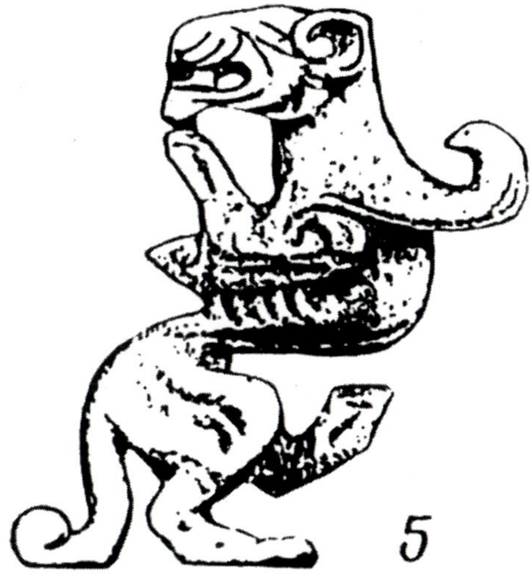

Plate 106: Tiger-griffin from Semirechye. Fifth century B.C.to fourth century B.C.

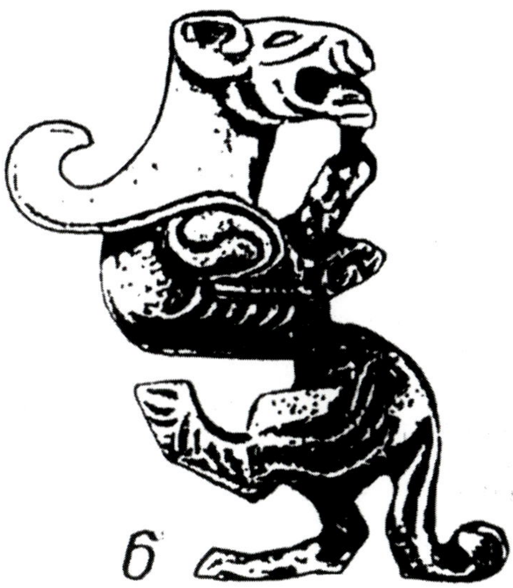

Plate 107: Tiger-griffin from Semirechye. Fifth century B.C. to fourth century B.C.

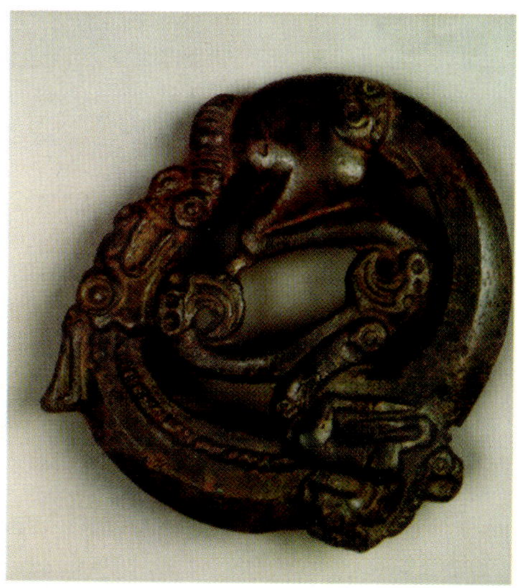

Plate 108: Bronze bridle plaque depicting a coiled-up wolf with additional stylized images of a recumbent goat, an elk's head and bird's heads on its body from Kulakovsky barrow. Early fifth century B.C.

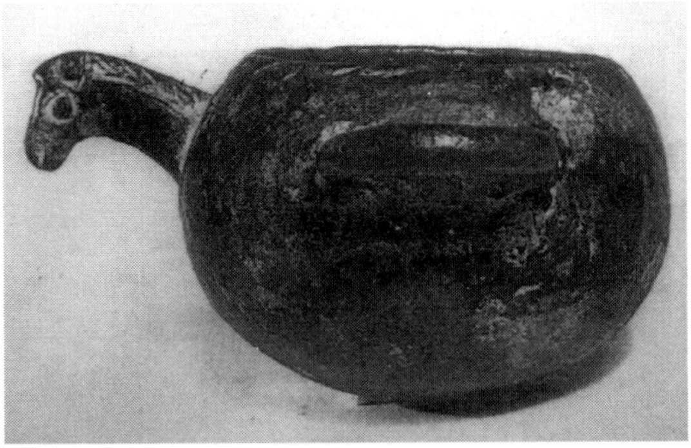

Plate 109: Small bronze cauldron from Ishkoman, Punyal. Second century B.C. to first century B.C.

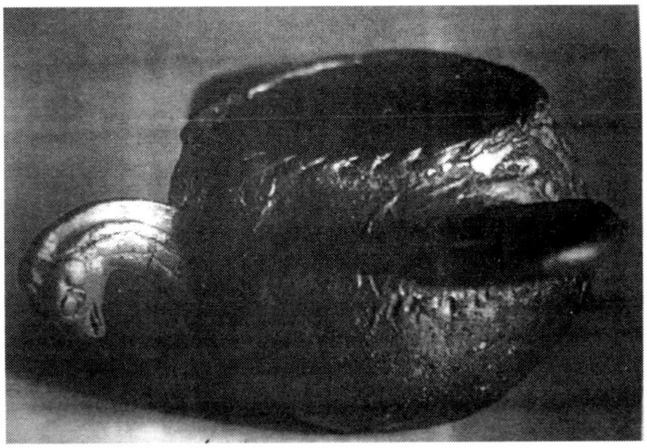

Plate 110: Bronze cauldron from Alicur II barrow 3. Second century B.C. to Late first century B.C.

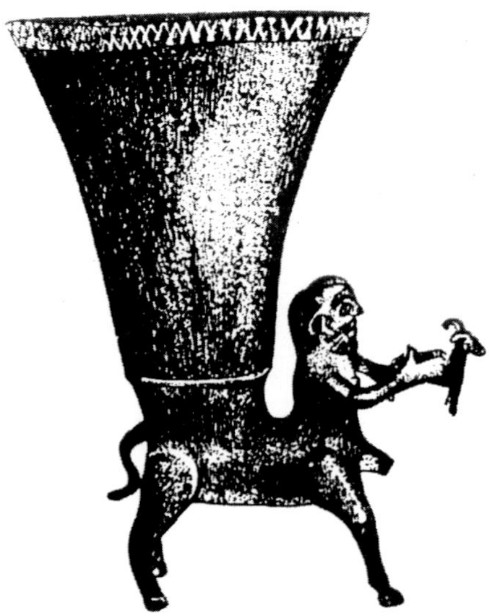

Plate 111: Rhyton from Imit. Second century B.C. to early first century A.D.

Plate 112: Bronze plaque acquired in the Kandia valley, now in The National Museum, Karachi. First century A.D. to second century A.D.

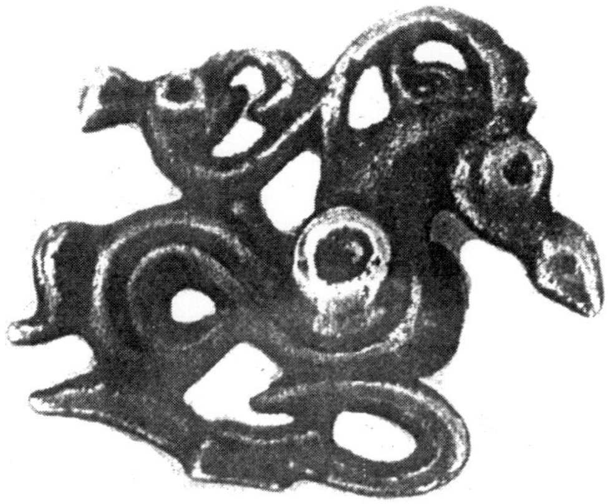

Plate 113: Pommel topping the hilt of an akinakes from Akbeit barrow 3. Fifth century B.C.

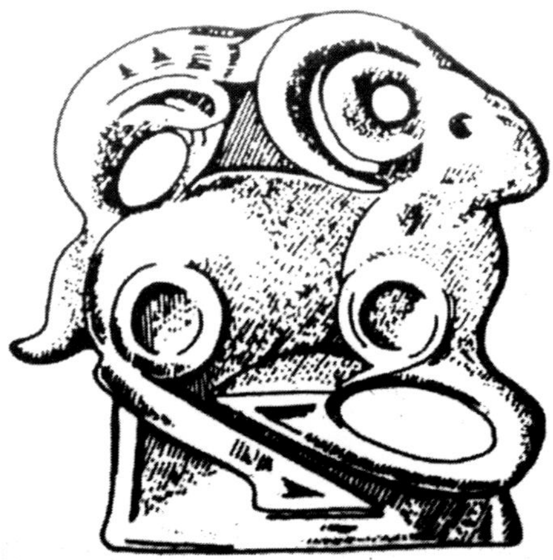

Plate 114: Plaque depicting a stag from Termansy. Fifth century B.C.

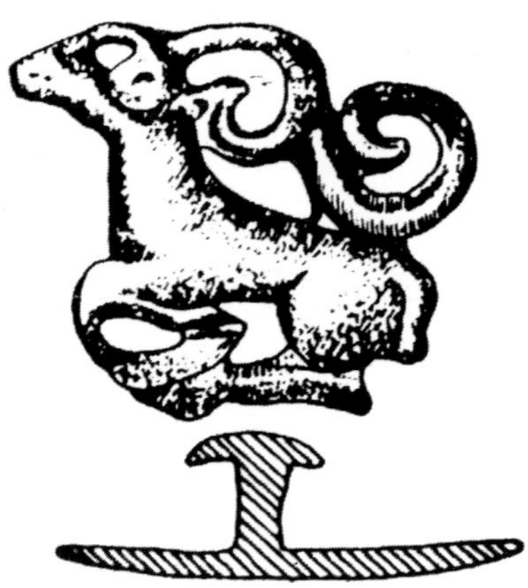

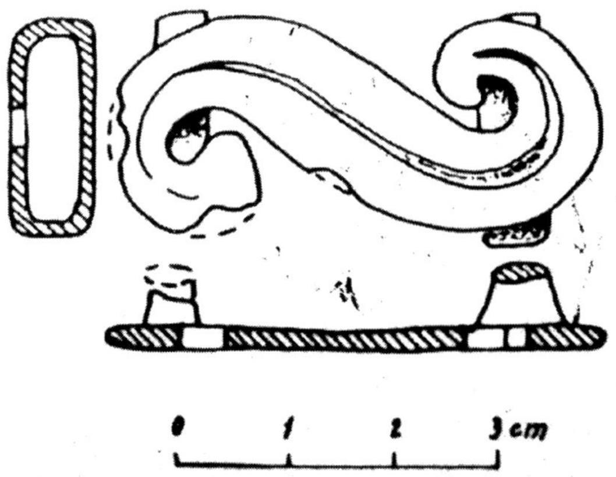

Plate 115: S-spiral used as abstract design on artifacts like the bronze one from Pamirskaja I. Fifth century B.C.

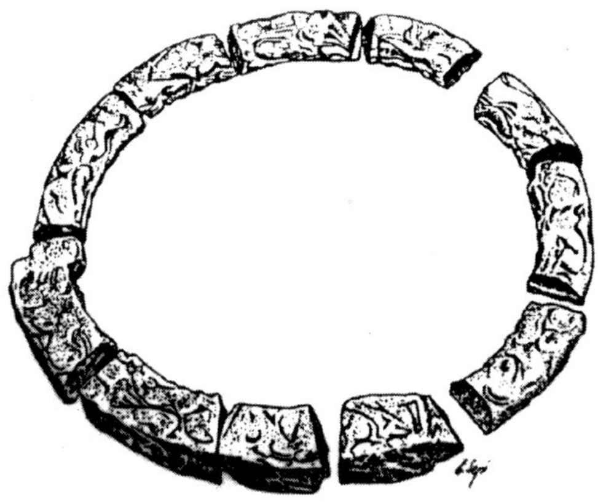

Plate 116: Gold ring of Pattan. Second to late first century B.C.

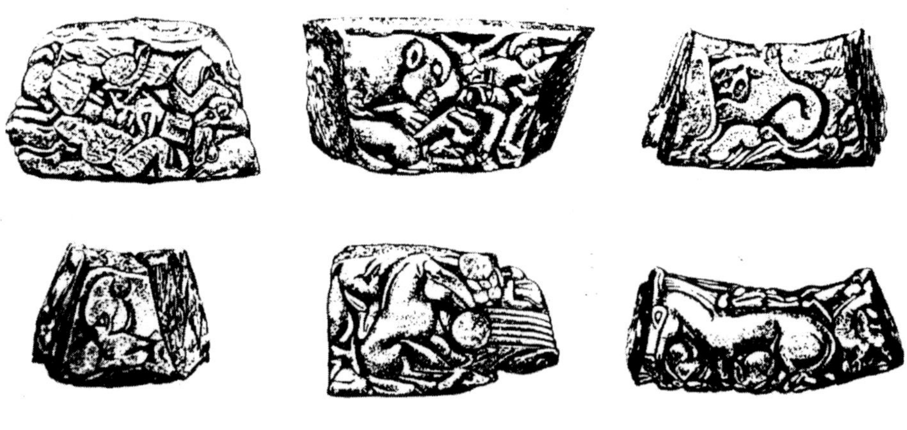

Plate 117: Details of gold ring of Pattan. Second to late first century B.C.

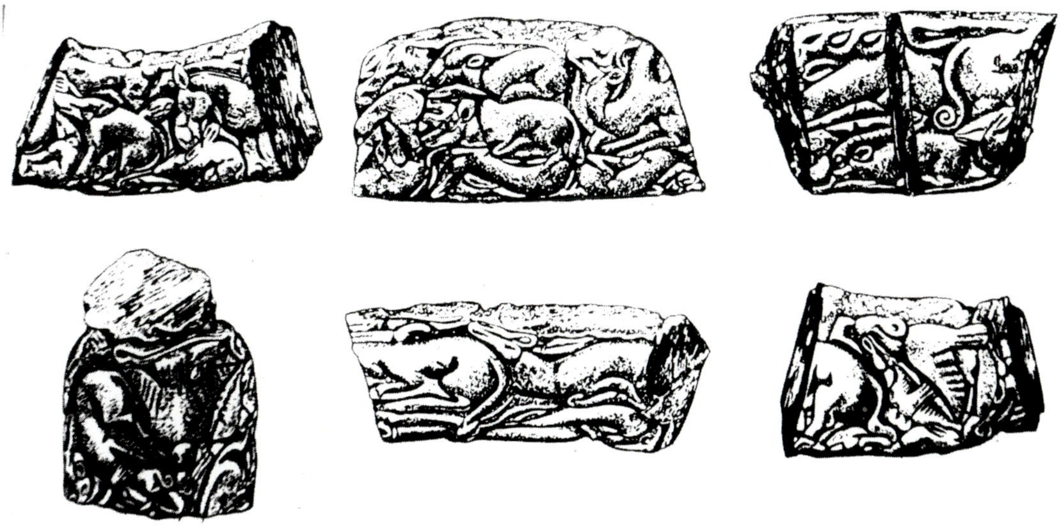

Plate 118: Details of gold ring of Pattan. Second to late first century A.D.

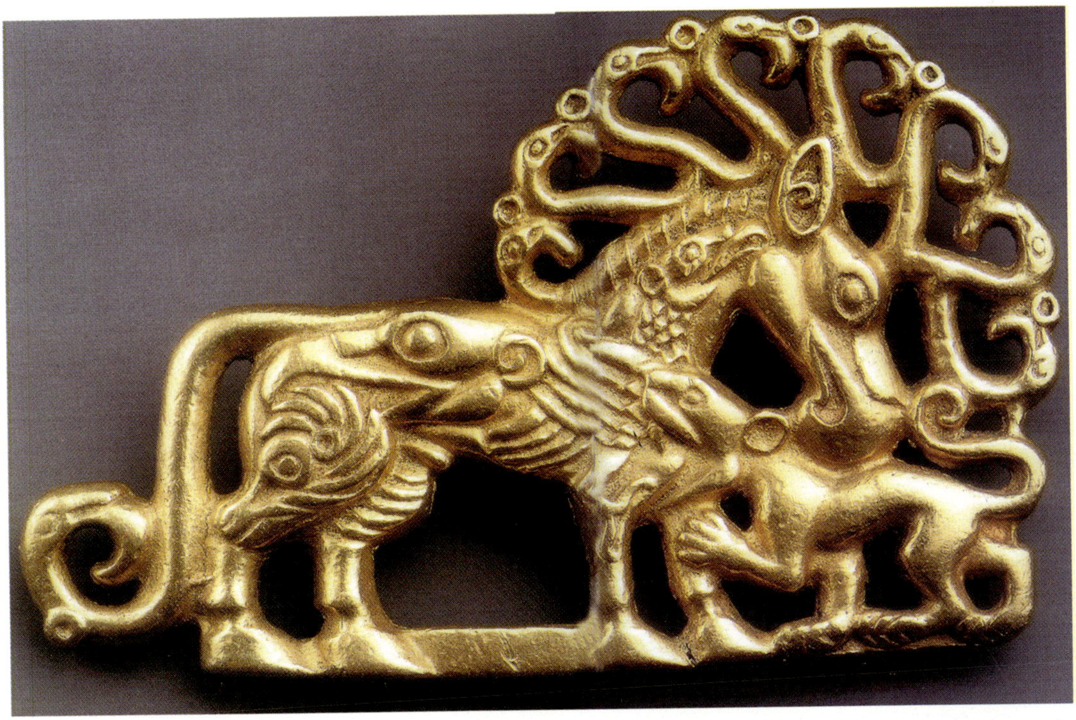

Plate 119: Gold belt plaque depicting a fantastic horselike animal from Lake Baikal area, Verkhneudinsk (modern Ulan-Ude), or from Mongolia. Fifth to fourth century B.C.

Plate 120: Bronze buckle for horse trappings from Ukraine barrow C, near the village of Zhurovka. First half of the fifth century B.C.

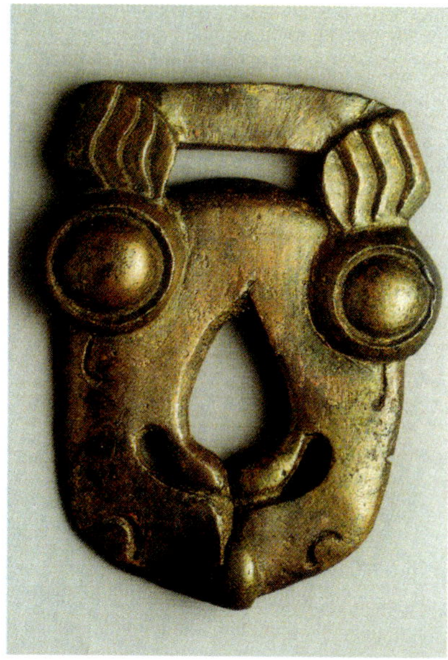

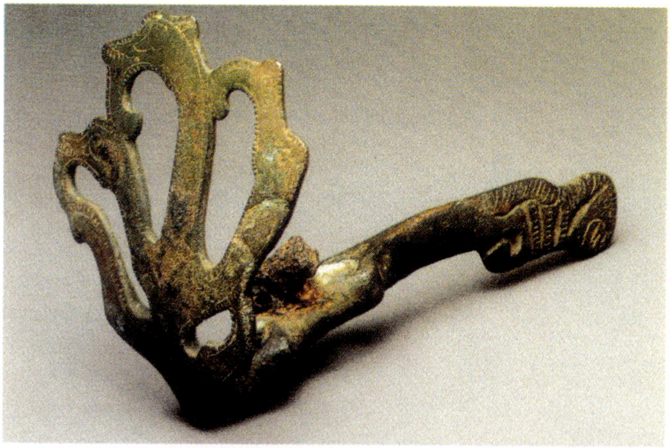

Plate 121: Bronze and iron bridle cheek piece from Elizavetinskaia barrow 7. Fourth century B.C.

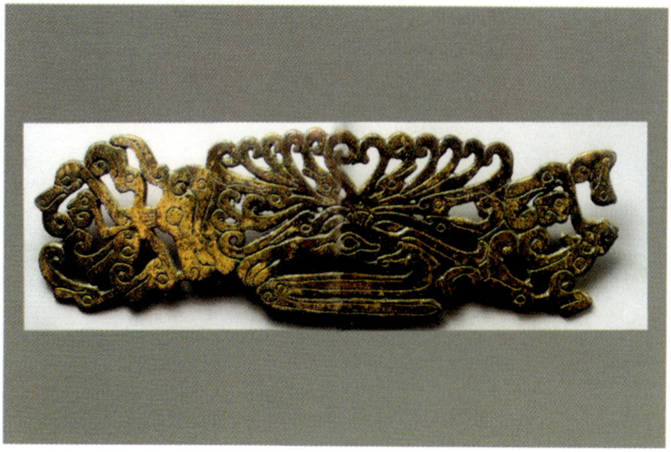

Plate 122: Bronze bridle attachment from Kuban region. Fourth century B.C.

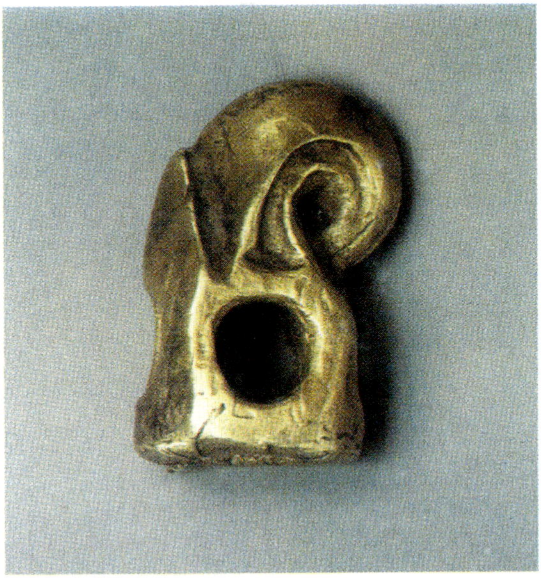

Plate 123: Bronze and gold eye-bars from Kelermes barrow. Late seventh or early sixth century B.C.

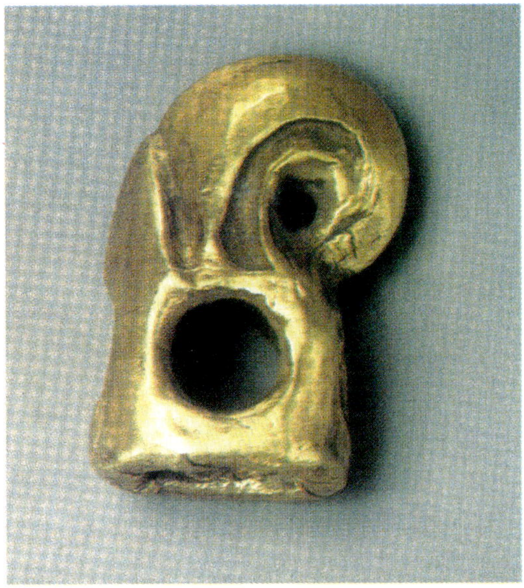

Plate 124: Eye-bars for linking bridle reins in the shape of stylized bird's heads from Kelermes. Late seventh or early sixth century B.C.

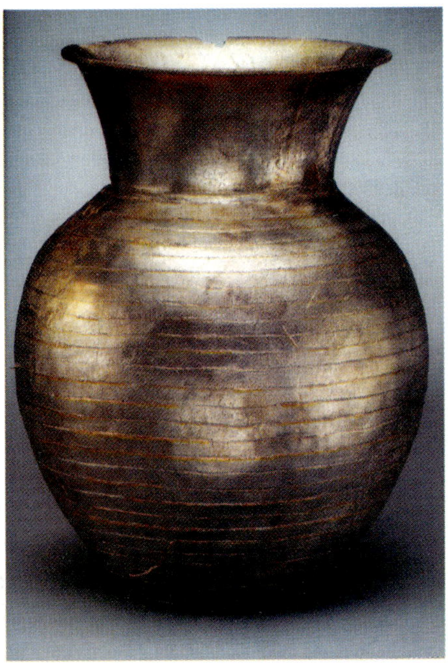

Plate 125: Silver and gold vessel with flaring neck from Filippovka, barrow 1. Late fifth to early fourth century B.C.

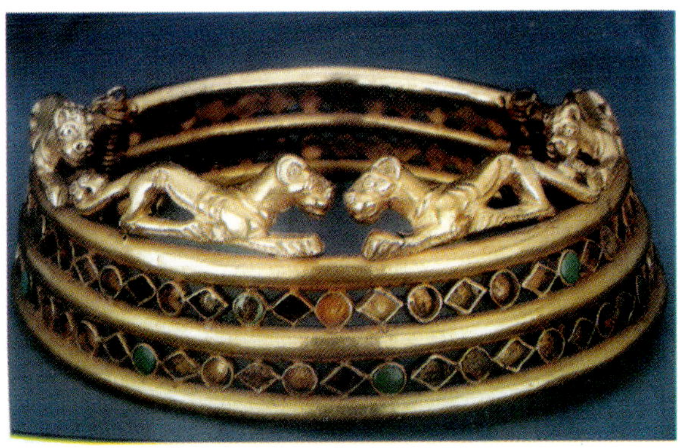

Plate 126: Gold turquoise, and coral neck ornament of Central Asian origin in the Siberian Collection of Peter I. Fifth to fourth century B.C.

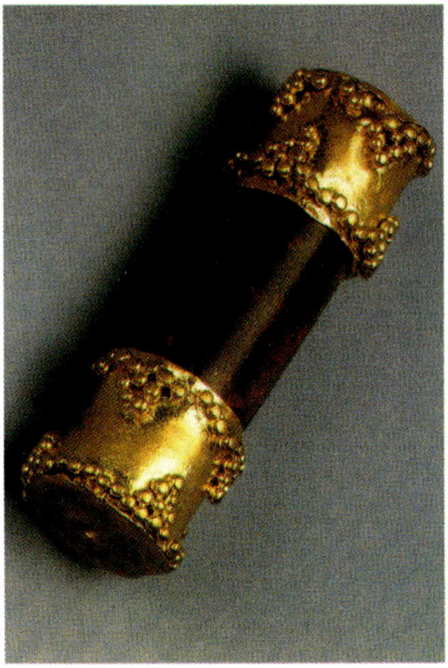

Plate 127: Agate and gold cylindrical bead from Filippovka barrow I. Fourth century B.C.

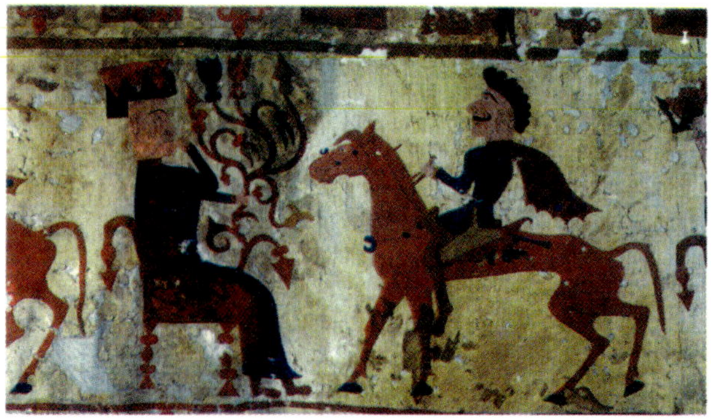

Plate 128: Rug fragment with an enthroned goddess and a horseman from Pazyryk barrow 5. Fifth to fourth century B.C.

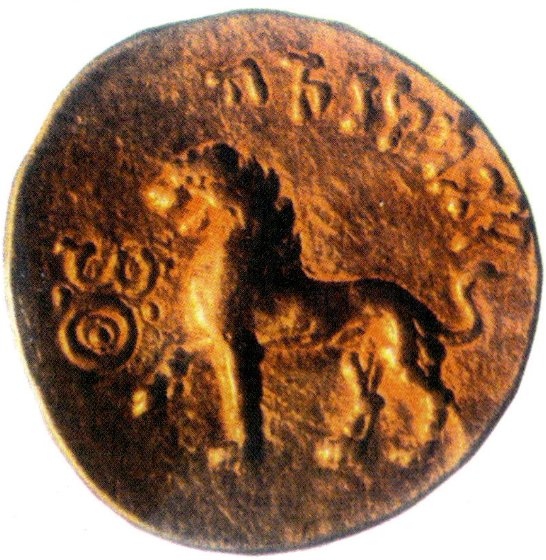

Plate 129 (A): Gold Indian coin from burial 4, Tillya-tepe. First century A.D.

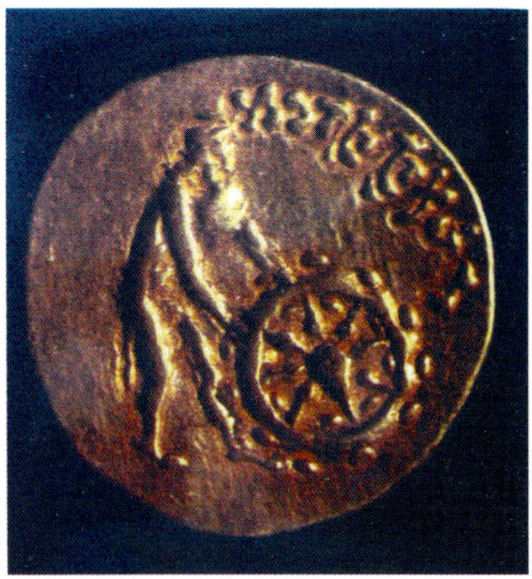

Plate 129 (B) : Gold Indian coin from burial 4, Tillya-tepe. First century A.D.

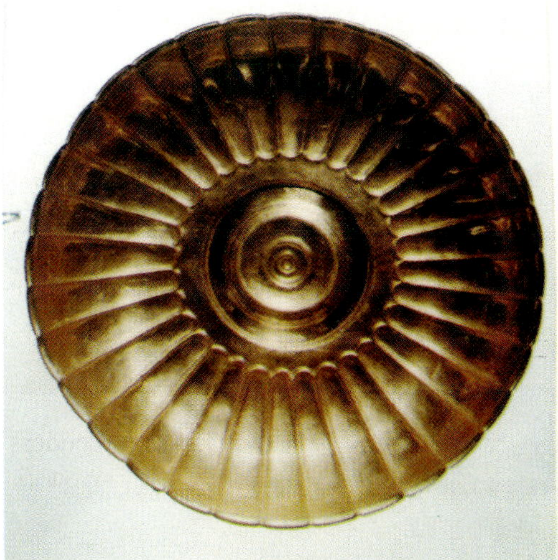

Plate 130: Gold phial from burial 4, Tillya-tepe. First century A.D.

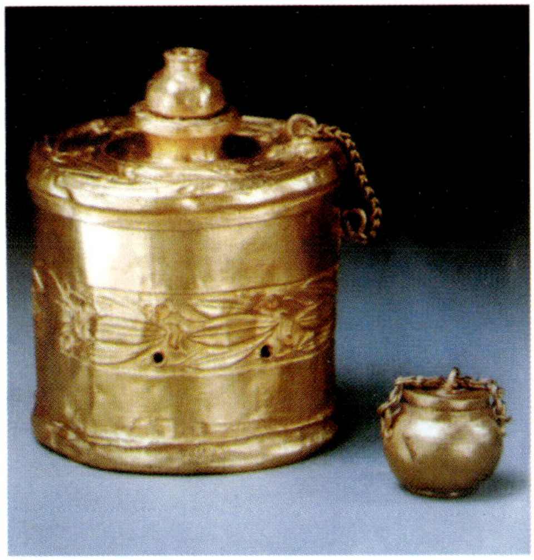

Plate 131: Gold cast flat bottomed pot from burial 3, Tillya-tepe. First century A.D.

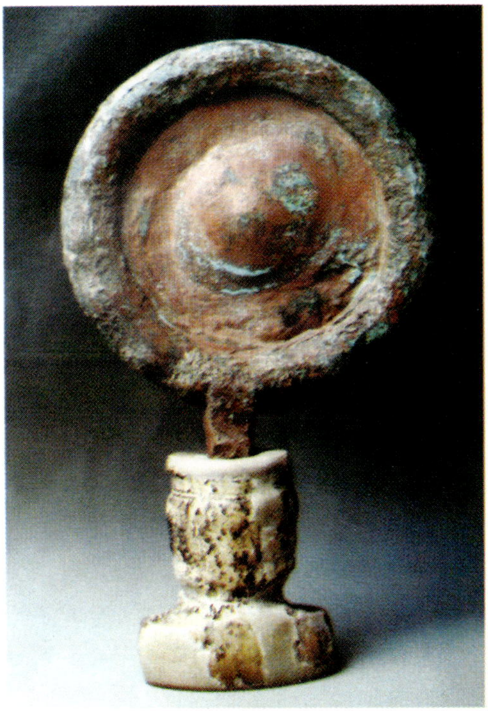

Plate 132: Mirror with ivory handle, from burial 3, Tillya-tepe. First century A.D.

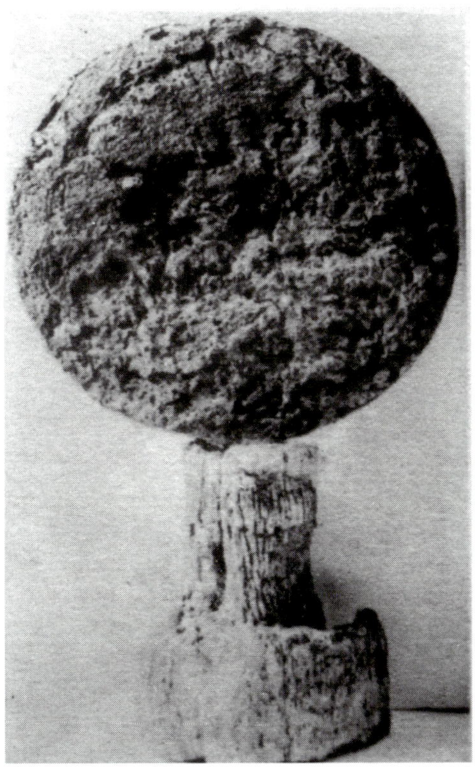

Plate 133: Mirror with ivory handle from Taxila. First to second century A.D.

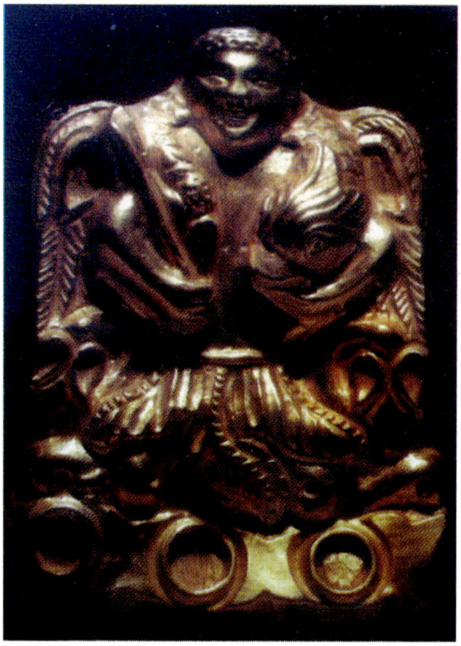

Plate 134: 'Man with a dolphin' plaque from burial 1, Tillya-tepe. First century A.D.

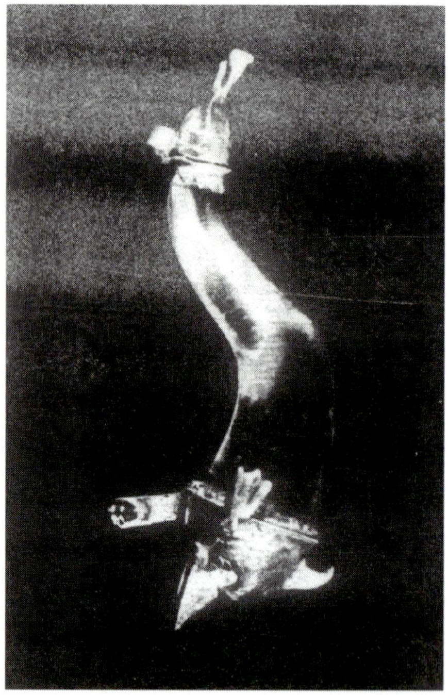

Plate 135: A fibula in the shape of a dolphin from the Nogaichik burial mound, Late first century B.C. to early centuries A.D.

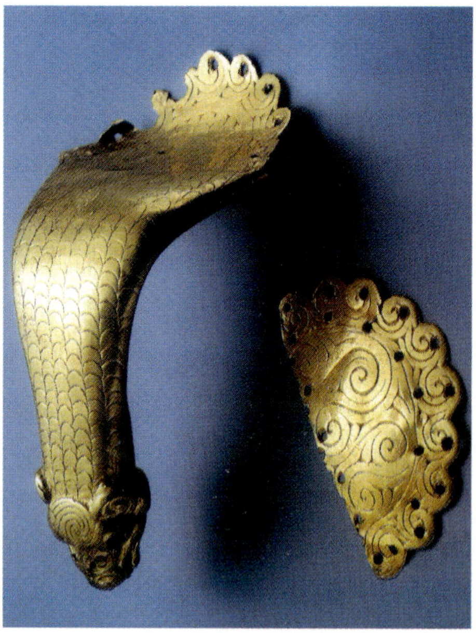

Plate 136: Gold plaque and gold griffin's — head handled from Filippovka barrow 1(now in the Archaeological Museum), Ufa. Fourth century B.C.

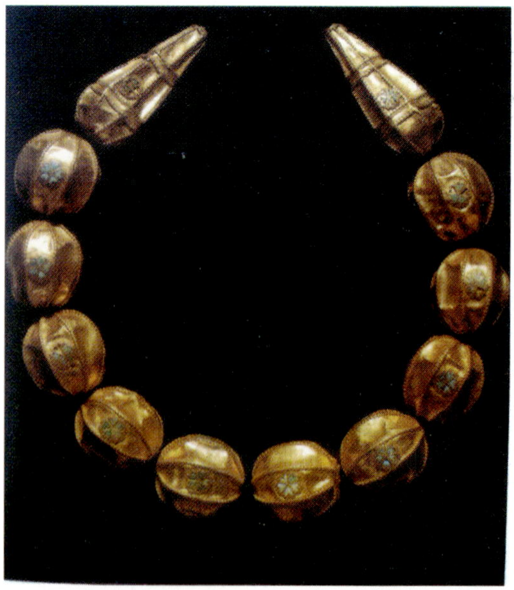

Plate 137: Necklace of gold beads from burial 6, Tillya-tepe. First century A.D.

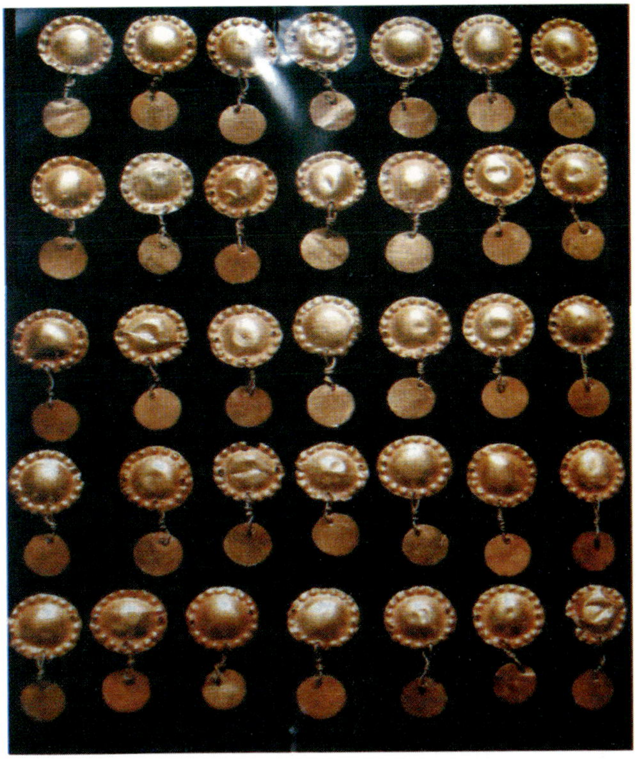

Plate 138: Gold pendants in shape of circles from Tillya-tepe. First century A.D.

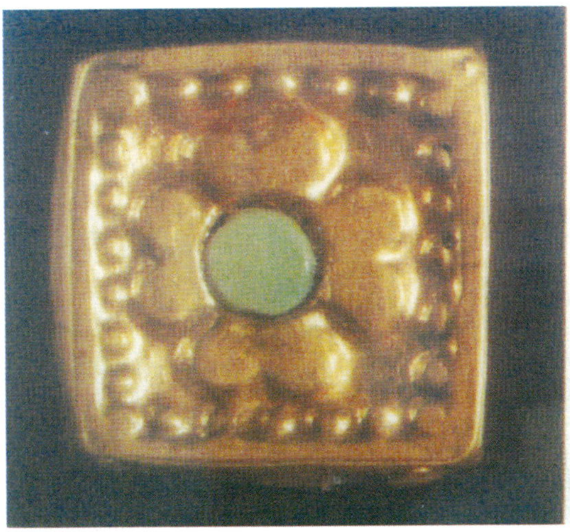

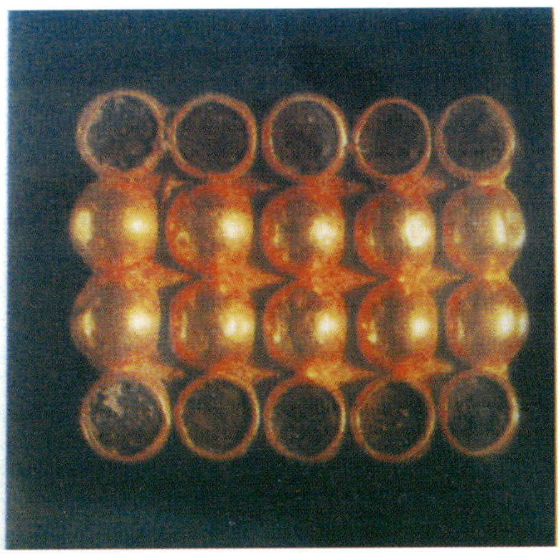

Plate 139: Gold plaque with four—petal rosette from burial 1,Tillya-tepe. First century A.D.

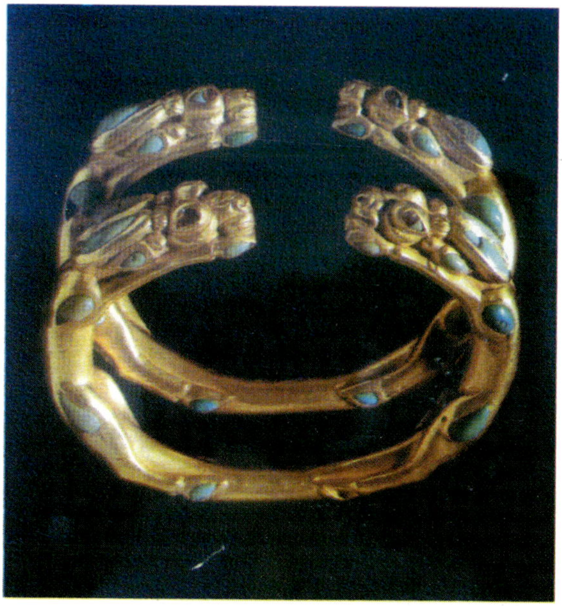

Plate 140: Gold bracelets with antelope terminals from burial 2, Tillya-tepe. First century A.D.

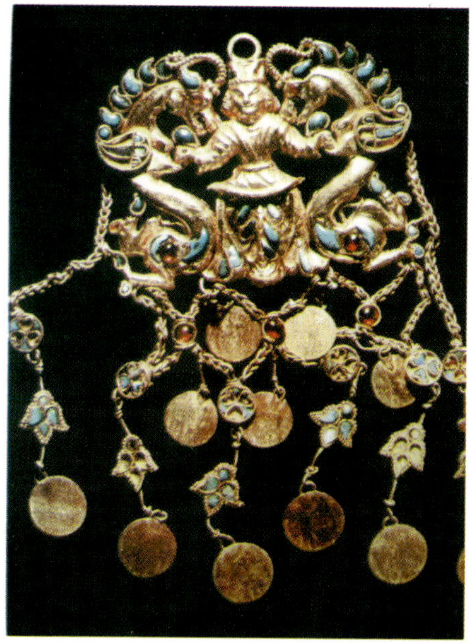

Plate 141: 'Mistress of animals' pendant from burial 2, Tillya-tepe. First century A.D.

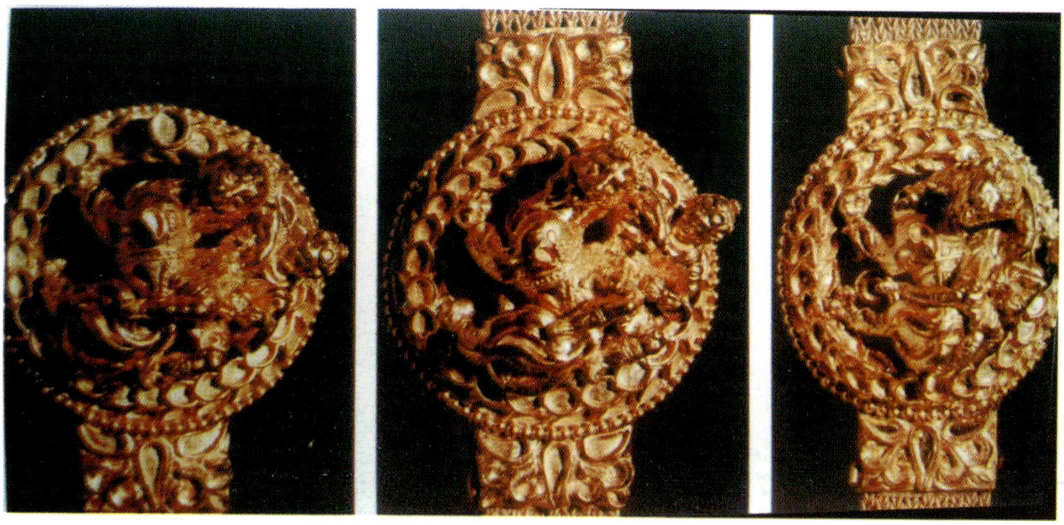

Plate 142: Details of the gold belt from burial 4, Tillya-tepe. First century A.D.

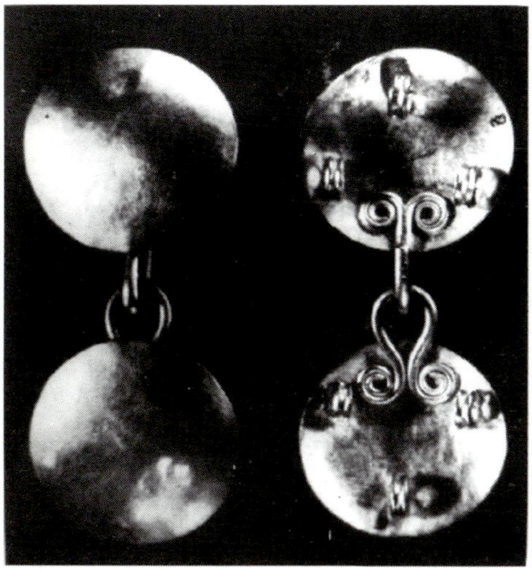

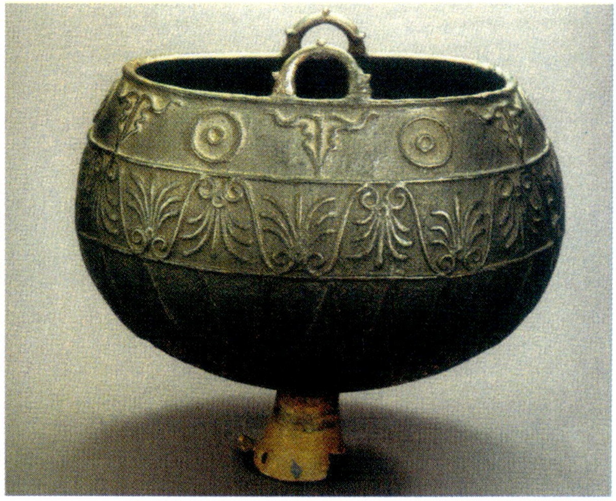

Plate 143: Clasp disks from burial 1, Tillya-tepe. First century A.D.

Plate 144: Bronze cauldron from Raskopana Mogila. Fourth century B.C.

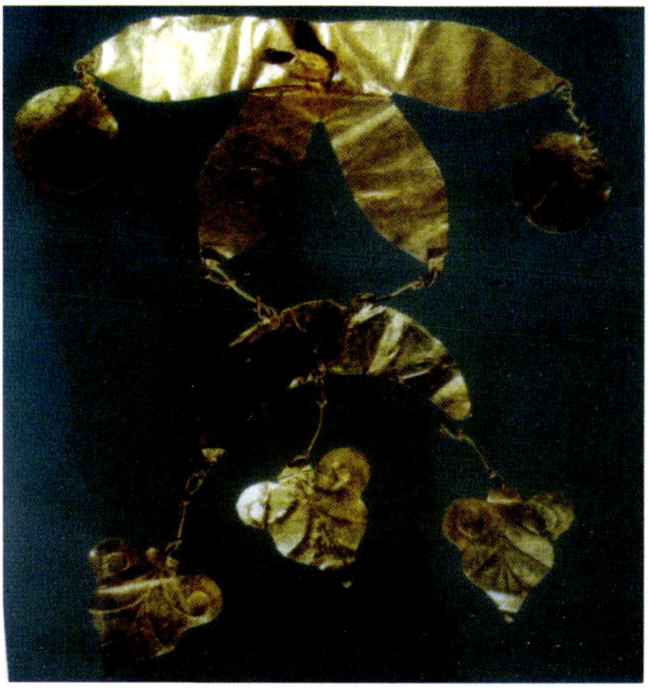

Plate 145: Hairpin of thin gold sheet from burial 1, Tillya-tepe. First century A.D.

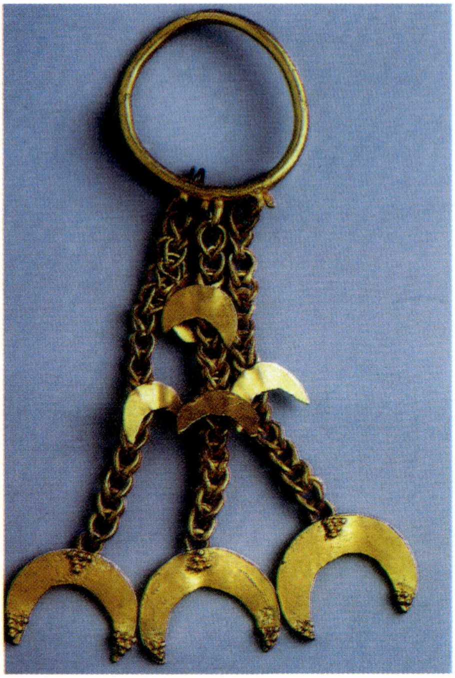

Plate 146: Gold headdress or hair ornament from Filippovka barrow 1. Fourth century B.C.

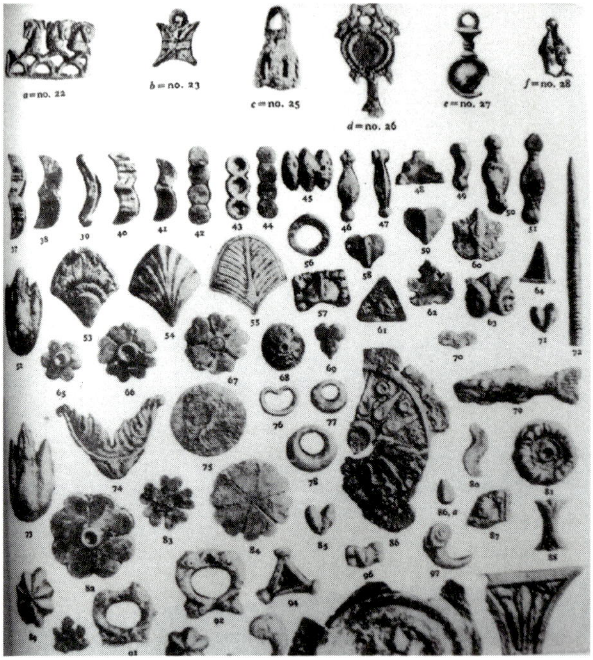

Plate 147: Copper, bronze and lead objects from Taxila. Nos.83,84 depict metal rosettes. First to second century A.D.

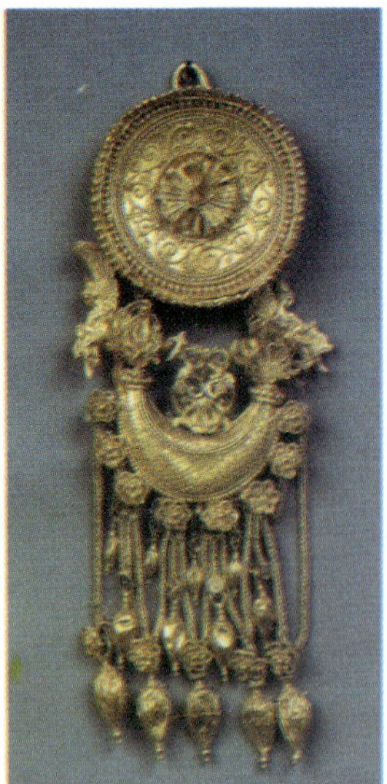

Plate 148: Gold disk pendant with a hanging boat-shape from Kul-Oba. Fourth century B.C.

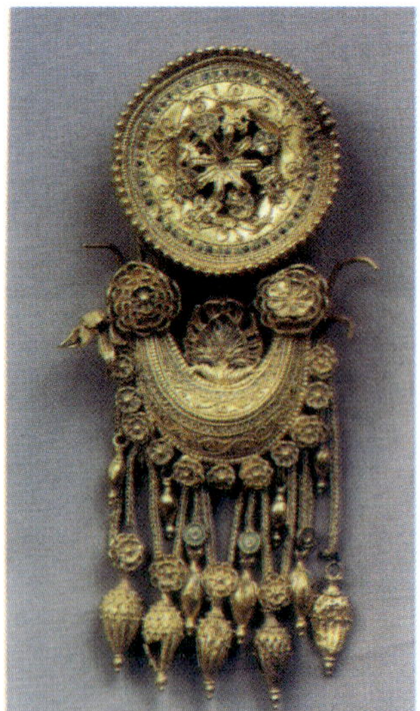

Plate 149: Gold disk pendant with a hanging boat-shape and ornamented chains from Kul-Oba. Fourth century B.C.

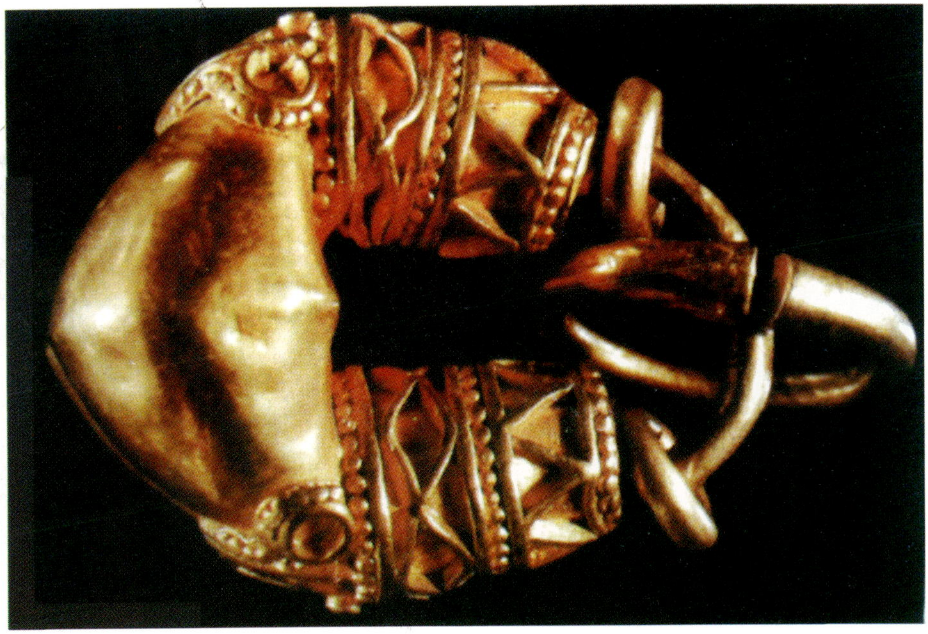

Plate 150: Gold earring clip from burial 1, Tillya-tepe. First century A.D.

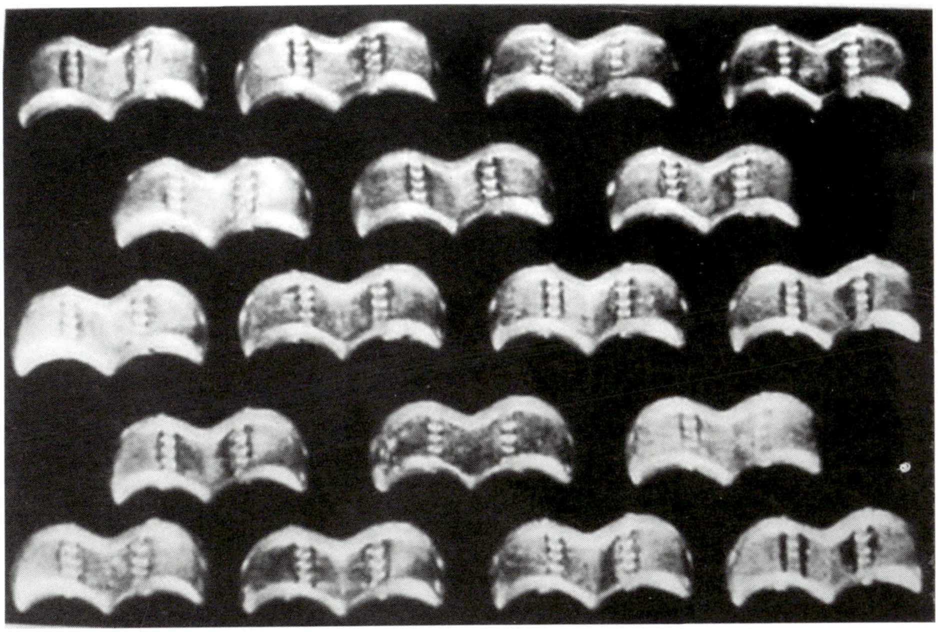

Plate 151: Large horned plaquettes from burial 3, Tillya-tepe. First century A.D.

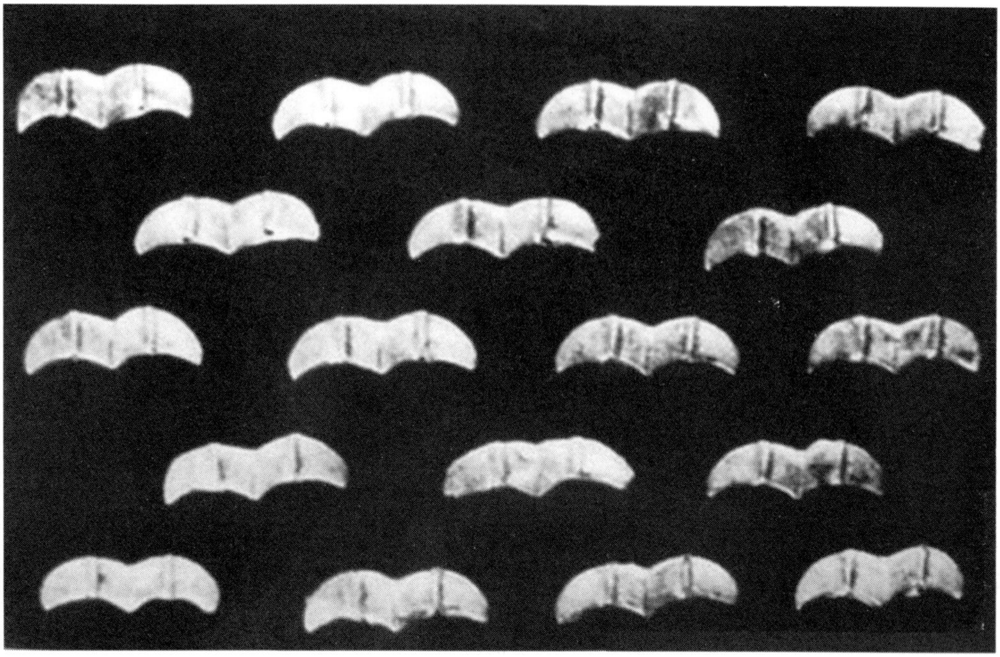

Plate 152: Small horned plquettes from burial 3, Tillya-tepe. First century A.D.

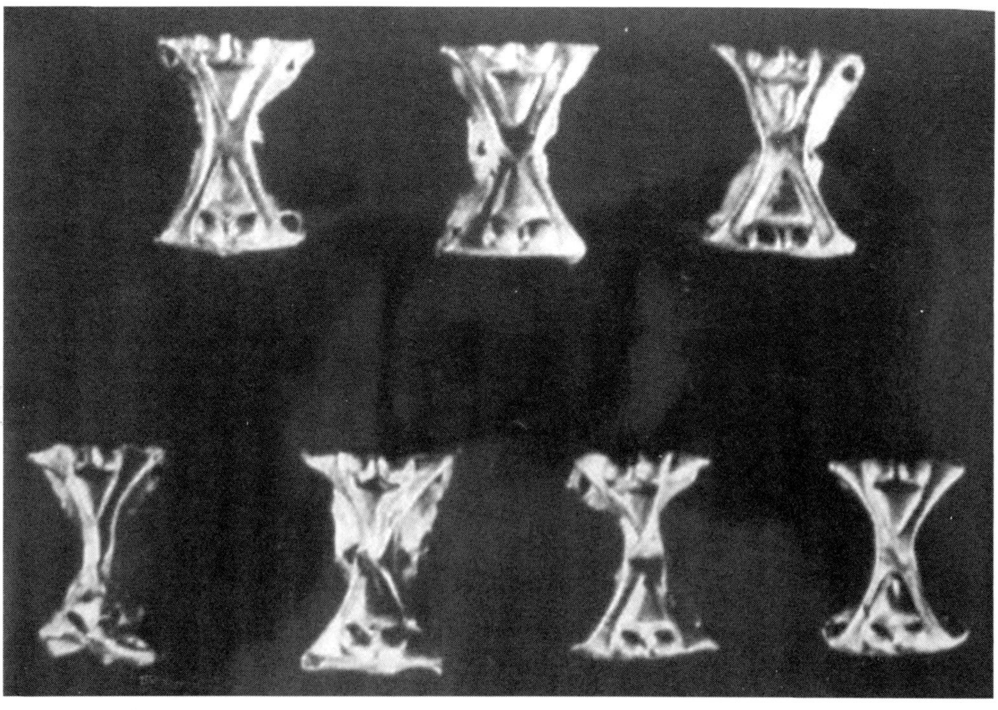

Plate 153: 'Bow with bosses' plaques from burial 1, Tillya-tepe. First century A.D.

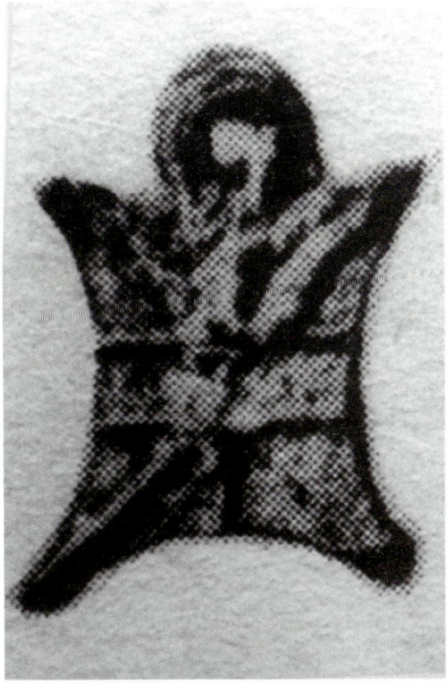

Plate 154: 'Bow with bosses' plaque from Taxila. First to second century A.D.

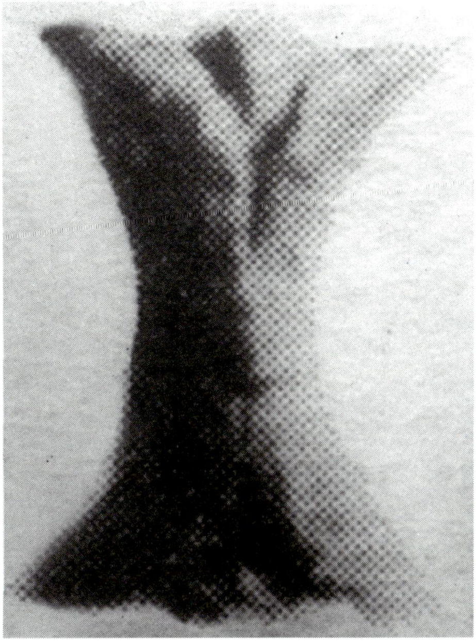

Plate 155: 'Bow with bosses' plaque from Taxila. First to second century A.D.

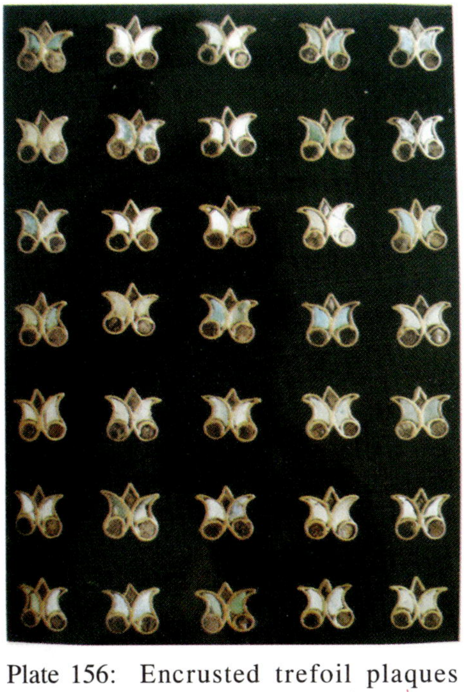

Plate 156: Encrusted trefoil plaques from Tillya-tepe. First century A.D.

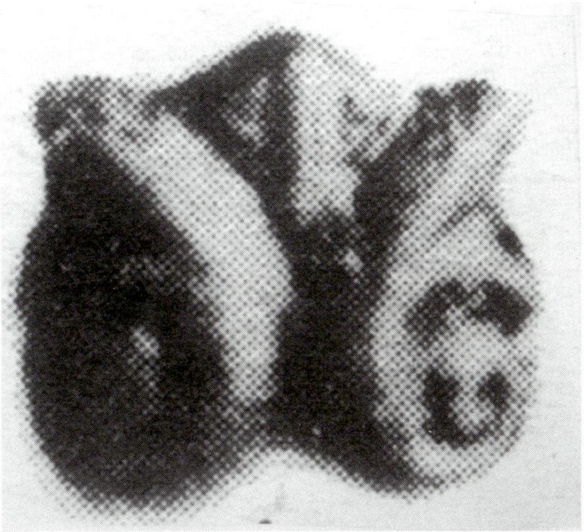

Plate 157: Metal trefoil plaque from Taxila. First to second century A.D.

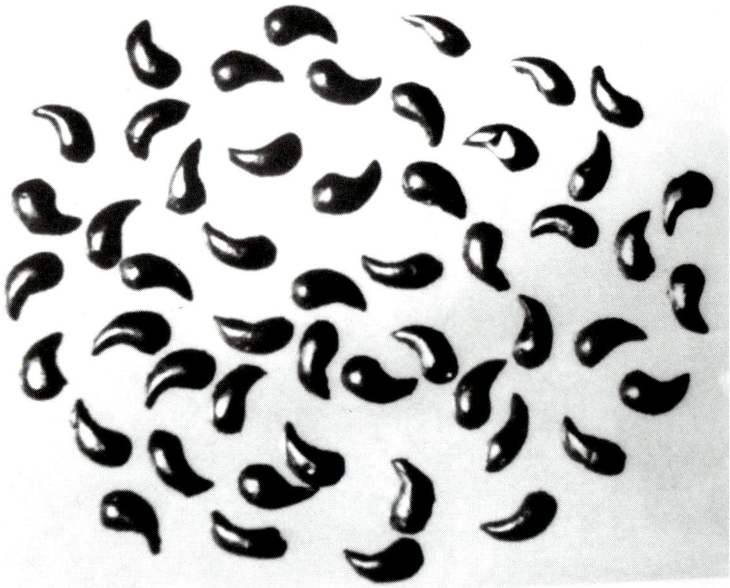

Plate 158: Pear-shaped plaques from burial 2, Tillya-tepe. First century A.D.

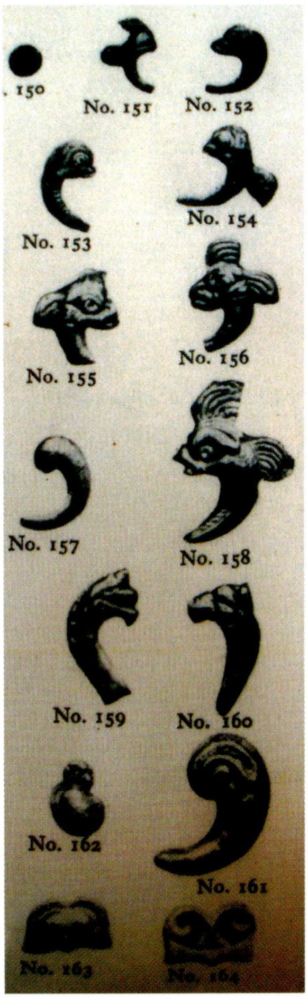

Plate 159: Variations of metal pear-shaped plaques from Taxila. First to second century A.D.

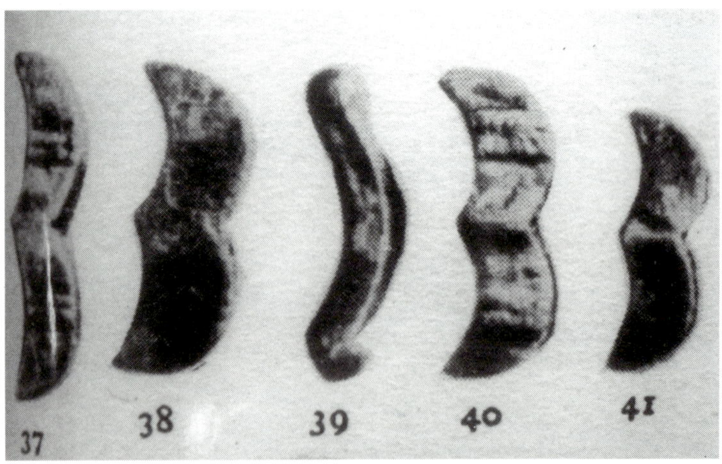

Plate 160: Horned plaquettes from Taxila. First to second century A.D.

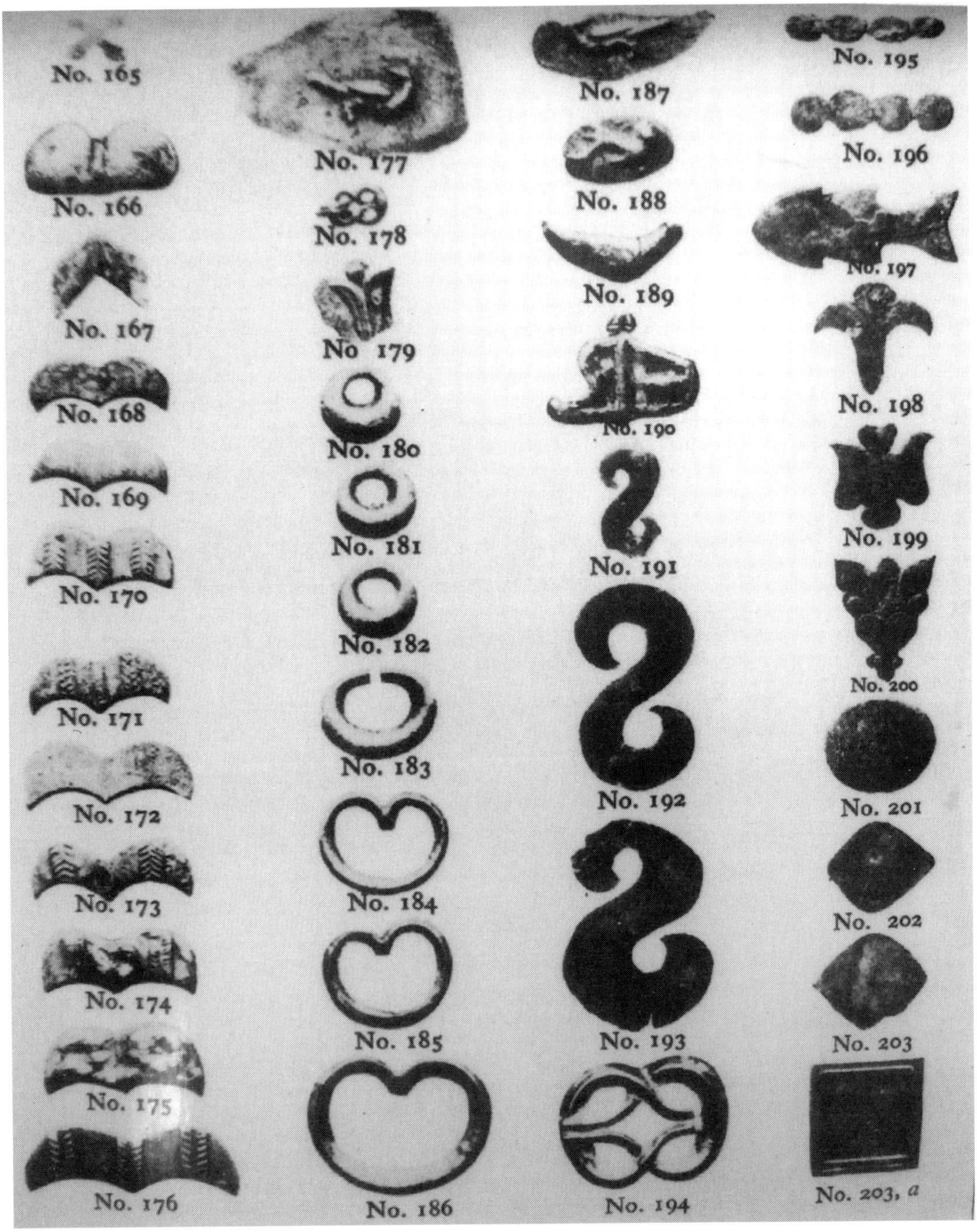

Plate 161: Numbers 168 to 176, depict horned plaquettes from Taxila. First to second century A.D.

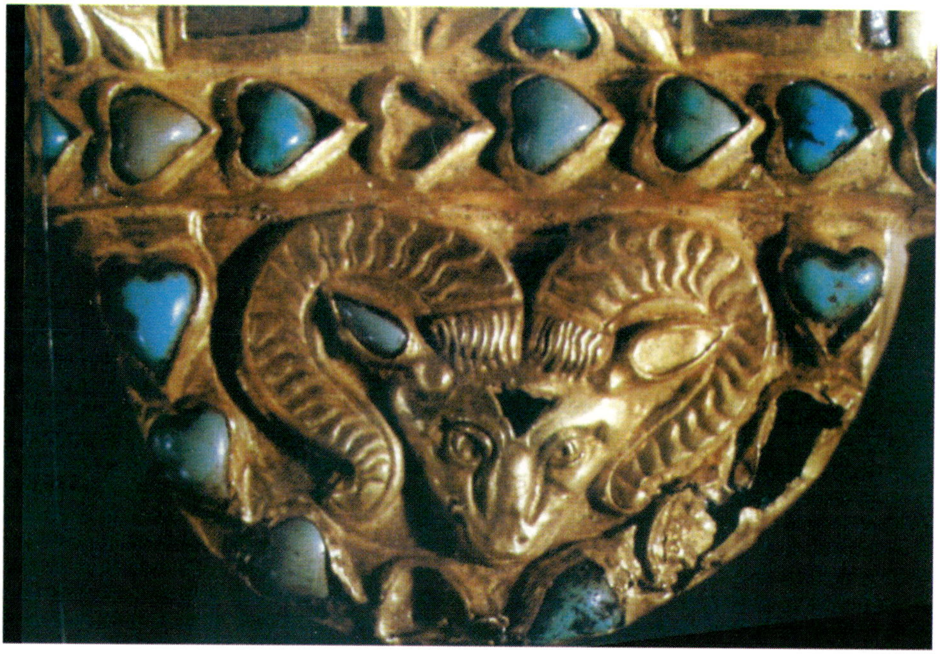

Plate 162: Details from the Tillya-tepe scabbard. First century A.D.

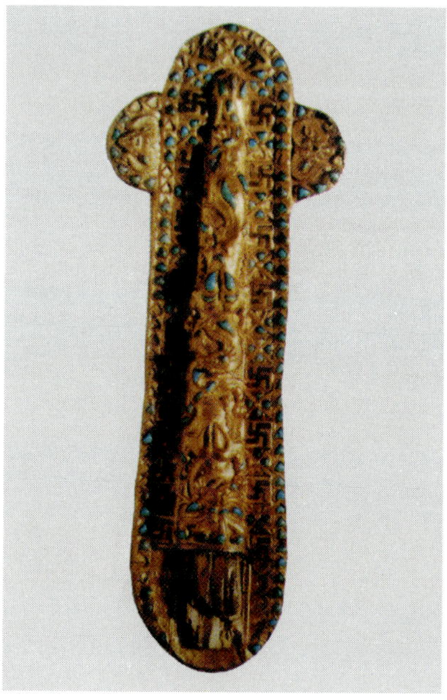

Plate 163: The Tillya-tepe scabbard. First century A.D.

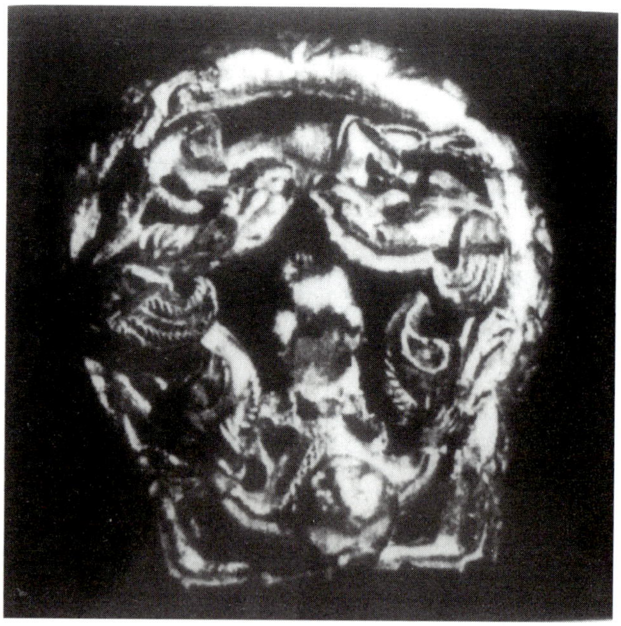

Plate 164: Gold clasp of the sword-belt from burial 1 near the village of Porogi. Late first century B.C. to first century A.D.

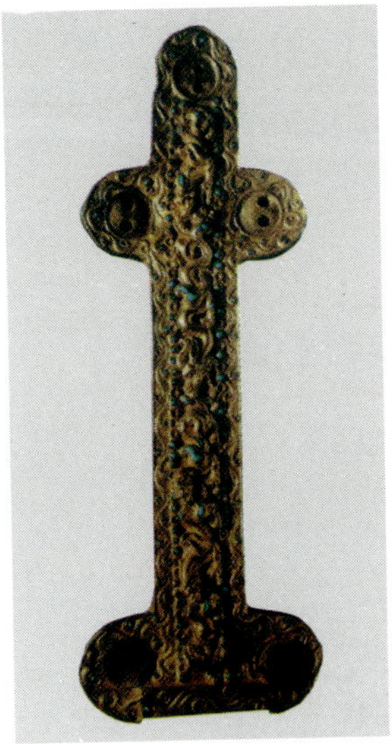

Plate 165: Tillya-tepe sheath ornamented with scenes of mauling animals. First century A.D.

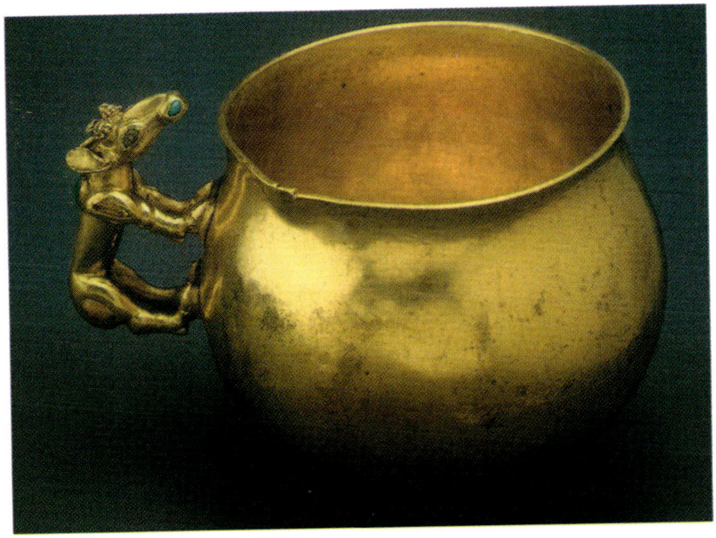

Plate 166: Gold vessel with zoomorphic handle from Khokhlach barrow. First century A.D.

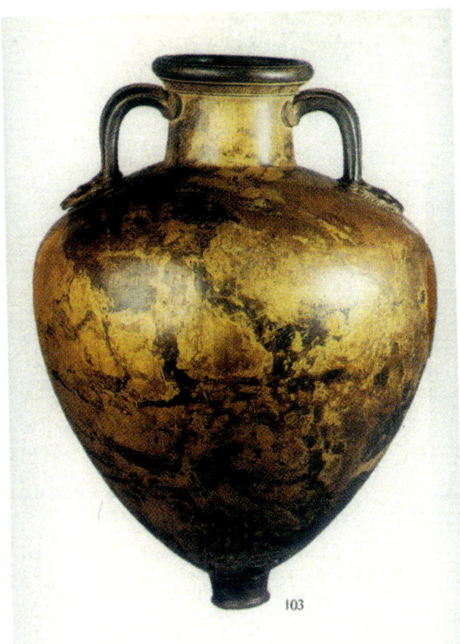

Plate 167: Bronze amphora from Peschanoye barrow, Late sixth century B.C.

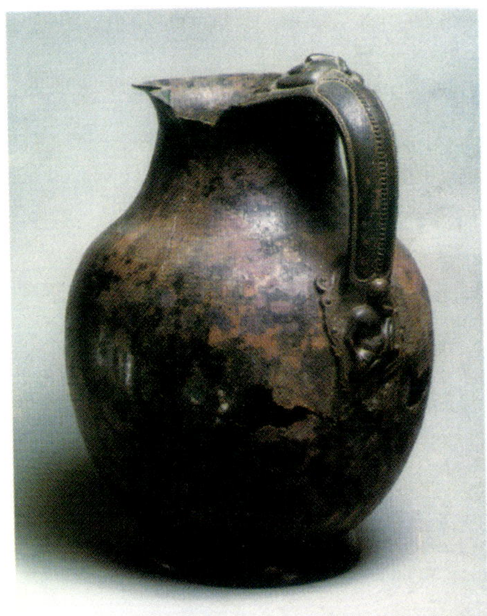

Plate 168: Bronze oenochoe from Nymphaeum, barrow 24 from Second quarter of the fifth century B.C.

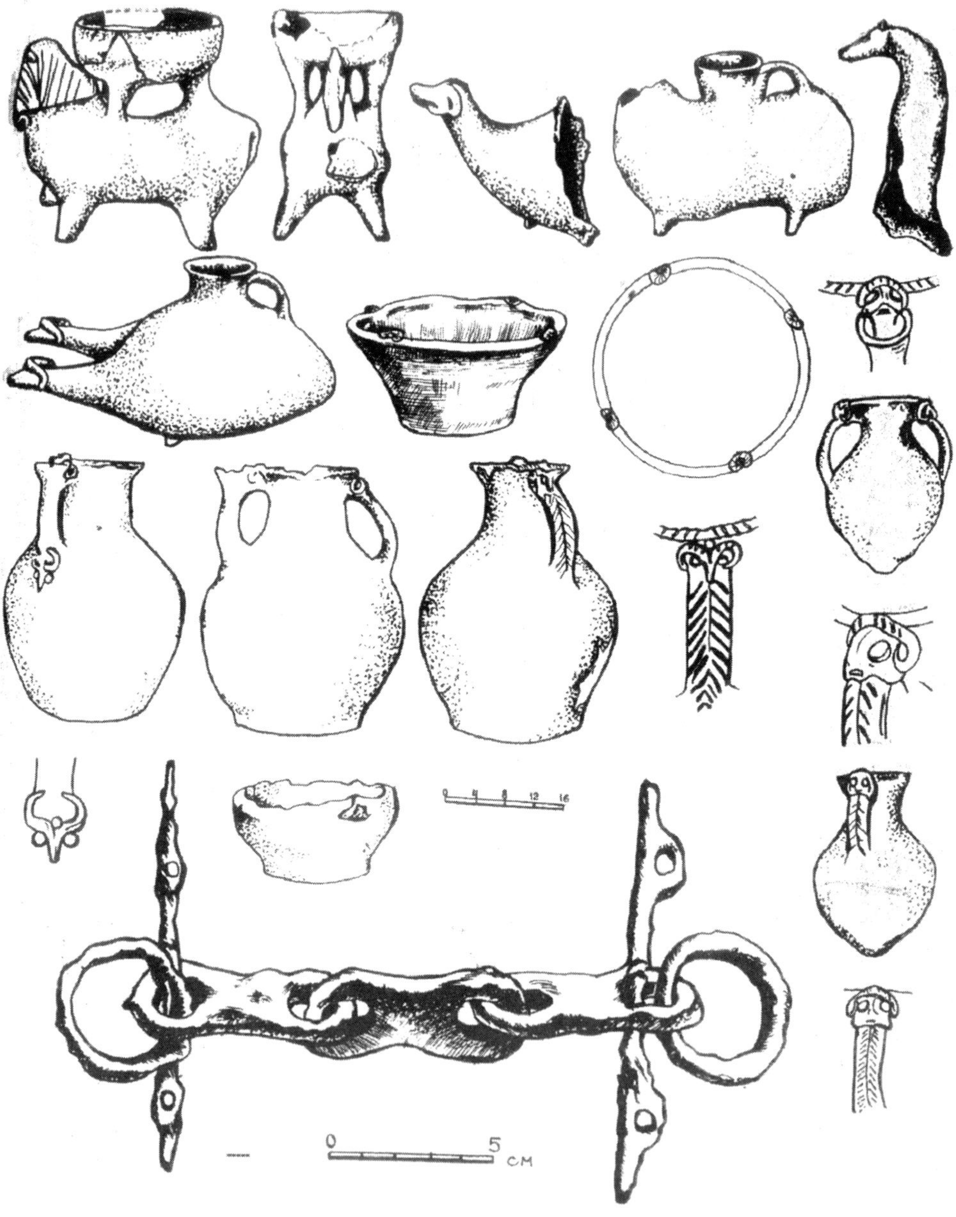

Plate 169: Vessels with zoomorphic handles from Amirtyuba burial, Azerbaijan. First century B.C. to first century A.D.

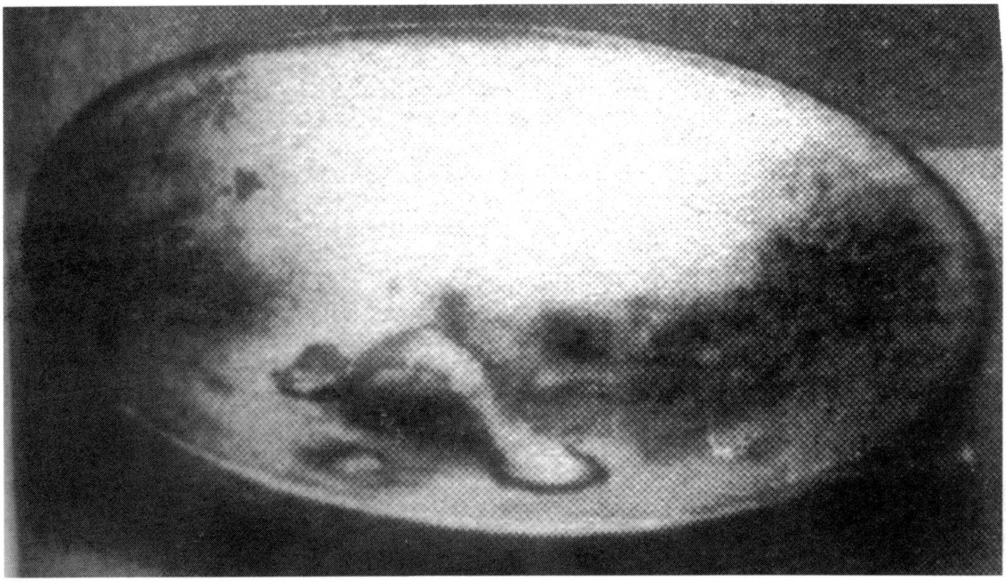
Plate 170: Silver lids with fish-shaped handles, Taxila. First to second century A.D.

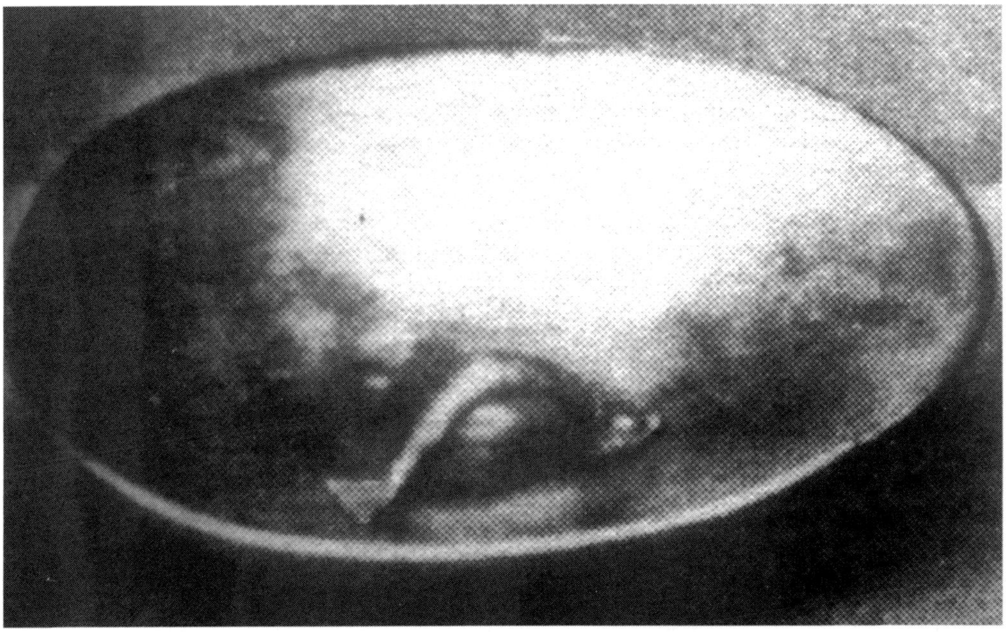
Plate 171: Silver lids with fish-shaped handles, Taxila. First to second century A.D.

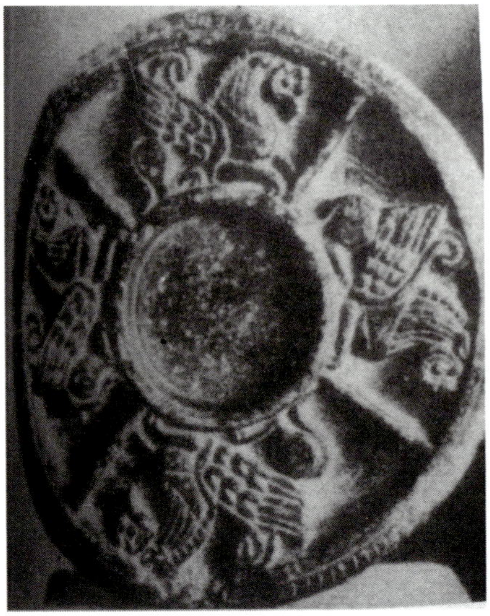

Plate 172: Stone tray from Taxila. First to second century A.D.

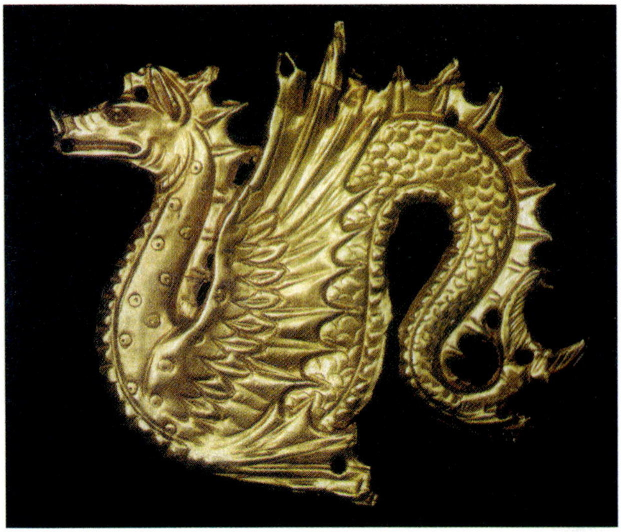

Plate 173: Gold plaque depicting a hippocampus from Kul—Oba barrow. Fourth century B.C.

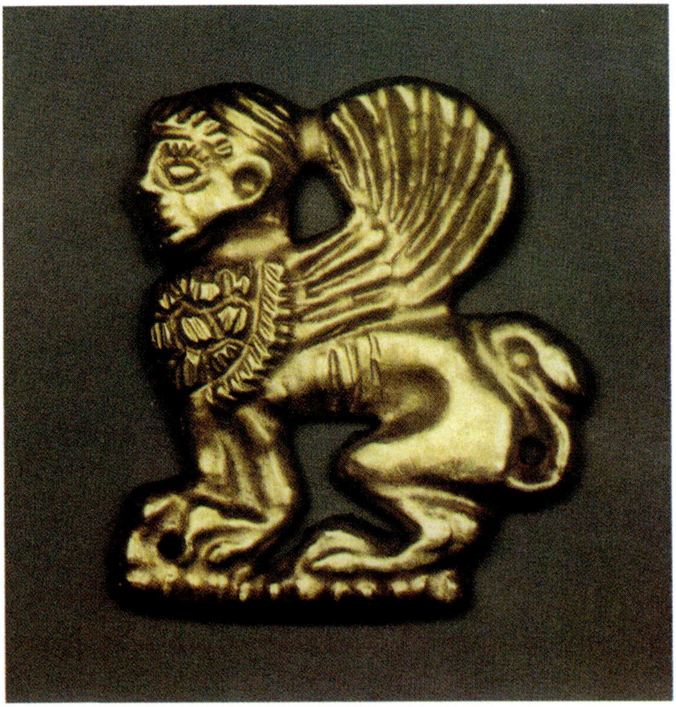

Plate 174: Gold plaques depicting sphinx from Seven Brothers barrow. Mid-Fifth century B.C.

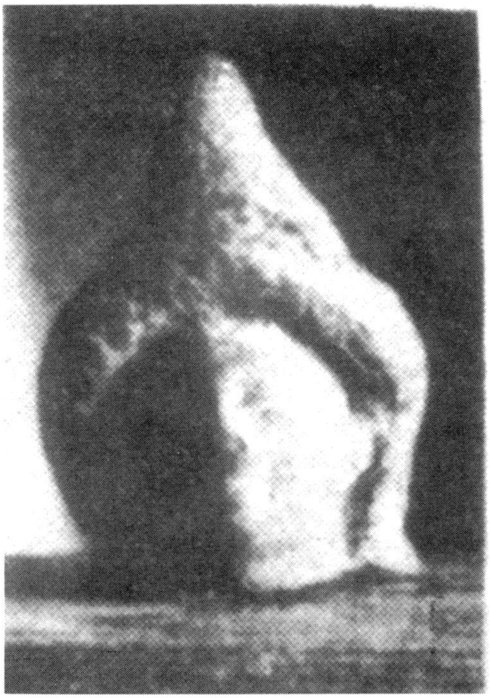

Plate 175 (A): Terracotta male heads with conical caps from Taxila. First to second century A.D.

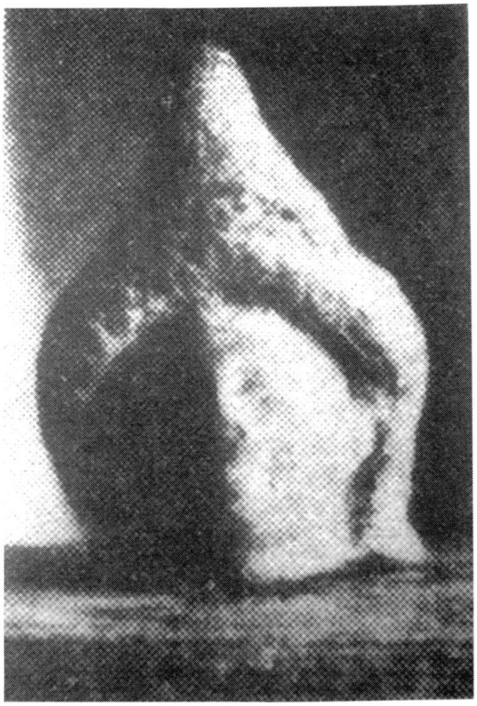

Plate 175(B) : Detail of Plate 175 A. First to second century A.D.

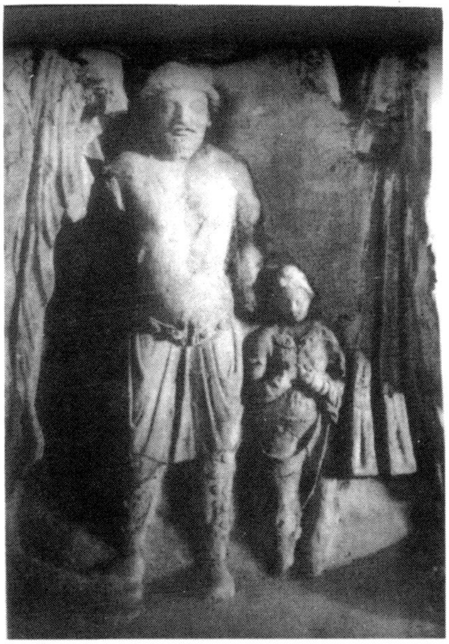

Plate 175 (C) : Stone sculptures with conical caps from Taxila. First to second century A.D.

Plate 176: Bronze ornamental buckle from Taxila. First to second century A.D.

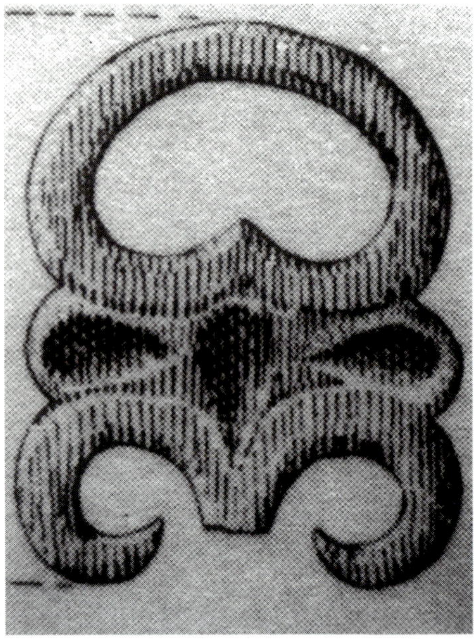

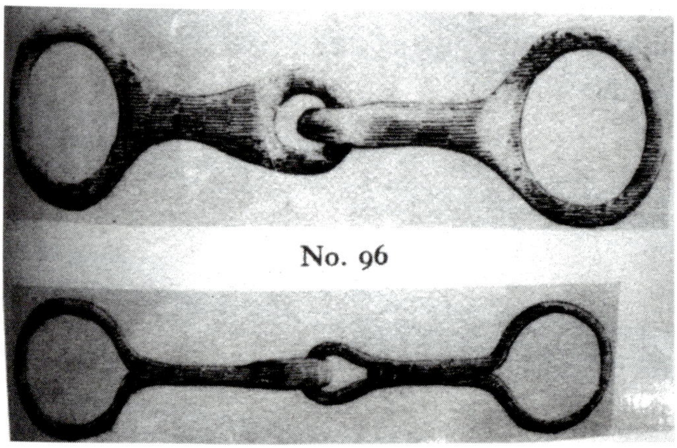

Plate 177: Iron horse-bits from Taxila. First to second century A.D.

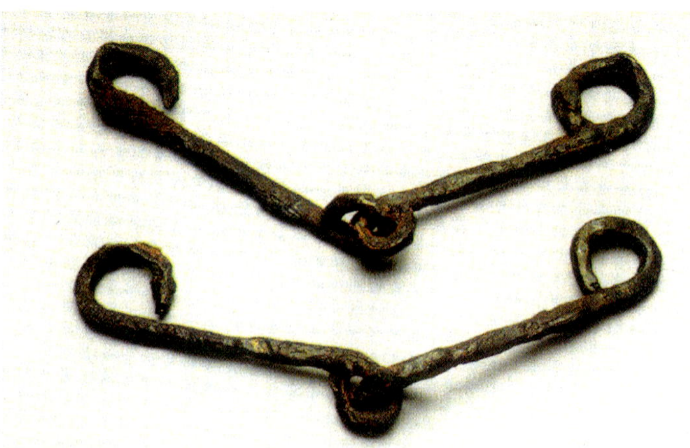

Plate 178: Iron horse bits from Filippovka kurgan 6. Fourth century B.C.

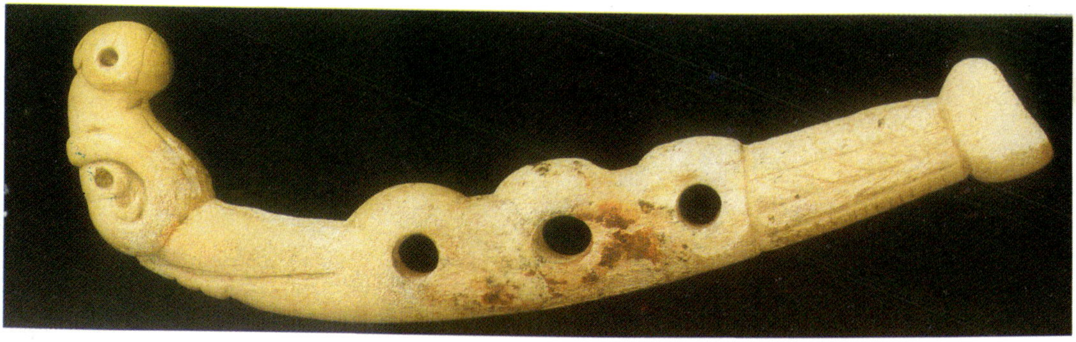

Plate 179: Bone psalia from Zhurovka. Fifth century B.C.

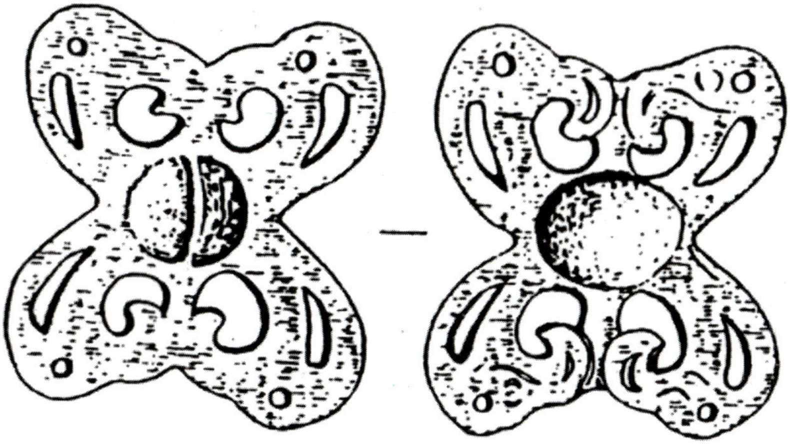

Plate 180: Bronze buckles from Otonkon hoard. Fifth to fourth century B.C.

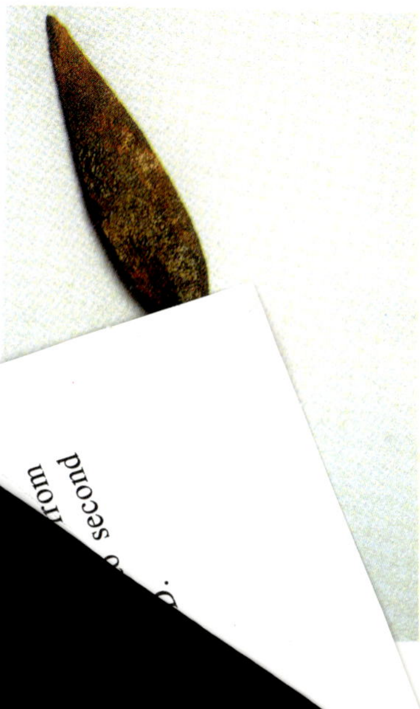

Plate 181: Iron leaf-shaped spear tip from Filippovka barrow 7. Fourth century B.C.

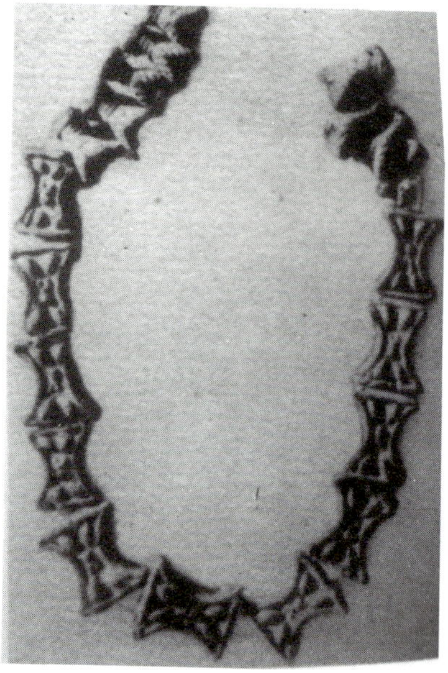

Plate 182: Necklace from Bhir mound, Taxila. First to second century A.D.

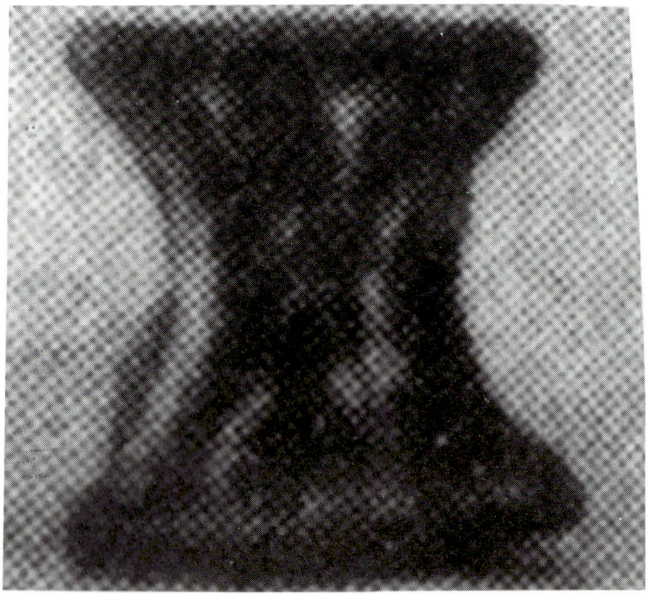

Plate 183: Bead from necklace from Bhir mound, Taxila. First to second century A.D.

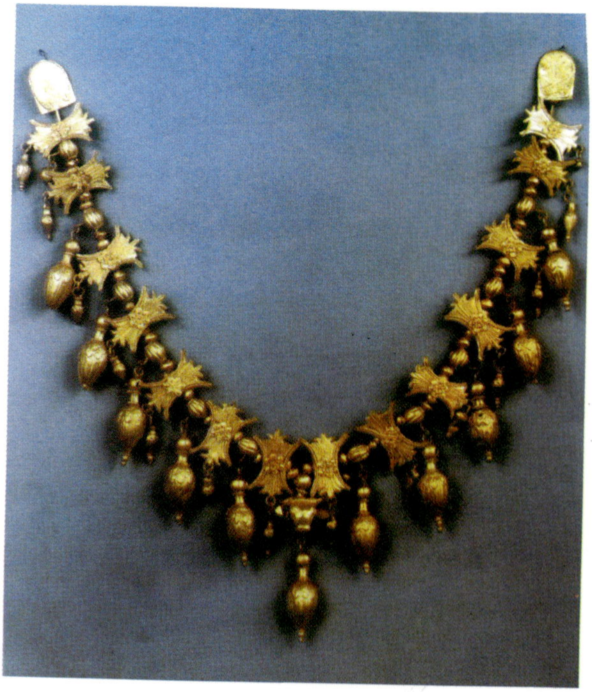

Plate 184: Gold necklace of beads, filigree plaques and pendants from Karagodeuashkh barrow. Late fourth century B.C.

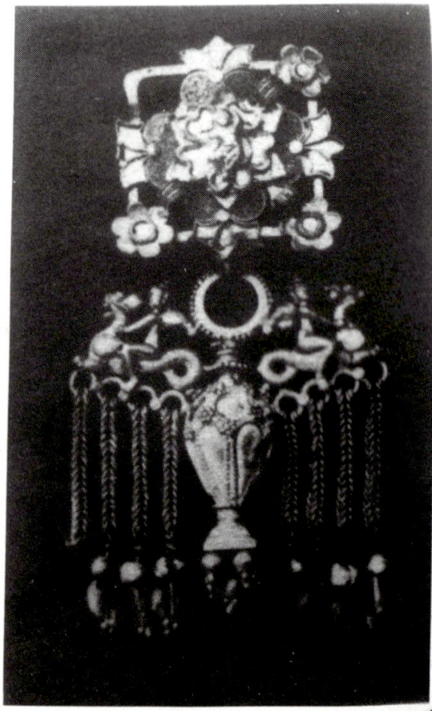

Plate 185: Gold ear pendant f
Taxila. First t
century A.D

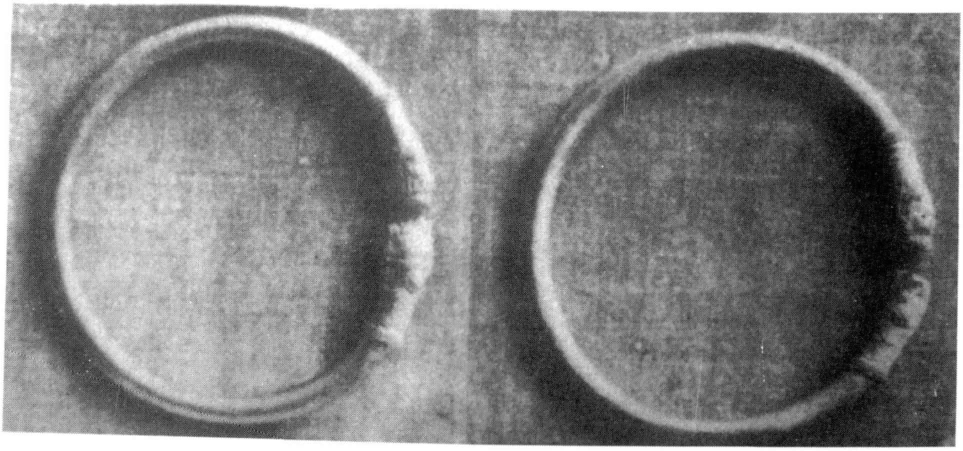

Plate 186: Gold bracelets from Taxila. First to second century A.D.

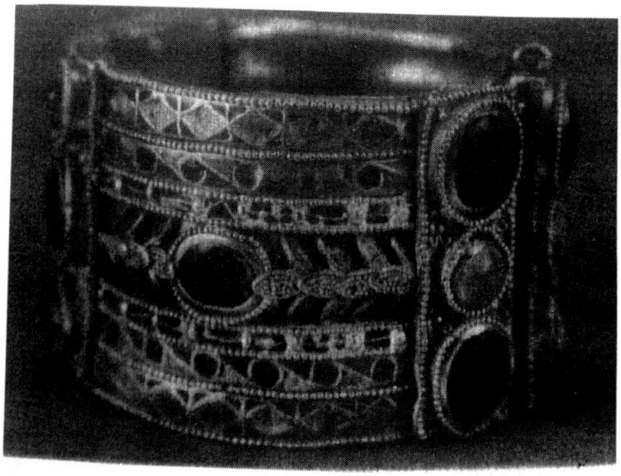

Plate 187(A) : Bracelet from Olbia. Fifth century B.C.

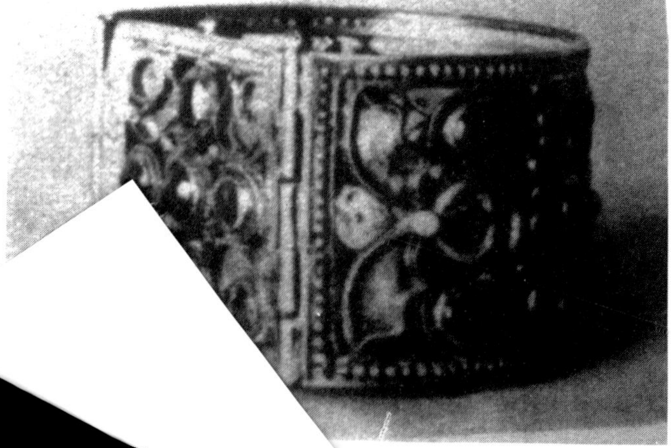

Plate 187(B) : Bracelet from Taxila. First to second century A.D.

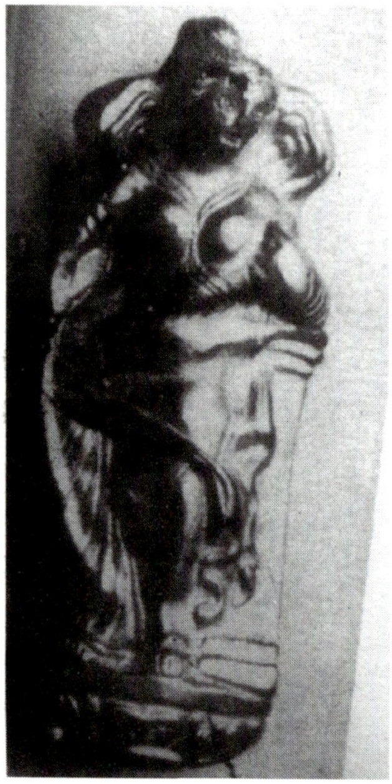

Plate 188: Gold brooch depicting winged Aphrodite from Taxila. First to second century A.D.

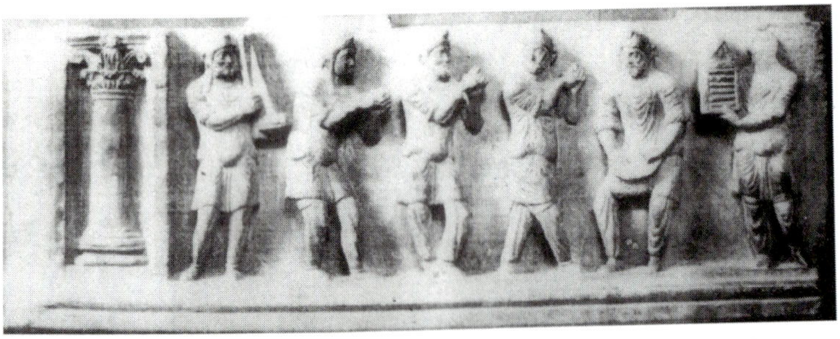

Plate 189: Musicians in Scythian costume from Buner. First century A.D.

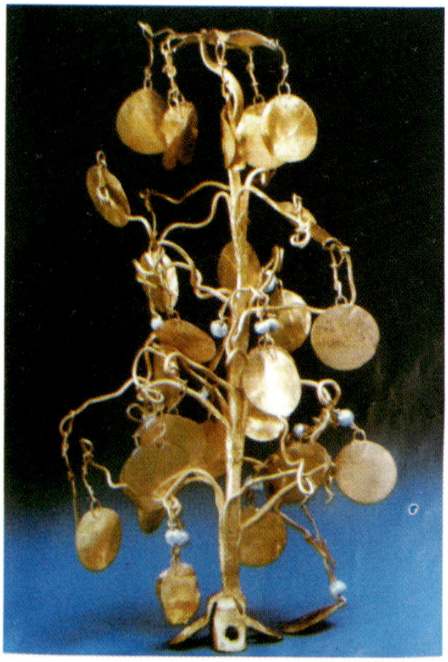

Plate 190: Gold scale model of a tree from burial 4, Tillya-tepe. First century A.D.

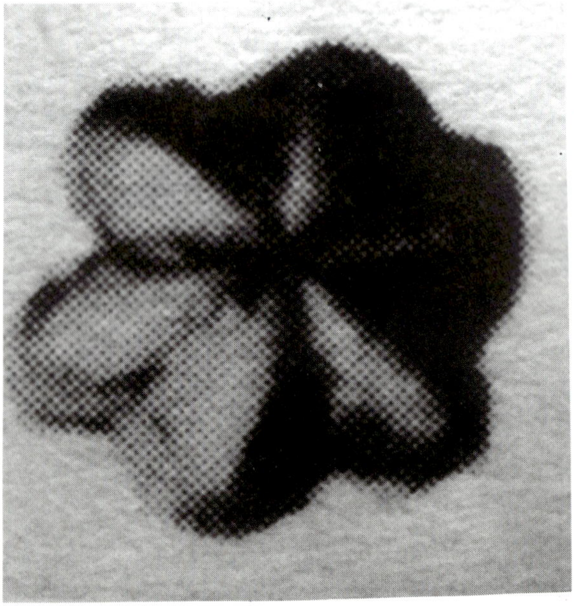

Plate 191: Detail of rosette from Taxila. First to second century A.D.

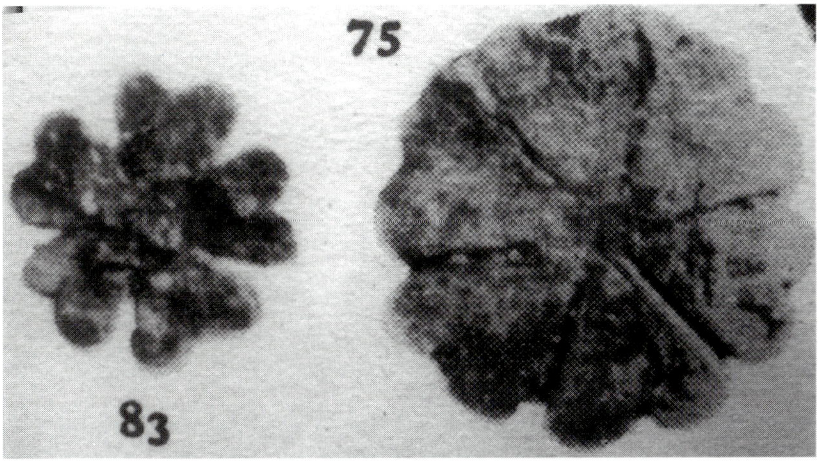

Plate 192: Detail of rosette from Taxila. First to second century A.D.

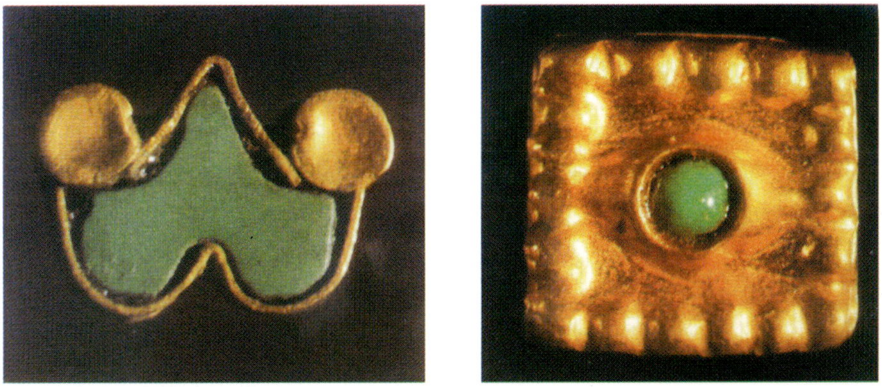

Plate 193: Trident-shaped plaques with circlets and eye-pupil plaques from Tillya-tepe. First century A.D.

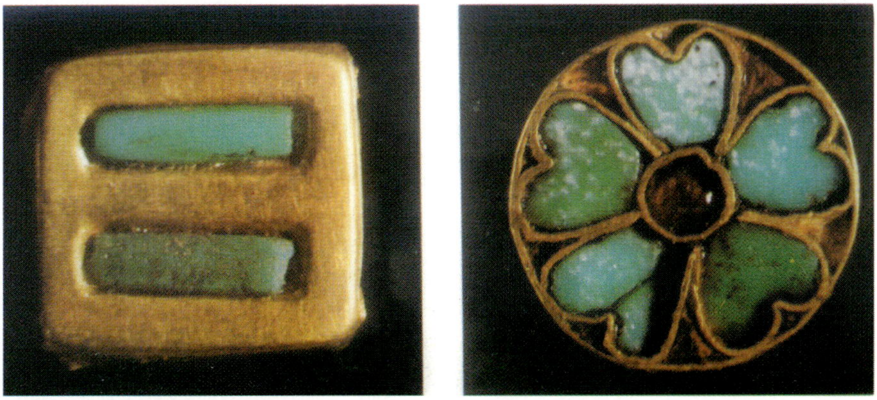

Plate 194: Plaques with elongated insets and flowerlet plaques from Tillya-tepe. First century A.D.

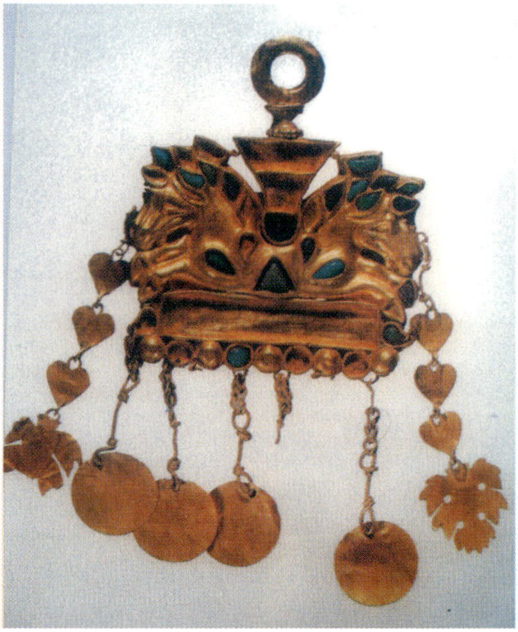

Plate 195: Gold temple pendant from Tillya-tepe. First century A.D.

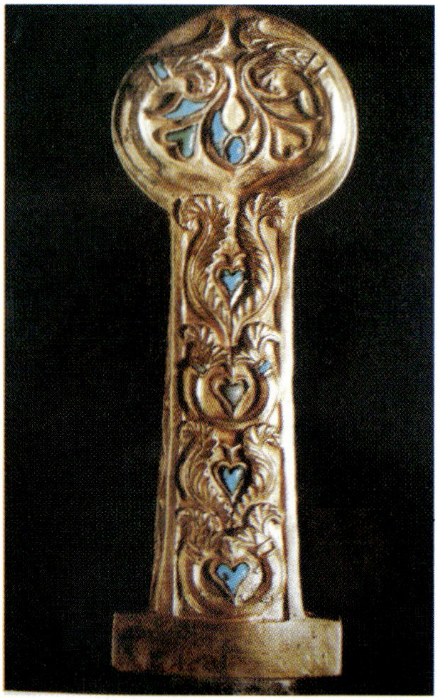

Plate 196: *Nandipada*—like patterns on Tillya-tepe weapon handle. First century A.D.

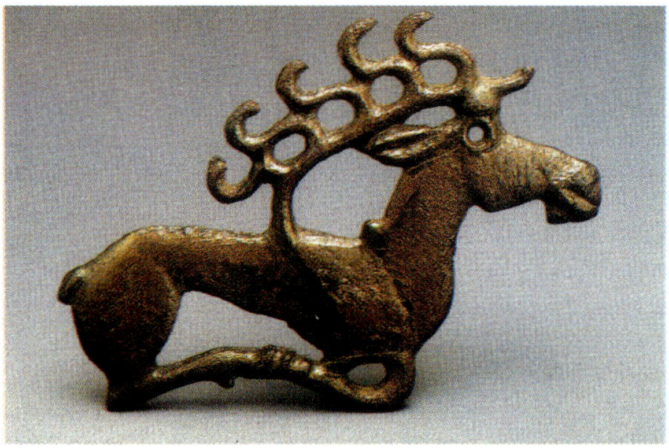

Plate 197: Bronze stag from Razliv burial site, barrow 3, Tagar culture. Seventh to sixth centuries B.C.

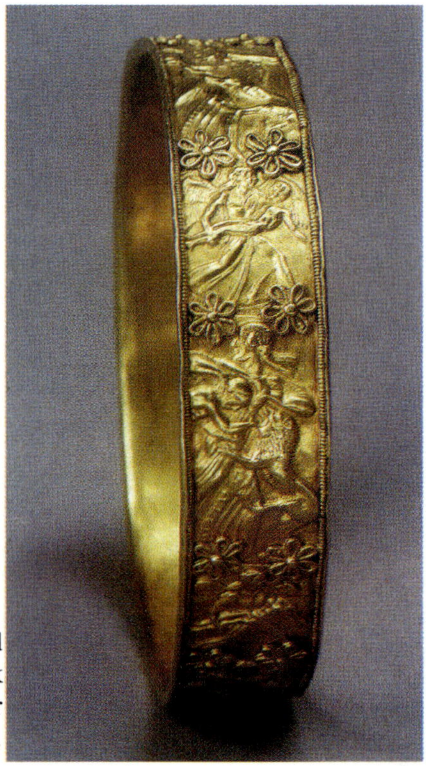

Plate 198: 'Greek art in Scythian barrow'. Gold two layered bracelets with relief images from Greek mythology and appliquê rosettes on the outer ring from Kul-Oba barrow. Fourth century B.C.

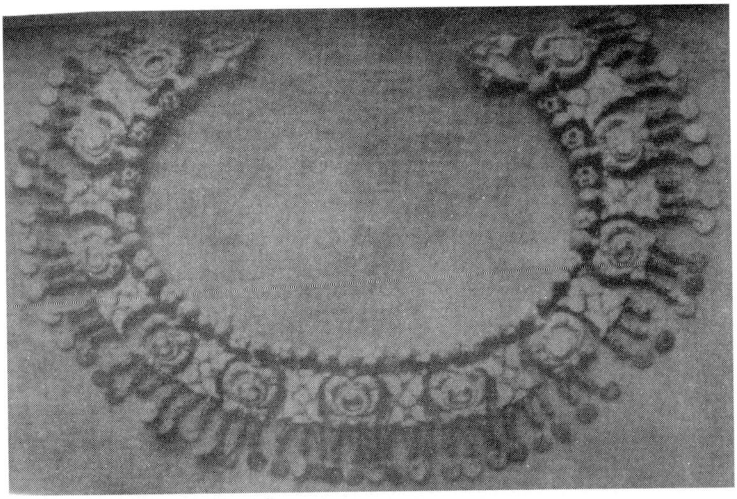

Plate 199: Necklace from Taxila. First to second century A.D.

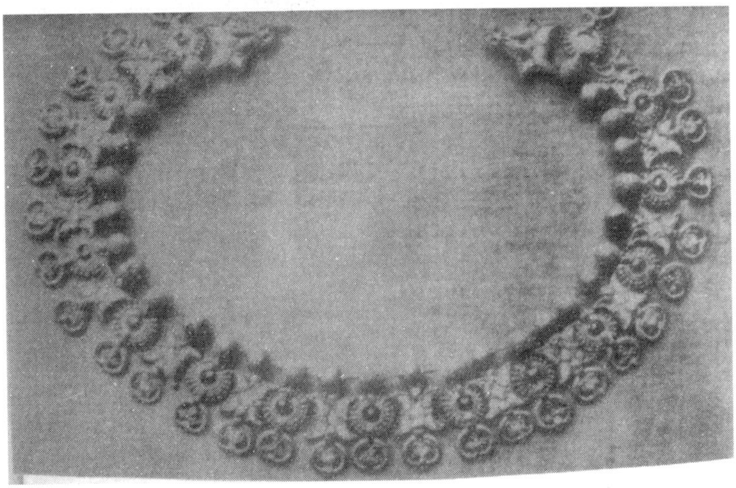

Plate 200: Necklace from Taxila. First to second century A.D.

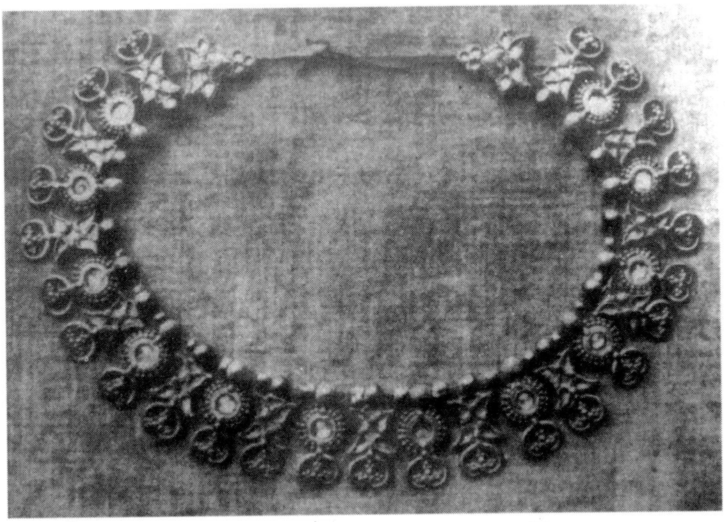

Plate 201: Necklace from Taxila. First to second century A.D.

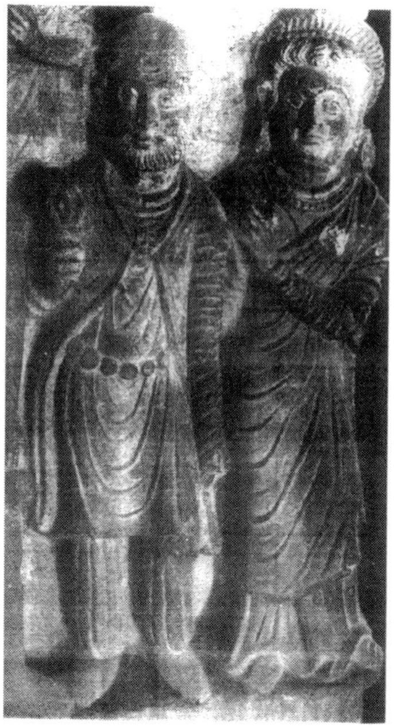

Plate 202: Detail of two donors in nomadic costume from Shotorak. First to second century A.D.

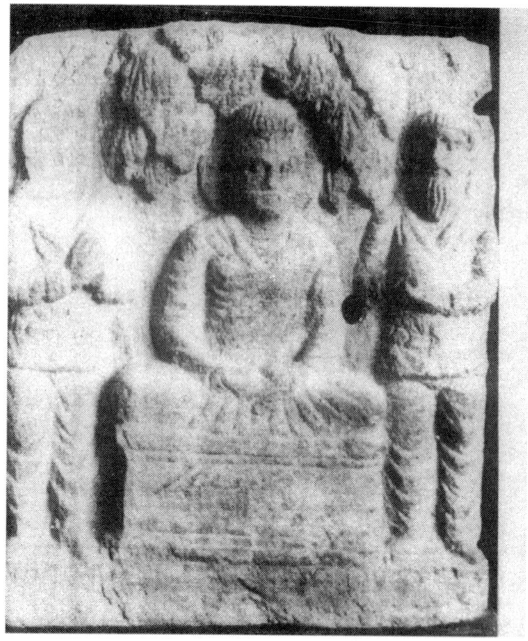

Plate 203: 'Trapuúa and Bhallika' flanking Úākyamuni, from Shotorak. First to second century A.D.

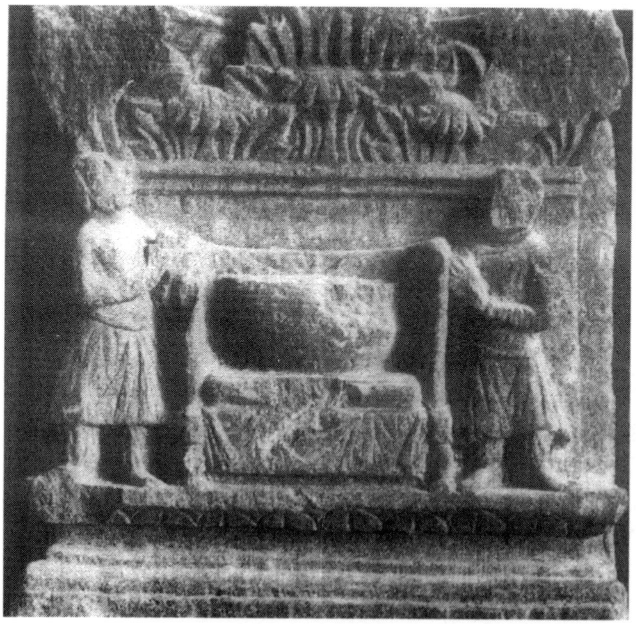

Plate 204: Worship of Úākyamuni's alms bowl from Shotorak. First to second century A.D.

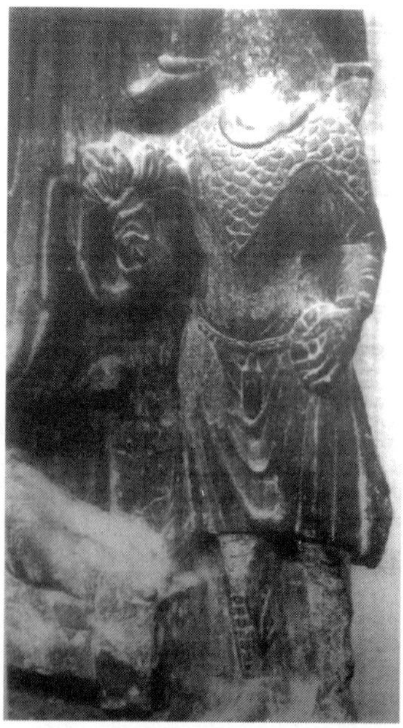

Plate 205: Detail of Indo-Scythian devotee from Takal. First to second century A.D.

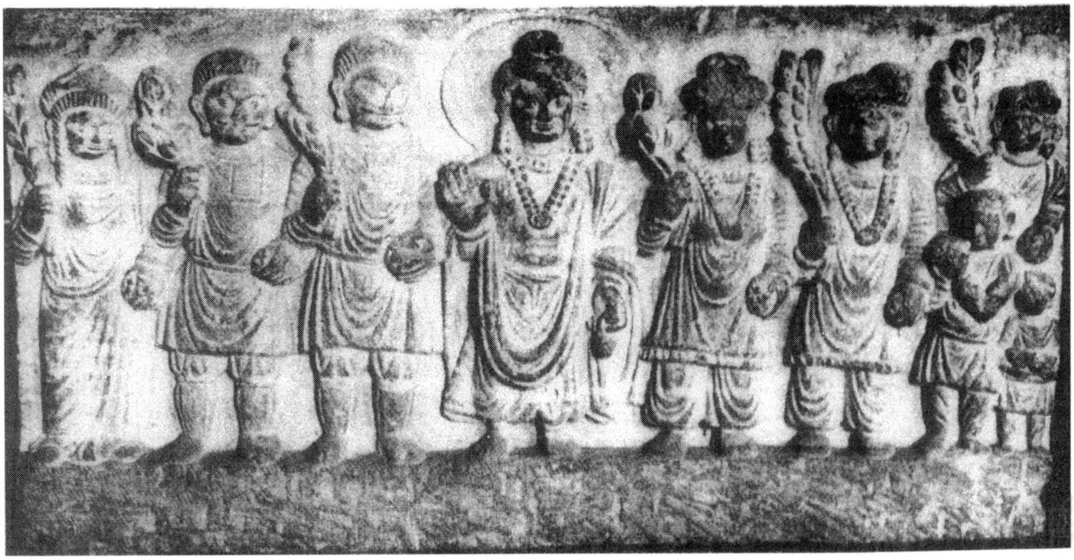

Plate 206: Image pedestal with Maitreya flanked by two groups of nomads from Paitava. First to second century A.D.

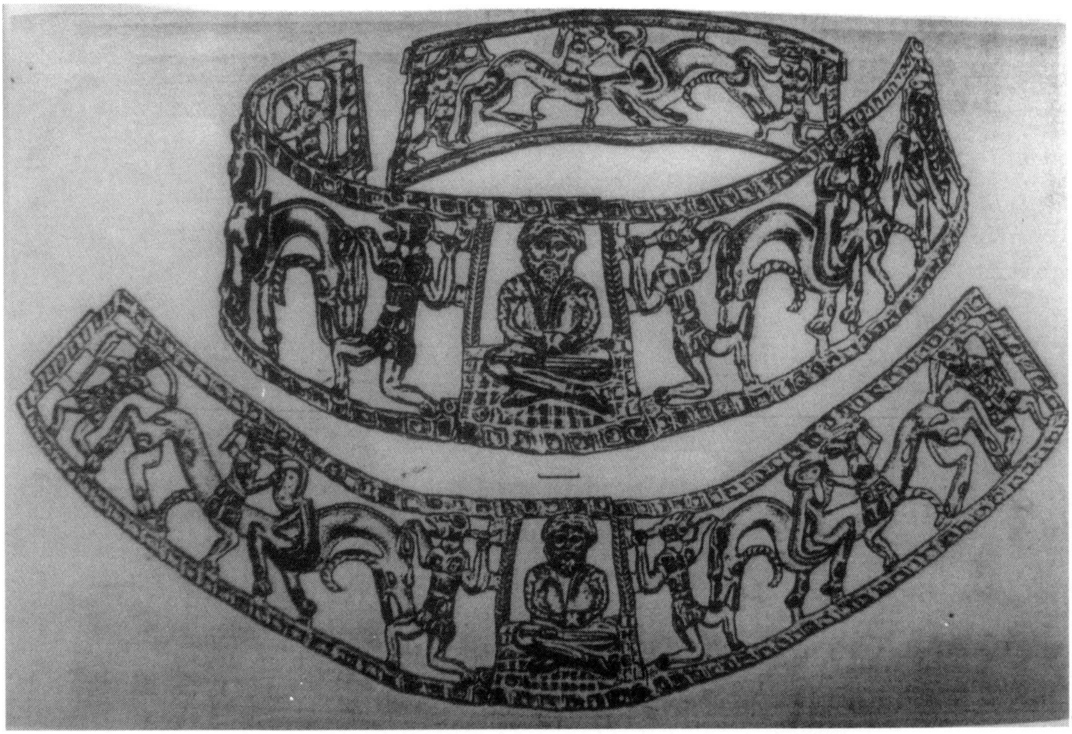

Plate 207: Torque from Kobya-Kovo barrow 10. First to second century A.D.

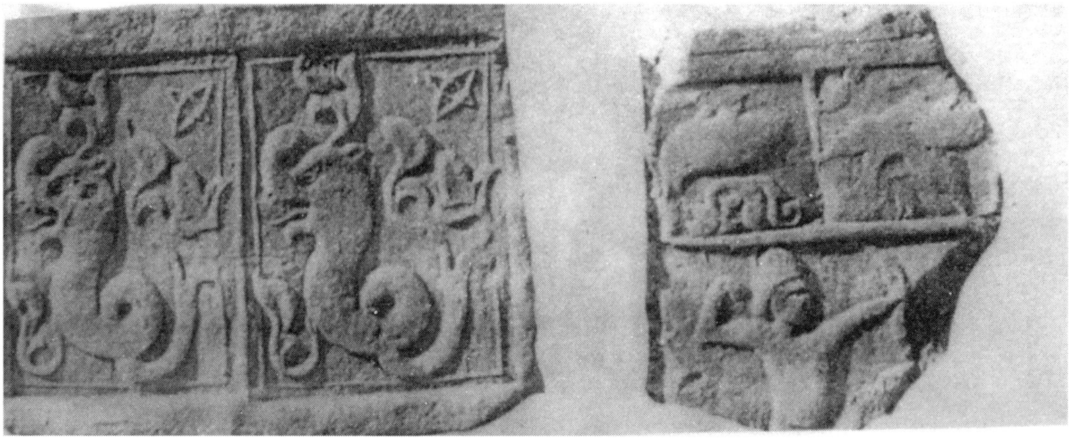

Plate 208: Left: Two impressions of a rectangle containing a dragon (*makara*) with foliate tail and crest and an upraised trunk-like snout from a Harwan tile. Right: An archer wearing conical cap from a Harwan tile. Second to fourth century A.D.

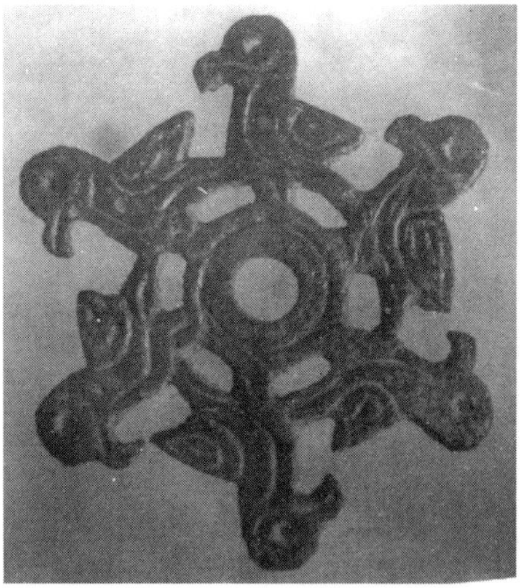

Plate 209: Bronze plaque (function unknown) from Iran. Tenth to ninth century B.C.

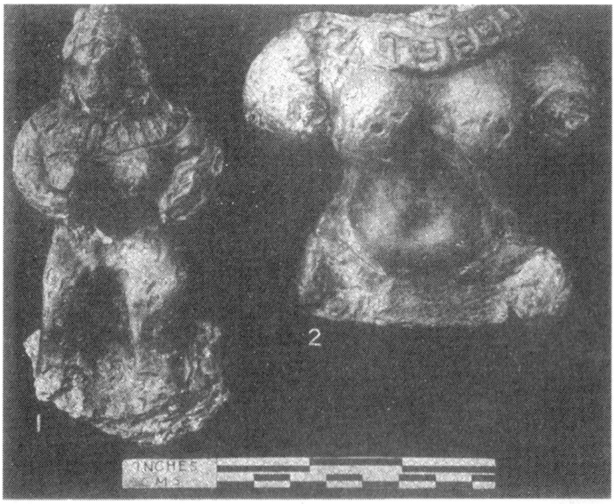

Plate 210: Terracotta figures from Śaka-Parthian levels at Kauúāmbī. First to second century A.D.

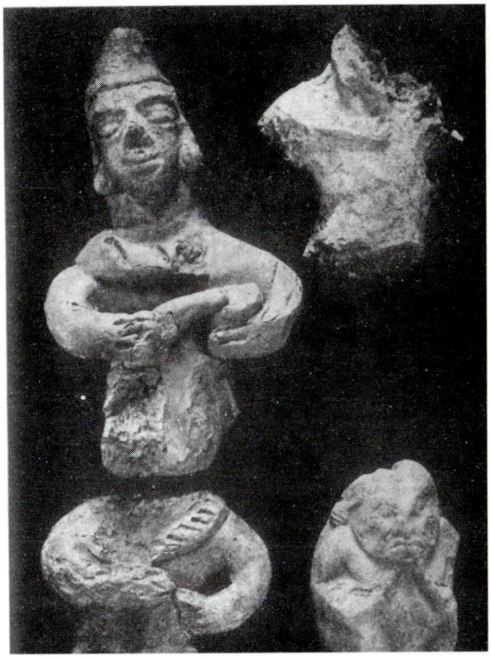

Plate 211: A terracotta drummer with a peaked cap from Śaka-Parthian levels at Kauúāmbï. First to second century A.D.

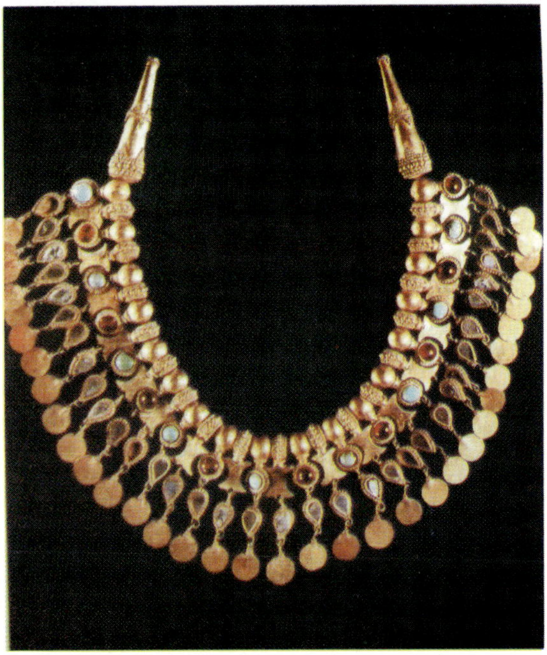

Plate 212: Necklace from burial 5, Tillya-tepe. First century A.D.

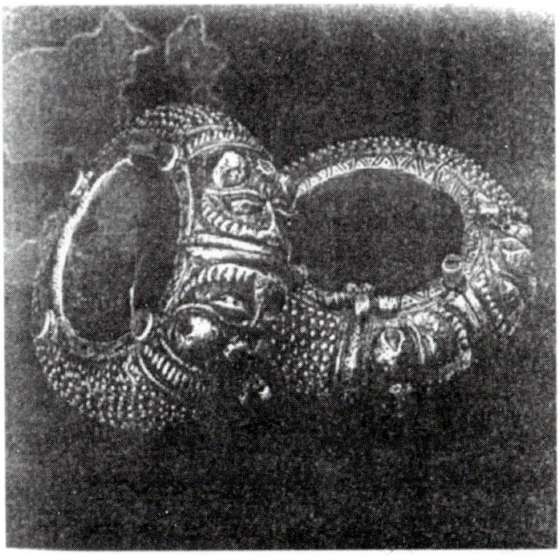

Plate 213: Silver 'tiger' anklets from Saurashtra, Gujarat. Twenty-first century.

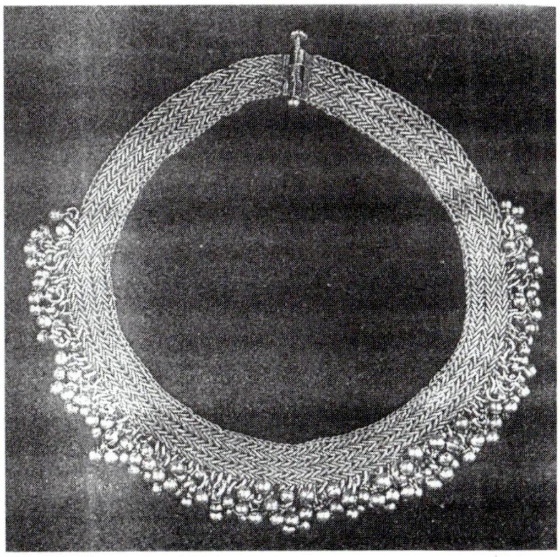

Plate 214: A necklace of linked silver chains and bell from Maharashtra. Twenty-first century.

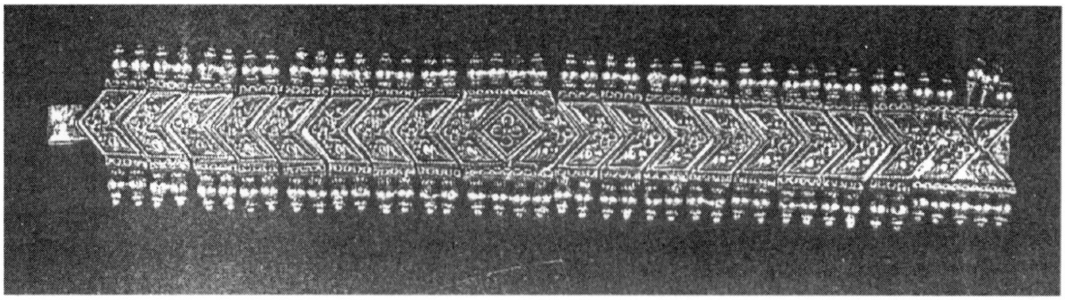

Plate 215: South Indian bracelet of linked silver repoussê elements. Twenty-first century.

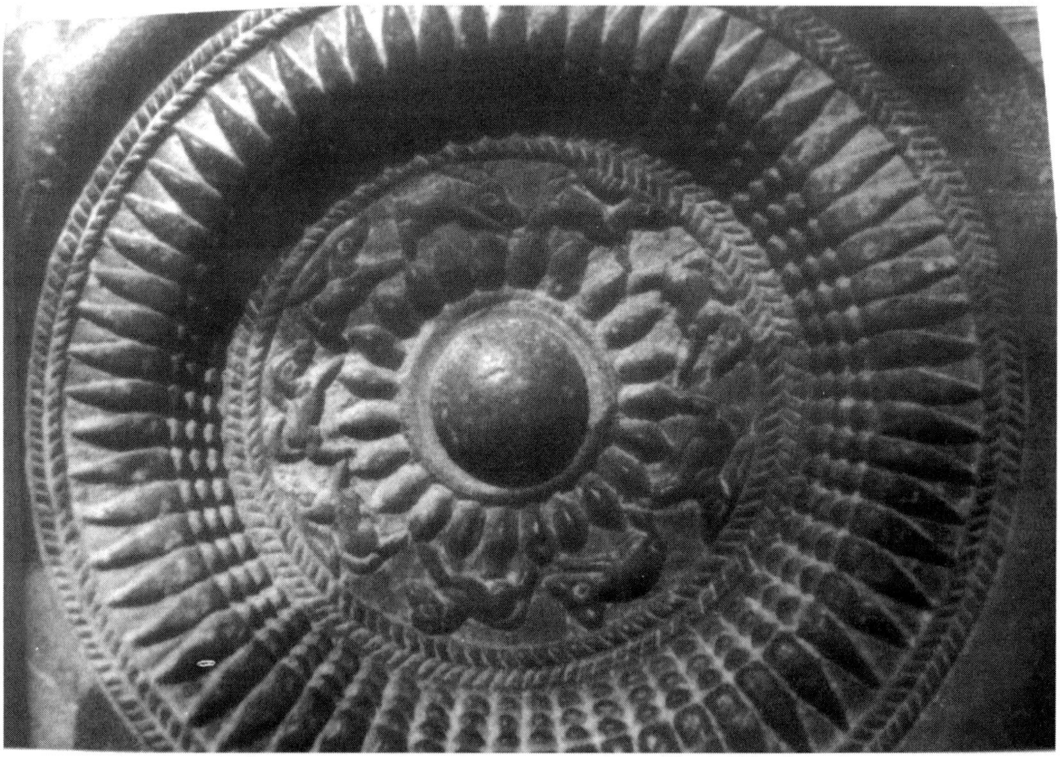

Plate 216: Stone disc from Rājghāt . Fourth to fifth century A.D.

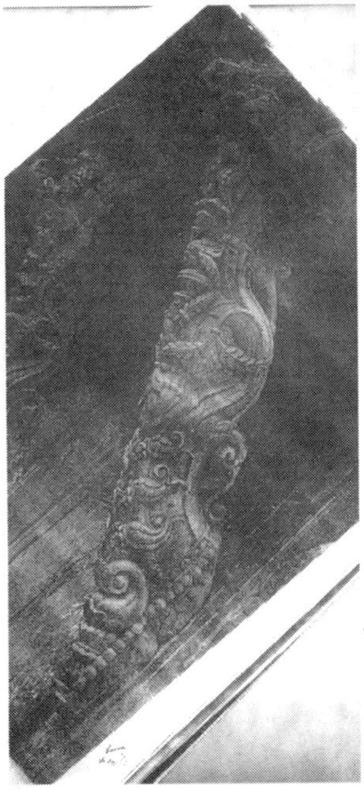

Plate 217: Wooden architectural decorations. Tenth to fourteenth century A.D.

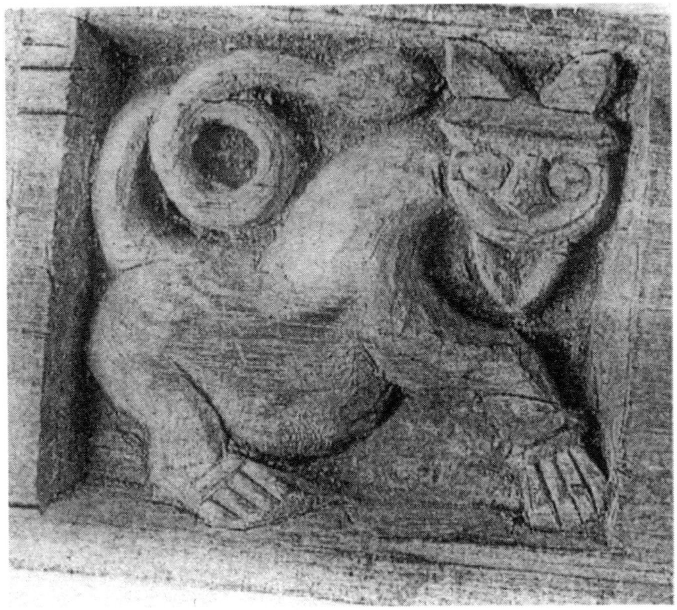

Plate 218: Wooden architectural elements from Saurashtra, Gujarat. Twentyieth century.

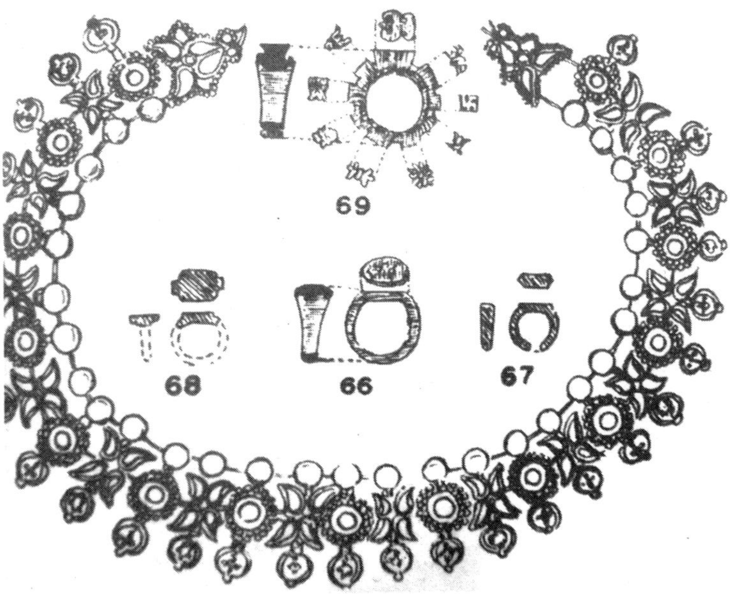

Plate 219: Necklace from Taxila. First to second century A.D.

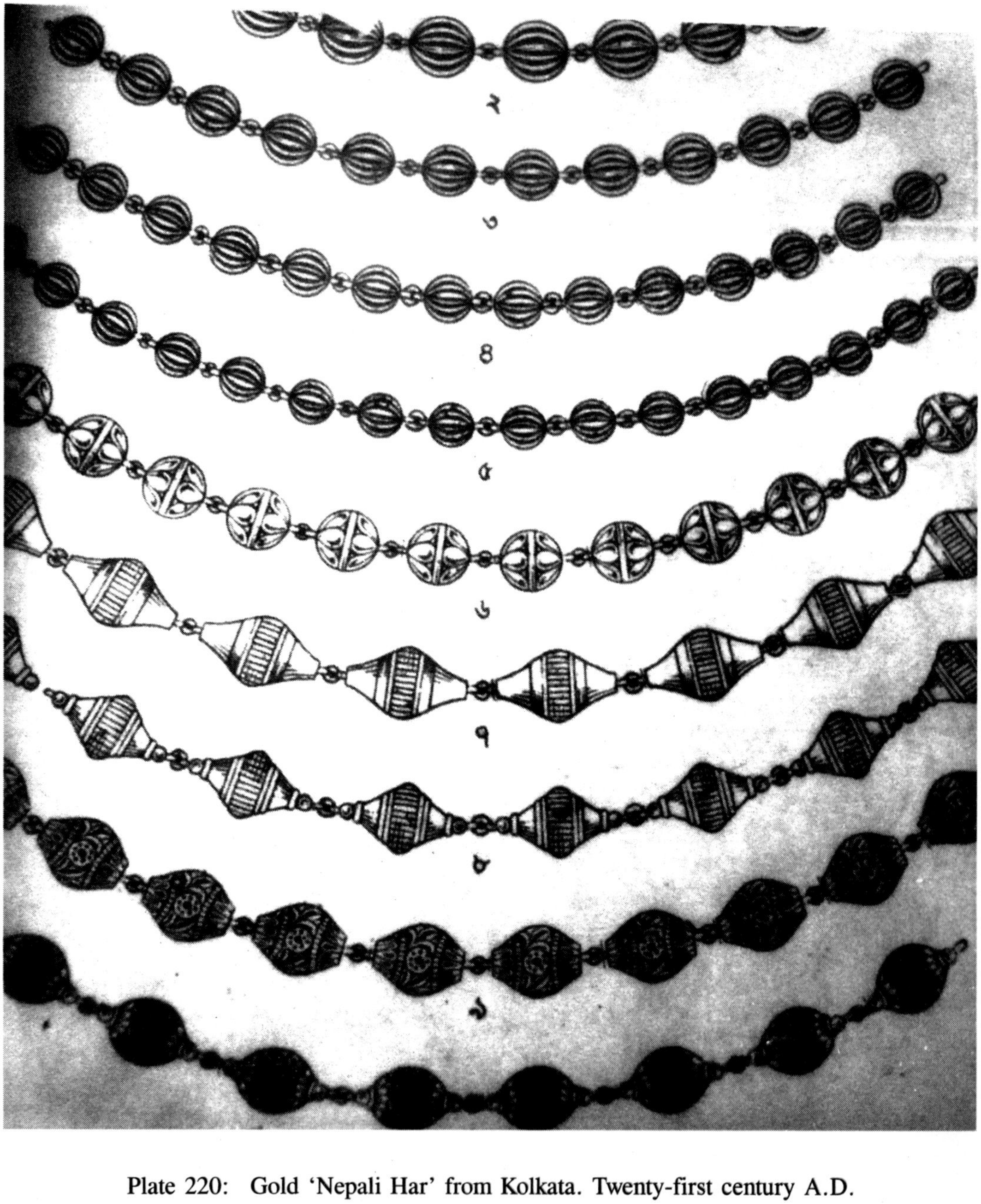

Plate 220: Gold 'Nepali Har' from Kolkata. Twenty-first century A.D.

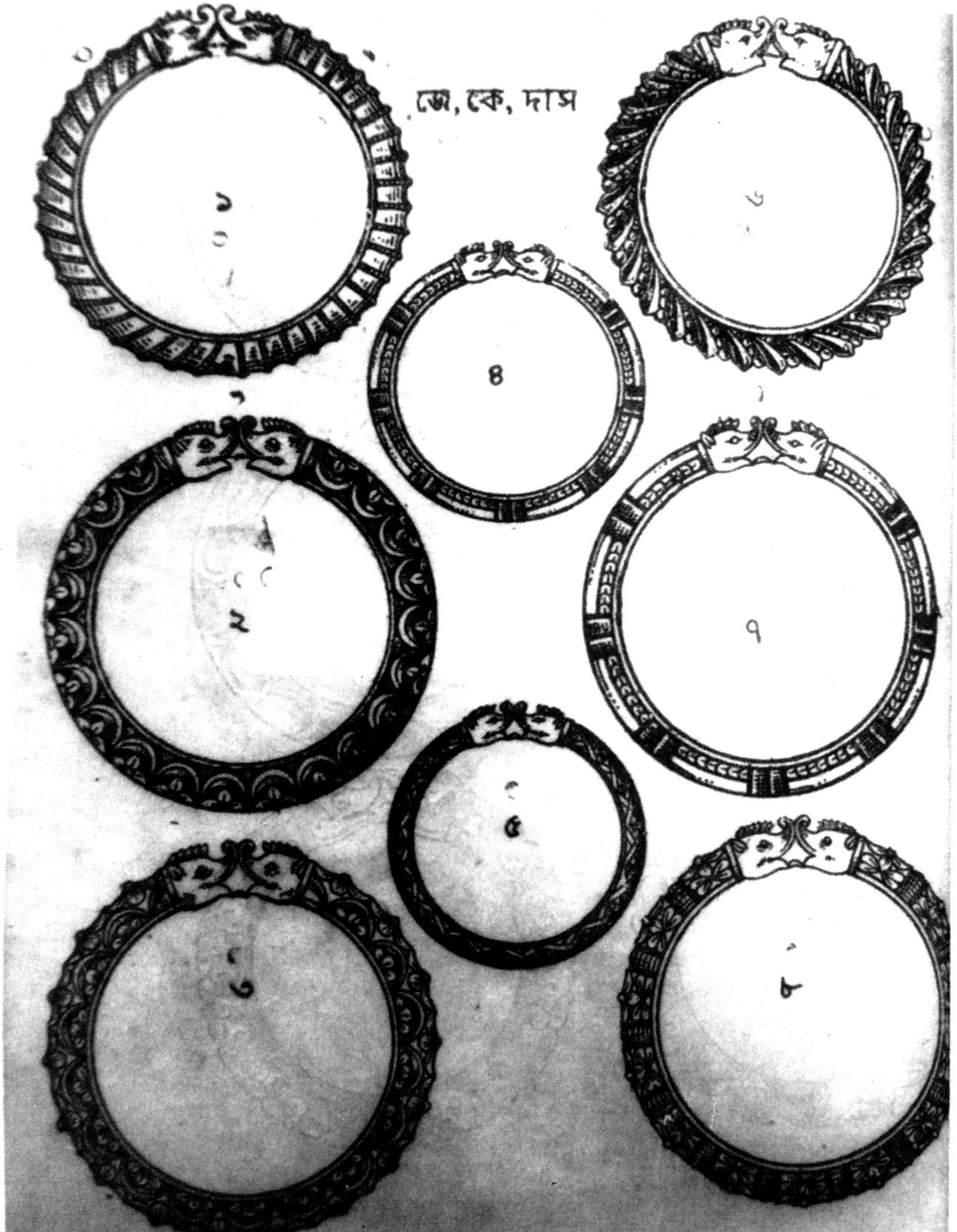

Plate 221: Bracelets with *makara* heads from Kolkata. Twenty-first century A.D. Also, see Plate 235.

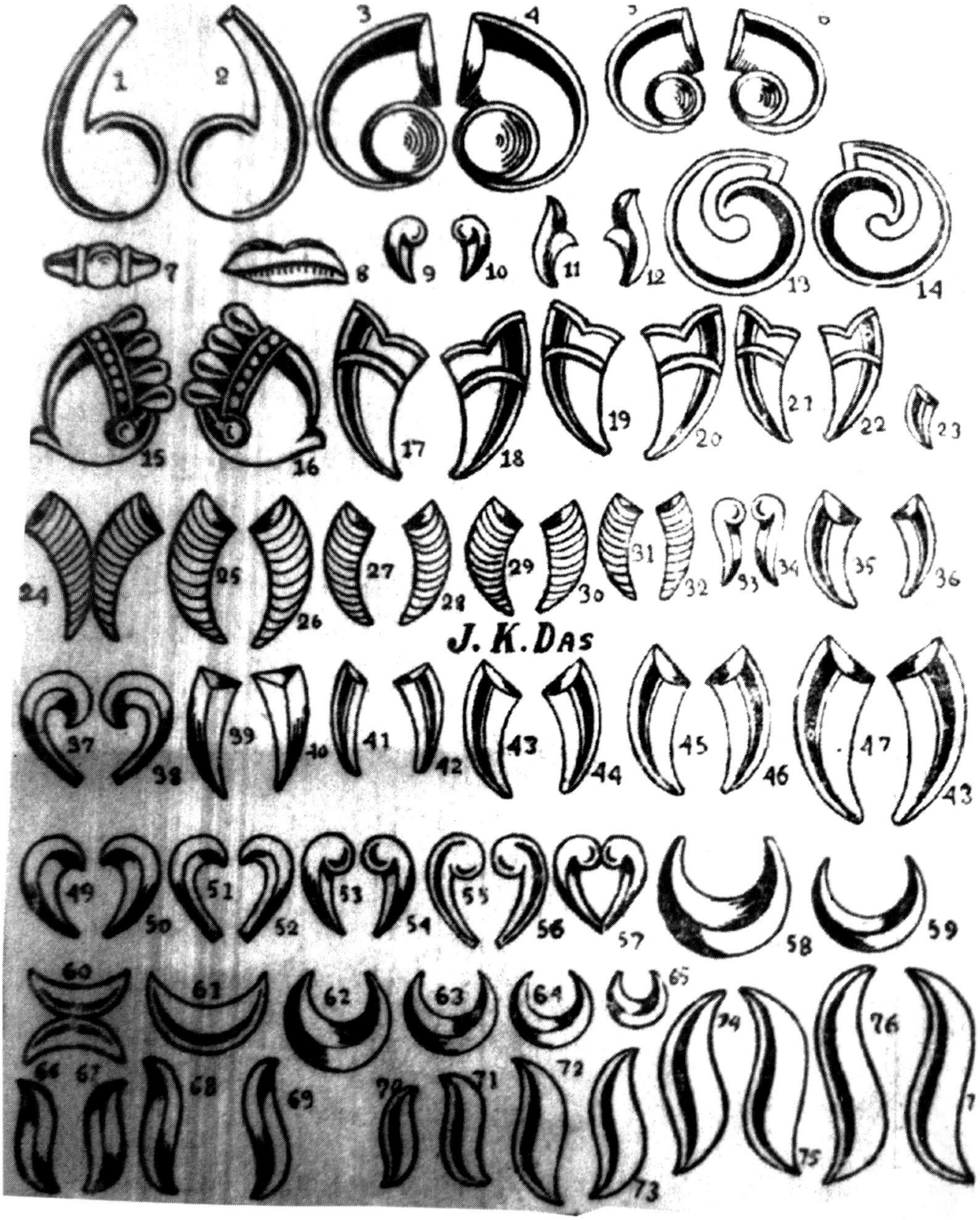

Plate 222: Plaques of various shapes used by the goldsmiths of Kolkata. Twenty-first century A.D.

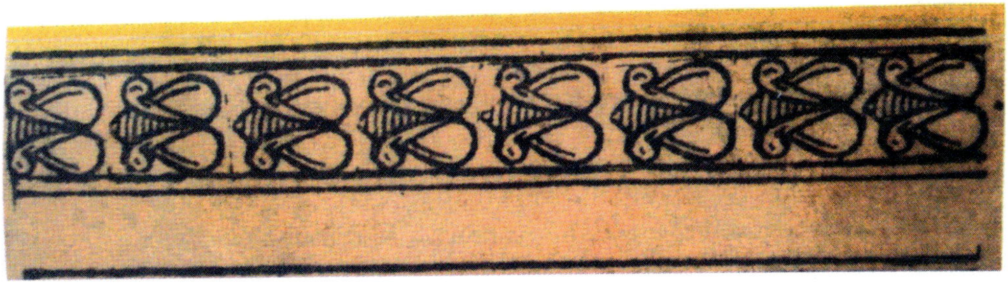

Plate 223 (A) : Chur, showing trefoil pattern, Kolkata. Twenty-first century A.D.

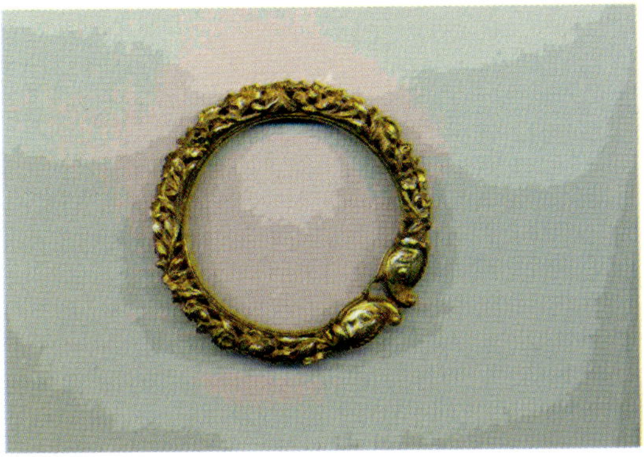

Plate 223 (B) : Gold arm ornaments, Kolkata, Twenty-first century A.D.

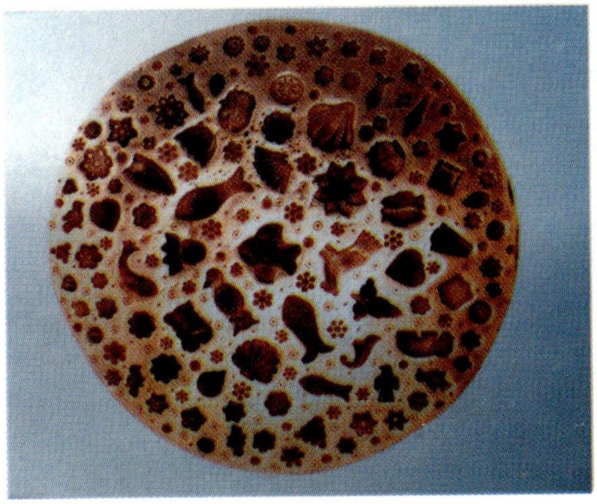

Plate 224: Jeweller's mould of cast brass, India. Twenty-first century A.D.

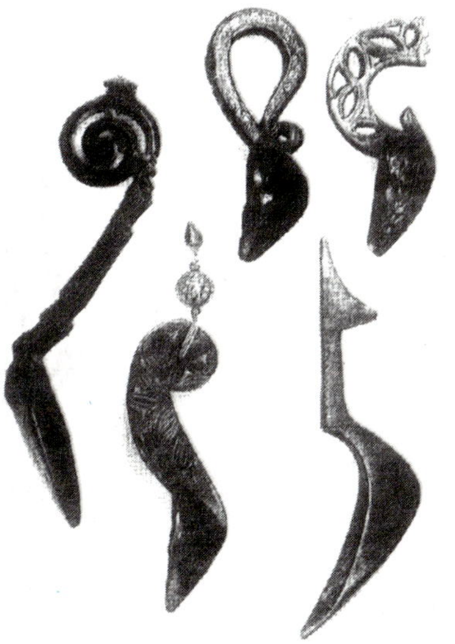

Plate 225: Medicine spoons from Swat valley. Twenty-first century A.D.

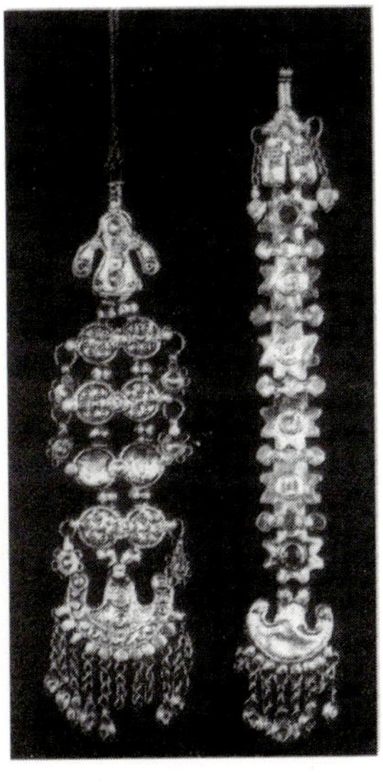

Plate 226: Pectoral ornaments from Swat, now in the Linden Museum. Twenty-first century A.D.

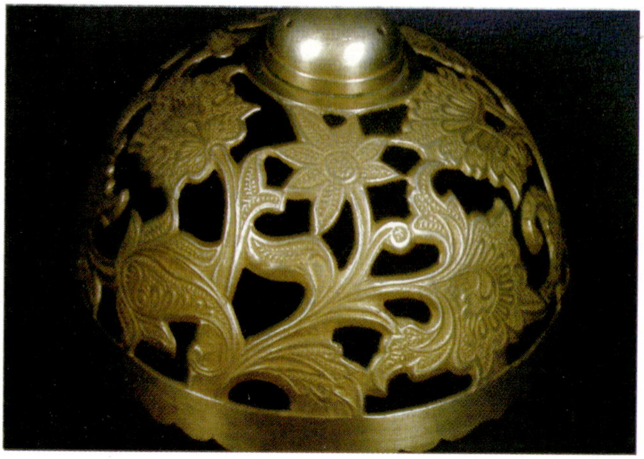

Plate 227: Brass lamp-shade from Uttar Pradesh. Twenty-first century A.D.

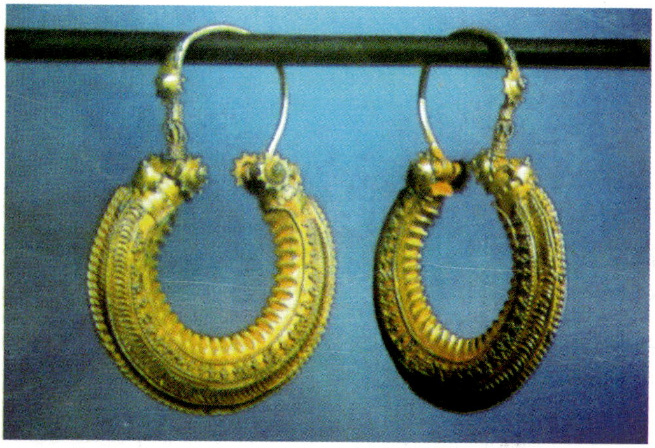

Plate 228: Gold earrings from Kutch. Twenty-first century A.D.

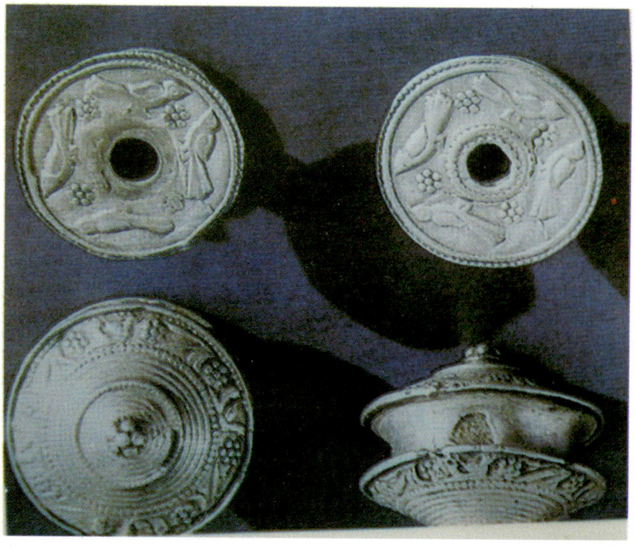

Plate 229: Silver discal earrings from Gujrat. Twenty-first century A.D.

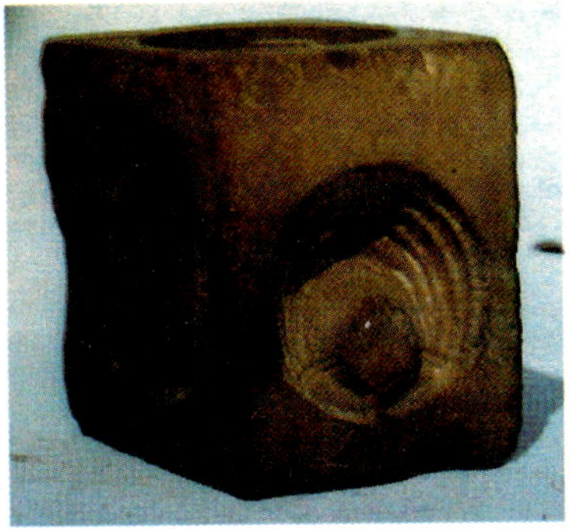

Plate 230: Cubic stone mould from Ter. Third century A.D.

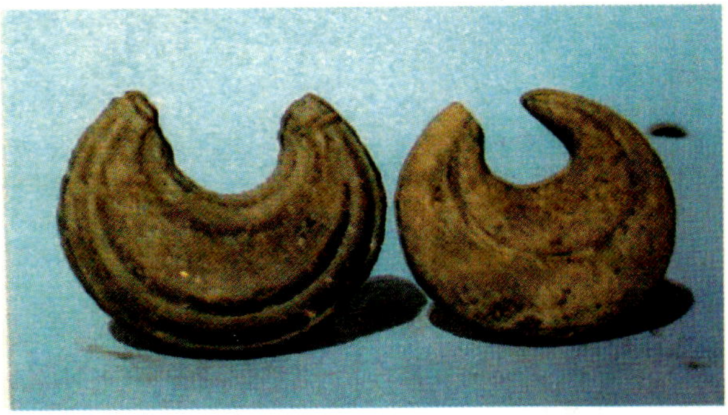

Plate 231: Crescent-type earrings from Ter. Third century A.D.

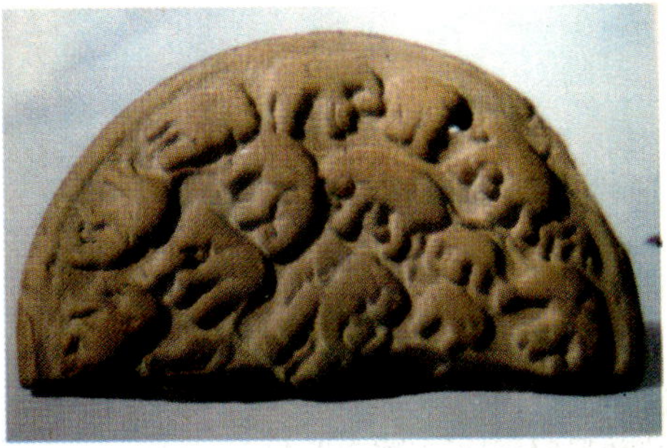

Plate 232: Beige terracotta pendant from Ter showing a herd of elephants. Third century A.D.

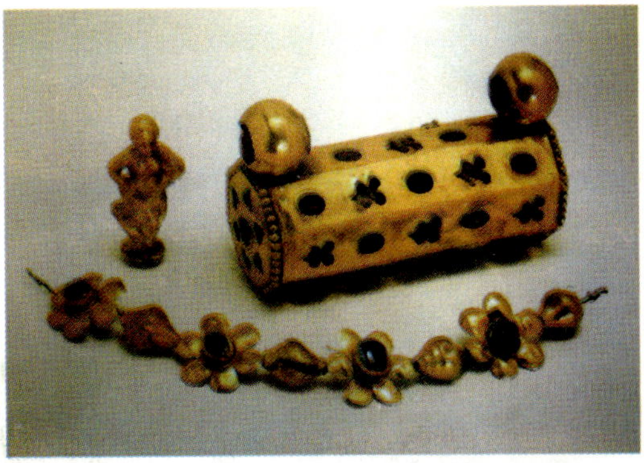

Plate 233: Gold amulet case from Ahin Posh, near Jalalabad. Second to third century A.D.

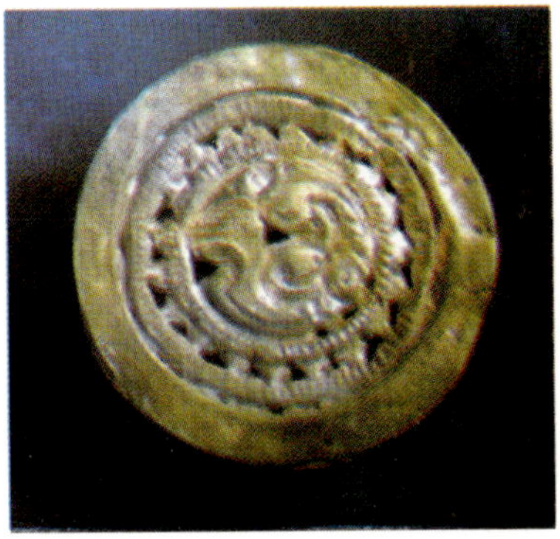

Plate 234: Discal ear ornament from Gandhāra. Third century A.D.

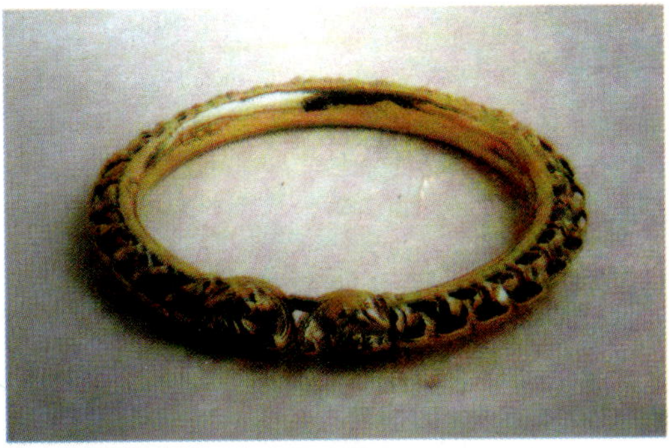

Plate 235: Elephant bracelet, gold, on a shellac core with ring-matting technique, Kolkata. Twenty-first century A.D.

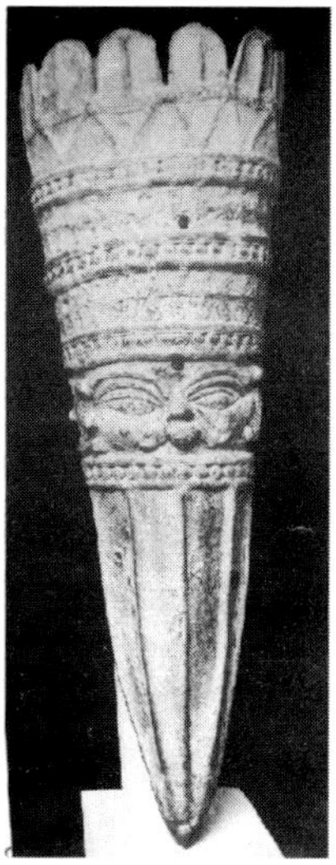

Plate 236: Posheri bronze cornucopia. Second century A.D.

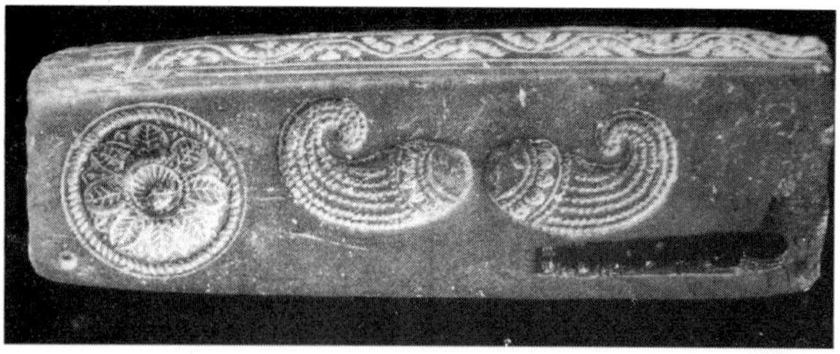

Plate 237: Jewellery moulds from Ter. Second to third century A.D.

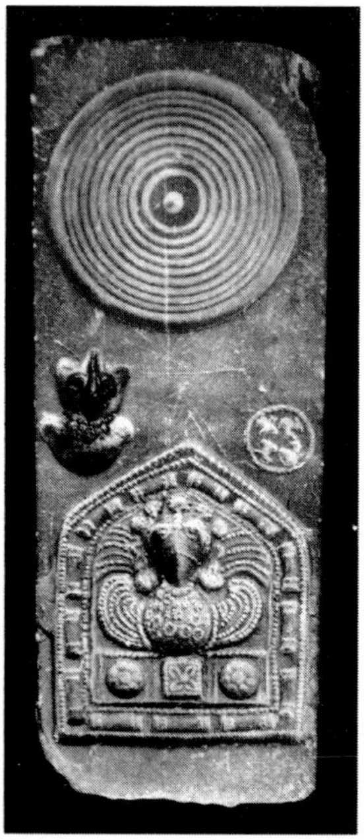

Plate 238: Jewellery moulds from Ter. Second to third century A.D.

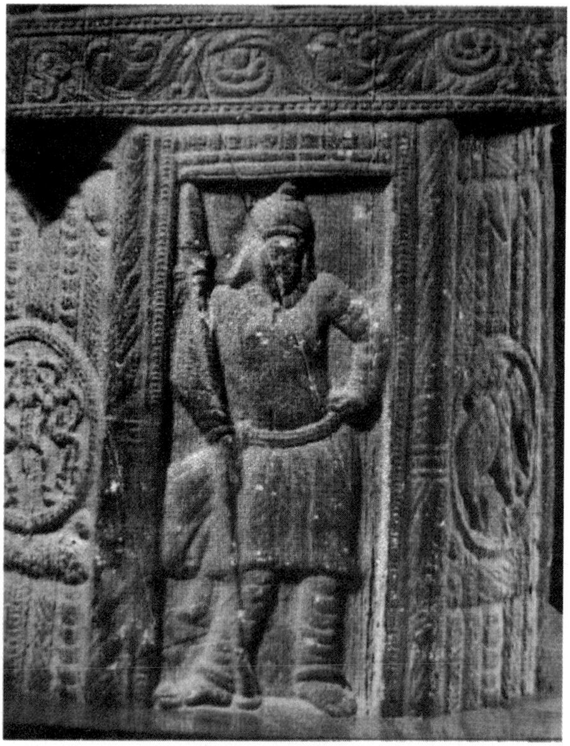

Plate 239: Pitalkhora sculpture showing Scythian dress.